NETWORKING AND INTERNET MANAGEMENT

ENCYCLOPAEDIA OF COMPUTER MANAGEMENT SERIES

NETWORKING AND INTERNET MANAGEMENT

Edited by

S.K. Goel

ANMOL PUBLICATIONS PVT. LTD.

NEW DELHI-110 002 (INDIA)

ANMOL PUBLICATIONS PVT. LTD.
4374/4B, Ansari Road, Daryaganj
New Delhi - 110 002

Networking and Internet Management

First Edition, 2000
ISBN 81-261-0346-9

PRINTED IN INDIA

Published by J.L. Kumar for Anmol Publications Pvt. Ltd., New Delhi and Printed at Mehra Offset Press, Delhi.

Contents

Preface

Management is defined as the process of achieving organizational objectives through the efforts of other people. Management is a process—i.e., management consists of a number of interrelated steps or function which, when satisfactorily performed, lead to the achievement of goals. The successful practice of management involves people working together in harmony to achieve desired results. The availability of quality information is, of course, a requirement for a smoothly functioning operation. The business manager is a practitioner of the art and science of management. It is his job to carry out the basic management functions necessary to attain company goals. Of course, the objectives pursued vary according to the manager's mission; however, the functions of *planning, organizing, staffing,* and *controlling* are performed by all managers. The planning function looks to the future; to plan is to decide in advance a future course of action. Thus, *planning* involves making decisions with regard to (1) the selection of both short-run and long-run business strategies and goals; (2) the development of policies and procedure which will help accomplish objectives or counter threats; (3) the establishment of operating standards which serve as the basis for control; and (4) the revision of earlier plans in the light of changing conditions. The organizing function involves the grouping of work teams into logical and efficient units in order to carry out plans and achieve goals. One aspect of the staffing consists of selecting people to fill the positions which exist in the organizational structure of the business. The staffing activity also includes the training of employees to meet their job requirements, the preparation of employees for promotion to positions of greater responsibility, and the reassignment or removal of employees when such action is required. Unlike planning, which looks to the future, the *control* function looks at the past and the present. It is a follow-up to planning; it is the check on past and current performance to see if planned goals are being achieved.

The process of management is a continuing one. In practice, however, managers carry out these functions simultaneously. Plans beget subordinate plans, old plans require modifications, and new plans develop while old ones are in effect. Thus, it is impractical to insist on a special time sequence for the various functions. Quality information could support good decisions; good decisions should lead to effective performance of managerial functions; and effective functional performance should lead to the attainment of organizational goals. It is not surprising, therefore, that the acquisition and use of a computer may have important managerial implications. We can consider this broad topic from at least three viewpoints. *First,* it is possible to look at the implications involved in *planning for computers. Second,* we can look at the impact of *planning with computers.* Finally, we can look at the computer-oriented *decision-making techniques* which are now gaining acceptance. In light of the importance of information in the decision-making process, it would be logical to assume that top executives have always actively participated in the planning and implementation of new systems which would influence their future decisions.

In short, many executive apparently felt that the introduction of a computer was primarily a technical problem. They were content to define the goals of the new system vaguely and then to turn the entire project over to data-processing specialists.

Top managers should realize that their serious involvement in planning for computers is perhaps the most important single factor determining the success or failure of a computer installation. They should also be aware of the magnitude of the problems which will have to be overcome. Firms which have been successful in making computers pay off have been through in the initial planning stages. Computer usage can certainly improve the effectiveness of managerial planning. But before leaving the subject of planning with computers, it should be emphasized that computers *do not* "make decisions." Rather, they follow program decisions made earlier by managers and programmers. Although experiments are being conducted by extremely able researchers attempting to improve the machines' ability to solve ill-structured problems, it is man who defines problems, selects strategies to follow, and formulates hypotheses and hunches. *Heuristic* is a word which means "serving to discover." Much of planning is judgmental or heuristic in nature, and man is far superior to machine in the heuristic area of intellectual work.

Editor

1

Computer Networking

The protocols used in a computer network are the mechanisms by which the hosts exchange information over physical distances. In the OSI model, the network layer is the primary layer for host-to-host communication. The network layer makes use of services from the link and physical layers; it also provides an end-to-end service to the transport layer. The network layer can utilise a number of physical networks to provide its services. The two services provided by the network layer are the connectionless services, and the connection-orientated service. This chapter begins by looking at the connection orientated service provided by the X.25 protocol. This protocol is important as it is being used on all public packet-switched networks operated by the PTTs. The X.25 protocol defines the necessary operation of layers one, two and three.

The X.25 protocol

Within any layer, a connection orientated protocol has two common tasks: error control and flow control. Error control is concerned with detecting, and correcting, errors that may have occurred in the information being transferred. Flow control is concerned with managing the resources of bandwidth and storage so that no single user can monopolise these resources, and the two endpoints are kept in step with each other. This is usually achieved by keeping the sending and receiving rates of information transfer approximately in step. The X.25 protocol covers the three lower layers of the protocol hierarchy. X.25 is defined as an access protocol, which means that it is used between a host and a node (in most X.25 networks the nodes are called 'exchanges') for the host to access the network so that communication between remote hosts is possible. The X.25 protocol has been adopted by the CCITT as a standard, which means that nearly all future networks will use it. The latest version of X.25 will be adopted by ISO as an international standard.

As well as describing the particulars of X.25, the principles of error and flow control will be shown and the mechanisms used to implement them in each layer explained. The description of level 2 is very detailed, as this is the first consequential level to be met in the bottom-up approach. The discussion of level 2 examines a number of problems which occur at many other protocol layers. For instance, the mechanisms used at level 3 for flow control and protocol synchronisation are very similar to those of level 2, so less detail is given in the level 3 explanation and references are made to the level 2 mechanisms.

In the X.25 parlance a host is called a DTE (Data Terminating Equipment) and a node is called a DCE (Data Communications Equipment). X.25 provides a standard mechanism for a DTE to access and use a DCE to transport data across a network to a remote DTE via its remote DCE. Figure 9.1 shows the DTE and DCE arrangement. The protocol used between the DCEs within the network does not have to be X.25, but would probably be very close to it. X.25 is a virtual call (connection-orientated) protocol.

X.25 level 1--the pPhysical circuit

This level provides the physical communication by specifying the electrical signals, voltages, plug shape and pin assignment that the DTE needs to connect physically to the DCE. In figure 9.2 the DTE/DCE boundary is shown on the host side of the MODEM at the host site. This would be the normal arrangement, as the supplier of the network (usually the PTT) will provide the MODEM link to the node (DCE) from the user's premises. The actual specification of level I is contained in the CCITT X.21 recommendation. For practical purposes the user will order a computer interface to this standard which plugs straight into the computer at one end and into the MODEM at the other. The user will normally also be able to buy the software necessary to handle the interface.

As the level 1 hardware is bought as a ready-made unit, no further discussion of it is necessary. The important information needed about level 1 is the type of interface it presents to level 2, and the functions it must perform. The level 1 will provide transport for a bit stream from the DTE to a (remote) DCE. The level 2 will present the level 1 with the bits which are then delivered to a level 2 at the DCE. The hardware of level 1 will also indicate if the physical circuit is working correctly, that is whether the MODEMs are switched on and able to exchange synchronised data. So the interface has two parts

1. the sending and receiving of a serial bit stream
2. the control signals indicating the status of the physical circuit.

X.25 level 2 -- link level

The purpose of level 2 is to control the physical link between the two ends of the level 1 circuit to provide a reliable transfer of information for level 3 between the DTE and DCE. X.25 level 2 uses a link control protocol based on the ISO HDLC (Higher Data Link Control) protocol. The advantages of using an existing protocol are greater than those to be gained from designing a new one. For instance, a new protocol would have to be adopted by a large number of people wishing to communicate; adoption of the protocol would then require a lot of effort. Other link protocols have been designed: IBM use one called SDLC (Synchronous Data Link Control) on their SNA network, which is not dissimilar to HDLC; DEC have their own as well.

Information is passed from level 2 to level 1 in blocks called 'frames'. The use of frames enables easier management of storage and error control. Each frame consists of some protocol information added by level 2, and possibly an information packet from level 3. 1 will use the convention of calling level 2 blocks frames and level 3 blocks *packets. The* functions performed by level 2 are

1. To establish the link connection to a level 2 at a remote site.
2. To transfer packets for level 3 securely, and in sequence.
3. To disconnect the link without loss of level 3 information.

To carry out these functions, the X. 25 level 2 uses three types of frame format. The uses of each format are shown in the next section, but first the fields in the frames are detailed

Flag field

This is a unique 8 bit pattern (01111110) which marks the beginning and end of each frame. The use of the flag as a delimiter presents a problem: to ensure that the end of the frame is correctly interpreted by the receiver, the flag pattern must not appear anywhere within the data in the frame. This means that the frame must be transparent to the hardware looking for a flag to mark the beginning or ending of a frame. The problem of transparency occurs in all link level protocols as they all use special bit patterns for synchronisation and for marking various parts of the frame. In X. 25 level 2 the flag is used as the level 1 synchronisation character (see chapter 2 on synchronous character frames). To ensure that the flag pattern does not occur within the frame, X.25 uses a technique called 'bit stuffing'. The bit stuffing technique involves the sender in inspecting the frame contents prior to transfer to level 1. Whenever a sequence of five Is occurs a 0 is inserted.

Notice that the 0 is inserted regardless of the value of the sixth bit. Bit stuffing in this way is easily implemented by hardware and only increases the length of the frame by 1 bit for every sequence of five Is. As the receiving hardware scans the incoming frame, a 0 following a sequence of five Is is removed. If the sequence of five Is is followed by a further 1, then the flag may have been found. The seventh bit is then inspected: if it is a 0 the flag has been found (01111110), whereas if the seventh bit is another 1 (01111111) then the frame is in error. Thus a sequence of seven Is is used to abort the frame.

There are other ways of providing transparency, such as using escape characters, or bit counts, but none is quite so efficient and flexible as bit stuffing.

Address field

This is really redundant in a point-to-point link. The intention in the HDLC protocol was to use this as an address for multipoint lines, but the present X. 25 recommendation does not include multipoint lines. However, X.25 uses the field as an additional check in the protocol, as well as having the field ready should multipoint lines be considered in the future. The addresses used in this field allow commands and responses to be separated. The level 2 link can be thought of as two separate channels.

Channel A for transferring data from the network (DCE) to the host (DTE) and

Channel B for transferring data from the host (DTE) to the network (DCE).

Any frames relating to information flow from the DCE to the DTE carry the address A (11000000) including any frames from the DTE to the DCE relating to information transfer from the network to the host; similarly for channel B (10000000). To help separate the channels, frames are divided into two classes: *commands* and *responses,* Commands always flow in the direction of information on a channel; responses flow in the opposite direction. Responses are obviously the receiver's replies to various commands.

Command field

This 8 bit pattern determines the type of the frame, as well as being used for sequence numbering and acknowledgement. The command field has a different meaning for the three types of frame (information, supervisory, unnumbered). Figure 9.4a shows the command octet format for an *information frame.* A 0 in bit 1 indicates that this is an information frame. An information frame is the only type that carries a level 3 packet in the information field. Bits 2, 3 and 4 contain the sequence number of this frame, bits 6, 7 and 8 contain the acknowledgement number. The sequence number and acknowledgement number are used in the ARQ techniques explained in chapter 6 for error correction and flow control. Level 2 uses a stop-go flow control. Bit 5 is the poll/final (P/F) bit. This is set in a command frame as a poll bit and the receiver will set the final bit in any response frame that is a reply to a command frame with the poll bit set. The use of the poll/final bit enables the sender of a command to recognise the corresponding response frame.

Bits 1 and 2 set to 10 indicate a supervisory frame. Bits 3 and 4 indicate which type of supervisory frame, Supervisory frames are not given sequence numbers as they do not contain any level 3 information, but they may be used to acknowledge information frames and so bits 6, 7 and 8 contain an acknowledgement number. Bit 5 is the poll/final bit which is the same as before.

The command field format for the *unnumbered frame,* so called because it contains neither sequence number nor acknowledgement number. Bits 1 and 2 set to 11 indicate an unnumbered frame and bit 5 is the poll/final bit. The remainder of the bits are used to indicate the type of unnumbered frame.

Information field

This field only occurs in information frames; it is the position in the frame where the whole level 3 packet is placed. The other level 2 fields provide an envelope for the level 3 packet during the level 2 transfer.

Frame check sequence

The FCS field is found by counting 16 bits back from the terminating flag. This is a 16 bit field to contain the CRC remainder used in error checking. The remainder is calculated using the CCITT recommended generating polynomial of $X^{16} + X^{12} + X^5 + 1$.

It is interesting to note that all the fields of the X.25 level 2 header and the CRC are multiples of 8 bits. This makes transmission easier, because the 8 bit byte is the lowest common multiple of most modern computer word sizes, as well as being the character frame size for synchronous transfer. However the information field and the CRC may be increased by bit stuffing for level 1 transmission.

Operation of X.25 level 2

This section describes the semantics of level 2, with the various commands and responses being explained in context. The level 2 at the DTE (host) end of the connection performs the protocol functions with the level 2 at the DCE, using the HDLC protocol over the level 1 physical connection.

Establishing the link connection

An earlier specification of the X.25 protocol included a lever 2 initialisation procedure called LAP (Link Access Protocol) This procedure has been superseded by a simpler *balanced* procedure called LAPB. The LAPB method of initialisation sets up both channels simultaneously.

Data transfer

Level 2 should provide a sequenced, error-free transport of lever 3 packers from the DTE to the DCE and vice versa. As only 3 bits are allowed for the sequence number and acknowledgement number in the C field, the maximum window size is 7. In X. 25 the link level window size is fixed when the subscriber first applies to use the network. The operation of the data transfer allows the use of limited buffers at the sender (no more than 7) and no requirement for extra buffers to handle out-of-sequence frames at the receiver. The cost of the small buffer requirement is extra channel capacity taken up with retransmission. The use of X.25 to connect hosts to networks would normally involve a fairly high-speed circuit between the DTE and

DCE The limiting factor in performance is more likely to be the network and level 3, so a superefficient level 2 is not necessary; thus simpler techniques, such as Go-Back-N, can be used.

The transfer of sequenced frames of information is straightforward but what makes the operation complex (and this applies to every protocol) is the handling of exceptions and errors. There are two basic errors that can occur during data transfer.

1. The frame check sequence indicates an error in the packet.
2. The packet appears to contain no transmission errors but the contents of the A and C fields are not those expected.

In case 1 above the frame is thrown away and no further action is taken by the receiver. Obviously when a frame is discarded the next frame received is not the one expected. In case 2 there are a number of inconsistencies that can be classed as errors. The most common would be a sequence error where a previous packet had been lost or discarded. To ensure that the frame sequence is maintained at the receiver, any frame that does not contain a sequence number matching that of the next expected frame variable, V(R), is an error. If the sequence number of the error frame is within the window, the receiver returns an REJ response to indicate, in the N(R) field, the frame from which the sender should retransmit. If the frame sequence number is not within the window then the sequence numbers of the two ends have become unsynchronised. The only way to recover from a synchronisation problem is to reset the sender and receiver to a known state. The CMDR (command reject) frame initiates a reset which is completed by going through the link establishment exchange. After a reset, the two end-stations will be in a known, initial state. The reset procedure is used to recover from all errors other than the loss of an information frame. A reset may be caused by the receipt of a command or response that is not expected; for instance, a UA if the data transfer is in progress, or the setting of the P/F bit in a response when no command has been sent with that bit set.

The RNR (receiver not ready) frame tells the data sender that the receiver will ignore any further information frames (flow control stop). Once the receiver has returned an RNR response to an information frame, no more information frames are accepted, but the *N(R)* field in the header of any further information frames is inspected so that information frames in the opposite direction are properly acknowledged. The RNR response only stops information on one channel; the other channel is unaffected. When the receiver has more buffer space, an RR (receiver ready) frame is sent to inform the information sender on that channel that more information frames may be transmitted (flow control go), starting at *N(R)*. Note that both RNR and RR have acknowledgement numbers, *N(R)*. The RR frame has another use: if the receiving station does not have any information frames to be sent on the opposite channel, the acknowledgements cannot be piggybacked, and the RR frame is then used to acknowledge the information frames.

A receiver, especially a DCE (node), may not have enough buffers to take a full window for every level 2 link to which it is connected. Instead a statistical allocation could be used which assumes that not all links will be fully active at the same time and that the data is forwarded within a given time. When the network becomes busy this allocation means that a receiver may run out of buffers and need to use some technique to stop the flow of data from one or more links. Every frame, whether it is data or control, needs some buffer space for its receipt. If all the buffers are used up by one link then none of the other links will be able to continue transferring information. Also, if every buffer is allocated, there may be no more buffers to receive a control frame acknowledging a data frame and releasing buffer space! To avoid these problems, complex buffer allocation methods may be used. Normally, enough free buffers are always kept to receive at least one frame on each link so that control information can be exchanged even if data cannot. An information frame would be received, the control information used (for example *N(R)*), and then the frame discarded so that the buffer may be used again.

The loss of information frames as a result of buffer starvation means that information is lost not only because of errors in transmission, but also because of the internal operation of the nodes of a network, especially when the network becomes heavily loaded.

Link disconnection

The LAPB procedure for closing a link requires an exchange of a DISC command and a UA response. The poll/final bit is used to obtain synchronisation between the DCE and DTE.

X.25 level 3 -- the network level

The function of level 2 is to carry a level 3 packet across a link. The function of the network level is to carry a piece of information from one host (DTE) to another via intermediate network nodes. The transfer of the level 3 information will involve a number of level 2 links. The X. 25 specification only covers the link between the DTE and DCE, but we will assume a similar protocol is used between each node of the network as well. Each level 3 packet contains a certain amount of level 3 protocol information in a header, and possibly some user data (from the transport level). The major differences between levels 2 and 3 are the use of addresses and logical channel numbers. Most hosts will be connected to the network by one level 2 link. This link then has to be used to enable the host to communicate with several other hosts by multiplexing logical channels on to the one physical link. Level 3 is used to achieve this multiple connection via a single link. Using level 3 a host establishes a logical channel to another host by making a connection request using the full address of the remote host. When the connection is established it becomes a logical channel with a unique number, the logical channel number. The logical channel number is unique only for each link. Using the logical channel concept, packets for several calls may pass across the same level 2 link as they are all identified by the unique channel number. At the DCE the channel number is used to decide which route the packet will take. The logical channel is in fact a virtual circuit.

The network level has the same basic functions to perform as the link level.

1. Connection establishment.
2. Data transfer.
3. Connection disconnection.

The difference for the network level is that these functions are now carried out (apparently) between two hosts.

Packet format

The X.25 level 3 headers are used to contain a variety of information, so they are not of uniform size like the level 2 frame headers. The level 3 headers are different for every type of packet, which makes the format quite complex. The general format identifier (GFI) field indicates which format of level 3 header follows. The logical channel group number and logical channel number provide a 12 bit channel-numbering field. Splitting the field may allow subdivisions to be used for, say, different services. Call request and incoming call packets contain the address of the remote host (DTE). The addresses may contain fields indicating a particular process on a host as well as identifying a host. The address fields are of variable length, preceded by a byte count.

Connection establishment

To begin a call, a host uses the full address of the remote host in a call request packet sent from the DTE to the DCE. The DCE will respond with either a call accepted packet if the request was successful, or a clear indication packet if the call was refused.

At the remote host the DCE will send an incoming call packet to the host to indicate that a remote call has been requested. The DTE receiving an incoming call packet will inspect the header to decide if the call is to be established or not. If the call is accepted a call accept packet is sent to the DCE; if the call is rejected a clear request is sent to the DCE. The channel number chosen for a new outgoing call by the DTE is the lowest available number. The channel number for an incoming call is chosen by the DCE as the highest available number. If the DTE and DCE agree on the channel numbers, and the DCE will accept the call, all subsequent packets on that call will only use that channel number, not the full address. A call has been established to a remote DTE when a host receives a call accepted packet having the same channel number as the call request packet. The call is established at the remote DTE when the call accepted packet is sent to the remote DCE.

Information transfer

Level 3 transfers data to the network in a sequenced stream using Go-Back-N ARQ. The techniques of sequence numbers, piggybacked acknowledgements, RNR, RR and REJ responses are the same as for level 2, but they control the data flow across the network and into the remote host for each, independent logical channel. The use of windows and sequence numbers was for error control in level 2 as the level 1 link was prone to errors. At level 3 the level 2 link is assumed to be error free so. the emphasis is different. The windows and sequence numbers are now used primarily for end-to-end flow control. The receipt of acknowledgements allows more information into the network, while the window limits the number of data packets in flight at any one time. Complete suspension of the data flow can be achieved by using a level 3 RNR, but the flow can be partially adjusted by the rate of acknowledgement.

Interrupt

An extra mechanism is used at level 3 to handle what is known as *out-of-band* transmission. Normal user data on an X.25 virtual call is kept in strict sequence; this is called *in band* transmission. However, a user application often requires a special signal which is not subject to the normal flow control. Such a signal is the abort character which a terminal user would type to stop a runaway program. X.25 level 3 uses an interrupt packet to carry this out-of-band signal. The interrupt is not subject to the normal information flow control, the idea being that the interrupt could overtake information packets already in the network. The interrupt packet contains a field to indicate the cause of the interrupt; it is up to the application to decide what to do both with the interrupt and any subsequent data. When the DTE sends an interrupt packet the DCE responds with an interrupt confirmation. The interrupt sequence is shown in figure 9.10. X.25 permits only one interrupt to be outstanding on a logical call at any one time.

Resets and restarts

In level 2 the reset was introduced as a mechanism for recovering from a protocol error where the two ends in the link became unsynchronised. The same thing can happen between the DTE and DCE at level 3, except that there are two areas where problems may occur.

The first problem is due to the information frames and sequence numbers becoming out of synchronisation on a single call. This may be detected by receiving a sequence number outside the window or an acknowledgement for a packet that was not sent. An error may also have been detected by a higher-level protocol, perhaps because of a network failure. In these cases only the one logical channel is affected so a *reset* is used. This sets the level 3 sequence numbers to 0 at the DTE and DCE. The reset will also be propagated to the remote DTE-DCE pair. The reset can be initiated from either the DTE or DCE and requires the usual request-confirmation exchange. A reset may cause the loss of any information packets within the network so a higher-level protocol will need to recover any lost data.

More drastic action is needed if the DTE and DCE become unsynchronised over global level 3 operation. An example is the choice of a channel number for a call request. If the DCE does not agree with the DTE over the chosen channel number (it should be the lowest free number) it means one of them thinks it has more logical calls opened than the other! The freeing of logical channel numbers correctly is the reason for the clear-request and clear-confirmation pair. When the whole level 3 needs resynchronisation a restart is initiated. This affects all the logical channels on the DTE-DCE link. A reset on the level 2 link is propagated as a restart at level 3.

Call disconnection

A DTE wishing to terminate a call issues a clear request packet, to which the DCE will respond with a clear confirmation packet when the call has been cleared in the DCE. This may involve waiting for the forwarding of any information packets still held there. When the clear confirmation is received the channel number is freed for further use. At the remote end the DCE wit send a clear indication packet indicating that the remote host has closed, and no more information packets will follow. The remote DTE will respond with a clear confirmation packet when all outstanding information packets have been acknowledged.

Data flow

The level 3 transport mechanism requires the data from the higher-level protocols to be broken into packets for transfer across the DTE-DCE interface. The X.25 recommendation specifies possible data lengths of 128 256, 512 and 1024 bytes, where 128 is the preferred maximum. It is probable that the PTT networks will guarantee 128 byte data packets. This means a user message must be broken into 128 byte sequences, the last one being perhaps less than 128 bytes. To enable the receiver to reassemble a message from multiple packets, level 3 uses a *more data bit* (M) in the information packet header to indicate that the current packet is not the last one of a message.

Just as the level 2 and level 3 need to include control information in the frames and packets as well as information from the next higher level, it is likely that a higher-level protocol would like to send control and data over level 3. The higher-level protocol may decide to add the control bits to the front of messages it passes to level 3. However, level 3 provides a mechanism that allows a higher-level protocol to multiplex data and control information on to the level 3 packet stream, thus maintaining the sequence of data and control across the network. This mechanism is the Q *bit*. The Q bit is set when the packet contains control information, and is clear when the packet contains data. Thus the higher-level protocol can quickly separate control and data information when receiving level 3 packets.

X.25 implementation

An advantage claimed for X.25 is that it only describes the host-to-node (DTE-to-DCE) interface. The network itself (internode) can use any convenient protocols, even completely different protocols, and the user would be unaware of them. In fact the proposed PTT networks are all planning to use X.25, or variations, within the networks for node-to-node transfer. The problem considered here is the implications of two methods of implementing an X.25 interface in a DCE that produce quite different results for the user. The discussion will show that even standards have complex problems of *meaning* (or semantics).

The two methods of implementation involve the mechanism for generating responses to various DTE packets at level 3. From the above description it can be seen that a command response sequence is used throughout level 3. The X.25 specification indicates quite clearly what responses are required, but leaves it up to the implementer to decide when, and under what criteria, the responses are made.

Consider the implementation that produces the DCE response as soon as the DTE's packet has been processed at the (local) DCE. This means the DCE's answer is sent to the DTE at the same time as the original request is forwarded across the network and well in advance of its arrival at the remote DTE. Such an implementation would give a very quick response to the user host. For instance, as data is passed to the DCE it is acknowledged immediately, even before it has crossed the network. The DCE-DTE flow control would ensure the DCE was not flooded with data, but large amounts could be in transit within the network before the call has been established at the remote end. This implementation would give the host the appearance of high throughput, as the DCE-DTE flow control would be the only restraint. If the DTE receives a level 3 acknowledgement for a data packet, does this mean that the remote DTE has received it, or only that the local DCE has? To be consistent in this implementation it would have to be the latter, so the DCE has taken on the responsibility for delivery of that data. A higher-level protocol would be needed, with its own flow control, to handle the host-to-host transfer.

This implementation has the effect, mentioned above, of apparently providing a fast throughput. A host may be able to open a call (to the local DCE), send data, and close the call, before the remote DTE has received any data. The network, however, will contain a large amount of unacknowledged packets as the DTE-DCE flow control will accept packets as fast as the DCE can forward them into the network. This makes end-to-end flow control in the network difficult and can quickly lead to congestion.

In the second implementation we only allow the DCE to respond to the DTE when the response from the remote DTE has been received by the local DCE. Data sent from the DTE is not acknowledged until the remote DTE has accepted the packet. This gives the host an impression of a long delay. In fact the delay is the round trip to the remote host, plus processing. This end-to-end use of the level 3 protocol reduces the amount of processing required from higher-level protocols. The sending DTE will only be able to have a window of packets outstanding which will represent the maximum number of data buffers which the whole network will need for the call. This makes the resource management within the network easier and is less likely to produce congestion. The cost is the lower performance seen by the user. Each packet takes longer to be acknowledged, thus reducing the throughput. There is also the problem of gaps which occurs when a window full of packets is sent rapidly, which is followed by a delay until the first acknowledgement comes back. This *bursty* mode of operation gives the network an uneven response and is difficult for both the host and DCE to manage.

The current X.25 recommendation allows a subscriber (DTE) to set a D bit in a data packet at level 3. This bit requires the acknowledgement to have end-to-end significance, as in the second example above. The D bit is an option, which means a network does not have to implement it.

Computer network technology

The communications techniques covered so far have been concerned with centralised systems. Terminal networks are all built around a central computer; similarly remote job entry stations are usually connected to a single computer. In the remaining chapters some of the problems and techniques of a network of intercommunicating devices are discussed. The devices at present connected to networks are usually generalpurpose computers, with their own terminal networks. One reason for networking multiaccess computers, rather than terminals or smaller devices, is that these computer systems already existed when networking was proposed. A second reason is that the protocols used in computer networks are very complex so that only a large computer system would have sufficient spare computing power to implement them. However, terminals can be directly attached to a network, by using a dedicated computer. In the near future computer networks will become as widespread as the telephone network, and large scale integration will enable cheap processors to handle the protocols. The result will be the networking of every sort of computing device. The current trends indicate that powerful, single user, workstations will replace terminals for network use. The workstations will be directly connected to a local area network and use the resources of larger computers via the network.

This chapter is primarily concerned with the technology used to connect the computers and devices that make up a computer network. For the purposes of description the range of technology has been divided into three areas

1. wide area networks
2. Radio and satellite broadcast networks
3. Local networks

The network technology includes the techniques used to interconnect the computing devices and physically transfer information from one computing device to another.

Wide area networks

The term 'wide area network' is applied to a network that covers a large physical area, say a whole country or large area under one administration. Such an area may be worldwide where a multinational organisation owns the network. The basic communication media used are dedicated circuits, usually of about 50 kHz bandwidth. Where digital circuits are available the bandwidth would be 64K bps. The recent introduction of fibre optics in longdistance trunks has make link bandwidth of 2-3M bps available. Wide area networks will be using these links over the next few years. Examples of such networks are PSS, ARPANET, Tymnet, Telenet, etc.; details of some of these networks are given at the end of this section. For reasons explained in chapter 3, the physical circuits are usually provided by a PTT, although in the case of PSS the whole network is also run by the PTT.

Although 50 kHz bandwidth seems to be a lot compared with the 3 kHz nominal bandwidth of the voice telephone line, it is not very much when highspeed or large-volume transfers of information are required. Even at these high speeds the channel capacity is a resource that needs to be used efficiently.

It is now necessary to see how information can be transferred from one computer to any other on the network. The problem falls into two parts. The first is that of transferring information via a medium, such as a wire. The second part is concerned with addressing and routing. If there were only two computers on a network, then they could be connected by two channels, one for each direction, and whatever one computer transmitted the other would be bound to receive. When more computers are added, the bidirectional connection solution can be extended by having each computer connected to every other computer by a full duplex connection. To send a message to a particular computer the appropriate connection is selected; thus the routing of a message is carried out by the sender. Using a dedicated connection between every computer on the network is very expensive. If there are n computers on the network then $n(n-1)/2$ lines are needed, and have to be paid for! As a single computer would not normally be communicating with every other computer on the network at the same time, most of the lines would be unused in a fully connected network. Therefore to increase the utilisation of the connection circuits, their number is reduced, and switching is introduced within the network.

There are three forms of switching that can be used in communications: circuit switching, message switching, and packet switching.

Circuit switching

Circuit switching is used on the PSTN to connect telephone subscribers. To use it for a computer network each computer would have a private circuit to a local exchange, and the exchanges would be connected to form a network.

Whenever two computers wish to exchange information, a physical path is established between them via the exchanges. The path is then disconnected when the connection is closed. The circuit has been ‚switched' by the exchanges. This method of connection is not used on established computer networks. The major disadvantages of circuit switching are

1. The cost of the equipment is very high, whereas the resulting circuit is not necessarily of high enough quality for computer communications.
2. The resulting circuit can only be used by the two computers on the call, thus the equipment is dedicated to the circuit. In particular the connection from the computer to the exchange is dedicated. To enable a single computer to communicate with more than one other computer at the same time, extra equipment is needed for each simultaneous call. If there are no connections all the equipment is idle but being paid for.
3. The time taken to set up the physical path can be very long in computer terms.

As high-speed connection using good-quality circuits is important for efficient computer networks, circuit switching is discounted in favour of the other methods. Circuit switching is used for some networks connecting computers-for instance, the Nordic Data Network.

Circuit switching has two advantages

1. Charges are made only for the time that a call is connected. If infrequent and short connections are all that is required, then circuit switching may be advantageous to the customer. It is expected that many slower devices, such as terminals, will be connected to national computer networks via the PSTN to gain this advantage.
2. Where a single device is used for long periods, such as a facsimile machine, circuit switching is economically advantageous. This is particularly true where digital facilities, such as X.21, are available.

The above discussion is based on the existing PSTN services offered by the PTTs. When the ISDN service is widely available, then it will be an attractive mechanism for some computer networks. Each host will be able to set up calls, use the 64K bps bandwidth, and quickly close the call, as required. The circuits will still carry packets for the end-to-end data transfer; but circuit switching will be the main link-switching mechanism. In the UK it is intended to bring all the PTT communications together into Integrated Digital Access (IDA). This will combine ISDN, X.25 networking and special digital services into a common access interface.

Message switching

To overcome problems in setting up and taking down physical circuits via exchanges, computer networks use permanent circuits and switch the data, A partially connected network is used in which each computer has a permanent circuit to a number of its neighbours, but not to all computers on the network. An example will illustrate the basic operation of *information switching* where the unit of information is a message.

If the computer at A wishes to send a message to B, the message must pass through either D or C. The points on the network are called *nodes. A will* address the message to B by placing the address of B in the message header. The message and address are then sent on the circuit to D. At D the node inspects the address; if the address is 'D' the message is given to the computer; if the address is not D the message is forwarded on a circuit that the node believes will enable the message to be delivered, In this case D will forward the message to B. Thus the node at D has switched the message on to the appropriate output circuit. In this example two major characteristics of a computer network can be seen.

Addressing

The message is addressed to a remote destination and sent on the next stage of its route.

Store and Forward

Each message is received into the node storage so that it can be processed as a whole unit. Usually an error check is carried out and the whole message has to be received before this can be completed. The message is then inspected for routing information so that the node can decide which output circuit to use to forward the message.

The nodes have been introduced in the network to carry out the functions of routing and store and forward, so the host computer is separated from the network operation as much as possible. The 'hosts' are the user computers which wish to use the network. Often a number of hosts will be attached to a single node.

The node computers are usually minicomputers chosen for their ability to respond in real time to the communications devices. Each node receives incoming messages and stores them. When a complete message has been received the destination address is inspected so that the message can be placed on the output queue of a circuit to forward the message. If the message is for a host attached to the node, the output circuit will be the one connected to the host. If the message is for a distant host the node must forward the message to another node on the route to the distant host. While the message is in the node store, waiting to be processed or waiting for output, it is, of course, being delayed.

The link into any one node may be used to carry messages from several different computers, as may the connection between the node and host. The physical equipment involved is used more efficiently than in circuit switching as a result of this multiplexing. Message multiplexing is the most important advantage of message and packet switching computer networks.

To distinguish between message and packet switching it is necessary to understand what a message is. This has already been introduced in earlier chapters, but a more detailed discussion is given here. The easiest way of defining a message is to say that it is a unit of information which is exchanged by users of a network. This means the characteristics of a message are only dependent on the user or the application. A message could be a few bits or a file, or even a whole database. In a message-switching network the whole message is passed from one node to another as a complete entity. Compared with circuit switching, a message-switching network has the following characteristics.

1. Any computer can communicate with any other computer without having a direct physical connection.
2. Any computer can communicate with several others using the same equipment by multiplexing messages.
3. There is no delay arising from circuit set up, but messages are delayed when they pass through a node *enroute.*

The messages can be transferred between nodes, and nodes and hosts, using an *ARQ* protocol.

Characteristic 3 implies that there is no delay arising from the use of a network other than the store and forward operation of the nodes. This is true in some networks using pure datagram techniques. However, in most networks the internode protocol used within the network introduces some delays. Any network using a virtual circuit protocol, at any level, will introduce a delay when the message or packet is given to the network. In many networks the local node negotiates for resources within the network before actually forwarding a message. This is true of an X.25 network when the call is first set up, and is true of every message on the ARPA network.

A user of a message-switching network will pass the network a message, together with a destination address, and the user will receive messages as single units.

Advantages and disadvantages

The advantages of message switching, over circuit switching are

- The sender may dispatch the message when convenient, even if the receiver is not ready, as the network will store the message for delivery, However, if network resources run out, an undelivered message may be deleted and thus lost; this depends on the network protocols.
- Computers can exchange information at different speeds, as the network will buffer the message.
- Broadcasting of a message may be possible.
- Equipment is used more efficiently.
- Messages may be handled by priority.

Each message is treated as a single unit. However, there are also some disadvantages.

- A very long message will hold up other, perhaps more urgent, messages as it monopolises a circuit for the duration of its transmission.
- As a message may be very large, the node computer may not have enough memory to store it before forwarding it; in this case the message is lost. Further, this message will never be delivered as the network does not have the required resources.
- A very large message may monopolise the storage of a node, because it cannot be delivered, so that other messages cannot be received by this node.

Packet switching

The disadvantages of message switching relate to the possible occurrence of *large* messages, where the exact value of 'large' will depend on the network. If a network could be certain of only handling small messages, the disadvantages would disappear. The transfer of messages is a user requirement, so a network that meets user needs must be able to handle very large messages as well as small messages. The solution to these two conflicting requirements is to break the user's message into small *packets* for transfer through the network and have the packets reassembled into the message by the receiver. Note that the message header is included as the data in the first packet and that each packet has its own header. This refinement produces packet switching, which is the most widely used switching technique for computer networks.

The physical organisation of a packet-switching network is the same as for message switching. The network is a partially connected mesh of nodes. For practical reasons most wide area networks use special node computers to perform the switching, with the user computers being attached to the nodes. The term 'host' is now widely used to mean a user computer system attached to a network. The nodes are part of the network, so the hosts use a well-defined interface for accessing the node to enable data transfer across the network. By using a node separated from the host, all of the packet-switching functions, such as storage and routing, are removed from the host. However, the host still needs considerable software to handle the protocols used to access the node and to transfer data to other computers on the network.

The advantages that packet switching has over message switching are

- The small maximum packet size makes storage allocation and management easier in the switching nodes, sufficiently so for minicomputers to be used.
- The multiplexing of packets enables several messages to be interleaved on one circuit, reducing the delay seen by the user.
- The total transmission time through the network is reduced. Figure shows a message passing from A to B which would normally require 6k + d seconds to reach B, where 3k is the transmission time of the whole message on one link and d is the node delay. If the message is broken into three packets, each taking k seconds to transmit, the whole message arrives at B in 4k + d seconds. The difference increases with the number of links traversed and the size of the message.

It would appear that packet switching solves all the problems of wide area network organisation: it uses fixed highspeed lines and minicomputers for nodes; it is also more efficient and responsive than message switching. However, although packet switching is a better technique with which to implement a computer network, users still want to transfer messages. Packet switching introduces another layer of complexity and translation between the user and the physical network transporting the bits. Fortunately, the cost of processing is falling so the extra cost is outweighed by the practical advantages. A second cost, not so easily overcome, is that each packet will have its own overheads as well as those used by each message; this will reduce the efficiency of the physical circuits.

The conclusion drawn from consideration of these three switching techniques is that packet switching, especially used in a partially connected mesh of nodes with wideband circuits, is currently the best technique for wide area computer networks. Packet switching is also used in other network technologies, rather than message switching, for the same reasons.

Wide area networks have been in existence since the early 1970s. The best known example is the ARPA network in the United States. This network was established by a government research agency to link together computer centres that had contracts for government research so that research workers could share the available computing resources. The network itself also forms part of a research project to evaluate the feasibility of a large computer network, and to investigate techniques that could be used in such a network. The ARPA network has been very successful in showing that the concept of resource sharing by use of a network is feasible. One of the most noticeable advantages that the network has introduced is a mail facility. This allows each user with access to a computer on the network to exchange mail with all the other network users. The mail facility is probably one of the main sources of traffic on the ARPA network and has certainly improved the amount of communication between researchers at different sites.

The basic techniques used within the ARPA network have been influenced by the defence aspects of the research, particularly the need for a fast response and resilience to the failure of any part. The network consists of a mesh of partially connected nodes called Interface Message Processors (IMPs). Each IMP can have up to eight hosts connected to it and may be connected to up to eight other IMPs. Each IMP accepts messages from the hosts of up to 8K bits in length. The IMP breaks the message into IK bit packets which are then forwarded through the network of IMPs to the IMP attached to the destination host. This destination IMP reassembles the message before delivering it to the destination host. If a host wishes to send a message of more than 8K bits it must break the message up itself, into 8K packets, and the destination host must reassemble the message from the 8K packets. Thus the translation between messages and packets takes place at two levels. Within the network of IMPs, packets (1K) are sent individually along whichever route is best at the time, so that packets in a single message may use different routes and may arrive at the destination IMP out of sequence. The destination IMP has to reassemble the message from the packets as they arrive. However, messages passed from the host to the IMP are delivered in the same sequence to the destination host. The technology developed for the ARPANET is now used in a number of commercial wide area networks all over the world.

The British Telecom network PSS (Packet Switching Stream) is an example of a network provided by a PTT as a public service. The design requirements for such a network are different from those of the ARPA network so they have resulted in a network with different characteristics. The network topology consists of a number of *exchanges* which are also partially connected. Each exchange is connected to a number of host computers in its area. The exchanges contain the node computers, the number of node computers in each exchange depending on the number of hosts attached to the exchange. The hosts use an access protocol called X.25 to enable them to make virtual calls to other hosts. A host will give the local exchange the destination address of the host with which it wishes to communicate. The network will route the call to the destination exchange which will then complete the call to the destination host. The call is represented by information kept at all the exchanges on the route. The information is then used to forward the packets transferred on the call. Once the call has been established the hosts may exchange their own information. This is very similar to circuit switching on the PSTN although it is provided using packet-switching techniques. The PSS network techniques are different from those on the ARPA network, where each message is addressed and transferred separately. The hosts can use a single link to the PSS exchange to carry a number of virtual calls to other hosts, thus the link is used to multiplex the calls.

Radio and satellite broadcast networks

These networks differ from wide area networks in the way in which the channel is used for communication between users. Broadcast networks use a channel to which all the users are connected, so all the users receive any transmission made on the channel. At present the two types of channel in use are local radio, covering up to a few hundred kilometres, and satellite channels which are used to span very large distances.

Networks using radio and satellite channels have special problems because noise in the channel can cause errors. There is also the problem of allocating the channel for transmission. The first operational broadcast computer network was built at the University of Hawaii using local radio transmission; many of the techniques and much of the terminology derive from this first network.

Every node receives all packets transmitted on the broadcast channel. When the received packet is complete, the node checks the packet for errors and then checks the destination address. If the address of the receiver matches the packet destination address, it is accepted; otherwise it is discarded. The problems particular to a broadcast network occur in the allocation of the channel to a node for transmitting a packet. Different solutions are used for radio and satellite links. Each node is only able to communicate with each other node via the common channel, so some scheme is needed to coordinate transmission. The schemes that have been proposed and used are discussed here in increasing complexity and are compared for channel efficiency.

The simplest transmission technique is called *pure aloha;* when a node has a packet to transmit it does so immediately. Having transmitted the packet, the node waits for an acknowledgement. This is therefore a positive acknowledgement protocol. If an acknowled-gement is not received within a time out period, the packet is assumed lost. Transmission collisions, which occur when two nodes transmit at the same time and thus interfere with each other's transmission, are detected by the time out mechanism. When a collision is detected, each node waits a period of time of random length before retransmitting the packet to of traffic increases, the rate of collision will increase and more re-transmissions will be needed. As the older packets are re-transmitted, more stations will have newer packets to transmit, causing more collisions, etc. Analysis has shown that a pure aloha scheme can only use a maximum of about 18% of the channel bandwidth. A node may transmit at any time, thus the maximum length of time the channel is wasted as a result of a collision is 2t, where t is the transmission time for one packet. The 2t period is the worst case, where one node begins transmitting just before the previous transmission is complete.

An improvement on pure aloha is *slotted aloha* in which the transmission channel time is divided into time slots of *t.* Each node is then only allowed to begin transmitting a packet at the start of a time slot. The nodes are kept in synchronisation by a time signal on the channel. Now if a collision occurs only one slot *is* wasted, so the maximum efficiency rises to about 34% of the channel capacity. When a collision is detected, a transmitter must wait for a random number of time slots before retransmitting. When the traffic is light the wait can be quite short, but as the traffic load increases the waiting period should be increased.

From the aloha schemes it can be seen that it is collisions that cause problems, so a collision avoidance mechanism should improve efficiency. In packet radio networks a scheme known as Carrier Sense Multiple Access (CSMA) is used. When a node is transmitting all other nodes can receive the transmission, so they can avoid a collision by not transmitting themselves until the channel is free. A transmission is detected by the presence of the carrier signal in the medium. When a node has a packet to transmit it looks for the carrier; if there is no carrier the packet is transmitted. If the carrier is detected the node waits for a random length delay and tries again.

Even in a radio broadcast the signal from a transmitter takes a finite amount of time to reach all the receivers in the network. When two nodes find the channel free, they may both begin transmission because neither has heard the other one. This case is most likely to happen when two stations are waiting for the channel to become free. The length of time it takes to propagate the signal to all receivers is the time band in which collisions may occur, but it is less than the total packet transmission time. As with the aloha technique, the CSMA technique can be improved by dividing the channel time into slots and only allowing the transmission of packets to begin at the start of a time slot. The slot length is set to the propagation delay, not the packet transmission time.

The CSMA technique has been further refined by modifying the action of the node when the channel is busy. When the node samples the channel again and finds it free, it transmits its packet with a probability p, or waits for a further delay of random length, with a probability (1-p). This is called persistent CSMA or p-persistent transmission. If p is high then the delay before transmission occurs is lower, but the possibility of collision increases if two stations are waiting for another station to finish. In persistent CSMA a trade off is made between channel efficiency and delay with the value of p. Channel efficiencies of about 80% may be achieved using these techniques.

Packet radio networks have a small delay between the start of a transmission and the detection of the transmission by all stations on the network. On a satellite broadcast network there is a very long delay between transmission and receiving, of the order of a quarter of a second. A satellite network operates by each transmitter sending its signal to the satellite. The satellite then broadcasts the signal to all of the Earth stations, which may be spread over a very large area. One satellite system currently used for packet switching connects nodes in England, Norway and North America using a satellite in stationary orbit over the North Atlantic. A different channel allocation technique is used on satellite broadcast networks because of the long propagation delay.

This satellite channel allocation technique involves making reservations for the future use of slots in the channel. The channel is divided into frames consisting of a number of reservation slots and a number of packet slots. Each reservation slot represents a packet slot in the second part of the frame. All ground stations are synchronised to the frame timing by the satellite transmission. During the first part of the frame the ground stations reserve slots for the packets they have ready by transmitting a marker during the reservation slot time. When the reservation slot is heard on the satellite down channel, the ground station inspects the slot to see if it contains its own marker. If so it can transmit a packet in the corresponding packet slot in the second part of the frame. This scheme uses some of the channel capacity to avoid the collisions which could reduce the network to a pure aloha scheme.

Obviously more than one ground station may attempt to reserve a particular packet slot by transmitting during the reservation slot time. There are a number of algorithms to overcome this, including allocating some slots to busy stations. Thus if a station successfully obtained a packet slot in the last frame, the same slot is allocated to that station in the next frame without competition. If an allocated slot is not used then the slot is open for competition in the following frame. Usually there are some slots that all stations can compete for in every frame. Another mechanism involves using a central allocation station to which each station sends its requirements and the central station allocates the slots. This has two disadvantages: firstly, the central station becomes a weakness in the network reliability, and secondly, the delay between requesting an allocation and receiving the allocation may be of the order of 1 or 2 seconds before the packet can be transmitted. A chapter in the book by Kuo is dedicated to broadcast satellite protocols.

Local area networks

A local, or private, network is a communication system connecting computers in a small geographical area, say less than a few kilometres between the furthest points. The network is wholly owned and run by one administration. There are currently two basic types of technology used on such a network: these are cable, or bus, technology and ring technology.

Whereas wide area networks and satellite networks use nodes to separate the internal network switching from the user hosts, local networks are meant to be as cheap as possible and so the separate node computer is omitted. In both local network technologies all the computers are directly attached to the transmission medium by a special interface, and all the interfaces receive all the packets. The difference between a ring and a bus system is the way in which the channel is allocated. Local networks are designed for use in local computing by allowing the interconnection of very small computers, such as microprocessors, personal workstations and peripheral devices. If the local network is to be useful, the cost of the computer interfaces into the network channel has to be low compared with the cost of the computer or peripheral, and microprocessors are very cheap in computer terms. A widely forecast use of local networks is connecting word processors within a set of offices for the exchange of information and electronic mail. The cost constraints, the limited processing power of the small computers and the protocols used on a local network are different from those used in wide area networks. A local network usually has a very high bandwidth channel of between I and 10 MHz and a very low error rate say one bit in several million might be corrupted. These characteristics permit the use of simple protocols. The lowest level protocol for using the transmission medium is built into the computer interface.

Cable or bus networks

These networks usually use a length of coaxial cable, or an existing cable such as that used for closed circuit television (CCTV). The medium is used in a broadcast fashion, exactly as described in the previous section on broadcast networks. The channel allocation techniques vary slightly on the theme of the CSMA techniques, or on a centralised slot allocation. The most popular broadcast local network is the Ethernet system developed by Xerox. The Ethernet principles can be used on any broadcast medium: radio, telephone lines, coaxial cable and optical fibres have all been used successfully. The Ethernet uses a base band signal, rather than a modulated signal, to simplify the broadcast transmitter and receiver, with a modified CSMA channel access technique. To obtain the maximum efficiency from the broadcast medium an Ethernet transmitter can listen to its own broadcast to detect a collision and abort the transmission. This extra complexity is known as CSMACD (CD = collision detection) or listen-while-talk. As with the other CSMA techniques a station does not begin transmitting until the broadcast medium is free. Two stations waiting for another station to finish a transmission will begin transmitting together, and thus interfere with each other. The collision is detected by the stations and they both abort the transmission immediately. To enforce the protocol a station that aborts a transfer then jams the ether. After a collision each station waits for a random time before trying again.

The CSMA-CD technique enables the Ethernet system to obtain up to 95% of the broadcast channel bandwidth. The improvement in performance over ordinary CSMA is due to the stopping of transmission as soon as a collision is detected. Note that no slots are used so a network-wide timing signal is not required. The transceiver handles all of the CSMACD access, including the retries and delay calculation which is varied with the traffic load. Thus only complete, and checked, packets are passed up to the station interface and only one request is made for a packet to be sent. The checksum generation and checking are carried out within the hardware: bad packets are discarded. A time out mechanism is used to retransmit packets that may have been lost as a result of errors.

Ring networks

The ring technique originated in the USA. The idea was then developed in parallel at Cambridge University in the UK and at two research centres in the USA. The version developed at Cambridge is known as the Cambridge ring in the UK. The computer interface is divided into two parts: the repeater and the interface proper. A ring uses a twisted pair of wires as the transmission medium. However, to improve reliability, the repeater is powered from the ring and electrically isolated from the computer interface, so four wires are used to connect the repeaters. The four wires are used as two pairs for signalling and carry sufficient power for the repeaters. In this way the computer can be switched off and removed from the ring without switching off the repeater. With the ring the medium is terminated at each station, whereas in the cable network it is not. Each station is represented by a repeater, several of which are then connected together into a ring. The repeater is a simple device containing a shift register and some logic to detect certain conditions in the information being passed around the ring. The repeater normally passes any information received on to the next repeater, so transmission only occurs in one direction. When a station transmits data, the repeater transmits the information from the station instead of the information received from the previous repeater.

Slotted ring

There are slight differences in the channel allocation mechanism used in the Cambridge ring and in those rings developed in the USA. In the Cambridge ring a fixed-size mini-packet is used which constantly circulates in the ring, and a special station called a monitor is used to ~generate and maintain the mini-packet and provide the power for the repeaters. In the American versions a variable-size packet is used which may be lost and regenerated as required by each repeater. The current format of the Cambridge mini-packet. Note that only 16 bits of information are carried in a ring mini-packet whereas the broadcast network packet may contain several hundred bytes. The assembly of information into a block has to be done by the computer. The monitor station also provides a buffer if the ring is not physically long enough to hold a complete mini-packet. The monitor performs a check on the mini-packet each time it passes to ensure that it is intact, and to replace it if not. The monitor is an obvious weakness in the Cambridge ring design so far as reliability is concerned; however, experience so far has shown that monitor failures are rare. The advantage of the monitor is that the repeaters can be very simple as well as cheap, which is the purpose of a local network.

To use the ring to send a packet of information, the station will wait until an empty mini-packet is detected by the repeater. When the full/empty bit in the mini-packet passes the repeater it is set to one. If the packet was already full no change has been made to the bit; if the packet was empty (full/empty bit = 0) the mini-packet is now reserved by this station, The repeater will use this mini-packet if the full/empty bit was received as 0. The addresses of the source and destination stations are placed in the address fields followed by the next 16 bits of the information that the station wishes to send; these are placed in the data field from the station buffer. The reserved mini-packet then travels round to all the other stations on the ring. Each station has a source select register in which an address is placed. If the source address in a mini-packet matches the contents of the source select register, and the destination address matches the station address, the data field is copied into the station receive buffer and the accept status is set at the end of the packet. If the packet is refused, or the destination station is busy, the destination repeater will set the appropriate value in the status bits at the end of the mini-packet. No other change is made by the receiving repeater, and all other repeaters will pass on the mini-packet unchanged. Special values which can be used in the source select register are: all ones, which means accept any source station address, and all zeros, which means do not accept the data from any mini-packets.

When the mini-packet returns to the sending station the full/empty bit is reset to 0 and the status bits are checked to see if the information was accepted. As an error check, the station also reads back the 16 data bits and checks them against the data in its buffer. Having reset the full/empty bit, the station must now wait for another empty mini-packet before it can send the next 16 bits of information. In this way the now empty packet becomes available to successive stations around the ring and the packet slot is allocated in a round robin fashion.

The variable nature of packet traffic in a local network makes it difficult to design a system that will provide a very fast response, especially when there is little traffic, and yet not become overloaded or unfair when the traffic becomes heavy. The broadcast techniques provide a low delay, especially in low-volume traffic, as the transmitter can usually send a packet as soon as one is available. However, as the volume of traffic increases, the broadcast system suffers from collisions and longer delays which can eventually lead to an unstable situation. In the slotted ring the channel is allocated by means of a round robin mechanism so collisions never occur, and during a burst of traffic each station is able to continue transmitting with only a larger delay. During periods of low traffic volume the ring does introduce a delay while a station waits for the empty packet to come round.

Proponents of both systems argue that because of the very high bandwidth available on the channel, and the low processing power of the computers attached to the local network, the volume of traffic is nearly always low in a broadcast network and the delay is negligible in a ring.

Token Ring

The token ring attempts to provide the advantages of broadcast access in low-volume traffic periods, with the inherent sharing of the slotted ring during high-volume traffic periods. The physical topology of the ring is the same, but instead of a circulating mini-packet there is a circulating token. Any host requiring access to the ring waits for the token to arrive; it then changes the token to indicate that a packet is following. The modified token is then followed immediately by the data packet, which can be of any size up to some system maximum. All hosts detect the modified token and examine the packet to see if it is addressed to them; if it is the packet is copied off the ring. The receiving host still sends the packet on though, so the data packet goes all the way round the ring to the sender. The sender takes the packet off the ring. Normally the sender receives the front of the data packet before it has finished transmitting the rest of the packet, owing to the short length of the ring. When the receiver detects the end of the data packet it marks its status by changing the last few bits, as in the Cambridge ring mini-packet; thus the sender knows if the packet was accepted or not. Immediately the sender has finished the packet it puts a token on the ring so another host may have a go.

The token ring is a simple idea, but it is more complex than the Cambridge ring and the interfaces are more expensive. The initialise sequence which is required to start the ring is quite complex as the token has to be put on the ring to start data transfer; of course there can only be one token. The mechanisms for detecting duplicate tokens and lost tokens, without the use of a monitor station, add to the cost of the computer interfaces. IBM carried out extensive tests and simulations of all the local area network technologies, and decided that the token ring was the best available. The company now intends to use the token ring as the basis of its local area network products.

Charater terminal networks

The majority of timesharing computers that are accessed from interactive terminals operate on a character by character basis using a full duplex connection. There are two basic network arrangements used for asynchronous terminals.

Star network This arrangement provides each terminal with its own physical connection to the main computer.

Remote multiplexer network Each terminal has a connection to the nearest remote multiplexer; then it shares a connection to the computer with other terminals.

Character codes

So far the discussion on information transfer has been limited to bit patterns. The bit patterns were grouped as characters but there was no discussion of what a character meant. When using a terminal the user is confronted with a keyboard containing recognisable characters. On the screen, or paper, similar characters will appear: these are called 'graphics characters', as they can be printed. There are functions such as a new line, back space, or tab that are represented by control characters, as they control the operation of the terminal. Each character is mapped into a particular bit pattern, so that as the user depresses a key the terminal will produce the appropriate bit pattern and send it as a character unit to the computer. At the computer the bit pattern will be inspected to try to discover which key was depressed and therefore what action is required. If the user presses the key marked `A' then it is useful if the computer recognises the resulting bit pattern as the character 'A'. To achieve this a standard mapping is required between the graphic characters, the control characters and the bit patterns actually transferred. Such a mapping is called a 'character code'.

The description above emphasises the need for a common understanding between two parties in a communication. Such an understanding is called a *protocol.* The use of the asynchronous character frame and V24 voltage levels is a protocol. Without protocols communication is impossible. It is important to realise that every standard is just a widely accepted protocol that makes widespread communication possible.

There are two main character code standards that have been adopted: they are ASCII (American Standards Committee for Information Interchange) and EBCDIC (Extended Binary Coded Decimal Interchange Code). The ASCII code is named after the committee in the United States that first proposed it; EBCDIC is a product of IBM and is used on their equipment. A third code called IA5 (International Alphabet number 5) is the standard of the CCITT. IA5 is almost exactly the same as the ASCII code except that it allows for one or two local variations such as different currency signs. The IA5 code is also the standard recommended by the International Standards Organization (ISO).

The ASCII code has been adopted by most computer manufacturers outside IBM influence. It is a 7 bit code, with no parity recommendation. 7 bits allow for 128 different symbols of which about 93 are graphic characters and 35 are control characters. The IA5 code is based on ASCII but uses even parity to produce an eighth bit. For most terminals the two codes are exactly the same; the eighth bit is often ignored.

The EBCDIC code is an 8 bit code invented and used by IBM. As a manufacturer IBM has sufficient domination of the computer market to have its own standards and not worry too much if they differ from everyone else's. The EBCDIC code covers nearly the same graphic and control characters as ASCII, but there are a number of the 8 bit patterns that are not allocated as character codes.

Some computer manufacturers have their own internal character codes, left over from days before standards were available. This means that the standard bit patterns have to be converted before they can be understood by the computer software, and of course converted back for communications use. Nearly all terminals available now use either ASCII or EBCDIC as their code.

The star arrangement

The components required to connect a single terminal to the computer are listed below:

a. a terminal with a UART,

b. a communication medium,

c. a UART at the computer end,

d. and an interface between the UART and the computer internal communication system.

A UART does not actually produce the V24 signal level voltages discussed in chapter 2; a second integrated circuit is needed to take the serial I/O from the UART and convert it to the V24 voltage signals. The use of a second chip merely allows the UART to be used with any voltage signalling system. A computer terminal usually comes complete and ready to plug into whatever medium is to be used. The plug would be standard, usually the V24 standard 'D' plug. A computer manufacturer will supply an interface containing a UART and a signal level converter which plugs directly into the computer. It comes with a standard plug ready to be attached to the communications medium. The medium could be, at the moment, either a length of wire or a PSTN connection involving two MODEMs.

1 Ensure the computer interface and the terminal are provided with compatible interfaces (V24).

2. Provide a suitable medium.

If MODEMs are used the purchaser should ensure that the terminal and interface plugs are for MODEM use, which is always a V24 (RS232C) standard. In the remainder of this chapter 'suitable medium' will mean either an in-house wire or PSTN connection, depending on the installation requirements. The use of the 'D' plug with the connections and signals arranged in the V24 standard now means that any terminal or computer can be attached to any medium using the standard connectors. Connecting a single terminal is reasonably easy, but connecting a large number, say one or two hundred, is slightly different. The obvious approach with a star network would be to use one computer interface for each terminal. As all the terminals are separate, each will have its own medium. However, a large number of interfaces on a computer causes problems in physically fitting them in, addressing each interface and other considerations of speed and efficiency within the computer. One solution adopted is to use a local multiplexer. *Multiplexing* is a technique which enables several inputs to be placed on one output; the reverse operation is called demultiplexing. A multiplexer normally performs both functions.

The terminal multiplexer is a device made by the computer manufacturer to enable several terminal lines to use one interface to the computer. The assumption is made by the designer of a terminal multiplexer that an asynchronous terminal will not be used continuously for very long, and even when a continuous stream of characters is being transferred the transfer rate will be very low compared with the capacity of the computer interface. A common number of terminals to put on a single local multiplexer is 16; thus if each one has a transfer rate of say 1200 bps then the total worst case rate is 16 x 1200 = 19,200 bps. A bus on a minicomputer could transfer over I million bps, so there is plenty of spare capacity in the computer for other transfers.

The multiplexer uses one UART for each terminal line and from the outside looks like a number of individual terminal interfaces, but there is only one computer interface for all of the UARTs. Where each terminal has its own computer interface the computer software can identify each terminal, and therefore the user, by the address of the interface. But when several terminals are using the same interface each terminal needs another address within the interface. Each terminal has its own port which consists of a UART and the signal level converter. The local multiplexer performs the function of multiplexing the terminals via the single computer interface. A common mode of operation of the multiplexer is to use a scanner register, to address each UART in a round robin sequence. The register is incremented as a modulo *n* counter where *n is* the number of terminal lines on the multiplexer. For this reason *n is* usually a power of 2 (8 or 16) as this makes implementing the counter easy. As a new number comes up in the scanner register the corresponding UART is tested to see if there is a character waiting in its receive buffer. If so, the character is removed and the present contents of the scanner register are added to make a line number/character pair. In this way each UART is given an address within the multiplexer and every character associated with that port is tagged by the port number.

After any received character has been dealt with, the multiplexer will look to see if there is a character to be sent out to the port; if there is, it is fetched and placed in the UART transmitter buffer register. The multiplexer scanner register is then incremented and the process repeated for the next port. As the scanning mechanism is implemented in hardware the whole process is very fast. The mechanisms by which characters are sent and received across the interface to and from the computer vary from computer to computer. Some manufacturers have more than one type of asynchronous terminal multiplexer to provide different levels of complexity at different prices.

Remote multiplexers

A star network consists of a number of terminals, each having its own suitable medium up to the computer interface which will be either a single line interface or a local multiplexer. A timesharing computer would have a combination of single line interfaces and local multiplexers to suit the exact needs of its users within the constraints imposed by the manufacturer's hardware. As each terminal has its own dedicated connection, all the bandwidth of the connection is available for information transfer. When the terminal is idle, then the connection and connection equipment are idle. If some terminals are at remote sites then the MODEM and the telephone charges for each line may become very high. As many timesharing systems have more physical terminals than the number of active terminals they can support, some connections will be idle for long periods.

The PTT's pricing policy for MODEM charges is such that a 2400 bps MODEM will cost only a little more than a 300 bps MODEM. So it makes economic sense to use the faster MODEMs if the total information rate justifies it. The star network is the obvious and natural first attempt at a terminal network design as it uses the simplest hardware and provides the best response. However if three or four, or even more, slow MODEMs can be replaced by one fast one, then the economics may justify a more complex network design. The use of remote multiplexers enables such a design to be used.

The operation of a local multiplexer was described as enabling several terminal lines to interface to a computer via a single interface. The remote multiplexer enables several terminal lines to use a single high-speed communications line. A number of terminals are connected by local PSTN lines or directly by wire to a remote multiplexer. The multiplexer is connected by a single high-speed line to the computer. The multiplexer is *remote* from the computer and very often involves a PSTN connection. The remote multiplexer has essentially the same function as the local multiplexer, except that its single high-speed side is serial. Using a remote multiplexer is more expensive in terms of equipment, because a computer interface is still needed and the remote equipment is extra. The choice of design is made by weighing up the extra capital cost of the equipment against the savings from renting a few high-speed lines instead of a large number of slow-speed lines from the PTT. Remote multiplexers are more economic on PSTN networks; however, some in-house wiring systems may be more economical if multiplexers are used instead of lots of dedicated circuits for each terminal. This is especially true if the multiplexer is intelligent and allows switching. Other factors are involved of course. For instance, a PTT is more likely to provide a couple of high-speed lines on time rather than say 100 slow-speed lines, as each line has to be individually supplied. A commercial timesharing bureau may decide to use a remote multiplexer in an area or town so that its customers need only pay local call charges by dialling-up the nearest multiplexer, rather than the computer which may be a long distance away.

Remote multiplexing techniques

The techniques used for multiplexing are quite simple: they are concerned with sharing the bandwidth of the fast communications channel amongst the slow terminal lines on the 'other side' of the multiplexer. The difference between multiplexing and concentration is difficult to separate as some techniques fall into both camps. There are two situations to consider.

1. *Input and output capacities are the same*

   A multiplexer has three slow-speed terminal lines attached to it with a single high-speed channel to the computer. If the capacities of each line are C_1, C_2, C_3, for the slow-speed lines and C_f for the high-speed channel. Then

   $$C_1 + C_2 + C_3 \leq C_f$$

   if the high-speed channel is to meet our requirement. The inequality (≤) is a practical consideration as the actual line speeds may not allow equality. For instance, if $C_1 = C_2 = C_3 = 300$ bps, then $900 < C_f$. As 900 bps is not a standard speed the actual value would be the next standard speed which is 1200 bps.

2. *The input capacity exceeds the output capacity*

   $$C_1 + C_2 + C_3 > C_f$$

   This is possible on a remote multiplexer with terminals, as the terminals are never used continuously because of thinking time and slow typing rates. So there are periods when each terminal line uses none of its capacity. What must be assured is that C_f is large enough for the average information rate on the terminal lines. Denoting ? as the average rate this gives

   $$c_1 + c_2 + c_3 \leq C_f$$

   The situation in case (1), equation 4.1 above, is usually called multiplexing'; the situation in (2) as described by equation 4.3 is usually called 'concentration'. The situation described by equation 4.3 can only be implemented by equipment sharing a channel and cooperating over its use. Concentrators use storage to even out fluctuations in the actual transfer rates. Usage of these terms by various groups of people within the computer industry has led to some ambiguity in their meaning in the communications context.

There are two ways of dividing the bandwidth of the fast channel

a. Frequency division multiplexing (FDM), and

b. Time division multiplexing (TDM).

Frequency division multiplexing is not used directly by computer communications equipment. It is used on the PSTN, and is described here in order to provide another illustration of the idea of multiplexing. Over a period of time it is required to share the bandwidth of the fast channel amongst the slower channels.

Frequency division multiplexing

By definition, the slow channels must have a narrower bandwidth than the fast channel. Frequency division multiplexing divides the frequency range of the fast channel into a number of narrower bands, each of which has the same bandwidth as a slow channel. In between each allocated band of frequencies is a guard band which is used to separate the narrow band channels, and avoid interference between them.

Frequency division multiplexing has certain characteristics which are worth noting.

a. Each slow channel has a permanently allocated channel on the fast channel.

b. If the slow channel is not being used at any time the corresponding channel on the fast line is wasted.

c. The slow channels have to be modulated up to the required frequency slots, and demodulated at the other end.

Frequency division multiplexing is useful for systems where the channel is in continuous use. For this reason FDM is used on the PSTN to carry a number of telephone connections on the high-speed channels used to connect telephone exchanges.

Time division multiplexing

The nature of computer communications makes the division of the high-speed channel along the time axis very easy, and more efficient. The information is always transferred in characters which are of fixed length (usually 8 bits). The time axis is divided into slots: each slot is of sufficient time to transmit a single character. The whole bandwidth on the high-speed channel is used to transmit the character, so it can be transmitted much more quickly than on a slow-speed channel. Figure 4.8 shows the bandwidth/time allocation in slots. If there are n slow-speed channels connected to the multiplexer then the time slots are allocated to each slow-speed channel in turn, so that every nth slot contains a character from the same slow-speed channel. There is no difficulty in receiving characters and deciding which terminal they belong to. The sender and receiver synchronise the slots by an internal mechanism, such as the use of SYN characters. After the sender and receiver on the high-speed channel have synchronised the slots, the first character will be for the first slow-speed channel, the second for the second slow-speed channel, an so on. When the last slow-speed channel character has been received in its slot, a character for the first slow channel is received next.

This multiplexing technique has some advantages for character-based computer communications, owing to the fixed size of the basic unit of information transfer. Ordinary TDM still has some of the disadvantages of FDM though in particular characteristic. If any slow channel does not have a character to send when its slot becomes available, perhaps because the user is thinking, then the slot remains empty in the high-speed channel. Usually a null character of zeros is sent in this case. This means that some of the bandwidth of the fast channel is wasted. However, the whole frequency range of the high-speed channel is used as there is no wastage in guard bands. A multiplexer used with asynchronous terminals on the slow channels will always have empty slots as there are usually some terminals not active; the percentage of time a character terminal is actually sending or receiving a character is quite small. More complex techniques have been devised, based on ordinary TDM, which use the fast channel more efficiently when interactive terminals are used on the slow channels. These techniques, described below, cross the boundary between multiplexing and concentration though they still have the title *multiplexing techniques.*

Intelligent or statistical time division multiplexing

With intelligent or statistical TDM the time axis is again divided into fixed slots; however, the slots are not allocated on a round robin basis but on a first-come first-served regime. As soon as a character arrives from a slow channel it is placed in the next free slot. This method raises two problems·

1. How does the demultiplexer at the other end know which slow channel any character came from?
2. What happens if there is no free slot?

The first problem is easily solved: the time slot is lengthened to take extra bits which identify the slow channel. For instance, a time slot of 16 bits could be used. This allows 7 bits for the slow channel number, 1 bit as a control bit, and 8 bits for the character. Remember the fast channel would probably be a synchronous connection, so allocating the slots in units of 8 bits is a good idea. The control bit can be used to identify this slot of 16 bits as a user character if it is 0 say; or if the control bit is 1, then the other 15 bits may contain control information passing between the multiplexer and demultiplexer at opposite ends of the fast channel. As the slots are not allocated to a fixed slow channel, it is easy to slip in control information about the status of the various slow channels for instance. The control slot is used to implement *intelligent* functions, such as switching, or automatic line speed control. It is possible to have variable sized slots; in that case a number of characters from the same slow channel are grouped together and sent as a unit preceded by some control information. Other complex framing schemes can be used, especially when a microprocessor is used to provide the intelligence in the multiplexer.

The second problem may be solved by some form of storage to hold the character until a slot is free; in this sense the intelligent multiplexer becomes a concentrator. The problem may also be solved by placing controls on the number and speed of the slow channels and then throwing away any characters that cannot be accommodated.

This statistical multiplexer relies on the sum of the average transfer rates for the slow channels not exceeding the capacity of the fast channel. This requires more intelligence than an ordinary time division multiplexer, and with the introduction of control information the equipment is capable of much more sophistication in error handling and traffic control, hence the term *intelligent.* This type of multiplexer is usually built around a microprocessor.

The choice of ordinary multiplexers or the intelligent type is a matter of economics. In terms of connecting more slow-speed channels on to the same high-speed channel the intelligent multiplexer is better but will cost more. The low price of microprocessors as a source of intelligence with better performance and more sophisticated control has in fact meant that most remote multiplexer networks use intelligent multiplexing techniques.

Multiplexer networks

A system using remote multiplexers requires an interface device at the computer to receive and send characters to the remote multiplexers, and interface in an appropriate way to the computer itself. Sometimes a high-speed direct memory access interface is used to reduce the load on the computer for character output to the terminals. Since the network is character based, the interface sends and receives the characters separately, which in the worst case may mean an interrupt for every incoming character on some computers! Even with a high-speed interface the processing required to handle the throughput of characters from an asynchronous terminal network can be very high. Many computers that have a terminal network use a front end processor (FEP) to handle the network and remove a lot of the character processing overhead from the main computer system. All of the local terminals and multiplexers will be interfaced to the FEP, which is usually a minicomputer. An FEP provides a number of advantages.

i. It can handle all character echo.

ii. It can edit lines before passing them to the main computer.

iii. When the main computer is down the FEP can be used to print a message to the terminal user.

iv. The FEP can perform monitoring and statistics collection on the network performance.

The front end processor communicates with the main computer through a shared processor memory area, shared disc or high-speed I/O channel.

With the extra processing power and flexibility of the FEP, very complex networks can be designed using cascaded multiplexers for remote terminals and star arrangements for local terminals. Cascaded multiplexers are used to save line charges by connecting multiplexers in series. In figure the multiplexers A, B and C are cascaded. The high-speed line for B needs to have the capacity to carry traffic from multiplexer B as well as the traffic from multiplexer C. The cascaded arrangement is cheaper in terms of line cost than connecting multiplexers B and C directly to the computer site. Usually cascaded multiplexers are of the intelligent type.

Designing an asynchronous terminal network

The choice of equipment and the planning of a connection layout is not easy for an asynchronous terminal network. The usual constraints are the number and position of the terminals and the position of the computer. Terminals local to the computer that do not need PSTN connection are best attached by a star arrangement, as this is cheapest and gives the best performance for the terminal user. Terminals needing a PSTN connection require more careful consideration. If only a few lines are involved a star arrangement may be cheaper; where a larger number are involved the saving in line rental by using a remote multiplexer will become more attractive. The crossover between a star design and a remote multiplexer has to be worked out for individual cases and must take into account other factors such as PSTN line availability and the facilities offered by the multiplexing equipment. For instance, to use remote multiplexers, a local multiplexer-demultiplexer is needed at the computer site. Often this multiplexer interface will also support local slow-speed terminals directly, enabling the entire network to use a single computer interface. The siting and choice of exact numbers of multiplexers to be used in a network design is an interesting exercise in its own right; more information can be found in the book by Schwartz.

Local area networks

A LAN can be considered to consist of four elements. The three hardware elements are a transmission medium, a mechanism for controlling transmission over the medium and an interface to the network for the host computer. The fourth basic element is the set of software required in the host computer to implement the protocols which control the communication from one host computer to another. The software functions at different levels to provide a number of protocol layers ranging from packetization to the appiication level. This combination of layered hardware and software is a noticeable feature of local computer networks. Inexpen-sive hardware, such as a twisted pair or coaxial cable, is used to interconnect systems. The characteristics of LANs are high bandwidth, low error rate and small delay. These characteristics enable LANs to interconnect processors to provide distributed multiprocessor systems which enable the sharing of resources such as secondary storage and other peripherals. The LANs described in this chapter are principally used for data transmission. Other forms of information, such as voice and video, are time critical and will not tolerate the variable delays of LANs.

Network topologies

There are a number of possible topologies for a computer network, the choice of which is usually determined by the purpose for which the network is installed and the physical location of the devices to be interconnected. The number of devices that are to be connected can dictate the choice of topology. If the number is very small, less than say 10 devices, then a point-to-point connection or polling system is possible, but as the number of devices to be interconnected increases then alternatives have to be considered. The basic alternatives, are: the star, where all devices are connected to a central point; the bus, where all devices are connected by a common link between them; the ring, where all devices are successively linked together and the ends of the connection are brought together again to complete a ring; and the unconstrained network, where links can exist between any one device and any number of other devices. There are variations of these basic topologies such as branching buses, trees, etc., but in general these can be considered to be extensions of the basic topologies in which the connected devices are components of another bus, star or ring.

Comparison of the basic topologies

The disadvantage of a star compared with a bus or a ring is that each device requires a connection to a central point which can become a bottleneck and, with a large number of connected devices, that the interconnection costs are comparatively high. The advantage of the star configuration is that the devices can use a simple point-to-point protocol rather than a common access protocol. The interconnection cost disadvantage can be reduced by providing device concentrators located adjacent to a number of devices. This saves the cost of individual connections, distributes some of the control and also allows the possibility of continued operation of parts of the network in the event of the failure of the central point.

The advantage of the bus and the ring is that a simpler interconnection strategy can be used that of single interconnection from one device to the next. A simple topology allows network configurations to be changed as the number of stations varies. With a bus, stations are simply connected to the bus cable. With a ring, the network is temporarily broken and a new station inserted between two existing stations. Most LANs are based on either a bus or a ring topology with common access protocols. The unconstrained topology is uncommon due to the necessity to handle the routing of data between devices and the problem of locating a path between devices. The passage of information through a node will affect its performance and will generally require a processor system of similar performance to the host system.

The physical connection between devices

The physical connection between devices on a LAN is characterized by

- The nature of the medium, e.g. fibre optic, coaxial cable, current loop, etc.
- The method of transmission, e.g. broadband, baseband.
- The signal levels and the modulation schemes used.
- The methods of signal coding.
- The types of connectors used and their pin allocations.
- The logic levels of the signals.
- The use of point-to-point or broadcast techniques.
- The synchronization method used.

Most LAN systems use synchronous schemes. The requirements of the link are specified in terms of data and error rates; this usually results in a compromise between performance and cost. Other important considerations in the selection of a physical medium are its integrity and reliability. These factors will seriously affect the performance of the network and its ease of use.

Some successful broadband LANs have also been implemented which carry information on channels of different frequencies. Often, one channel on a broadband network is shared using an access technique similar to those discussed below.

Medium access control techniques

The physical connection ensures that one device can communicate with another. In most LAN topologies part of the transmission system is shared, so some form of control is required to arbitrate between contending devices. This is called the *medium access control* (MAC). In this section, a broad outline is given of the variety of techniques available. In later sections, examples of these techniques are covered in more detail. The techniques to be discussed are token passing and contention for both rings and buses, and slotted and register insertion rings.

Common access control schemes: token passing

A token is a unique control message that conveys the right of access to the medium.

The token is passed between devices; the device that received the token most recently is said to hold the token and can access the communication medium. Token passing can be used with both broadcast (token bus) and sequentially connected (token ring) networks.

A number of potential problems exist in token passing systems. The systems must be able to detect and recover from lost or duplicated tokens. These problems have different solutions for ring and bus networks. In a token ring a unique marker is used to delimit the end of a transmission. When this marker is detected by the next device on the ring it looks for a pattern that represents the token and, if found, inserts its message into the ring. If this device does not wish to transmit, it passes the frame marker and token on to the next device. A token bus transmits a unique message for the token and monitors the bus for activity that indicates that the token was successfully received. If this is not so then a token recovery procedure has to be started.

Common access control: contention

Contention control is a distributed control scheme where each device attempts to gain control of the transmission medium. Each device competes against the other devices, so, to ensure fairness, each device must follow a precise set of rules for accessing the medium. LAN contention schemes are derived from the ALOHA and slotted ALOHA approach to multiple access to broadcast networks.

Contention control for network systems

Contention access control methods allow any device to attempt transmission and then take steps to resolve and limit the collisions that will occur. In a LAN, the prevention of collisions is attempted by sensing the activity on the bus before transmission is attempted. Any activity on the bus can be detected by looking for the presence of the carrier on which the data is encoded. This is known as *carrier sense.* The detection of a carrier can be used to prevent a device from corrupting the transmission in progress.

An algorithm is needed to specify what a station should do if the medium is found to be busy. Three approaches or persistence algorithms are possible:

1 *Non-persistent.* The station backs off a random amount of time and then senses the medium again.

2 *1-persistent.* The station continues to sense the medium until it is idle and then transmits.

3 *p-persistent.* The station continues to sense the medium until it is idle and then transmits with some probability p. Otherwise it backs off a fixed amount of time and then transmits with probability *p* or continues to back off with probability (1-p).

The non-persistent algorithm is effective in avoiding collisions; two stations wishing to transmit when the medium is busy are likely to back off for a different amount of time. The drawback is that there is likely to be wasted idle time following each transmission. In contrast, the 1-persistent algorithm attempts to reduce idle time by allowing a single waiting station to transmit immediately after another transmission. Unfortunately, if more than one station is waiting, a collision is guaranteed. The p-persistent algorithm is a compromise that attempts to minimize both collisions and idle time.

If two devices find that the bus is free then both may start to transmit at the same time and their messages will collide. This is detected by each station monitoring its signal on the bus. This is known as *collision detection.* To ensure that the collision is detected by all devices on the network, the devices must continue to transmit for a period after the detection of a collision. After the collision both devices will then wish to transmit. To prevent an immediate collision a random back off delay is used. The system just described is called carrier sense multiple access with collision detection (CSMA/CD).

Other access control techniques for ring systems

A ring can be configured to contain a number *of* circulating data minipackets; this allows two methods of access. In the first method, if a device is able to determine if a packet is empty it can fill this with data. This is called a slotted ring. Alternatively, a device can detect the end of a packet and insert its own packet between two existing packets; this is known as *register insertion*.

Allocated control for buses

In a bus system the access to the bus can be controlled by allocating time slots to connected devices. The simplest form is to divide the time equally between each device using time division multiple access (TDMA). This has the disadvantage that if a device does not wish to communicate then its allocated time is unused and resources are lost. Polling schemes can be used in which one device is allocated the role of bus master to handle requests. When a device wishes to transmit, it waits to be polled by the bus master and either transmits its message or declines the offer.

Both of the above schemes have high overheads when the network traffic is low. This has led to the development of combined contention and allocation schemes. In a combined scheme contention control is used when the load is light and the probability of collisions is low, resulting in low overheads. As the network utilization increases the chances of collisions increases and the throughput decreases. When this occurs an allocation scheme is utilized to ensure the maximum use of the network without contention. For example, see Kleinrock and Yemeni.

Local area network standardization

Local area networks have developed rapidly over a short period of time, presenting the prospective user with a wide choice of systems. To help the prospective users and suppliers, national and international standards bodies have produced standards specifically for LANs, concentrating on the lower levels of the OSI model. The standards developed for wide area networks will also be applicable to the higher levels of LANs. The IEEE is the organization principally involved with the standardization of the lower levels of LAN systems. The standardization was started by the IEEE Computer Society in 1980 by the formation of the IEEE Standards Project 802 whose role is to standardize the means *of* connecting digital equipment within a local area.

The project has noted that one single standard will not suffice and has accepted three main access methods. The first is the CSMA/CD bus (802.3) and the other two are token passing rings (802.5) and token passing buses (802.4). All three are designed to provide for the transmission of data over the network and are generally not suitable for the transmission of time critical information such as speech and video.

Standardization in metropolitan area networks is closely following that of LANs and will be important for LAN users wishing to interwork between LANs interconnected via gateways to the larger MANs.

The IEEE 802 standardization

The IEEE 802 committee has developed an overall structure into which a family of substandards. These standards have also been adopted by the International Standards Organization (ISO) with the series numbers 8802 (i.e. IEEE 802.2 is the same as ISO 8802/2). The individual IEEE standard numbers are:

802.1 Relationship between the 802 standards and the OSI model

802.2 Logical link control

802.3 Carrier sense multiple access with collision detection

802.4 Token passing bus access method

802.5 Token passing ring access method

802.6 Metropolitan area networks

In addition the following Technical Advisory Groups (TAG) have been initiated which may subsequently produce standards:

802.7 Broadband TAG

802.8 Fibre optic TAG

802.9 TAG concerned with the integration of LANs and digital telephony

IEEE 802.1 standard and the OSI model

The IEEE standard 802.1 describes the interrelationship between the members of the IEEE 802 standard family and their relationship to the ISO OSI reference model for LANs. Each of the access methods includes both physical layer components and a medium access control technique. The 802.2 logical link control (LLC) standard describes a network-independent protocol set used for passing data over any of the standardized systems 802.3-5; The combination of the MAC and LLC layers can be considered to form layer 2 of the OSI model.

The principles adopted for local area computer network systems introduced in the previous sections have been incorporated into many experimental and commercial systems.

The ethernet

The majority of installed LANs are based on Ethernet, which is a passive bus network that utilizes CSMA/CD. The system was developed, in 1976 by Metcalfe and Boggs. The original system operated with a data rate of 3 Mbit/s connecting up to 256 stations with a maximum network length of 1km. The system has evolved into a commercially available system operating at 10 Mbit/s, connecting a maximum of 1024 stations over a branching bus with a maximum network length of 2.5 km. Three of its major manufacturers, Xerox, Intel and DEC, have produced the industry standard definition which has been accepted by the IEEE. The advantages of the Ethernet system are its commercial standard and the fact that commercial interfaces are available for most common computer buses. Two of the disadvantages of the full specification system are the cost per connection and the cabling costs. A number of manufacturers now provide lower cost connection and cabling systems called Cheapernet or thin Ethernet. This has a reduced specification for the number of devices and cabling lengths, but is very suitable for small-scale networks.

IEEE 802.3 CSMA/CD bus

The IEEE standard 802.3 describes a LAN system using a multiple access, broadcast, baseband transmission medium with CSMA/CD.

Physical layer

The 802.3 standard specifies the physical layer of the system which has the following characteristics:

- *Transmission.* Baseband signalling over shielded coaxial cable.
- Topology. Branching non-rooted tree.
- *Network length.* Maximum cable segment length is 500 in, which may be interconnected via repeaters to a maximum system length of 2500 in.

- Data rate. 10 Mbit/s.
- Maximum number of stations. 1024

Frame format

When the frame is transmitted a minimum size limit of 46 data octets is imposed. Shorter, blocks of information presented for transmission are padded to the limit using the PAD field. This is to ensure that a frame will have been sensed by all stations on a maximum sized network before the transmission is completed. The time taken by any transmission must be longer than the *slot time,* that is the maximum propagation time from one end of the network to the other and back. This enables the deference and collision detection procedures to operate correctly.

The *preamble is* a 7-octet field with a bit pattern that results in a transmitted signal of half the transmission frequency; this has a polarity transition at the centre of each symbol time which simplifies synchronization. The SFD is the start of frame delimiter and signifies the start of the frame. The *destination* and *source address* fields are either 2 or 6 octets in length. The address length is constant for a network implementation. The *length* field contains the number of octets in the data field. The *LLCData* field contains the *LLC* information and information from higher layers. The FCS (frame check sequence) field contains a 32-bit cyclic redundancy check (CRC) computed on both address fields, length, LLCData and PAD fields.

Transmission without contention

Transmission is initiated by the MAC on reception of data from the LLC. The MAC constructs a frame, to the above format, with the data provided by the LLC. The MAC monitors the medium for the presence of a carrier, indicating that a transmission in progress, and defers to passing traffic. When the medium is clear transmission is started.

Reception without contention

All stations listen to the network; a reception is begun by the detection of the preamble which is used for clock synchronization. The bit stream up to the end of the start delimiter is discarded and then the frame is reconstructed. The destination address of the incoming frame is checked to see if it should be received by the station, if not it is discarded. If the address matches and the reception was completed without error, this is signalled by the MAC to the LLC and the address and data fields are passed to the higher layer.

Access contention

If more than one station attempts to use the medium at the same time they will interfere with each other, causing a collision between the signals of the two stations. A station can experience a collision during the initial part of its transmission transmitted signal has had time to propagate to all stations on the medium. Once the window has passed, the station has the medium and collisions will be prevented by other stations deferring to it. When a collision is detected the MAC enforces the collision by transmitting a bit sequence called a *jam*. The duration of the jam is sufficient to ensure that all stations will detect the collision. After the jam has been sent transmission is stopped. Transmission is rescheduled to occur after a random period of time, called the back off. If on re-transmission a further collision is detected, the jam and back off sequence is repeated with an increase in the back off. This is continued until a maximum number of retries have been exceeded, in which case a transmission error is signalled to the LLC layer.

Network management and initialization

The CSMA/CD MAC scheme has no separate network management functions to provide detection, control and recovery from abnormal network conditions. This is because these functions are essential for the operation of the CSMA/CD control and are incorporated within it. In addition, as the network is a passive medium with fully distributed control, no medium or common network control initialization is required.

IEEE 802.4 token passing bus

The IEEE standard 802.4 describes a LAN based on a broadcast bus medium with a token passing access control scheme. The physical layer specifications cover a number of coaxial cabled systems with hardware derived from cable television (CATV) systems. The number of stations connected and the total length of the network depend on the physical layer scheme used.

Physical layer

Three different physical layer options are described in the standard. These are:

- An omnidirectional bus using phase continuous frequency shift keying at I Mbit/s.
- An omnidirectional bus using phase continuous frequency shift keying at 5 or 10 Mbit/s.
- A directional bus with active head end repeater using multilevel duobinary amplitude modulation/phase shift keying at 1, 5 or 10 Mbit/s.

Each physical layer option provides a generic interface to the medium access control and to the station management. The MAC interface provides four primitives to control the operation of the physical layer. These are transmission initiation, reception notification, transmission mode control and end of reception indication. The station management interface provides primitives for the configuration and control of the physical layer.

Medium access control

The medium access control scheme used is a token-based system where the token passes sequentially around a logical ring formed between stations on the network. The MAC provides the standard functions of data buffering, station address recognition, frame encapsulation, FCS generation and valid token recognition. The MAC also provides facilities for the maintenance of the logical ring. These are lost token recovery, token holding time-outs, distributed initialization, node failure error recovery and logical ring member addition. The passage of the token between stations on the logical ring has little relationship to the physical connectivity of the stations. The logical ring consists of stations A→B→E→G→C→A; the token is passed between these stations sequentially. Stations D and H are connected to the physical layer and can therefore receive messages but cannot initiate transmission. However, they can transmit a response when a station which is a member of the logical ring issues a *request_with_response.*

Frame formats

The start and end delimiters are unique octets that contain a special symbol which will never be present in the data. This *nondata* symbol is to aid in the identification of the delimiters.

PREAMBLE	SD	FC	DA	SA	DATA_UNIT	FCS	ED

PREAMBLE	Pattern for clock sync
SD	Start delimiter
FC	Frame control
DA	Destination address
SA	Source address
DATA_UNIT	Information, 0 or more octets
FCS	Frame check sequence
ED	End delimiter

Token bus frame format

MAC operation

The operations performed by the MAC layer involve the management of ordered access to the medium, providing a means for the addition and subtraction of stations and fault handling. The operation of the MAC is based on the following observations about a station's operation:

1 When a station transmits to the medium its signal can be received by all stations; no station can predictably alter the transmission but a transmission can be corrupted.

2 The transmitting station can assume that all active stations received some transmission but cannot assume that its message was received correctly by any station.

3 When a station successfully receives a frame it can assume that all other stations were aware of the transmission.

4 It is not necessary for all stations to be involved in the transmitted sequence, i.e. be members of the logical ring.

5 Each station must be able to handle multiple or lost tokens; there is no common monitor to perform this function.

MAC management functions

The normal operation of the network, when the logical ring has been established and is not changing, simply involves the passage of the token between a station and its logical successor after it has completed its transmissions. A station holding the token may temporarily delegate its right to transmit to any station, including those not in the logical ring, by sending a *request_with_response* data frame. When a station receives a *request_with_response* it can respond with a *response* data frame; after this the right to transmit returns to the original station. After a station passes the token it listens to ensure that its successor sends a valid frame indicating that the token was accepted successfully. If no valid frame is heard the sender attempts to determine the reason why the token was not transferred.

If the sender hears noise or an invalid frame it must attempt to recover the token. If it was just to repeat the token, it could create two tokens in the network. If the station hears a noise burst it continues to listen for four more *slot times*. If nothing more is heard it assumes that its own token was corrupted and as in the case of no activity, repeats the token. The second token is monitored as before; if there is still no activity the sender assumes that its successor has failed. It then attempts to find out its own place in the logical ring by transmitting a Who_follows frame with its previous successor's address. All stations check the address and the station whose predecessor was the successor of the current station responds with a *Setsuccessor* frame. If there is still no response the token holder has to find another station on the logical ring by sending a *Solicit successor* frame containing its own address. Any station wishing to be part of the logical ring responds using a *response windoiv.* A response window is a controlled interval of time after the transmission of a MAC control frame during which the sender waits for a reply to be started. If the attempts to solicit a successor fail, either all stations have left the logical ring or an error condition exists and the logical ring needs to be re-established.

Stations are added to the logical ring by active stations sending a *solicit_successor* frame. This specifies a range of addresses between the sender and its successor.

Stations in this range respond during the response window. It is possible that more than one station will wish to respond. If contention occurs the sending station starts an arbitration procedure by sending a *resolve_contention* frame. A station that responds chooses a delay of 03 slot times before transmitting. If during the delay another transmission is heard the station removes itself from the contention resolution. If nothing is heard it replies, this initiates further *resolve contention* requests. Finally only one station will successfully respond, resolve the contention and become the successor.

The initialization of the logical ring is a special instance of adding stations. This action is started when the bus has been idle for too long. When this occurs, a station transmits a *claim_token* frame and contention is resolved in a similar manner as before. The station that wins the contention holds the token; it can solicit a successor and build the logical ring.

IEEE 802.5 token ring

The IEEE standard 802.5 describes a ring LAN using a token passing access control scheme for the connection of up to 250 stations with multiple levels of message priority. Information is transmitted sequentially from one station to the next, each active station acting as a repeater for the information. The destination station copies the information from the ring. The information is removed from the ring by the source station. Error detection and recovery facilities and control of the number of bits in the ring are provided by one of the stations acting as a network monitor. This is protected by backup capability in all other ring stations.

Physical layer

The IEEE token ring uses shielded twin twisted pair cable with data transmission at either I or 4 Mbit/s. The frequency is fixed for a particular implementation of the system. Each station is connected into the ring via a trunk coupling unit (TCU) that enables an active station to be inserted into the ring or by-passed from the ring when inactive or failed. Symbols are transmitted to the medium using differential Manchester-type coding which is characterized by having two signal elements per symbol. Two non-data symbols are used within the frame delimiter octets.

The active monitor

The physical layer requires that all stations have the capability to become the network monitor. Only one station acts as the active monitor and signals its presence by regularly broadcasting active monitor present (AMP) MAC frames. The first station to receive the AMP frame resets a timer and sends a standby monitor present (SMP) frame. If the timer expires, indicating the failure of the active monitor, the standby monitor starts the procedure of becoming the active monitor. The SMP frame is passed between all other stations; these stations use a similar procedure to backup the first standby monitor. The active monitor checks the ring for correct transmission and will attempt to restore correct operation when an error is detected. It also checks for AMP frames that are not its own, indicating that two active monitors are in operation. If this occurs it returns to the standby state.

The active monitor station provides a variable-length delay buffer, the *latency buffer,* that maintains the minimum length of the ring, specified in bit times. This must be greater than the number of bits in the token sequence, 24 bits. The active monitor also acts as the master oscillator for the network, providing the clock to which all other stations synchronize. Although this provides the frequency to which all segments of the ring should be synchronized, it is possible for segments of the ring to be operating at slightly different frequencies and thereby change the total ring latency. These errors can be up to +- 3 bits, so to maintain a constant ring latency of $\geq$ 24 bits, a variable length buffer, of up to 6 bits, is added to the buffer.

Format of transmitted information

Two formats of information are transmitted around the ring, tokens and frames. The token represents the right for a station to transmit. The frame format is used for the transmission of medium access control (MAC) and logical link control (LLC) messages between stations. To meet the requirements of the LLC each station should be capable of receiving frames up to and including 133 octets. The *end delimiter* contains an intermediate frame bit, I, and an error detected bit, E. The I bit is set to a I to signify that another frame from the same transmitter will follow, and is set to 0 for the last or only frame transmitted. The E bit is set to 0 by the source transmitter. Each station in the ring checks tokens and frames for errors as they are repeated. If an error is detected the E bit is set to I in the frame in error: otherwise the E bit is repeated as received. The *access control field* contains bits for the identification and control of tokens, for message priority and monitor control. The token bit is set to 0 in a token and I in a frame. The priority bits specify the priority of a token allowing a station to determine if it can use the token. There are eight levels of priority with level 0 being the lowest. A station that has a protocol data unit (PDU) awaiting transmission with equal or higher priority than the token's priority may change the token to a start-of-frame sequence and commence transmission of the PDU.

The *monitor* bit is set by the transmitter to 0 in all frames and tokens. When a monitor bit of 0 is detected by the active monitor it is converted to a I to mark its first passage around the ring. If the active monitor detects an access control field with the monitor bit set to I and a priority greater than 0 then the frame or token is aborted; this is because a frame or token should have been removed by its transmitting station. The exception is a priority 0 token which will circulate around the ring when the network is idle.

The frame status field is used to enable the trans-mitting station to receive information about the passage of a frame around the ring. Two bits, the address recognized, A, and frame copied, C, are sent as 0 by the transmitting station. If a station recognizes the destination address of the frame as its own it sets the A bit to 1. If the station also copies the frame into its buffer, it sets the C bit to 1. From the possible combinations of these bits the originating station can determine:

1 If the destination station is inactive on this ring.

2 If the station exists but did not copy the frame.

3 That the frame was copied by the destination station.

Medium access control

The access to the ring, or medium, is controlled by the token. MAC rules specify the usage of the token, the control of the priority of messages and management of the network in the case of errors or failures.

Frame transmission

For transmission, the MAC formats the frame by adding the address and control fields and then waits for the reception of a token with a priority equal to or less than that of the awaiting frame.

When a usable token is received it is converted into a start-of-frame sequence and the frame transmission is started. The frame check sequence is calculated and appended to the information field. Frame transmission will continue until either there are no more queued PDUs with the same or higher priority than the current service priority or the *token holding time* (THT) would be exceeded by transmitting the PDU. The THT ensures that one station does not hog the network and allows fair network usage. When a station has a PDU of higher priority than the current service priority it requests a priority token. This is done by raising the value of the reservation bits of a repeated token or frame using the following algorithm:

if (PDU priority > received priority) set reservation bits else leave reservation bits unchanged

Token transmission

A transmitting station checks that it receives its own frames by looking at the source address of the incoming frames and also checks the response bits to determine if each frame was successfully received. When it has completed its transmissions, it sends a token and continues to receive until all frames that it transmitted have been cleared from the ring. It then repeats the incoming signal. When a token is inserted in the ring it may be necessary to increase its priority either because the received reservation value or the priority value of a frame still queued is higher than the priority of the received token. The station transmits a token of raised priority with the reservation bits set to zero. A station that raises the priority level has the responsibility for subsequently resetting it.

The Cambridge ring

Although there have not been as many implementations of slotted rings as of other LAN types, the most recent approaches to multiservice networks are based on multiple access to a slotted network structure. For this reason it is valuable to discuss the Cambridge ring as an example of a slotted ring LAN. The Cambridge ring was developed, from 1975, by Wilkes, Wheeler and Hopper at the University of Cambridge Computer Laboratory. It has been a popular choice in the UK academic community where it has formed the basis for research into such areas as distributed systems and network interconnection. Up to 254 stations can be connected to a single ring, the total ring length being limited only by the total ring delay. Devices are connected to the ring by *repeaters* which pass on the circulating bit stream. Various technologies can be used in the ring transmission system to cater for differing interrepeater distances. Information is written into a circulating slots in the form of a *minipacket.* The slot structure is established by a special station: the monitor. In addition to initial start-up the monitor provides the facility for the control of lost minipackets.

Physical layer

The basic transmission scheme uses a twin twisted pair cable providing reliable communication at 10 Mbit/s. The system uses a modulation scheme that enables a 10 Mbit/s data and clock to be transmitted while keeping the bandwidth used to 10 MHz. The scheme uses the two pairs, changing the state of both pairs to indicate a 1, and alternately changing pairs to indicate a 0. This scheme will suffer from any differential delays between the two pairs; this is a significant factor in limiting the interrepeater distance over copper cables to 200 metres. For greater distances fibre optic links can be used to extend the network over a wide physical area.

Ring access scheme

The latest Cambridge rings use a 40 bit minipacket separated by a gap of at least 4 bits. The type bits are used to distinguish between different sequences of minipackets. The data is transmitted at approximately 10 Mbit/s; the frequency is adjusted to ensure that the ring delay is equal to a whole number of bit times. In small rings, where the ring length is less than 44 bits, the ring is padded by a delay in the monitor so that a whole minipacket and a 4-bit interpacket gap exist. An empty minipacket is filled by the transmitting station which sets the full bit and fills in the address and data fields as required. When the minipacket is received by the destination it copies the address and data fields into its internal buffer and sets the response bits to indicate that it *accepted* the data. If the destination station's register is full it sets the response bits to busy. Each station has a source select register which can be set to any station, a specific address or no station. This register is used to control reception so that minipackets from other stations do not interfere with a sequence of minipackets from one station. If the source of the minipacket is from a station the destination has not selected, the station does not copy the data, but sets the response bits to *unselected.* If the destination is inactive or not present on the ring the response bits return *unchanged,* to indicate that the minipacket was ignored by all stations on the ring. The transmitting station waits for the minipacket to return, sets the full bit to empty and stores the response bits for the controlling software. The restriction of waiting for the minipacket to return limits the maximum data rate achievable in a ring with more than one minipacket. The system also prevents a station from reusing the same minipacket, forcing it to send it empty to the next station on the ring. This prevents one station from hogging the ring, resulting in load sharing among the ring stations.

Ring error control

The Cambridge ring uses the monitor station to maintain the ring size and detect circulating minipackets. The monitor station is also used to fill empty minipackets with random data which is checked for errors if the minipacket returns unused to the monitor, so that the error performance of the ring can be monitored. With the Cambridge ring it is possible to determine if the device is inactive by examining the status of the response bits of the minipackets sent to it. If these return ignored then the device is off the ring. This method is used in the Cambridge distributed system where a logging device sends minipackets at regular intervals to known devices on the ring and logs any change of status.

Cambridge ring standardization

The system has received considerable interest in the United Kingdom and is available commercially from a number of manufacturers. The standard consists of two documents, one defining the hardware and its interface and the second defining the protocols for communication using the ring. These standards are known as the CR 82 standards.

The fibre distributed data interface (FDDI)

The fibre distributed data Interface (FDDI) is a token ring network that has many similarities to the IEEE 802.5 standard but is specifically intended for the faster speeds offered by optical fibres, and is designed to run at 100 Mbit/s. Optical fibres have the additional advantages of being lightweight and unaffected by electromagnetic interference. The FDDI was designed to be compatible with the IEEE 802 LAN standards and shares the common LLC level, thus making it particularly suitable as a backbone to interconnect IEEE 802 LANs. It was also envisaged as a general purpose interface channel between processors. The physical medium is multimode optical fibre using light emitting diodes (LEDs) transmitting at 1300 nms. The FDDI can support up to 500 stations with a maximum distance between stations of 2 km and a maximum ring circumference of 200 km. It uses a 4 out of 5 code which implies signalling at 125

Mbit/s, and is intended to achieve error rates of less than 1 in 2.5 x 10^{10}. Clock synchronization is obtained not by transitions in every symbol as in the Manchester code, but by the receiver synchronizing to a stream of signals at the beginning of each frame. Of the 32 available bit patterns in the 5-bit code, 16 are used for data, 8 are used for delimiters, control and hardware signalling and the remaining 8 to ensure that signal transitions are sufficiently frequent. The maximum frame size is 4500 octets. FDDI products are now commercially available.

An FDDI network consists of two counterrotating rings. Stations are of two types: those of type A which require a high level of reliability are connected to both rings, stations of type B are connected to one of the rings. Reliability is provided by three techniques-station bypass switches, ring connections that allow reconfiguration and the provision of wiring concentrators. The concentrators allow alternative paths to be formed and also allow type B stations which have a single connection to the concentrator to make use of its reconfiguring properties.

FDDI tokens, which offer a priority mechanism similar to IEEE 802.5. Information is transmitted in a frame when the token is held. Frames may carry either synchronous or asynchronous traffic depending on token priority. The frame status (FS) field is set by the destination and checked by the source station which removes its frame from the ring and generates another token. Unlike IEEE 802.5 it is possible for several frames to be carried on the ring at the same time, enabling the much larger potential size of an FDDI ring to be used efficiently. Thus a station will transmit a token immediately after it has completed its transmission, even if the transmitted frame has not started to arrive back. A station further round the ring is allowed to insert its own frame after the frame from station and before regenerating the token.

To ensure a guaranteed bandwidth for synchronous traffic, the FDDI uses a timed token rotation protocol. Synchronous traffic using the token passing portion of the ring is given a guaranteed bandwidth by ensuring that the token rotation time does not exceed a preset value, If not required, this bandwidth is made available to asynchronous traffic. A target value of the token rotation time (TRT) is agreed when the ring is initialized. A station is allowed to capture an arriving token and transmit synchronous traffic provided it has sufficient synchronous allocation. Asynchronous traffic may only capture a token when the time since it last received a token is less than the TRT. The MAC protocol ensures that on average the TRT is less than the target TRT and that the maximum TRT is not more than twice the target TRT.

A later version of the protocol called FDDI-2 has a more complex protocol and carries circuit switched traffic. It is compatible with FDDI-1 networks and reverts to this mode if no circuit switched traffic is being carried. For circuit switched traffic the capacity of the ring is divided into cycles by a master station, part of each cycle still being available for use under the token passing scheme. Circuit switched traffic is allocated in increments of 6.144 Mbit/s to isochronous channels, in which information at a guaranteed bandwidth is carried from a fixed source to a fixed destination at an agreed fixed position in the channel. The circuit switched option makes FDDI-2 particularly suitable for the connection of PABXs.

Personal computer networks

There have been a number of developments for personal computers (PCs) and their clones to support communications between hosts. There are a considerable number of proprietary implementations of networking systems by manufacturers, for example:

NETBIOS
Novell's Netware
3-Com Networks
IBM PS/2 LAN interfaces
SUN's NFS for PCs
The Macintosh network system Appletalk

NETBIOS

IBM's network basic input/output system (NETBIOS) was announced in 1984 and provided a basic building block for networking. IBM published the details of the NETBIOS interface to encourage other manufacturers to emulate their own NETBIOS products. IBM was committed to NETBIOS as the interface on future LANs and for the IBM PS/2 range of computer systems. NETBIOS provided the mechanism for PC-to-PC communication without the previously used approach of having an intermediate disk server to control the PC network. The aim of NETBIOS was to provide a fixed interface between the operating system and the LAN which was independent of the network hardware or software. It was effectively an extension to the standard PC basic input/output system (BIOS).

NETBIOS may be viewed as an interface between the presentation and session layers of the ISO reference model, thus offering peer-to-peer communication. It has support for both virtual circuits and datagram services. Implementation may be provided as a ROM, which is often located on the network card itself. The IBM PC network and token ring use a card with its own microprocessor which relieves much of the network protocol load from the host PC. To communicate with NETBIOS, an application must give the system commands in the form of a data structure called the network control block, which is used to pass information in both directions across the NETBIOS interface. Up to 32 independent sessions may be supported simultaneously. NETBIOS uses a distributed LAN management approach. If one PC wishes to access a named resource on another PC, it broadcasts its request and all PCs on the network must interpret the request; if the resource is found then a connection is made. When a new resource is named, the name is broadcast to ensure that it does not already exist.

This broadcasting strategy represents a significant overhead on the PCs and some manufacturers have modified this approach to provide a centralized hierarchical method to naming.

The PC network program produced by IBM for their CSMA/CD-based PC network, and later for the token ring, provides simple techniques for file serving, printer spooling and simple PC-to-PC messaging. When the token ring product was released, IBM provided an extension to their existing systems network architecture (SNA) products. This was machine and operating system independent, and enabled personal computers with a 3270 connection card to emulate an IBM terminal or printer, to execute host application programs, or to transfer files and use host printers or disks.

LAN: Performance and Reliability

Network dependent performance

For the lower levels of a local area network, the performance may be measured in terms of the utilization of the capacity of the network. For an individual node, performance is measured in terms of its mean data rate or the mean delays in transmission. Measurements of actual network installations show that most computer networks are rarely used to their full capacity, with typical usage figures of less than 10 per cent. Under these conditions most networks will appear to give the full capacity of the network to an individual node for the duration of the communication. Performance evaluations are, however, undertaken at a much higher network utilization when it is likely that a number of simultaneous transmission attempts will occur. This is valid, as studies have shown that most data communi-cation is of a 'bursty' nature with periods of high data transfer followed by idle periods. If the bursts of a number of transmissions occur at the same time, the presented load may be higher than the maximum network capacity so delays are introduced. It is the performance evaluation *of* the different networks during these periods of high utilization that gives the most interesting results.

Slotted and register insertion rings

For these networks, as more devices attempt simultaneous transmission, the mean delay between packets transmitted from a station increases. This is because the number of free packets is restricted. For a *slotted* ring each device may not reuse a slot after a transmission, so this slot is made available to the next device. This means that the available network capacity is evenly shared between the competing devices. Also, the worst case delay, before a station can transmit again, is defined as the time for a minipacket to be inserted by all other stations, i.e. one slot delay per station. For a *register insertion ring* the delay increases as more registers are inserted into the network.

Multiple access bus with CSMA/CD

For a contention network, as the number of devices attempting to transmit increases, so does the probability of collisions. The utilization of the network therefore depends on the ability of the system to prevent and detect collisions. The effect of collisions and subsequent retries depends on the size of the data packets sent, because for smaller packets the proportion of time spent in resolving collisions to that spent transmitting data is higher. These effects mean that under high loads the system performance is probabilistic and hence that the delay in transmitting a packet is indeterminate. This can be a problem in certain applications, particularly where real time data transmission is required.

Token passing systems

With token passing systems there is the overhead of the transmission of the token, but, as the load is increased, the probability of the token being passed to a device that does not require to transmit is reduced. The throughput of the system will not be wasted in collisions, so high utilization can be achieved. The delay for the transmission of a packet depends on the action of the other devices; it also depends on the token holding time. If the packets have a maximum size then the maximum delay can be calculated.

Performance comparisons

Executing fair performance comparisons is difficult due to the differences between systems and the variance in the parameters for a single system. Performance comparisons have therefore concentrated on specific pairs or groups of LAN systems.

The simple comparison presented here, which follows the technique discussed in Stuck, shows the effect of token passing on the data rate achievable from one station. For the *token ring,* the point-to-point data rate between two stations, ppDR, can be calculated as follows. It is assumed that only one station requires to transmit data in fixed size frames, whose data portion is of length Framesize.

CSMA/CD compared with earlier contention systems

The ALOHA and slotted ALOHA protocols were introduced and an analysis given of the throughput against offered load. Throughput S against offered load G for ALOHA, slotted ALOHA, nonpersistent CSMA and nonpersistent CSMA/CD, all assuming a Poisson arrival distribution.

Comparing token passing with CSMA/CD

A performance comparison between CSMA/CD, token ring and token bus systems is presented in Stuck. Stuck derived performance equations for the three systems; the calculations were for the total network data rate, not that achievable between individual stations. If the load sharing is fair then each station will achieve an equal portion of the network data rate. The analysis of the different systems yielded the following conclusions:

1. For the parameters used, the smaller the mean packet length, the higher the maximum mean throughput rate for token passing compared with that for CSMA/CD. This reflects the fact that, for a given amount of data, smaller packets suffer more collisions under CSMA/CD.
2. The token ring is the least sensitive to applied load.
3. CSMA/CD offers the shortest delay under light load, whereas it is the worst under heavy load.
4. When a single station is transmitting, the token passing bus is the least efficient due to the high overhead of the token passing.

Cambridge ring performance

A detailed performance study of a slotted ring, the Cambridge ring, was Made by Blair. The Cambridge ring transmission access rules restrict the maximum slot utilization for one transmitter to be one slot in every $(n + 2)$ slots, where n is the number of slots in the ring. This is because the station must wait for a minipacket to return around the ring and pass the slot on empty, to enable sharing. It then has to examine the response bits at the end of the minipacket, to determine the next minipacket for transmission; while this happens the next slot is allowed to pass.

Comparing CSMA/CD with slotted and token rings

The performance comparison between CSMA/CD and slotted rings is quite difficult due to the variation of the performance of rings when their parameters are changed. The significant parameters are:

- *Slotted ring.* Slot size, overhead bits per slot, ring length, number of slots.
- *CSMA/CD.* Slot size, network length, number of stations.

The delay/throughput performance of CSMA, slotted and token rings operating under similar conditions at 10 Mbit/s. CSMA/CD shows the best performance at low loads, but for loads greater than 0.4 the delay increases rapidly, showing the degradation due to collisions. The token ring has much more stable delay characteristics. The slotted ring performs worse than the token ring, largely because of the minipacket overheads and the delay caused by the destination release of slots. Blair and Shepherd comment that, although the delays for the Cambridge ring are greater than for Ethernet, the Cambridge ring does have the advantage of a lower variance of delay and the hardware construction of the network interface is simpler and therefore of lower cost and higher reliability.

Network reliability and fault detection

The usability of an LAN is strongly affected by the reliability of its components, the ease with which any faults can be detected and located and the measures taken to repair the faults.

Network reliability

The reliability of an individual device connected to a network is usually considered to be less important than the reliability of the total network. If an individual device connection fails, this only affects the processes running on the device and other processes wishing to access the device. If the network fails then all communication processes are affected. Therefore networks are designed so that failures are unlikely to affect the network as a whole.

All systems are susceptible to the failure of the interconnecting cable. In a star topology, any failure will only cause the loss of the device connected by the faulty cable. In a ring or a bus a shorted cable will cause the failure of the network section. An open circuit cable will cause the complete failure of a ring system but will divide a bus into two sections which may continue to operate.

Reliability in bus networks

In a bus system, the control is decentralized and the connection is usually made to the cable using passive taps. This reduces the possibility of a single failure causing the system to become inoperative. Failures such as shorting the bus, permanently transmitting data and incorrect access behaviour can cause a complete or partial interruption to other devices on the bus.

Reliability in ring networks

In a ring system, the transmitted data is repeated at each device, requiring an active component to be included in the ring. A single failure can thus cause the system to become inoperative. In most systems the operation of the repeater is very simple, consisting of regeneration and re-transmission of the incoming signal, the value of the signal only being changed when data is transmitted. Such repeaters must always be active; they must be provided with a power supply even when the connected device is turned off or if the device is disconnected. This is arranged by distributing the power to the repeaters round the ring, often using the same cores in the cable as used by the signals.

Fault detection and location

The location of faults, particularly intermittent ones, can also be improved by the connection of devices that are dedicated to the monitoring of the network performance and error detection. The Cambridge distributed system incorporated an error logger which produced a hard copy of the source and type of errors detected. The printout produced enabled failing devices to be identified and, due to the error reporting of the

Cambridge ring hardware, ring breaks or repeater failures to be detected. In all ring systems individual stations can detect errors in the structure of the incoming signal stream.

On CSMA/CD networks two methods of fault detection are possible. Firstly, periodic enquiries can be made to determine which stations are active. This can be combined with a knowledge of the network configuration to locate faults in sections of the system. Secondly, special monitor stations can be provided which act in promiscuous mode Abnormal behaviour of individual stations can then be detected.

Improving reliability

A possible protection against failure is to provide an alternative communication path. For a bus system the communication path is duplicated to provide an alternative path for use when the main path fails. For ring systems, extra links between repeaters can be added. Then it becomes possible either to form an alternative route for the ring using the extra data paths or to bypass nodes completely. Further discussion of providing alternative communication paths to overcome failures is provided by Zafiropulo.

Wire centres for ring networks

Location and circumvention of faults can be difficult in a ring network which snakes in and out of many offices. One solution employed, for example, in some IEEE 802.5 ring installations is to wire stations in a star arrangement, bringing the wires together at *wire centres* where the ring is completed. It is then a simple matter to remove one of the stations from the ring using bypass relays. For example, station B can be excluded by completing the bypass relay from X to Y. One disadvantage of this method is that, in normal operation, the length of the ring is increased.

LAN management

Most LANs are operated by a single organization and employ a distributed access protocol, so management techniques for LANs must address slightly different problems from those for WANs. Fault management can be carried out as discussed above. The performance of a LAN can be assessed using a promiscuous station to determine, for example, network utilization and to give an early indication of possible overload conditions. This technique can also be used for accounting management.

Protocols above the MAC layer

The discussions above and in the preceding chapter have been concerned with the operation of the lower levels of a LAN system. To consider the operation of a full system, the higher levels have to be included. These higher levels consist of protocol suites or families. Different protocol types have developed to meet system requirements and provide various levels of service to the user processes. In general, the higher the level of service and the more features provided, such as guaranteed delivery, the greater the complexity of the protocol and hence the overhead of operation. Three classes of protocols can be defined: connectionless, transaction and connection-oriented protocols. In general, transaction protocols are considered as special options of connectionless protocols. Each of the different protocol types may support three modes of addressing that control the number of stations to which a message is sent:

1 Individual addressing. Sent to one station only.

2 Multicast addressing. Sent to a group of stations.

3 Broadcast addressing. Sent to all stations on a network.

Addressing types 2 and 3 are more suited to connectionless protocols. In principle, once the details of the network are hidden, i.e. once we get above the transport layer, any accepted protocol can be used. Protocol suites have been developed for each major LAN type. In addition, the IEEE 802.2 LLC offers a standard to complete the data link layer for both connectionless and connection-oriented protocols.

IEEE 802.2 logical link control

Logical link control provides that port' on of the data link layer which is common to every IEEE 802 access technique. The specification details the service interfaces with the adjacent levels and the protocol with peer LLC entities across the network. Two classes of procedure may be supported. Class I is just the connectionless service. Class II provides both connectionless and connection-oriented services. The fundamental unit of information that is passed between two LLC endpoints is the LLC protocol data unit (PDU).

The control field is used by the LLC to indicate which type of data transfer is being carried out—datagram or connection-oriented. In addition, this field contains further control parameters associated with the data being transferred, such as sequence numbers used for flow control. Finally, the information field is made available to the higher level software. This field contains an integral number of octets and can be zero. The maximum size of the information field depends on the MAC layer that the LLC is using for the data transfer. The protocol suffers from only having 8 bits for the service point address and has to incorporate facilities for the control of duplicate addressing within a connected system. If more bits were used the chance of duplicate addressing would be considerably reduced and is generally avoided by other protocol suites.

Cambridge ring protocols

The protocols for the Cambridge ring have been developed to provide connectionless, transaction and connection-oriented communications. Connectionless communication is provided by the basic block protocol (BBP). All the other protocols rely on the BBP to provide a packet or frame communication similar to that supported by the MAC levels in the IEEE 802 systems.

Basic block protocol

Because the Cambridge ring delivers only 16 bits of data in every minipacket, some method had to be devised to send longer packets of information between two stations on the network. A sequence of such minipackets sent between two stations is called a basic block. The first minipacket of the block contains a header that indicates that this is a basic block. The next minipacket is optional and contains the count of octets in the basic block, enabling both stations to know when the block has been completely transmitted and received. The route minipacket includes a 12-bit field called a *port* which is used to address a specific application process in the destination system.

Single shot protocol

The Cambridge ring protocols provide a transaction protocol called the *single shot protocol* (SSP) for simple request/reply transactions. The request contains the port to which the reply should be returned; the station addresses will be found in the ring minipacket and the destination port in the BBP header of the basic block in which the request is sent. Although all this information is in different places, the request includes the full identification of both the destination and the address for the reply.

Byte stream protocols

In order to provide a reliable stream of bytes in both directions between two processes and to ensure that no data is lost, corrupted or duplicated, the *byte stream protocol* was devised. The BSP protocol fragments the user process' byte stream into BSP packets which are sent using the basic block interface. Acknowledgements are used by the BSP protocol to ensure data integrity. However, as the ring error rate is low no negative acknowledgement is used for packets in error; instead a time-out is implemented at the transmitter to recover from unacknowledged packets and retransmit them. During periods when there is no data to send or no available receive buffer, the transmitter or the receiver can stop the traffic and resume responsibility for restarting it. To enable a broken connection to be distinguished from a stopped connection an idle handshake is used in which the two parties infrequently exchange their last messages. This is particularly useful when operating through interconnected rings as it will prevent the path from timing-out and being cleared by the interconnecting systems.

The transport service byte stream protocol (TSBSP) is a superset of the BSP including primitives for the provision of a full transport level service in line with interim UK standards.

DARPA internet protocols

Many computer systems attached to LANs implement the Internet protocol (IP) and the transmission control protocol (TCP) at the higher levels. These protocols are collectively known as TCP/IP. This suite of protocols has much wider significance than its use for LANs, as it is the basis for an Internet-a system of interconnected networks of many types. In particular, most of the major research organizations and universities in the United States are connected by an Internet called the Defense Advanced Research Projects Agency (DARPA) Internet, and since 1983 all hosts connected to the DARPA Internet have been required to use TCP/IP. A full description of TCP/IP principles, protocols and architectures can be found in the book by Comer.

The IP is a connectionless network layer protocol; the Internet control message protocol (ICMP) is used for network control messages. Above the IP, connection-oriented working is provided by the transport level TCP; for applications requiring only datagram reliability the connectionless user datagram protocol (UDP) is provided. Above the TCP and UDP, application protocols such as file transfer protocol (FTP) and remote log-in use the TCP or UDP as appropriate.

Internet addressing

In order to provide a user perspective of an Internet in which all hosts appear to be accessible, a standard form for network addressing is necessary. For every host on the DARPA Internet, a network connection is assigned a unique 32-bit *Internet address.* A host that exists on more than one network will have an address for each network on which it resides since the address defines a host's connection to a particular network and not an address for a specific host computer. The three highorder bits are used to indicate which form of addressing is applicable. The three main address formats are assigned different sized fields for network address (netid) and host address (hostid), appropriate to networks of large, intermediate and small sizes, respectively. To ensure that hosts of different architectures understand the Internet address, the Internet specifies that bytes should be sent in the big-endian format. The 32-bit address is usually written in a form described as the *dotted notation.* Thus an Internet address may be written as four decimal integers separated by dots where each integer gives the value of one octet.

Address resolution protocol (ARP)

The knowledge of a host's Internet address Is not sufficient to allow communication with it; the physical hardware address is also required. In order that applications can be written which require only a knowledge of the Internet address, a mapping must occur at a lower level. This mapping is commonly known as *address resolution.* One mechanism for address resolution would be for hosts to keep tables consisting of pairs of Internet and physical addressees. Alternatively, the physical address could be mapped using some algorithm to the Internet address. Both methods are unattractive, particularly for Ethernet, which has a large physical address space of 48-bits assigned by the interface or chip manufacturer. The Internet solution is both simple and elegant—a low level protocol provides dynamic binding of addresses. When a host wishes to find the physical address of another host on the Internet, it broadcasts a packet which contains the Internet address of the required host, requesting it to respond with its physical address. All hosts on the network receive the request, but only the host with the specified address should respond. The physical address in the response can then be used for direct communication with the specified host. To reduce the overhead of broadcast packets caused by the protocol, a table of ARP replies is held in a cache on each system for future reference. Also, the initiator of the ARP request sends its own physical address and Internet address in every ARP request, enabling recipients to update the binding information in their local ARP caches. The ARP message is treated as data in the Ethernet frame; details can be found in RFC 826.

The Internet protocol (IP)

The fundamental data delivery service of the TCP/IP suite is the IP which provides a connectionless datagram delivery service, i.e. an unreliable but best attempt packet delivery service. The IP datagram is *encapsulated* in the MAC data frame. The IP datagram contains both header and data parts. Ideally the IP datagram should fit into one MAC frame, making the transmission fairly efficient. Ethernet allows a data unit of 1500 octets but some networks have much smaller data units available. To maintain efficiency on networks such as Ethernet and yet allow networks with a smaller frame size to carry IP datagrams, a strategy of splitting datagrams into fragments is used. These fragments, which are identified by bits in the header, must be reassembled at the destination. The major items of interest concerning the header will be briefly presented. However, the detail of this packet header is not discussed here and the reader is referred to RFC 791 and RFC 894 for details of transmission of the IP across an Ethernet. The *version* field is used to check that all packet handlers are operating with the same version of software for IP data handling. The *length* field specifies the size of the header counted in 32-bit words. The *total length* is the length of the whole datagram including the header and data and is counted in octets. The *type of service* field has several parts. The *precedence* part is generally unused but would allow control messages to be given a higher priority over standard data messages, for example, to implement congestion control. Quality of service can be specified using the D, T *and* R bits: D requests low delay, T requests high throughput and R requests high reliability. The type of service field may be consulted at gateways and applied to the selection of a particular route from several alternatives.

The *ident, flags and fragment offset* fields control fragmentation and reassembly. The ident field together with the source address allows the destination to associate the packet fragment with the correct datagram.

The *time to live* field specifies the time that the datagram should be allowed to remain in the Internet and hence ensures that datagrams do not travel around the Internet forever if routing difficulties occur. The field is decremented by one unit at each gateway on the assumption that each traverse between networks takes one unit of time; when it reaches zero, the datagram is discarded. The *proto* field is used by higher level protocols to specify the protocol in use. The *header checksum is* used to ascertain the integrity of the header field data, the *options* field is largely used for testing and the remaining fields should be self-explanatory.

The internet control message protocol (ICMP)

The ICMP protocol is used by gateways and hosts to send messages concerning error detection and network control. The ICMP messages are transmitted in the data part of an IP datagram and allow messages between the Internet software in two machines. An Internet host might, for example, send an echo request message; if a reply is received the destination is alive and hence reachable. Details of ICMP message types can be found in RFC 792.

The user datagram protocol (UDP)

The Internet user datagram protocol (UDP) provides a datagram service to allow user application programs to send messages to other programs with a minimum of protocol mechanism. The protocol does not guarantee delivery or provide protection. The UDP is achieved by an abstraction for subaddressing called a port. The data is thought of as originating from or being directed to a host at a specific port number. The UDP protocol is normally implemented with a user interface which provides the following:

1. The ability to create new receive ports.
2. Receive operations on the receive ports which return the data octets and an indication of source port and source address.
3. An operation that allows a datagram to be sent, specifying the data, source address and port and destination address and port.

UDP port numbers may be permanently assigned or bound to an application when it is initiated. The UDP protocol is described fully in RFC 768.

The transmission control protocol (TCP)

The TCP makes few assumptions about the underlying network over which it runs. It provides a reliable stream transport mechanism for data and consequently its implementation is rather more complex than the previously discussed Internet protocols. The TCP is responsible for delivering error free data to the destination in the same order as it left the source. The TCP provides a virtual connection which will remain established while the stream is operating. TCP connections are established using a three-way handshake which enables both parties of the communication to be ready for transfer and allows them to agree on the initial sequence numbers. Control packets offer facilities for setting up calls, sending and detecting acknowledge-ments, flow control, multiplexing and security. Data transferred across the network is buffered to provide efficient transfer of data in reasonable sized datagrams, but this may be overridden by a push mechanism, forcing data to be transferred immediately.

The data byte stream is divided by the TCP into entities called *segments,* and each segment is transmitted in an IP datagram. A sliding window protocol at the byte level is used which allows multiple segments to be sent before an acknowledgement arrives, hence providing an efficient data transmission and flow control mechanism. All bytes in the stream are numbered sequentially and three pointers to the byte sequence numbers are maintained:

1. The sequence number reached for bytes sent and not yet acknowledged.
2. The highest sequenced numbered byte which may be sent before more acknowledgements are received.
3. The current byte count for transmission.

The size of the window may be changed dynamically since the acknowledgement contains information on the number of additional bytes that the receiver is willing to accept. The TCP uses a go-back-N scheme and employs timeouts to ensure re-transmission if acknowledgements are lost. The length of the time-out can be adapted to reflect the round-trip delay encountered on a particular virtual circuit. Details of mechanisms for window management may be found in RFC 813. The header contains a number of fields including the source *and destination ports* which are used as in the UDP for directing a stream to the correct application program. The *sequence number* identifies the position in the transmitted byte stream of this data segment. The *acknowledgement number* is used to indicate the sequence number of the highest byte received in the return data stream. Further detail on the fields in the header may be found in RFC 793.

Xerox network systems protocols

The Xerox network systems protocols were principally developed for operation over Ethernets and the interconnection of Ethernet systems over public packet networks. All the protocols are built on the lowest level protocol, the Internetwork datagram protocol (IDP).

Internetwork datagram protocol

Both addressing fields fully specify the location of the source and destination of the datagram. The packet type field, identifies the function of the packet and its association, if any, with a higher level protocol. The checksum provides for additional error detection for the complete datagram, in addition to that provided by the MAC layer.

Packet exchange protocol

The XNS packet exchange protocol (PEP) is the transaction protocol of the XNS protocol suite. PEP is implemented above the IDP and uses type 4 packets. When a packet has been sent the sender will expect a reply. Timeouts are used to retry the exchanges. The ID field is unique for each exchange and is used to identify request and reply pairs.

Sequenced packet protocol

The sequenced packet protocol (SPP) is a connection-oriented protocol which guarantees the integrity and sequence of the packet flow and undertakes re-transmission in the event of errors. The protocol offers three services:

1 Message service, in which a message may comprise a number of packets.

2 Sequenced packet service, in which message boundaries are not distinguished.

3 Reliable packet mode, in which packets are presented in order of arrival without duplicates.

The data is carried by type 5 IDP packets. Connection identifiers (IDs) are unique and identify the call; the call establishment involves the process of agreeing IDs between the parties. The caller has the responsibility for terminating a call, which is achieved by sending an 'end' packet.

Software interfaces for LAN protocols

The above discussion has concentrated on the requirements of network protocols and the facilities provided by implementations. For any protocol implementation to be useful, a software interface has to be provided for the applications programmer. This interface should ideally be uniform between different protocol families and implementations so the programmer can produce portable programs. Uniform interfaces are required for both connectionless and connection-orientated protocols.

As an example, the Berkeley UNIX interprocess communications environment offers an endpoint of communication, called a socket, for different protocol families. Three separate domains are supported: the UNIX domain for processes on the same system, the Internet domain for processes communicating between machines using the DARPA Internet protocols and the NS domain for processes communicating between machines using the XNS protocols.

LAN development direction

The development of local area networks has reached a state where stable commercial products are established in the market place. This does not mean that development and research have stopped but the direction has been changing from new concepts to new applications. The increase in interworking between computers enabled by local area networks is creating an increasing need for interworking between systems on different networks via gateways and bridges. As network interfaces and protocols are standardized, interworking will be simplified, enabling a wide variety of networks and systems to coexist commercially. As a wider choice becomes available the cost/performance of a network will become the overriding factor in choosing a network for an application. Terminals will be interconnected via low-cost networks offering local services and shared resources. These networks will be interconnected by gateways to higher performance networks connecting mini and mainframe systems offering large-scale applications. Again these networks will be interconnected on a metropolitan, regional or national level.

Two areas of development that will have a great influence on local area networks are optical networks, offering higher performance systems, and large-scale integration, which will enable the cost of a network to be reduced due to the scale of manufacturing production.

Network Interconnection

Networks must be interconnected to allow a user on one network to access services or information located on another network. To satisfy immediate needs it may be possible to connect the two networks together directly or in some ad hoc fashion, but in the more general case it will be necessary to interconnect a variety of networks to achieve communication between many different endpoints, and indeed to transport information between two networks that are situated a long distance apart. A wide variety of networks already exists: proprietary networks such as SNA, heterogeneous WANs based on X.25, token passing and contention based LANs. Standardization should reduce this diversity, but even the standards offer choices and there is a transitional phase as standards are specified, refined and adopted. Networks are often chosen for their suitability for their main body of users, rather than for ease of connection. Also, new types of network are likely to be introduced implying a continuing need for interconnection strategies.

LANs have size limitations, so that interconnection with other networks is essential for wider geographical coverage. All networks must be maintained and managed; separate networks offer a well defined boundary for management control, decisions about the installation and security of a particular network being the responsibility of a single organization. Small networks offer better reliability and performance than large networks; by interconnecting a number of small networks in which the majority of communication takes place within individual networks these advantages can be preserved while wider interworking is made possible.

The nearer the architectures of the networks concerned, the easier it is to connect them. Linking a datagram network to a virtual circuit network presents obvious problems, as does connecting a highspeed local area network with simple access mechanisms to a slower more complicated wide area packet switched system. The following list shows some of the characteristics, which may differ between network architectures and which will therefore have to be considered:

- Addressing and routing
- Multiplexing
- Maximum packet size
- Directionality
- Packet sequencing or resequencing
- Error control
- Connection-oriented and connectionless working
- Flow control
- Expedited flow
- Classes of service

Terminology

A network interconnection system usually connects two networks, but some connect more than two.

1. A *repeater is* often used to connect segments of a LAN and is an extension at the physical level, layer I of the OSI model.
2. A *bridge* connects LAN's at the medium access control layer; bridges may connect similar or dissimilar LANs.
3. A *gateway is* the term normally used when interconnecting two unlike networks, e.g. connecting a LAN to a WAN; the connection is made at layer 3.
4. A *protocol converter is* needed where protocols differ between interconnected networks. This could conceivably be at any level, but the term has been used to describe interconnection at a higher level, e.g. to convert between two message handling systems.

Bridges, gateways and protocol converters generally consist of both hardware and software. A gateway would, for example, have to be capable of implementing protocols on both or all of its interconnected networks up to layer 3, and would also have to make routing, accounting and other decisions associated with information crossing between the networks. Because the actual implementation of such a system may well be at the boundary of two different organizations, or the boundary between a public and a private network provider, in practice a gateway often consists of two processing systems separated by a communications link. In this case the gateway functions are split and each system is called a *half gateway* The interconnection problem is then reduced to agreeing a protocol along the communications link connecting the two half gateways.

A strategy for the interconnection of LANs on a single site is to connect each of the LANs to a *backbone network.* Over a wider area LAN interconnection can be achieved though a metropolitan area network.

Internetworking in the OSI framework

In the OSI model, the decisions and actions involved in forwarding information between open systems are called *relaying.* The highest layer at which relaying can be done is the network layer. Thus the network service ensures that the transport and higher layers need not be concerned with routing and relaying. Indeed, in OSI terms open systems may communicate over a network consisting of a variety of interconnected subnetworks, each of which may, for example, be a LAN, a public WAN or a private data network. There should be no problems in interconnecting subnetworks that provide the full OSI network service. An individual subnetwork will need to use its own lower level services and must be modified to converge with standard relaying functions in order to comply with other subnetworks.

How should the gateway look to the rest of the subnetwork

Should a gateway look like a host or a packet switching exchange to the rest of the subnetwork? If the two subnetworks are very similar, the switching exchange solution may seem easier as the gateway can perform similar functions such as flow control and routing. However, there are problems of addressing. Each exchange will have to know about the address space of the other subnetwork in order to perform routing. If the interconnected subnetworks have totally different strategies for routing and flow control, the problem becomes very complex and a common access interface is needed. If the gateway looks like a host, the operation of the exchanges of the subnetwork is not affected. This technique is suited to the transmission of datagrams, where there is no requirement for packet sequencing or guaranteed delivery. A datagram typically will be wrapped up in the protocol of a specific subnetwork for its passage through the subnetwork, and then unwrapped at the destination host or ongoing gateway.

Approaches to network interconnection

Because requirements have predated the availability of standards, there have been and continue to be a number of ad hoc solutions to network interconnection. However, there are three main areas where standards work has been most evident. The first is the CCITT X.75 recommendation which is intended for the interconnection of connection-oriented public packet switched networks. The second are *Internet* protocols which have been used for some time on the DARPA Internet and offer a connectionless service, and form the basis of an ISO standard. Thirdly, for the interconnection of local area networks, the IEEE project 802 has been looking at LAN bridges for the various IEEE medium access control options. We shall be looking at each of these three areas in more detail, but first discuss more general approaches.

Connection-oriented versus connectionless working

The arguments as to whether interconnection should be based on a connection-oriented or connectionless approach are very similar to those between the two techniques in a single subnetwork. With a connection-oriented approach it will be necessary to enhance connectionlesss subnetworks by providing virtual circuit facilities, and this may be very difficult. However, the advantages of shorter headers, packets being kept in sequence and quick recovery from errors are maintained. Where reliability and predictable response time are of prime importance the connection-oriented approach is preferred With the connectionless approach it is much easier to provide connectionless facilities on a connection-oriented subnetwork, and packets can be routed individually thus offering robustness in the event of gateway failure. However, any error correction or flow control must take place end to end at a higher layer. The connectionless approach may also be suitable for services such as packetized speech which do not require every packet to be delivered reliably.

A general approach to protocol conversion

The following general technique for protocol conversion between different subnetwork architectures which is based on the OSI model was put forward by Green. We can consider conversion as a *mapping* between the protocols of one subnetwork architecture to those of another subnetwork architecture. The first step is to concentrate on the differences between the architectures. In particular, we must find an appropriate conversion level in the hierarchy of each network. In general it will be necessary to map the top of the Nth layer of architecture X onto the top of the Mth layer of architecture Y. The level of interconnection is often dictated by existing system structure, for example specialist hardware may be available to implement the protocols up to a certain level in one subnetwork. The technique can be applied to both host-based and exchange-based gateways, and to a number of conversion methods such as protocol substitution or enveloping one protocol inside another.

Having decided to connect subnetwork X at level N to subnetwork Y at level M, the next step is to examine the services provided by the N-layer and M-layer protocols and look for differences. The protocols of layers M and N must also be taken into account. Since each protocol may have a variety of transient or steady states it is also necessary to examine differences over a certain length of time. Having done this comparison we are left with a well-defined protocol *mismatch,* which must be corrected. This may be very simple. It may prove impossible. Green calls this a *hard mismatch.* On the other hand, it may be possible to perhaps impose some degradation of performance such as extra delay. The gateway must then overcome the mismatch;

in the case of a hard mismatch this may be achievable only by inserting an extra complementary layer to enhance the existing architecture.

Service versus protocol data unit mapping

In a more recent paper, Bochmann and Mondain-Monval distinguish two approaches to the mapping between subnetworks—a vertical approach and a horizontal approach. When mapping service primitives there are three main options:

1. Reduce the service available to a minimum level provided by both networks.
2. Enhance the services in one network to correspond to the more powerful services of the other.
3. Provide a common set of extra services on top of existing ones which can be used to enhance both networks to an agreed common level.

The advantages of the service approach are that it is conceptually simple and can use existing protocol implementations which provide the existing services of the interconnected subnetworks. In the protocol conversion approach, the protocol data units (PDUs) from one subnetwork are converted to PDUs of the other subnetwork, thus conforming to the appropriate protocol in each network. This approach is more complex and more difficult to implement than the service mapping approach, but is easier to optimize.

Addressing

The problems of addressing are similar to those within a single subnetwork. The options are

1. *Unique global addresses* This would be the simplest scheme to implement but very hard to manage, and it is already too late to include all subnetworks. The IEEE 802 standard LANs support global addressing with I bit in the 48-bit address field being used to indicate whether addresses are administered universally or locally.
2. *Address mapping* Addresses from outside a sub-network are mapped onto unused addresses within the subnetwork. By performing the mapping only while a call is in progress, a small range of addresses is needed, though care has to be taken not to reuse addresses too soon. This technique was used, for example, in the Universe project, an experiment in highspeed LAN/WAN interconnection
3. *Hierarchical schemes* The address contains a field specifying the subnetwork agreed globally and a field for the address within that subnetwork allocated by the managing body for each subnetwork. It is probably the simplest and most satisfactory solution when different organizations are involved. Variations of this method are used in X.75 and for the Internet protocols as discussed later.

Routing

Gateways and bridges must keep routing tables which may be fixed or may change. Connectionless schemes offer more flexibility than connection-oriented ones, allowing each datagram to be routed independently and quickly adapting to fluctuations in subnetwork availability. Another desirable feature *is source routing* in which the user specifies the route to be taken. For example for security purposes the user may wish to avoid traversing a subnetwork operated by a rival organization or a user may wish to ensure that a single satellite subnetwork is used rather than a concatenation of several interconnected terrestrial subnetworks.

Packet size and fragmentation

All packet networks have a maximum packet size. When a packet enters a subnetwork whose maximum packet size is less than the length of the packet, it must be fragmented by the gateway. Each fragment must be appropriately addressed and labelled. Fragmentation is relatively easy, but at some point the fragments must be reassembled. If the packet is destined for a host on a subnetwork of small maximum packet size, that host can be expected to cope with reassembly. If the packet is simply passing through such a subnetwork there are two options:

1. Reassemble the packet at the outgoing gateway. Packets travelling through a succession of subnetworks may be subjected to this procedure several times. The gateways must provide buffer space and avoid reassembly lockup.

2. Reassemble only when the packet reaches the destination host. In this case the host must be aware of the fragmentation procedure, but it will save effort and memory in the intermediate gateways.

It may be necessary to indicate within fragments whether the receiving host is capable of reassembly; if not then reassembly must be done by the gateways.

Connection-oriented approaches

In this model the transport layer asks the network layer to open a connection to a specific destination, and that connection will consist of a sequence of virtual circuits created across each subnetwork between source and destination. Each gateway must provide resources, remember all the paths which are currently active, and provide appropriate conversion of packet formats. The result is a transport layer end-to-end connection. Obviously all packets on a single call must pass through the same sequence of gateways.

CCITT recommendation X.75

The CCITT recommendation X.75 is principally aimed at international data communications between public switched data networks. It is based on the virtual circuit model and defines the interface between signal termi-nating equipments (STEs) in two packet switched networks. The STEs must be implemented in the exchanges of each network. X.75 is very similar to X.25 on which it is based. In X.75, the call request packet must contain the full CCITT X. 121 address. The X.75 call request packet has a field for utilities specific to network interconnection such as transit network identification and throughput class. The user facilities of the X.25 call which is being carried are conveyed transparently in the X.75 call request packet. Additional diagnostic codes are defined in the clear request packets which will be conveyed across each of the virtual circuits in turn to the source or destination host.

Connectionless approaches

The ISO *Internetwork protocol (IP)* standard (ISO 8473) is based on an earlier US Department of Defense (DOD) standard. It offers a connectionless service, with the ability to send and receive datagrams, and the protocol is effectively a common datagram format. Since the standards are based on the DARPA Internet protocol we now describe this.

The DARPA Internet protocols

One of the best examples of practical network interconnection is the Defense Advanced Research Projects Agency (DARPA) Internet. The Internet consists of over 150 subnetworks of several types including packet radio networks, LANs, commercial networks, satellite networks and the ARPANET. It is in everyday use as a vehicle of communication between researchers in the United States and Europe.

The Internet protocol (IP) is implemented by all the hosts attached to the Internet and is based on the connectionless approach. Reliability and sequenced delivery are provided if necessary by the transmission control protocol (TCP), a higher level protocol imple-mented in the hosts and offering end-to-end flow control.

The gateways of the Internet have several functions including store and forward for the datagrams, providing interfaces to the appropriate networks, routing, monitoring and control facilities. The Internet address uses a common format, and is therefore easily interpreted by each gateway. IP datagrams are enclosed within the local subnetwork header for transmission across each subnetwork, The local header is stripped off when a datagram arrives at the gateway. A datagram may be destined for the gateway itself, for a host on the connected network or for a host on another network. In the last case the gateway chooses the most appropriate neighbouring gateway for the datagram's onward route, wraps it in the subnetwork's local header and sends it to that gateway. Datagrams are fragmented by the gateway if necessary and reassembled at the destination host. Gateways communicate with each other by a special protocol which allows them to send out echo and probe packets to determine the status of their neighbours. The information obtained is then sent to other gateways as routing updates so that a gateway's view of the status of the network is obtained by dynamic learning. To avoid datagrams circulating endlessly within the Internet each datagram has a *time to lire* field which is decremented on its passage through a gateway. Monitoring systems poll the gateways to collect information on traffic carried.

Bridges

A bridge connecting two identical highspeed LANs is much simpler than a gateway. The interface on each side is identical and some buffering is needed in case the receiving network is busy, but the main objective is to forward information as quickly as possible. Bridges normally make 'best efforts' to forward packets but may discard them if congestion occurs. The IEEE 802 standardization procedure has resulted in three MAC options: CSMA/CD (802.3), token bus (802.4) and token ring (802.5). Interconnection of the three MAC types is not trivial. Tanenbaum gives a detailed picture of some of the problems which we summarize here. Each standard has a different frame format requiring translation in the bridge. They have different data rates making congestion more likely when forwarding, for example, from 802.3 (10 Mbit/s) to 802.5 (4 Mbit/s). They all have different maximum frame lengths. This is very serious as no MAC can cope with fragmented frames, so frames that are too long to be transported have to be discarded. The result of these mismatches makes bridge architecture complicated and in general a degradation of facilities occurs when interconnecting unlike LANs. The IEEE 802 committee have also produced two options for the routing strategies for bridges. The first, produced as an extension to IEEE 802.1 and applicable to all IEEE 802 networks, is the *transparent bridge,* which can simply be plugged in and will learn from its environment. Initially all frames are flooded onto all possible connected networks. As each frame arrives its source address indicates where a particular host is situated, so that the bridge learns which way to forward future frames to that address. To prevent looping, the bridges form a *spanning tree,* a tree structure that has one bridge as a root and in which there is exactly one route between any two bridges. The second bridge type, developed for IEEE 802.5 token rings, is the *source routing bridge,* which requires users to specify the route to be followed. A user can discover a route by sending a discovery frame which proliferates through the network using all possible paths to the destination; each frame gradually collects bridge addresses as it goes. The destination responds to each frame and the source chooses an appropriate route from these responses, for example the route with the minimum number of hops. Thus shorter paths may be found for source routing than for users in an unfortunate position relative to the root of the spanning tree in transparent bridging. However, the proliferation *of* discovery frames can exert a serious extra load on the network. A comparison of the two techniques is made by Soha and Perlman.

FDDI/LAN interconnection

As an example of practical interconnection problems, we consider the use of FDDI as a backbone to link together several lower-speed LANs. This raises a number of issues for bridge design. The issues can be resolved reasonably easily if all the LANs are of the same type, but more complexity is introduced if it is required to have more than one bridge to a single LAN, to interconnect LANs of different types or to allow access to systems directly connected to the FDDI backbone network.

FDDI bridges will adopt one of the LAN bridge routing techniques. We will briefly discuss some other interconnection issues: frame size, frame check computation and MAC address interpretation. It should be noted that there are further issues such as response bit setting for token rings. The maximum size of a frame on a CSMA/CD network is 1518 bytes, on a token ring it can be more than 2048 bytes and on FDDI the frame size could reach 4500 bytes. This can pose problems for frames that are too large to be forwarded onto a network of small maximum size. The easiest solution to this problem is for bridges to discard such frames. Extensions to the LLC layer which allowed fragmentation and reassembly might be possible, but seem less practical.

The second problem is what to do about frame check sequences—should these be passed on unchanged or should they be recomputed by the bridges? Different frame check algorithms are used for each LAN type so recomputation is essential when connecting LANs of different types. For bridging networks of the same type, it would seem sensible to leave the check field unchanged, but as the checksum is often provided by the LAN interface hardware recomputation may be easier. Any doubt about the validity of a checksum at this level may be removed by providing higher layer reliability when it is needed, e.g. at the transport layer.

The third problem, which is considered to be the most serious, is the interpretation of the MAC address. CSMA/CD networks transmit MAC addresses starting with the least significant bit of each byte; token rings start with the most significant bit of each byte. This is not a problem for the bridge as the appropriate bit order can be provided for each LAN, but it Is a problem when the MAC address is used as data by a higher layer. A late decision by the IEEE 802.1 committee is that the least significant bit should be sent first; this implies that all token ring interfaces should be changed, a daunting task. A similar problem could apply if CSMA/CD stations wish to communicate directly with FDDI stations because FDDI is based on token ring conventions.

Commercial Ethernet to FDDI bridges are available, most of which employ *encapsulation,* that is the whole of each Ethernet frame is carried unchanged within an FDDI frame across the FDDI network, and the receiving bridge simply extracts the Ethernet frame for transmission onto the destination Ethernet. This technique, although simple, is not easily extended to enable other networks to be attached or to allow communication directly with FDDI stations.

Network Management

Open systems interconnection (OSI) standards have been ten years in development, yet the subject of network management has become a significant part of this activity only relatively recently. It is not that the need has only just been realized. That was foreseen at the outset. Rather, the delay has been caused by the difficulty in agreeing:

1 What the scope of network management is,

2 Why it is needed.

3 Where its requirements can be supported through open management standards.

By seeking answers to these questions we shall obtain an overview ot, where OSI management standards are today and identify where further research and development is needed. To be a viable facility, network management must be as appropriate for interconnected international networks to which many businesses are attached as it is for local area networks. In this context a business may be a national or multinational enterprise operating over one or several industrial/commercial sites, it can be government, an academic or similar research community. At each site we may postulate the existence of one or more local area networks, connected to each other and to networks at remote sites as dictated by local technical needs and management policies. This scenario helps to bring out the key features of network management:

1. There are many independent management domains which have to be able to interact meaningfully yet safely.
2. There are many areas which, while not truly independent have a measure of local autonomy.
3. There will be different communication technologies involved in the networking.
4. The networks can be large and they are a strategic component of many industries.
5. The networks will evolve over time,

Although much of this chapter concerns OSI management, currently the subject of standards' activity, communications is but one of the services to be managed when information processing is distributed. Other information processing resources and activities need to be managed too, e.g. data storage, peripheral devices and processors. 'Network management' should properly include all these within its scope.

Business is dynamic. Consequently there is matching growth and decay of the networks that support the business. New requirements may lead to different types of equipment being connected to the network, or different networking technologies, with different behavioural characteristics may be introduced to meet changing workloads. As old equipment becomes obsolete and harder to maintain, it will be phased out to be replaced by newer technology. A network makes such evolution possible. Network management assists the evolutionary process and ensures that it is controllable. Management concerns the *planning, organizing, monitoring, accounting* and *control* of resources and activities. Business enterprises establish policies and provide human structures to carry out the planning and organizational activities to effect a particular management policy. Although computers will probably be used to plan and organize, this use of information technology is usually regarded as lying outside the scope of network management. Rather, network management is more concerned with the day-to-day, operational aspects of maintaining a viable network environment; that is it is concerned with the accounting, monitoring and control functions of management. A particular aspect of management policy in many systems concerns the availability and effective use of resources. The policy may also influence the security of information and its processing in the distributed processing environment. Where the policy demands availability, it is the task of network administrators to achieve this, for example by providing duplicate resources. Where the policy also demands economy, they will find cost effective ways of providing backup. Where security is important they will ensure that the network is operated in such a manner as not to compromise user and management data.

Whereas these tasks can in principle be carried out by people, the responsiveness demanded for monitoring and the complexity of management information is such that many of the tasks are handled by the distributed information processing system itself. The network management team interacts with the processing environment to effect management policies and to provide feedback to policy makers on network behaviour. In short, network management can be implemented as an interactive, distributed processing application where the application task is that of managing the distributed processing environment.

Not all parts of a large network need the same degree of management control, not all will be subject to precisely the same policies. The network environment is therefore composed of many domains of management. We define a *domain* as:

> A set of managed objects that are grouped together, for the purpose of management organization, to support a particular aspect of management.

At the outermost level, domains are determined by the boundaries of different organizations. Within organizations there can be a hierarchy of subdomains, each responsible for a given subset of resources and activities. Domains may also be established on the grounds of delegated responsibility, security, operational reporting, resource naming, etc.

Modelling concepts in network management

A model for network management must cover three main aspects:

- The sphere of management responsibility.
- The delegation of management responsibility.
- The objects of management concern.

The principles of management authority and responsibility require that managers exercise control within their own management domain but that they cannot exercise control outside them. Yet, to provide effective management, managers will need information about activities in other domains which may influence their own domains. They will seek to access that information and even request the delegated authority to effect controlling actions on behalf of particular distributed applications. Management responsibility may be delegated within the management domain. A management entity lying within a domain and carrying out particular management activities is termed an *agent.* These requirements lead to the following dialogue types:

- Manager to manager: to obtain information or authority for control.
- Manager to manager: to request control be exercised on a manager's behalf.
- Manager to management agent: to invoke a management operation.
- Management agent to manager: to report the occurrence of a situation.

A collaborative project in the United Kingdom to develop an advanced network system architecture has adopted a four-level hierarchy of management in which administrators respond to the directives of policy makers and effect management activities. At the base of this hierarchy are the primitive management operations. Control is exercised down the hierarchy and management information flows in the reverse direction. This simple model can be further elaborated to allow for information filtering and for feedback at intermediate levels in the hierarchy.

When a domain is distributed, the interaction between managers and agents becomes explicit. At the operations level there are no peer information flows but at higher levels there can be both peer communication and manager-to-agent communication.

At each level, control is exercised over managed objects and data values are obtained from them. Objects may be passive having values assigned to them or data read from them. Some objects may be active, i.e. changed by agencies external to management activity. Such objects may 'spontaneously' report changes in the values of their attributes to their managers.

Functional areas of management

It is generally accepted that network management covers five areas:

- Fault handling.
- Performance monitoring.
- Accounting.
- Security management.
- Configuration management.

Analysis of these areas identifies the management requirements, specific management functions and the types of managed objects involved. The following examples briefly illustrate this functional decomposition.

Fault handling is concerned with responding to situations when a system no longer meets its specification. For example, comparing a count of the successful number of transactions with a count of failed transactions will show if the error rate for a system has risen to unacceptable levels. A fault-reporting algorithm may contain a threshold to identify the level at which a fault report will be generated.

Performance monitoring records the actual behaviour of systems. For example, operations could monitor the values of the same two counters identified above to see what grade of service was being provided and if the system was meeting its management objectives. Alternatively, the rate at which transactions occur could be monitored to determine throughput.

Accounting management establishes the use that is made of the networked resources, essentially for the purpose of making a charge. Again, counters will be read that total the 'cost' of using a resource. Accounting management can also be used to exercise control over the use of resources by sanctioning only a given amount of resource to be used before warning that an accounting threshold has been reached. A further use of accounting management concerns the maintenance and communi-cation of account records.

Because management operations influence system and network wide behaviour, it is essential that they be properly controlled. Like many other distributed applications, network management will have to demonstrate that authority exists before certain operations can be performed. The need for access control and the authentication of management actions are not of themselves aspects of network management. Rather, *security management* is the set of activities that maintain the security of the environment by controlling the way access permissions are communicated and exercised. Security management also includes activities that monitor the success with which security policies are enforced by, for example, maintaining security audit trails.

Configuration management is needed because the network and the activities within it change. As the network evolves new resources are added and old ones are discarded. The detection and rectification of faults also affects the availability of networking components. Configuration management monitors and controls the following:

- The state of resources and activities.
- The relationships between resources.

- The introduction and removal of resources,

Status is characterized both by administrative and operational attributes. Administratively a resource can be *available, unavailable* or *under test.* Operationally it may be *active* or *inactive.* Relationships characterize resource alternatives and the interconnectivity of resources. In the networking environment, configuration management controls and reports upon the path or route taken to communicate between resources. These aspects of configuration management and the need to create or delete references to both types and instances of managed objects may involve passing considerable amounts of information between systems, for example to update control tables or specify revised management algorithms.

These examples show that individual managed objects do not necessarily belong uniquely to a particular management functional area. Managed objects and their attributes, as typified by counters, gauges, reports, etc., are found in all aspects of management, and although some policy objectives may be satisfied by simple operations of the type described, many will require these simple operations to be compounded into more complex management procedures, For example, a report on the presence of a fault may lead to a check on performance. If this fell below the norm, it could lead to a change of configuration. The faulty component could be placed 'out of service' and made the subject of diagnostic tests to track down the nature of the fault in more detail.

Management standards

The scope of management standards

Users investing in distributed information technology want an open market for equipment in order to avoid being tied into a single vendor situation. They therefore welcome standardization which also brings the benefit of defined functionality and provides a yardstick against which to judge claims of conformance. These benefits of standardization apply equally to management standards though, because of the diversity of management requirement, the standards are both harder to define and to apply. Standards apply to interfaces and functions, not to the way systems are implemented. Having identified management functions, what are the interfaces? Network management is a distributed processing activity which requires a symbiosis between people and their computing systems. We identify three interfaces of concern to network management:

1. User-system.
2. System-system.
3. Application program-system.

The first two require some form of command and response language. Although the semantic requirements of such languages are similar, the syntax of the first interface is oriented towards human expression. The second interface can be optimized for efficient communication between computer systems. The third interface also concerns language but this time it is the binding between conventional programming languages and the objects of concern to management. These allow systems programmers to write programs to carry out monitoring and controlling operations. All three interfaces provide mechanisms to express the activities which a system is required to perform but, whereas the first and third are handled locally, the second interface involves the communication of the management information between systems. Thus, system-system interfaces require us to consider two aspects of standardization: (1) the end system activity and (2) the open communications between systems. The latter are expressed through open systems interconnection standards.

This distinction between the standards needed to specify the management objects and their associated operations, on the one hand, and the communication standards, on the other, is being developed in a standard document which gives an *overview* of the set of OSI management services. This standard is essentially concerned with the services to manage the OSI environment, that is the communications environment. However, research suggests that the principles it embodies are applicable to the wider aspects of management which are the subject of this chapter. An analysis of the requirements of the open communications environment shows that the OSI basic reference model has to be augmented to handle management. This extension to the reference model is specified in the OSI management framework.

The OSI management framework

The purpose of this standard is twofold:

1. It augments the protocol architecture of the OSI basic reference model by describing the principles of communication in the OSI environment when applied to communication management activities.

2. It is prescriptive of some of the management standards that will be needed.

The basic reference model encapsulates the concept of protocol exchange between peer entities at seven layers. The service provided by each layer adds value to the communication service provided by lower layers and so provides an enhanced service to a higher layer. The highest layer specifies the application specific protocol. Network management is a distributed processing application so it is not surprising that the system-system communications discussed above should be conveyed by application layer protocol exchanges. This aspect of OSI management is defined as *systems management.* However, some management information is of necessity communicated also in lower layer protocols. This may occur during failure conditions, during system boot-strap or re-configuration. To handle these management communications, the OSI management framework defines the concept of *layer management*. It specifies the circumstances when layer management is appropriate and the constraints upon its use. For example, a network layer operating the X.25 protocol can provide accounting information relevant to a particular instance of communication as a normal part of the layer protocol. Alternatively, in a local area network that offers a broadcast facility, it is appropriate to use data link layer protocols to identify which of the attached systems is acting as manager to control the operation of the network at that level. Systems management is however specified as the norm. Whereas normal protocol exchanges ultimately serve inter-application communications, layer management exchanges are only between the systems connected at that level of protocol. However, the information being transmitted may be destined for a further system or may be transmitted as a result of a request from a distant system. Consider the example of system A requesting system B to place a remote modem into the loop-back test mode. The communication between A and B is a systems management exchange, that between B and the modem occurs through layer management protocol. How the information is handled within system B is an implementation matter. However, the OSI management framework provides an important modelling concept, the *management information base* to cover this type of communication. The management information base is a conceptual repository of information which is accessible for management purposes.

Management information services

OSI management standards encompass the following:

- Those parts of layer protocol standards that help to maintain layer activity on behalf of all users of the layer service.
- Specifications of managed objects that are the subject of systems and layer management communications.
- A naming structure to identify managed objects.
- Abstract definitions of management information together with the specification of operations on the information.
- Procedures that may be invoked to carry out management activities.
- Operations to perform management tasks for a specific management functional area
- The definition of a common application layer service for communicating management operations between open systems.
- A protocol specification for that communication service.
- Mappings between the definition of managed objects and their operations onto their representation in protocol exchanges.

Of these standards, those for the common management information service and protocol are the most advanced. These standards set out the rules for open communication between a manager and a management activity operating as a management agent. The standards are independent of specific management procedures and are applicable to all management functional areas. They distinguish between communications that notify managers of event reports in the agent system and operations that the manager requests of the agent. The general form of the latter is:

< operation type > < managed object identifier > < access right token > < value >

where the operation type is currently defined as one of the following:

- *Get* the value of the identified object.
- *Set* the value of the identified object.
- Perform a given *action* on the identified object.
- *Create* a managed object of a specified type.
- *Delete* the identified object.

Other operations, now being appended to the above list, are those to *cancel* a get operation and to *add* and *remove* members from a set of managed objects. The *cancel get* operation has been introduced to deal specifically with the prospect that a large amount of data may be returned to a manager who has requested a *get* operation of an agent. When network traffic is particularly heavy or the manager does not wish to be overburdened, this operation allows the original *get* to be terminated. The operation may be cancelled at any time. The protocol will ensure that the manager will know, unambiguously, whether the *get* finished normally or prematurely. Because a *get* operation leaves the agent system unchanged, there is no uncertainty concerning the state of the agent system after an early cancellation. There are also proposals to be able to cancel *set* and *action* operations, but these are meeting with resistance because they would leave the state of the agent undefined. Although the common management information protocol is seen as the principal mechanism for the transfer of management information, there is no reason in principle why file transfer protocols should not be invoked for the transfer of very large volumes of information.

All operations and notifications may require the agent system to respond to the communication to acknowledge that the operation has been performed or the notification has been dealt with. However, these standards are not concerned with the consequences of the semantics of the end system operation; these are defined by the specific management information services for each functional area and by the definitions of managed objects.

Some of the standards relating to the fault and configuration management functional areas are well advanced and draft proposals for international standards have recently been registered. One of the difficulties of standardization in this highly integrated area of OSI management standards is establishing an effective structure for the standards documents and meaningful crossreferences between standards. It would be im-practical to publish the whole of OSI management as a single standard since management is a potentially open-ended activity and new aspects of the standards could be added continually. Even if a reasonable subset were to be identified, publishing all those together represents a major editorial task which would delay stable parts of the standard while the less developed parts were refined.

Two sets of documents help to maintain the coherence of this set of standards. One, the management information services overview, has already been mentioned. The other set recognizes that many objects and operations are common to several different management functions. A group of documents defines the structure of management information, the common information types, their attributes and the operations upon them, The documents provide a prescriptive method for specifying new managed object types. For each type the following information is needed:

- The individual *items* of information that can be invoked by management.
- The *permitted* operations on those items.
- The *inherent* properties of the object.
- The *implicit* relations with other information elements.
- The *specific* properties for each instance of an object type.

The documents define such objects and attributes as: status, counter, gauge, threshold, event and log. One aspect of OSI management not included in this figure is the way conformance to management standards is defined. This area still needs further exploration since not only must implementations of the standard conform to the rules of the protocol exchanges but they must also conform to the definitions of the semantics of operations that take place in the end systems where management operations are performed. This presents an interesting problem since tests for conformance cannot expect common implementations of particular management operations. Therefore, indirect methods are needed to test for conformance to a distributed management algorithm and demonstrate that the desired operations have been performed correctly. The difficulties of testing for conformance are further compounded by the nature of the management operations themselves. For example, when testing for conformance to standards related to fault reporting, it is necessary to cause a system to simulate faults to carry out the specified procedure. However, responses may be generated spuriously when the system under test is itself faulty. Also, how may one test for performance without compromising the performance one is seeking to test? Even more significantly, how does one test security management functions without compromising system security? Finally, will it be possible to check re-configuration procedures in such a way that recovery is still possible even if the implementation of the standard under test fails to conform to requirements?

Further developments in open management

Those developing OSI management standards are well aware of the above issues and that they are only scratching the surface of the possible set of management activities that may need to be expressed as standards. So far, most operations and most objects are very simple as are their mappings onto management protocol. Also, they represent only those objects of concern to the open communications environment. It is the author's contention that, in the long run, all aspects of management have to be handled in a coherent manner whether they relate to communications objects, processing resources and activities or to data storage. It will not be possible for managers to monitor and control their distributed processing environments effectively if these areas of their responsibility are handled separately.

Research into distributed systems is now sufficiently mature as to show the appropriate architectures for distributed systems. This is now being complemented by the development of standards for open distributed processing (ODP). More recent work has extended these architectural approaches to encompass management by implementing distributed systems management activities in a wide area networked test bed. As a result, there is growing confidence that the current approach to OSI management is capable of handling all aspects of management. This requires that the current standards are developed with an eye to their eventual extension. Failure to do so runs the risk of constraining the development of open distributed management standards or, worse, of developing mutually incompatible sets of standards requiring different implementation approaches. The consequences for manufacturers would be increased development cost and this would be reflected to users in the costs of products.

What then must be done to extend OSI management? Firstly, the set of objects of concern to all of management and the operations upon them must be defined. Secondly, an extended set of management procedures is needed, though these are still likely to fall within the five functional areas of management that have been established. Then the objects, their operations and the procedures have to be mapped onto the services needed to communicate the management requirement between systems. This will call for extensions to the set of common management information services and protocol. One type of extension will allow for typical control structures to be communicated, for example to express conditional constructs or to request that a set of operations be repeated. Since these constructs can be nested, the syntax of information transfer will take on some of the aspects of a block structured language. A second type of extension will concern the conditions under which groups of activities will be performed. It will define relative priorities for remote operations and whether a group of operations shall be processed as an atomic action or whether a more relaxed processing regime is permitted. Many of these extensions will add to the functionality of the local operating system enabling its functionality to be extended over the distributed processing environment. This will assist in realizing the concept of a distributed operating system when interworking between existing systems with conventional operating systems.

One further benefit which is implicit in this approach to the development of open distributed management is that it handles the open endedness of management requirements and the need to allow managers to manage their systems according to their own policies; that is there is HU requirement to specify a standard way in which management is performed. Drawing upon the analogy of a programming language we see that, by adopting a language structured approach to management communications with a well-defined syntax and semantics we can generate any management procedure *in a standard way* and have it communicated and interpreted *according to a standard* so that it is understood, without having to standardize the procedure itself. With such a language, procedures for remote operation can be specified for immediate action or transferred as named procedures to be invoked by a subsequent *action* primitive.

Current practice

Although progress towards management standards has been slow and there are, as yet, only proposed functional standards for OSI management, manufacturers have recognized the need for some management tools to handle their proprietary networking products. These provide facilities for gathering performance related data, carrying out tests and performing re-configuration of network resources. The products are largely related to managing the communications infrastructure though some local area networking products for personal computer and workstation systems do permit their users to manipulate remote processing and storage resources.

Space does not permit a full analysis of existing products. However, the current ranges of products tend not to integrate their management functions into a single package. Rather, management is performed by a loosely coordinated group of software packages. Nor is communications management coordinated with distributed processing or distributed data management. Many of the current products are concerned solely with the local area communications network on which they reside. They are frequently installed within an IBM personal computer and observe network traffic as it passes; that is on a CSMA/CD network the interface would be instructed to operate in a 'promiscuous' mode, listening to all packets on the network cable. A similar operation is possible on token ring networks and though the packet is not processed by the management computer, it is able to monitor all traffic. Such management devices are well able to produce network traffic statistics, report packet collisions and detect ring failures. They are essentially monitoring devices. Some control can be exercised where such systems are used as filtering bridges between network segments. Also, where networks provide mechanisms for terminal multiplexing, some manufacturers offer proprietary products that restrict the services that may be accessed from a given terminal or by a given user at a terminal.

In some manufacturer's offerings the different aspects of management may have to be performed from different network management devices. For example, some of the products that support the interconnection of local area networks through fibre optic cable only allow the cable environment to be managed from a special management terminal. Management of the attached local networks must be done from other terminals while management of attachments must be done from yet another control system.

These are implementation matters, for even if there is a coherent set of management standards, manu-facturers will not be obliged to place all their management functionality into one box. However, offering a coherent set of standards increases the likelihood of their doing so and, having a compatible set of management standards, allows the users to purchase networking products knowing them to be accessible, for management purposes, in a common way.

Network management has become a critical issue, especially in heterogeneous and multivendor computer networks. Also, for the success of client-server computing, effective and proper implementation of network management is essential. Client-servers with a large number of workstations need network management to manage and control the networks and the components of networks with their associated hardware and software. Like other areas of the computer industry, network management has been undergoing rapid technological advances to meet ever increasing challenges.

It is worth mentioning that, these days, the *computer* has expanded to include desktop computers popularly known as personal computers, workstations, laptops, palm-held computers, and other computing devices, which have the intelligence to do computation and also to communicate with each other. With computer technology growing at an incredibly fast pace, it may not be proper to place limitations on what a "computer" can be. Computers can connect to one another to form a *local area network* (LAN). In LANs, there are two important computer networking scenarios. The most popular scenario is known as *client-server* computing. In client-server computing, a client requests a service from a server and the server provides the service to the client. As an example, compiling a computer program in a client can be done by the compiler located in a server. On the other hand, in *peer-to-peer* computer networking, there are no fixed roles such as that of client or server, and any computer in the network can be a client or server. For our discussion purposes, we include both computer networking scenarios under LANs.

The evolution from hostcentric computer networks to heterogeneous LAN networks has been gradual. This transformation to LAN computing and networking is further complicated by existing applications and protocols from different standards bodies and vendors. However, the limitations of technology, protocols, and topology impose restrictions on the number of computers that can be connected to form LANs. Therefore, clusters of networks have become the trend. Once these islands of networks come into existence, the issue of connecting and managing networks becomes important.

To get a better appreciation of the problems involved in the present-day network management of LANs, let us look at some of the possible LAN environments. Some networks can be connected by *bridges* with similar LAN protocols. Here, networks A and B use similar protocols, and they are connected by bridges. Sometimes, network A and network B are known as *segments.* Here one network is using a token ring and the other network is using Ethernet. *Routers* are used to connect these networks to the backbone network. There are also cases where dissimilar networks have to be interconnected. In this case, as shown in Figure 1.3, *gateways* are used for connecting the networks. Here one network may be using TCP/IP, and another one may be using Open Systems Interconnection (OSI) or System Network Architecture (SNA). Also, these LANs may span buildings and cities to form a *metropolitan area network* (MAN). An extension of the MAN can be found in the *wide area network* (WAN), which covers a larger area than a MAN does.

After having discussed some of the LAN scenarios, let us take some simple examples of problems involved in managing different components of a network. Suppose we have to apply a software fix to all the computers in a network. How do we do it? We cannot take a diskette and apply the fix to all the computers, especially if there are thousands of them. Or what about isolating a fault in one computer? How can we say with certainty that a problem has occurred in X computer? And we need to be sure what caused the problem, and how it can be rectified.

These sets of problems assume serious proportions if computers are from different vendors. These computers may be using different software and hardware architectures. There are various ways of reporting the problems and different ways to rectify them. In some cases, these architectures may be such that the computers attached to different LANs may not communicate with each other. In some cases, it may be necessary to connect these networks to a centralized computer. How do we connect these LANs from different vendors and then manage them from a single, central point?

All of these factors make the network management of computer networks and their components, which may be widely dispersed with multivendor origins and multiprotocol operation, a highly challenging task. How we meet it is the topic of this book.

Network management uses distinctions described by *open systems interconnection* (OSI) seven-layer architecture, it is imperative that we look into it right up front. The International Standards Organization (ISO) brought out the OSI architecture of seven layers for computer networking. The main idea behind partitioning computer networking functions into separate, independent subfunctions is to standardize each layer of activity more easily and expeditiously. Each layer is expected to carry out a set of functions and provide services to the layer above it.

As defined in OSI, a *system* includes computer hardware and peripherals, software, and applications, including those used for communications. *Open system* has different interpretations and connotations. We prefer the following definition: A system is said to be *open* if it supports a widely accepted and well-published set of standards. Openness is not concerned with the system technology, implementation, or how the systems are connected to one another.

The seven layers are as follows:

1. The *physical layer* deals with physical interfaces and details of the physical medium used to connect two open systems. It is concerned with mechanical, electrical, optical, functional, and procedural characteristics of the links used in data transfer.

2. The *data link layer is* responsible for reliable data transfer between two linked open systems. This may require flow control, error control and recovery, and synchronization.

3. The *network layer* provides a path for data transfer between end systems. In this layer, routing of data through a network of intermediate systems may be required. As a consequence, this layer is responsible for making connections when required, maintaining them, and terminating the connections when they are no longer needed.

4. The *transport layer* is concerned with data transfer from one end to another end. For this purpose, end-to-end error recovery and flow control may be required. Note that the network layer is concerned with data transfer from one system to another, whereas, in the transport layer, we are talking about end-to-end data transfer.

5. The *session layer* is responsible for sessions between applications. This layer also provides services for establishing, maintaining, and terminating these sessions.

6. The *presentation layer* is primarily responsible for resolving differences in the way data is represented between two applications on either end. As an example, ASCII to EBCDIC translation, or vice versa, may be done in this layer. This layer also may provide services such as encryption and data compression.

7. The *application layer* provides services and functions required by user applications. In other words, this layer provides applications and services which are not provided by lower layers to support communication between the systems. In this layer, we may include *commitment, concurrency, and recovery (CCR).* Applications such as electronic mail and network management belong to this layer. Network management applications, which use network management, also form part of this layer.

Network management, systems management, and *enterprise management* have been variously defined. This can lead to a lot of confusion and we will therefore clearly define what these terms will mean in this book. We define *management* as monitoring and controlling the resources in computers, the resources used in the connection and communication of computers, and the applications used in the computers. There are, broadly, two models for *network management,* based on how the management activities are accomplished. This, in turn, is dependent on the computing environment. A LAN is a typical *distributed-computing environment.* Management of LAN environments can be done by peer-to-peer network management. Sometimes, this is also known as *distributed-network management.* Here managers, which undertake the network management activities, act more as peers, and there is no one central manager.

The other model is *hierarchical,* or *centralized, network manageinent. In* this model, the network management is controlled from a single point, known as a *manager.* This manager may manage network resources from a centralized computing environment. This may cover the cases where one supermanager or one centralized controlling manager may manage devices via some intermediate managers. This supermanager is also known as the *manager of manager* (MOM). All these cases are grouped under *hostcentric network management.* Some-times, this can also be termed *enterprise management.*

Many definitions are in vogue for network management. We use the one provided by IEEE Standard 802.6-1990. "Network management provides mechanisms for the monitoring, control, and coordination of all managed objects within the Physical Layer and Data Link Layer of a node." The same document also defines systems management as follows: "Systems management provides mechanisms for the monitoring, control, and coordination of all managed objects within open systems. Systems management is effected through application layer protocol." Here we have to note that *skinny stacks* or trivial upper layers can also be used. From the definitions provided by the IEEE, it is apparent that network management is a subset of the activities in systems management. In the preceding definitions, we have to be clear on the terms *monitoring, control,* and *coordination.* This is central to the concept of systems management. Let us examine the term *monitoring* first. Resources used in computer networks have to be continuously watched, and any untoward behavior leading to the deterioration of functioning of a resource, resources, or network has to be rectified. This is more a proactive action than a reactive one.

The resources have to be controlled. This means that we should be able to control how the resources behave so that they function properly. When resources have to be monitored and controlled, there is a necessary factor: coordination. If there is no coordination, the situation is a free-for-all, and chaos ensues. Not only do the activities of the managed resources have to be coordinated, but so do the facilities that monitor and control them.

Unfortunately, *systems management is* a very generic term. Readers can confuse it with management of systems used in other disciplines. This confusion is compounded by the use of different terms in the computer industry.

While treating the topics of OSI and SNA, especially in the peer-to-peer arena, *systems management* is the popularly used term; thus, it is better to use this term when dealing with these protocols. In Internet, *network management* is the prevalent term; hence, this term will be used when discussing this topic. While discussing IEEE-related management of resources and layer management, we will also use the term *network management.* In other places, where it is not specifically required to make distinctions between network management and systems management, the term *network management* has been used, as well.

Goals

The goals of network management are:

Higher network availability: This involves improving the operational efficiency, which means reducing system and network downtime and improving response times. Problems in a network should be responded to as quickly as possible. In many cases, it should be possible to rectify the problems unattended. But the access and transfer of management information will require processing power and involve network traffic. Therefore, performance must be considered in the design and installation of network management.

Reduce network operational cost: Ultimately, cost reduction is one of the primary motives behind network management. Because the technology changes rapidly, management of heterogeneous systems and multiple protocols is desirable.

2

Understanding Internet

Most countries have a government body to run the telephones. In the United States a number of private companies are given licences by the Federal Communi-cations Commission (FCC) which oversees the arrangements. Such licensees are known as common carriers in the USA. The effect of the monopoly given to the licensees is that only the licensee can erect systems to carry signals such as telephone conversations or computer data. The licensees are usually called PTTs and this reflects the arrangements more common in the rest of the world rather than those in the USA. In economically advanced countries the PTTs have established a comprehensive network of telephone connections specially designed to carry speech. This network is called the Public Switched Telephone Network (PSTN). Even if the PTTs did not have a monopoly it would make sense to try to use this existing network for long-distance computer data communications, as all the cables are readily available.

The major problem with the PSTN is that it was designed before anyone even thought of computers. The telephone system is ideally suited to carry speech where a human being can concentrate on decoding the received sounds and try to understand them. There are a number of factors contributing to the PSTN being a poor medium for the type of signals.

Firstly, the equipment has a frequency range of 3003400 Hz, which is not very wide for high-speed data traffic. Secondly, the frequency range is not continuous; some frequencies may be used to operate equipment at exchanges, which explains how phone freaks in the USA can make calls by whistling into the telephone handset and causing the exchange to set up the call. If a data signal produces the wrong frequency the call may be disconnected, This problem is taken up in the section on modulation. Finally, to protect the exchange equipment from damage, no DC (direct current) is allowed through the local exchange. By looking at the type of wave produced by speech against a data signal, in figure, it can be seen that the speech signal never has the same voltage continuously, whereas the data signal consists almost entirely of a continuous voltage at one of two levels. The continuous voltage is the DC part which would be removed by the exchange. Removing the DC part would seriously distort a digital data signal.

The PTTs provide four solutions to these problems

1. Special equipment to convert digital data signals into audio signals which can easily be transmitted through the PSTN.
2. Private four-wire connections to the local exchange, then a fixed circuit to the remote site. This cuts out some parts of the PSTN that cause problems, but not all of them.
3. Direct links of high bandwidth most of the way between sites.
4. More recently, some PTTs now offer digital services directly to the customer, in multiples of 64K bps.

Each of these solutions represents increasing cost, but results in a higher information rate.

Solution 1—This involves the use of a MODEM (MOdulator DEModulator) on the ordinary telephone line, which converts the binary signals into audio signals and back again. Only one two-wire circuit is used, but the available bandwidth is divided to provide two channels, one in each direction. One medium — two channels.

Solution 2—When the bandwidth in solution I is insufficient, an extra two wires are added, and all the wires permanently connected. This means that some of the lost frequencies can be used.

Solution 3— Because of the way the telephone exchanges are connected together, solution 2 does not normally require special connections between exchanges. However when a high bandwidth connection is needed, say 50K bps, then some extra inter-exchange connections have to be made. If special connections are made right through, then modulation techniques may not be required.

A normal telephone handset is connected to the local exchange by two wires, which is sufficient for an electrical circuit. The subscriber can dial any other subscriber on the PSTN by passing through the local exchange. At the exchange, connections are established through a hierarchy of other exchanges. The exchanges are connected together by wideband channels which are subdivided into smaller channels; each small channel is sufficient for one call. When a call is connected the caller is allocated a series of small channels between the exchanges through to the subscriber that is being called. The subscriber can dial-up any other subscriber only by passing through the local exchange which sets up the connection.

The first solution above allows a subscriber to dial-up anywhere and then transfer data by using equipment that will pass data signals through the exchange. This equipment, a slow MODEM, does not have a very high data rate: 300 bps full duplex or 600/1200 bps half duplex. To improve the data rate the local exchange has to be bypassed, but this means the dialling facility is lost. Normally British Telecom provide a four-wire connection bypassing the exchange with a small channel permanently allocated through to the destination. This through connection is called a private circuit as it can only be used by the two subscribers, one at each end. Different MODEMs can be used on private circuits to provide a faster data rate on the better bandwidth. The noise levels on a private circuit are normally lower than on a dialled connection.

The third solution is used to provide a faster data rate. For this, direct connections bypassing several exchanges are made so that the required bandwidth and noise level can be obtained. All of these three methods use some of the existing telephone system. British Telecom have a special data transfer network which is designed for computer data, but uses as many of the existing methods as possible. This data network, known as PSS (Packet Switching Service).

The introduction of digital telephone exchanges will enable the provision of digital circuits direct to ordinary subscribers in the near future. The major piece of equipment needed to transfer data through the PSTN is the MODEM. Modulation is a technique that can enable information signals to be passed through a medium not really suited to them. The original, and still the major, use of modulation is in radio transmission. By using that analogy it is possible to see how modulation can be used to pass digital data signals, through a medium designed to carry voice signals. The human voice does not travel very far on its own, and if more than one person were to try broadcasting at the same time it would be very difficult to separate out the messages. The frequency range of an original signal is called the *base band;* for the human voice a base band of 300 to 3300 Hz is used on the telephone though a wider range is possible. When two people talk at once close together, they confuse listeners because they are both using the same frequency range, the base band. To transmit speech over long distances very much higher frequencies have to be used, and care must be taken to ensure that different frequencies are used for each different transmission. The original base band frequencies have to be increased and no two transmissions should use the same frequency range. The only problems now are how to increase the frequency of the base band signal without losing any information in the signal, and then how to recover the original signal so that the transmission can be heard in the base band. The problems are solved by modulation.

Modulation, very simply, involves superimposing the information signal on to a simple carrier signal in such a way that one, or more, components of the carrier are modified to carry the information.

The technique known as 'differential phase modulation'; there are four possible phase changes (0°, 90°, 180°, 270°) so each possibility represents two bits of data. A continuous frequency simple wave is used so that only the phase component changes; figure shows the phase changes. To be able to detect the phase changes a complete wave, or cycle, is used. In any one cycle there are four possible changes that could occur, so each cycle represents two bits of information. For instance, if we use a frequency of 1200 Hz we can have an information rate of 2400 bits per second. If a stream of zeros is transmitted, no phase change occurs during that time so the receiver and sender (modulator and demodulator) can become out of bit synchronisation. To overcome this an alternative differential, phase modulation encoding scheme is used on newer MODEMs. Notice that every code now has a phase change from the previous cycle, enabling the bit synchronisation to be maintained.

Quadrature amplitude modulation

This modulation technique combines changes in phase with different signal amplitudes. The data is encoded into a specific phase change and signal amplitude. For instance, if there are four possible phase changes and each one can be paired with one of two different signal amplitudes, then there are now eight different combinations giving three bits of information in each baud. This idea is being used on the faster MODEMs above 2000 bps to increase the information rate without increasing the signal frequency. The amplitude of a signal is more likely to be changed by noise than the frequency or phase, so it is not very suitable for use as a modulation parameter for data communication on its own.

The MODEM

This section describes three MODEMs to illustrate the practical arrangements made to use the PSTN for binary data using the modulation techniques previously described. The frequencies mentioned are standard CCITT recommendations; they are not the same as those used on some MODEMs in the US.

A Timesharing Terminal MODEM

A timesharing terminal is restricted by the typing and reading speed of a human being, and as such it has a relatively low data rate. The terminal also needs a full duplex connection. The MODEM used to provide the timesharing terminal with a connection to a remote computer divides the bandwidth on the PSTN into two parts to provide two channels. Normally this MODEM is connected to an ordinary telephone line, allowing the user to dial any computer he wishes, but of course this means passing through the local exchange using a two-wire circuit. The timesharing MODEM uses frequency shift keying to implement the two channels; the frequencies are

Channel 1	binary 0	1180 Hz
	binary 1	980 Hz
Channel 2	binary 0	1850 Hz
	binary 1	1650 Hz

Modulation techniques

This discussion is only related to techniques currently used in MODEMs on the PSTN.

Frequency shift keying (FSK)

The digital data is recoded as frequencies. The binary signal, such as V24 voltage levels, can only have two values, so only two frequencies are needed. This technique is used on slower MODEMs. In FSK the two values of voltage are converted into one of two different frequencies; this is done by a modulator. The electrical circuit *modulates* the input voltage to produce the output. The receiver performs the opposite process, it takes in the frequency signal and *demodulates* it to produce the original voltage signal. Using this technique on the telephone lines is fairly easy; the frequencies can be in the range 3003300 Hz so they are easily passed through the PSTN just as if they were speech signals. The major problem lies in the choice of frequencies, for which there are a number of constraints.

- The chosen frequencies have to be fairly far apart on the frequency range. That is, the cycle time for one should be measurably different from the other.
- In order to detect the actual frequency, half a wave, or cycle, must be transmitted. This means the input digital wave cannot change faster than twice the lowest frequency output from the modulator. Thus the lowest frequency used must be greater than the baud rate of the data signal.
- Certain frequency ranges on the telephone circuit are reserved for use by the switching equipment.
- The higher frequencies on a telephone circuit are attenuated.

Phase modulation

A newer technique that is used to provide a higher information rate whilst using the same frequencies involves coding the data into the phase of a wave. Remember that phase is measured between two waves; it can also be measured between the same signal wave at different points in time. If a wave has phase p_1 at time t_1, we can measure the phase at time t_2 relative to the phase at time t_1. It is very difficult to measure small changes in phase, so MODEMs mainly use large changes.

If channel 1 is used by one MODEM to transmit on a connection it must be used by the other MODEM for receiving, and vice versa. The timesharing MODEM can be used at either end of a connection, terminal or computer. A mechanism is needed to decide which channel should be used for transmitting and which channel for receiving at each end. By international agreement the following mechanism is used. When a MODEM is switched on, but before being connected for a data transfer, it is set to transmit on channel 1 and receive on channel 2. One of the MODEMs in a connection pair must change if data transfer is to proceed: by agreement this is the MODEM associated with the called computer or terminal. The normal situation is for the computer MODEM to be called by the user. Where a MODEM may be used to receive a call, such as at a computer site, the MODEM is arranged so that the incoming call switches the called MODEM over.

This type of MODEM arrangement is the most commonly used; it has been arranged so that a device known as an acoustic coupler can be used to replace the caller's MODEM. An acoustic coupler does not need installation directly into the telephone system. An acoustic coupler uses the same frequencies as the ordinary MODEM, but instead of placing them directly on to the telephone line it whistles into the mouthpiece of a telephone handset and takes the received signals from the earpiece. The acoustic coupler is a very cheap and convenient way of connecting a terminal to any telephone. Unfortunately, using the handset allows other noises from the room to interfere, so it is not as reliable as an installed MODEM.

Higher-speed asynchronous MODEM

Sometimes a faster rate of data transfer is required, say for printing messages, though the input may still be slow. The bandwidth available on the PSTN is not sufficient, given the noise, to allow a full duplex connection faster than 300 bps. However, research is continuing on modulation techniques to achieve faster data rates. A second type of MODEM is used to provide a higherspeed in one direction, but a much lower speed in the other direction. Up to 600 bps can be guaranteed on the PSTN in the UK, passing through the exchange in one direction, whilst the return channel has only 75 bps. The return channel is called a 'supervisory channel' and is not expected to carry much data.

Up to 1200 bps may be obtained using a dial-up connection if the noise is very low, but a 'private circuit' will provide a guaranteed 1200 bps. If a connection of 600/1200 bps is needed in both directions, then two MODEMs are needed at each end. If the PSTN is used via a dial-up line only a half duplex connection is possible, because the circuit can only manage 600/1200 bps in one direction at a time. If a private four-wire circuit is used then a full duplex connection is possible. Because the direction of the main data transfer is fixed, one type of MODEM is used for sending on the fast channel (600/1200 bps) and receiving the supervisory channel (75 bps), whilst a different model performs the reverse operation at the other end. The 600/1200 MODEM uses frequency shift keying as the modulation technique, with the following frequencies.

Up to 600 bps	binary 1	1300 Hz
	binary 0	1700 Hz
Up to 1200 bp	binary 1	1300 Hz
	binary 0	2100 Hz

The receiving MODEM can always tell if the sender is using 600 or 1200 bps as the idle frequency is different for the two data rates. Note that the frequency range 13002 100 Hz fills the middle of the available frequencies on the PSTN. This means that the supervisory channel is relegated to using the low frequencies, and therefore has a low data rate. The frequencies for the supervisory channel are

binary 1 390 Hz
binary 0 450 Hz

The dial-up MODEM using 1200/75 bps is becoming popular for use with teletex services.

Fast synchronous MODEM

A popular speed for synchronous transfer is 2400 bps. This is provided by a group of MODEMs that use differential phase encoding to obtain the higher data rate within the frequency range of the PSTN. The connection pattern is the same as for the 600/1200 bps MODEM; a simplex connection is available on the two-wire circuit via the exchange with a sending and receiving MODEM. If a sending and receiving MODEM are provided at each end, a half duplex connection can be made by sharing the two-wire circuit. A full duplex connection can be obtained by using a private four-wire circuit. A 2400 bps MODEM is available for use over the PSTN using a dial-up line, but may be limited to 1200 bps by noise. The 2400 bps main data connection can be augmented by a 75 bps supervisory channel in the reverse direction, as in the 600/1200 MODEM. The differential phase encoding uses four possible phase changes on a 1200 Hz signal to obtain the 2400 bps data rate. MODEM speeds of 4800 bps and 9600 bps are also available, but only using private circuits.

Very high-speed MODEMs

For use in inter-computer communications, an arrangement is available for data rates between 40.8K bps and 50K bps over 48 kHz wide band circuits. Some of the larger exchanges in the PSTN are connected by very wide band circuits. These can be utilised for data transfer, although a private high-speed circuit may have bypassed several exchanges on the way to the large exchange. For the high-speed circuit four MODEMS are used, one pair to reach the large exchange, and another pair at the other end. Between the end pairs of MODEMs the data is passed in the base band frequency of the data signals on a special private circuit.

The main uses of MODEMs are listed below.

1. To connect a teletype or slow VDU (110/300 bps) to any computer in full duplex, by dialling through the PSTN.
2. To connect a faster terminal (600/1200 bps); but to get a full duplex connection a permanent private circuit is needed, so only one computer can be used.
3. To provide a synchronous connection using higher data rates (1200/2400, 4800, 9600 bps); but again a private circuit is needed for full duplex and full speed operation.
4. A very high data rate can be achieved, but at a higher cost, using base band signalling for part of the distance on a special circuit.

In terms of cost the acoustic coupler represents the cheapest modulation equipment. The cost then rises through the four types of MODEM described above. The higher the data rate, the higher the cost; however, the relationship is not linear. A 1200 bps service does not cost four times as much as a 300 bps service: it is more likely to cost only about twice as much to install, especially if a private wire is needed, but the rental may only be half as much again. Thus the problem of obtaining the optimum cost/service is not easy.

Digital Data Network

So far in this chapter we have been concerned with using an analogue PSTN that was designed to carry speech signals. The PTTs are currently investing very large sums of money in converting the existing analogue telephone equipment to use digital technology. This digital telephone service is known as ISDN; there is an international standard for this service which includes the interface for connecting private equipment. In the UK, British Telecom are installing equipment to provide the ISDN service in a number of new exchanges and gradually replacing old exchanges and equipment.

The new digital systems convert the analogue speech signal into digital signals using a technique called 'pulse code modulation'. The encoded speech signals are carried through the network as digital signals and converted back to their analogue form for the receiver. Using digital signals for transferring analogue information has a number of advantages.

a. The effects of noise are considerably reduced.

b. Digital multiplexing techniques can be used to make more efficient use of the trunk network.

c. The subscriber circuits can be switched by digital processors using information embedded in the encoded signal.

d. The very cheap VLSI technology developed for computers can be used, thus allowing considerable intelligence to be built into the telephone network.

A further advantage for users of computer communications is that the PSTN can be used directly, and therefore more efficiently. The digital information from the computer is passed directly into the digital network where it is transferred in its original form.

The basic ISDN connection consists of two 64K bps channels, primarily for speech, and an 8K bps channel for control. It is expected that the control channel will be available for data use; this will have a major impact on home computing and personal information services. If required, either or both of the 64K bps channels can be used for data as well.

Standards

The PTTs from all over the world work through a body called the CCITT. The CCITT is a part of the United Nations. It is concerned with enabling the individual PTTs from all over the world to cooperate and provide an international service. The CCITT is one of the most authoritative standards organisations in communications, so any standard adopted by the CCITT is very important.

All of the MODEMs discussed in this chapter conform to international standards for their operation, so it is possible for a terminal user in the UK to use a timesharing computer in Germany by dialling the computer. The German computer uses a German MODEM, while the UK user has a UK MODEM, but because they conform to the same standards they will be able to operate together. The CCITT have had a tremendous impact on computer communications by standardising various interfaces between computing equipment. The most important interface is that between the MODEM and the user's equipment. For instance, for asynchronous terminals the interface standard is called V24. The V24 standard defines all of the control and data signals used to enable the MODEM and the user's equipment to operate together and pass data, including the signal levels.

The result of the standards and their widespread adoption by equipment manufacturers means that any terminal having a V24 interface can be plugged into any MODEM, anywhere. Furthermore computer manu-facturers now use the V24 standard for connecting local terminals as well. This compatibility between equipment is very important in allowing various different types of equipment, from different manufacturers, to be interchangeable. Because the manufacturers in the United States dominate the computer industry the standards adopted by the United States often become the international standards of the CCITT. One of the US standards called RS232C is in fact the same as the V24 recommendation and preceded it. RS232C was the name given to the standard in the US before it became an international recommendation. Many US manufacturers still refer to it as RS232C rather than V24.

The CCITT have defined a standard interface for connecting communications equipment to a digital switched network: this standard is known as X.21. A second interface standard, known as X.21(bis), allows the same mechanisms but over the analogue PSTN, because there are still so few digital services available. The packet switched network access interface, X.25, is defined to used X.21 as its lowest level. However, X.21 (bis), or even V24, may be used where a digital network is not yet available.

Computer network technology

The communications techniques covered so far have been concerned with centralised systems. Terminal networks are all built around a central computer; similarly remote job entry stations are usually connected to a single computer. In the remaining chapters some of the problems and techniques of a network of inter-communicating devices are discussed. The devices at present connected to networks are usually general-purpose computers, with their own terminal networks. One reason for networking multiaccess computers, rather than terminals or smaller devices, is that these computer systems already existed when networking was proposed. A second reason is that the protocols used in computer networks are very complex so that only a large computer system would have sufficient spare computing power to implement them. However, terminals can be directly attached to a network, by using a dedicated computer. In the near future computer networks will become as widespread as the telephone network, and large scale integration will enable cheap processors to handle the protocols. The result will be the networking of every sort of computing device. The current trends indicate that powerful, single user, workstations will replace terminals for network use. The workstations will be directly connected to a local area network and use the resources of larger computers via the network.

This chapter is primarily concerned with the technology used to connect the computers and devices that make up a computer network. For the purposes of description the range of technology has been divided into three areas

1. wide area networks
2. Radio and satellite broadcast networks
3. Local networks

The network technology includes the techniques used to interconnect the computing devices and physically transfer information from one computing device to another.

Wide area networks

The term 'wide area network' is applied to a network that covers a large physical area, say a whole country or large area under one administration. Such an area may be worldwide where a multinational organisation owns the network. The basic communication media used are dedicated circuits, usually of about 50 kHz bandwidth. Where digital circuits are available the bandwidth would be 64K bps. The recent introduction of fibre optics in longdistance trunks has make link bandwidth of 2-3M bps available. Wide area networks will be using these links over the next few years. Examples of such networks are PSS, ARPANET, Tymnet, Telenet, etc.; details of some of these networks are given at the end of this section. For reasons explained in chapter 3, the physical circuits are usually provided by a PTT, although in the case of PSS the whole network is also run by the PTT.

Although 50 kHz bandwidth seems to be a lot compared with the 3 kHz nominal bandwidth of the voice telephone line, it is not very much when highspeed or large-volume transfers of information are required. Even at these high speeds the channel capacity is a resource that needs to be used efficiently.

It is now necessary to see how information can be transferred from one computer to any other on the network. The problem falls into two parts. The first is that of transferring information via a medium, such as a wire. The second part is concerned with addressing and routing. If there were only two computers on a network, then they could be connected by two channels, one for each direction, and whatever one computer transmitted the other would be bound to receive. When more computers are added, the bidirectional connection solution can be extended by having each computer connected to every other computer by a full duplex connection. To send a message to a particular computer the appropriate connection is selected; thus the routing of a message is carried out by the sender. Using a dedicated connection between every computer on the network is very expensive. If there are n computers on the network then $n(n-1)/2$ lines are needed, and have to be paid for! As a single computer would not normally be communicating with every other computer on the network at the same time, most of the lines would be unused in a fully connected network. Therefore to increase the utilisation of the connection circuits, their number is reduced, and switching is introduced within the network. There are three forms of switching that can be used in communications: circuit switching, message switching, and packet switching.

Circuit switching

Circuit switching is used on the PSTN to connect telephone subscribers. To use it for a computer network each computer would have a private circuit to a local exchange, and the exchanges would be connected to form a network.

Whenever two computers wish to exchange information, a physical path is established between them via the exchanges. The path is then disconnected when the connection is closed. The circuit has been ‚switched' by the exchanges. This method of connection is not used on established computer networks. The major disadvantages of circuit switching are

1. The cost of the equipment is very high, whereas the resulting circuit is not necessarily of high enough quality for computer communications.
2. The resulting circuit can only be used by the two computers on the call, thus the equipment is dedicated to the circuit. In particular the connection from the computer to the exchange is dedicated. To enable a single computer to communicate with more than one other computer at the same time, extra equipment is needed for each simultaneous call. If there are no connections all the equipment is idle but being paid for.
3. The time taken to set up the physical path can be very long in computer terms.

As high-speed connection using good-quality circuits is important for efficient computer networks, circuit switching is discounted in favour of the other methods. Circuit switching is used for some networks connecting computers-for instance, the Nordic Data Network.

Circuit switching has two advantages

1. Charges are made only for the time that a call is connected. If infrequent and short connections are all that is required, then circuit switching may be advantageous to the customer. It is expected that many slower devices, such as terminals, will be connected to national computer networks via the PSTN to gain this advantage.
2. Where a single device is used for long periods, such as a facsimile machine, circuit switching is economically advantageous. This is particularly true where digital facilities, such as X.21, are available.

The above discussion is based on the existing PSTN services offered by the PTTs. When the ISDN service is widely available, then it will be an attractive mechanism for some computer networks. Each host will be able to set up calls, use the 64K bps bandwidth, and quickly close the call, as required. The circuits will still carry packets for the end-to-end data transfer; but circuit switching will be the main link-switching mechanism. In the UK it is intended to bring all the PTT communications together into Integrated Digital Access (IDA). This will combine ISDN, X.25 networking and special digital services into a common access interface.

Message switching

To overcome problems in setting up and taking down physical circuits via exchanges, computer networks use permanent circuits and switch the data, A partially connected network is used in which each computer has a permanent circuit to a number of its neighbours, but not to all computers on the network. An example will illustrate the basic operation of *information switching* where the unit of information is a message. If the computer at A wishes to send a message to B, the message must pass through either D or C. The points on the network are called *nodes. A will* address the message to B by placing the address of B in the message header. The message and address are then sent on the circuit to D. At D the node inspects the address; if the address is 'D' the message is given to the computer; if the address is not D the message is forwarded on a circuit that the node believes will enable the message to be delivered, In this case D will forward the message to B. Thus the node at D has switched the message on to the appropriate output circuit. In this example two major characteristics of a computer network can be seen.

Addressing

The message is addressed to a remote destination and sent on the next stage of its route.

Store and Forward

Each message is received into the node storage so that it can be processed as a whole unit. Usually an error check is carried out and the whole message has to be received before this can be completed. The message is then inspected for routing information so that the node can decide which output circuit to use to forward the message.

The nodes have been introduced in the network to carry out the functions of routing and store and forward, so the host computer is separated from the network operation as much as possible. The 'hosts' are the user computers which wish to use the network. Often a number of hosts will be attached to a single node.

The node computers are usually minicomputers chosen for their ability to respond in real time to the communications devices. Each node receives incoming messages and stores them. When a complete message has been received the destination address is inspected so that the message can be placed on the output queue of a circuit to forward the message. If the message is for a host attached to the node, the output circuit will be the one connected to the host. If the message is for a distant host the node must forward the message to another node on the route to the distant host. While the message is in the node store, waiting to be processed or waiting for output, it is, of course, being delayed. The link into any one node may be used to carry messages from several different computers, as may the connection between the node and host. The physical equipment involved is used more efficiently than in circuit switching as a result of this multiplexing. Message multiplexing is the most important advantage of message and packet switching computer networks.

To distinguish between message and packet switching it is necessary to understand what a message is. This has already been introduced in earlier chapters, but a more detailed discussion is given here. The easiest way of defining a message is to say that it is a unit of information which is exchanged by users of a network. This means the characteristics of a message are only dependent on the user or the application. A message could be a few bits or a file, or even a whole database. In a message-switching network the whole message is passed from one node to another as a complete entity. Compared with circuit switching, a message-switching network has the following characteristics.

1. Any computer can communicate with any other computer without having a direct physical connection.
2. Any computer can communicate with several others using the same equipment by multiplexing messages.
3. There is no delay arising from circuit set up, but messages are delayed when they pass through a node *enroute.*

The messages can be transferred between nodes, and nodes and hosts, using an *ARQ* protocol. Characteristic 3 implies that there is no delay arising from the use of a network other than the store and forward operation of the nodes. This is true in some networks using pure datagram techniques. However, in most networks the internode protocol used within the network introduces some delays. Any network using a virtual circuit protocol, at any level, will introduce a delay when the message or packet is given to the network. In many networks the local node negotiates for resources within the network before actually forwarding a message. This is true of an X.25 network when the call is first set up, and is true of every message on the ARPA network.

A user of a message-switching network will pass the network a message, together with a destination address, and the user will receive messages as single units.

Advantages and disadvantages

The advantages of message switching, over circuit switching are

- The sender may dispatch the message when convenient, even if the receiver is not ready, as the network will store the message for delivery, However, if network resources run out, an undelivered message may be deleted and thus lost; this depends on the network protocols.
- Computers can exchange information at different speeds, as the network will buffer the message.
- Broadcasting of a message may be possible.
- Equipment is used more efficiently.
- Messages may be handled by priority.

Each message is treated as a single unit. However, there are also some disadvantages.

- A very long message will hold up other, perhaps more urgent, messages as it monopolises a circuit for the duration of its transmission.
- As a message may be very large, the node computer may not have enough memory to store it before forwarding it; in this case the message is lost. Further, this message will never be delivered as the network does not have the required resources.
- A very large message may monopolise the storage of a node, because it cannot be delivered, so that other messages cannot be received by this node.

Packet switching

The disadvantages of message switching relate to the possible occurrence of *large* messages, where the exact value of 'large' will depend on the network. If a network could be certain of only handling small messages, the disadvantages would disappear. The transfer of messages is a user requirement, so a network that meets user needs must be able to handle very large messages as well as small messages. The solution to these two conflicting requirements is to break the user's message into small *packets* for transfer through the network and have the packets reassembled into the message by the receiver. Note that the message header is included as the data in the first packet and that each packet has its own header. This refinement produces packet switching, which is the most widely used switching technique for computer networks.

The physical organisation of a packet-switching network is the same as for message switching. The network is a partially connected mesh of nodes. For practical reasons most wide area networks use special node computers to perform the switching, with the user computers being attached to the nodes. The term 'host' is now widely used to mean a user computer system attached to a network. The nodes are part of the network, so the hosts use a well-defined interface for accessing the node to enable data transfer across the network. By using a node separated from the host, all of the packet-switching functions, such as storage and routing, are removed from the host. However, the host still needs considerable software to handle the protocols used to access the node and to transfer data to other computers on the network.

The advantages that packet switching has over message switching are

- The small maximum packet size makes storage allocation and management easier in the switching nodes, sufficiently so for minicomputers to be used.
- The multiplexing of packets enables several messages to be interleaved on one circuit, reducing the delay seen by the user.
- The total transmission time through the network is reduced. Figure shows a message passing from A to B which would normally require 6k + d seconds to reach B, where 3k is the transmission time of the whole message on one link and d is the node delay. If the message is broken into three packets, each taking k seconds to transmit, the whole message arrives at B in 4k + d seconds. The difference increases with the number of links traversed and the size of the message.

It would appear that packet switching solves all the problems of wide area network organisation: it uses fixed highspeed lines and minicomputers for nodes; it is also more efficient and responsive than message switching. However, although packet switching is a better technique with which to implement a computer network, users still want to transfer messages. Packet switching introduces another layer of complexity and translation between the user and the physical network transporting the bits. Fortunately, the cost of processing is falling so the extra cost is outweighed by the practical advantages. A second cost, not so easily overcome, is that each packet will have its own overheads as well as those used by each message; this will reduce the efficiency of the physical circuits. The conclusion drawn from consideration of these three switching techniques is that packet switching, especially used in a partially connected mesh of nodes with wideband circuits, is currently the best technique for wide area computer networks. Packet switching is also used in other network technologies, rather than message switching, for the same reasons.

Wide area networks have been in existence since the early 1970s. The best known example is the ARPA network in the United States. This network was established by a government research agency to link together computer centres that had contracts for government research so that research workers could share the available computing resources. The network itself also forms part of a research project to evaluate the feasibility of a large computer network, and to investigate techniques that could be used in such a network. The ARPA network has been very successful in showing that the concept of resource sharing by use of a network is feasible. One of the most noticeable advantages that the network has introduced is a mail facility. This allows each user with access to a computer on the network to exchange mail with all the other network users. The mail facility is probably one of the main sources of traffic on the ARPA network and has certainly improved the amount of communication between researchers at different sites.

The basic techniques used within the ARPA network have been influenced by the defence aspects of the research, particularly the need for a fast response and resilience to the failure of any part. The network consists of a mesh of partially connected nodes called Interface Message Processors (IMPs). Each IMP can have up to eight hosts connected to it and may be connected to up to eight other IMPs. Each IMP accepts messages from the hosts of up to 8K bits in length. The IMP breaks the message into IK bit packets which are then forwarded through the network of IMPs to the IMP attached to the destination host. This destination IMP reassembles the message before delivering it to the destination host. If a host wishes to send a message of more than 8K bits it must break the message up itself, into 8K packets, and the destination host must reassemble the message from the 8K packets. Thus the translation between messages and packets takes place at two levels. Within the network of IMPs, packets (1K) are sent individually along whichever route is best at the time, so that packets in a single message may use different routes and may arrive at the destination IMP out of sequence. The destination IMP has to reassemble the message from the packets as they arrive. However, messages passed from the host to the IMP are delivered in the same sequence to the destination host. The technology developed for the ARPANET is now used in a number of commercial wide area networks all over the world.

The British Telecom network PSS (Packet Switching Stream) is an example of a network provided by a PTT as a public service. The design requirements for such a network are different from those of the ARPA network so they have resulted in a network with different characteristics. The network topology consists of a number of *exchanges* which are also partially connected. Each exchange is connected to a number of host computers in its area. The exchanges contain the node computers, the number of node computers in each exchange depending on the number of hosts attached to the exchange. The hosts use an access protocol called X.25 to enable them to make virtual calls to other hosts. A host will give the local exchange the destination address of the host with which it wishes to communicate. The network will route the call to the destination exchange which will then complete the call to the destination host. The call is represented by information kept at all the exchanges on the route. The information is then used to forward the packets transferred on the call. Once the call has been established the hosts may exchange their own information. This is very similar to circuit switching on the PSTN although it is provided using packet-switching techniques. The PSS network techniques are different from those on the ARPA network, where each message is addressed and transferred separately. The hosts can use a single link to the PSS exchange to carry a number of virtual calls to other hosts, thus the link is used to multiplex the calls.

Radio and satellite broadcast networks

These networks differ from wide area networks in the way in which the channel is used for communication between users. Broadcast networks use a channel to which all the users are connected, so all the users receive any transmission made on the channel. At present the two types of channel in use are local radio, covering up to a few hundred kilometres, and satellite channels which are used to span very large distances.

Networks using radio and satellite channels have special problems because noise in the channel can cause errors. There is also the problem of allocating the channel for transmission. The first operational broadcast computer network was built at the University of Hawaii using local radio transmission; many of the techniques and much of the terminology derive from this first network.

Every node receives all packets transmitted on the broadcast channel. When the received packet is complete, the node checks the packet for errors and then checks the destination address. If the address of the receiver matches the packet destination address, it is accepted; otherwise it is discarded. The problems particular to a broadcast network occur in the allocation of the channel to a node for transmitting a packet. Different solutions are used for radio and satellite links. Each node is only able to communicate with each other node via the common channel, so some scheme is needed to coordinate transmission. The schemes that have been proposed and used are discussed here in increasing complexity and are compared for channel efficiency.

The simplest transmission technique is called *pure aloha;* when a node has a packet to transmit it does so immediately. Having transmitted the packet, the node waits for an acknowledgement. This is therefore a positive acknowledgement protocol. If an acknowled-gement is not received within a time out period, the packet is assumed lost. Transmission collisions, which occur when two nodes transmit at the same time and thus interfere with each other's transmission, are detected by the time out mechanism. When a collision is detected, each node waits a period of time of random length before retransmitting the packet to of traffic increases, the rate of collision will increase and more re-transmissions will be needed. As the older packets are re-transmitted, more stations will have newer packets to transmit, causing more collisions, etc. Analysis has shown that a pure aloha scheme can only use a maximum of about 18% of the channel bandwidth. A node may transmit at any time, thus the maximum length of time the channel is wasted as a result of a collision is 2t, where t is the transmission time for one packet. The 2t period is the worst case, where one node begins transmitting just before the previous transmission is complete.

An improvement on pure aloha is *slotted aloha* in which the transmission channel time is divided into time slots of *t*. Each node is then only allowed to begin transmitting a packet at the start of a time slot. The nodes are kept in synchronisation by a time signal on the channel. Now if a collision occurs only one slot *is* wasted, so the maximum efficiency rises to about 34% of the channel capacity. When a collision is detected, a transmitter must wait for a random number of time slots before retransmitting. When the traffic is light the wait can be quite short, but as the traffic load increases the waiting period should be increased.

From the aloha schemes it can be seen that it is collisions that cause problems, so a collision avoidance mechanism should improve efficiency. In packet radio networks a scheme known as Carrier Sense Multiple Access (CSMA) is used. When a node is transmitting all other nodes can receive the transmission, so they can avoid a collision by not transmitting themselves until the channel is free. A transmission is detected by the presence of the carrier signal in the medium. When a node has a packet to transmit it looks for the carrier; if there is no carrier the packet is transmitted. If the carrier is detected the node waits for a random length delay and tries again.

Even in a radio broadcast the signal from a transmitter takes a finite amount of time to reach all the receivers in the network. When two nodes find the channel free, they may both begin transmission because neither has heard the other one. This case is most likely to happen when two stations are waiting for the channel to become free. The length of time it takes to propagate the signal to all receivers is the time band in which collisions may occur, but it is less than the total packet transmission time. As with the aloha technique, the CSMA technique can be improved by dividing the channel time into slots and only allowing the transmission of packets to begin at the start of a time slot. The slot length is set to the propagation delay, not the packet transmission time.

The CSMA technique has been further refined by modifying the action of the node when the channel is busy. When the node samples the channel again and finds it free, it transmits its packet with a probability p, or waits for a further delay of random length, with a probability (1-p). This is called persistent CSMA or p-persistent transmission. If p is high then the delay before transmission occurs is lower, but the possibility of collision increases if two stations are waiting for another station to finish. In persistent CSMA a trade off is made between channel efficiency and delay with the value of p. Channel efficiencies of about 80% may be achieved using these techniques.

Packet radio networks have a small delay between the start of a transmission and the detection of the transmission by all stations on the network. On a satellite broadcast network there is a very long delay between transmission and receiving, of the order of a quarter of a second. A satellite network operates by each transmitter sending its signal to the satellite. The satellite then broadcasts the signal to all of the Earth stations, which may be spread over a very large area. One satellite system currently used for packet switching connects nodes in England, Norway and North America using a satellite in stationary orbit over the North Atlantic. A different channel allocation technique is used on satellite broadcast networks because of the long propagation delay.

This satellite channel allocation technique involves making reservations for the future use of slots in the channel. The channel is divided into frames consisting of a number of reservation slots and a number of packet slots. Each reservation slot represents a packet slot in the second part of the frame. All ground stations are synchronised to the frame timing by the satellite transmission. During the first part of the frame the ground stations reserve slots for the packets they have ready by transmitting a marker during the reservation slot time. When the reservation slot is heard on the satellite down channel, the ground station inspects the slot to see if it contains its own marker. If so it can transmit a packet in the corresponding packet slot in the second part of the frame. This scheme uses some of the channel capacity to avoid the collisions which could reduce the network to a pure aloha scheme.

Obviously more than one ground station may attempt to reserve a particular packet slot by transmitting during the reservation slot time. There are a number of algorithms to overcome this, including allocating some slots to busy stations. Thus if a station successfully obtained a packet slot in the last frame, the same slot is allocated to that station in the next frame without competition. If an allocated slot is not used then the slot is open for competition in the following frame. Usually there are some slots that all stations can compete for in every frame. Another mechanism involves using a central allocation station to which each station sends its requirements and the central station allocates the slots. This has two disadvantages: firstly, the central station becomes a weakness in the network reliability, and secondly, the delay between requesting an allocation and receiving the allocation may be of the order of 1 or 2 seconds before the packet can be transmitted. A chapter in the book by Kuo is dedicated to broadcast satellite protocols.

Local area networks

A local, or private, network is a communication system connecting computers in a small geographical area, say less than a few kilometres between the furthest points. The network is wholly owned and run by one administration. There are currently two basic types of technology used on such a network: these are cable, or bus, technology and ring technology.

Whereas wide area networks and satellite networks use nodes to separate the internal network switching from the user hosts, local networks are meant to be as cheap as possible and so the separate node computer is omitted. In both local network technologies all the computers are directly attached to the transmission medium by a special interface, and all the interfaces receive all the packets. The difference between a ring and a bus system is the way in which the channel is allocated. Local networks are designed for use in local computing by allowing the interconnection of very small computers, such as microprocessors, personal workstations and peripheral devices. If the local network is to be useful, the cost of the computer interfaces into the network channel has to be low compared with the cost of the computer or peripheral, and microprocessors are very cheap in computer terms. A widely forecast use of local networks is connecting word processors within a set of offices for the exchange of information and electronic mail. The cost constraints, the limited processing power of the small computers and the protocols used on a local network are different from those used in wide area networks. A local network usually has a very high bandwidth channel of between I and 10 MHz and a very low error rate say one bit in several million might be corrupted. These characteristics permit the use of simple protocols. The lowest level protocol for using the transmission medium is built into the computer interface.

Cable or bus networks

These networks usually use a length of coaxial cable, or an existing cable such as that used for closed circuit television (CCTV). The medium is used in a broadcast fashion, exactly as described in the previous section on broadcast networks. The channel allocation techniques vary slightly on the theme of the CSMA techniques, or on a centralised slot allocation. The most popular broadcast local network is the Ethernet system developed by Xerox. The Ethernet principles can be used on any broadcast medium: radio, telephone lines, coaxial cable and optical fibres have all been used successfully. The Ethernet uses a base band signal, rather than a modulated signal, to simplify the broadcast transmitter and receiver, with a modified CSMA channel access technique. To obtain the maximum efficiency from the broadcast medium an Ethernet transmitter can listen to its own broadcast to detect a collision and abort the transmission. This extra complexity is known as CSMACD (CD = collision detection) or listen-while-talk. As with the other CSMA techniques a station does not begin transmitting until the broadcast medium is free. Two stations waiting for another station to finish a transmission will begin transmitting together, and thus interfere with each other. The collision is detected by the stations and they both abort the transmission immediately. To enforce the protocol a station that aborts a transfer then jams the ether. After a collision each station waits for a random time before trying again.

The CSMA-CD technique enables the Ethernet system to obtain up to 95% of the broadcast channel bandwidth. The improvement in performance over ordinary CSMA is due to the stopping of transmission as soon as a collision is detected. Note that no slots are used so a network-wide timing signal is not required. The transceiver handles all of the CSMACD access, including the retries and delay calculation which is varied with the traffic load. Thus only complete, and checked, packets are passed up to the station interface and only one request is made for a packet to be sent. The checksum generation and checking are carried out within the hardware: bad packets are discarded. A time out mechanism is used to retransmit packets that may have been lost as a result of errors.

Ring networks

The ring technique originated in the USA. The idea was then developed in parallel at Cambridge University in the UK and at two research centres in the USA. The version developed at Cambridge is known as the Cambridge ring in the UK. The computer interface is divided into two parts: the repeater and the interface proper. A ring uses a twisted pair of wires as the transmission medium. However, to improve reliability, the repeater is powered from the ring and electrically isolated from the computer interface, so four wires are used to connect the repeaters. The four wires are used as two pairs for signalling and carry sufficient power for the repeaters. In this way the computer can be switched off and removed from the ring without switching off the repeater. With the ring the medium is terminated at each station, whereas in the cable network it is not. Each station is represented by a repeater, several of which are then connected together into a ring. The repeater is a simple device containing a shift register and some logic to detect certain conditions in the information being passed around the ring. The repeater normally passes any information received on to the next repeater, so transmission only occurs in one direction. When a station transmits data, the repeater transmits the information from the station instead of the information received from the previous repeater.

Slotted ring

There are slight differences in the channel allocation mechanism used in the Cambridge ring and in those rings developed in the USA. In the Cambridge ring a fixed-size mini-packet is used which constantly circulates in the ring, and a special station called a monitor is used to ~generate and maintain the mini-packet and provide the power for the repeaters. In the American versions a variable-size packet is used which may be lost and regenerated as required by each repeater. The current format of the Cambridge mini-packet. Note that only 16 bits of information are carried in a ring mini-packet whereas the broadcast network packet may contain several hundred bytes. The assembly of information into a block has to be done by the computer. The monitor station also provides a buffer if the ring is not physically long enough to hold a complete mini-packet. The monitor performs a check on the mini-packet each time it passes to ensure that it is intact, and to replace it if not. The monitor is an obvious weakness in the Cambridge ring design so far as reliability is concerned; however, experience so far has shown that monitor failures are rare. The advantage of the monitor is that the repeaters can be very simple as well as cheap, which is the purpose of a local network.

To use the ring to send a packet of information, the station will wait until an empty mini-packet is detected by the repeater. When the full/empty bit in the mini-packet passes the repeater it is set to one. If the packet was already full no change has been made to the bit; if the packet was empty (full/empty bit = 0) the mini-packet is now reserved by this station, The repeater will use this mini-packet if the full/empty bit was received as 0. The addresses of the source and destination stations are placed in the address fields followed by the next 16 bits of the information that the station wishes to send; these are placed in the data field from the station buffer. The reserved mini-packet then travels round to all the other stations on the ring. Each station has a source select register in which an address is placed. If the source address in a mini-packet matches the contents of the source select register, and the destination address matches the station address, the data field is copied into the station receive buffer and the accept status is set at the end of the packet. If the packet is refused, or the destination station is busy, the destination repeater will set the appropriate value in the status bits at the end of the mini-packet. No other change is made by the receiving repeater, and all other repeaters will pass on the mini-packet unchanged. Special values which can be used in the source select register are: all ones, which means accept any source station address, and all zeros, which means do not accept the data from any mini-packets.

When the mini-packet returns to the sending station the full/empty bit is reset to 0 and the status bits are checked to see if the information was accepted. As an error check, the station also reads back the 16 data bits and checks them against the data in its buffer. Having reset the full/empty bit, the station must now wait for another empty mini-packet before it can send the next 16 bits of information. In this way the now empty packet becomes available to successive stations around the ring and the packet slot is allocated in a round robin fashion.

The variable nature of packet traffic in a local network makes it difficult to design a system that will provide a very fast response, especially when there is little traffic, and yet not become overloaded or unfair when the traffic becomes heavy. The broadcast techniques provide a low delay, especially in low-volume traffic, as the transmitter can usually send a packet as soon as one is available. However, as the volume of traffic increases, the broadcast system suffers from collisions and longer delays which can eventually lead to an unstable situation. In the slotted ring the channel is allocated by means of a round robin mechanism so collisions never occur, and during a burst of traffic each station is able to continue transmitting with only a larger delay. During periods of low traffic volume the ring does introduce a delay while a station waits for the empty packet to come round.

Proponents of both systems argue that because of the very high bandwidth available on the channel, and the low processing power of the computers attached to the local network, the volume of traffic is nearly always low in a broadcast network and the delay is negligible in a ring.

Token Ring

The token ring attempts to provide the advantages of broadcast access in low-volume traffic periods, with the inherent sharing of the slotted ring during high-volume traffic periods. The physical topology of the ring is the same, but instead of a circulating mini-packet there is a circulating token. Any host requiring access to the ring waits for the token to arrive; it then changes the token to indicate that a packet is following. The modified token is then followed immediately by the data packet, which can be of any size up to some system maximum. All hosts detect the modified token and examine the packet to see if it is addressed to them; if it is the packet is copied off the ring. The receiving host still sends the packet on though, so the data packet goes all the way round the ring to the sender. The sender takes the packet off the ring. Normally the sender receives the front of the data packet before it has finished transmitting the rest of the packet, owing to the short length of the ring. When the receiver detects the end of the data packet it marks its status by changing the last few bits, as in the Cambridge ring mini-packet; thus the sender knows if the packet was accepted or not. Immediately the sender has finished the packet it puts a token on the ring so another host may have a go.

The token ring is a simple idea, but it is more complex than the Cambridge ring and the interfaces are more expensive. The initialise sequence which is required to start the ring is quite complex as the token has to be put on the ring to start data transfer; of course there can only be one token. The mechanisms for detecting duplicate tokens and lost tokens, without the use of a monitor station, add to the cost of the computer interfaces. IBM carried out extensive tests and simulations of all the local area network technologies, and decided that the token ring was the best available. The company now intends to use the token ring as the basis of its local area network products.

The protocols used in a computer network are the mechanisms by which the hosts exchange information over physical distances. In the OSI model, the network layer is the primary layer for host-to-host communication. The network layer makes use of services from the link and physical layers; it also provides an end-to-end service to the transport layer. The network layer can utilise a number of physical networks to provide its services. The two services provided by the network layer are the connectionless services, and the connection-orientated service. X.25 protocol is important as it is being used on all public packet-switched networks operated by the PTTs. The X.25 protocol defines the necessary operation of layers one, two and three.

The X.25 protocol

Within any layer, a connection orientated protocol has two common tasks: error control and flow control. Error control is concerned with detecting, and correcting, errors that may have occurred in the information being transferred. Flow control is concerned with managing the resources of bandwidth and storage so that no single user can monopolise these resources, and the two endpoints are kept in step with each other. This is usually achieved by keeping the sending and receiving rates of information transfer approximately in step. The X.25 protocol covers the three lower layers of the protocol hierarchy. X.25 is defined as an access protocol, which means that it is used between a host and a node (in most X.25 networks the nodes are called 'exchanges') for the host to access the network so that communication between remote hosts is possible. The X.25 protocol has been adopted by the CCITT as a standard, which means that nearly all future networks will use it. The latest version of X.25 will be adopted by ISO as an international standard.

As well as describing the particulars of X.25, the principles of error and flow control will be shown and the mechanisms used to implement them in each layer explained. The description of level 2 is very detailed, as this is the first consequential level to be met in the bottom-up approach. The discussion of level 2 examines a number of problems which occur at many other protocol layers. For instance, the mechanisms used at level 3 for flow control and protocol synchronisation are very similar to those of level 2, so less detail is given in the level 3 explanation and references are made to the level 2 mechanisms. In the X.25 parlance a host is called a DTE (Data Terminating Equipment) and a node is called a DCE (Data Communications Equipment). X.25 provides a standard mechanism for a DTE to access and use a DCE to transport data across a network to a remote DTE via its remote DCE. The protocol used between the DCEs within the network does not have to be X.25, but would probably be very close to it. X.25 is a virtual call (connection-orientated) protocol.

X.25 level 1--the pPhysical circuit

This level provides the physical communication by specifying the electrical signals, voltages, plug shape and pin assignment that the DTE needs to connect physically to the DCE. This would be the normal arrangement, as the supplier of the network (usually the PTT) will provide the MODEM link to the node (DCE) from the user's premises. The actual specification of level I is contained in the CCITT X.21 recommendation. For practical purposes the user will order a computer interface to this standard which plugs straight into the computer at one end and into the MODEM at the other. The user will normally also be able to buy the software necessary to handle the interface.

As the level 1 hardware is bought as a ready-made unit, no further discussion of it is necessary. The important information needed about level 1 is the type of interface it presents to level 2, and the functions it must perform. The level 1 will provide transport for a bit stream from the DTE to a (remote) DCE. The level 2 will present the level 1 with the bits which are then delivered to a level 2 at the DCE. The hardware of level 1 will also indicate if the physical circuit is working correctly, that is whether the MODEMs are switched on and able to exchange synchronised data. So the interface has two parts

1. the sending and receiving of a serial bit stream
2. the control signals indicating the status of the physical circuit.

X.25 level 2 -- link level

The purpose of level 2 is to control the physical link between the two ends of the level 1 circuit to provide a reliable transfer of information for level 3 between the DTE and DCE. X.25 level 2 uses a link control protocol based on the ISO HDLC (Higher Data Link Control) protocol. The advantages of using an existing protocol are greater than those to be gained from designing a new one. For instance, a new protocol would have to be adopted by a large number of people wishing to communicate; adoption of the protocol would then require a lot of effort. Other link protocols have been designed: IBM use one called SDLC (Synchronous Data Link Control) on their SNA network, which is not dissimilar to HDLC; DEC have their own as well.

Information is passed from level 2 to level 1 in blocks called 'frames'. The use of frames enables easier management of storage and error control. Each frame consists of some protocol information added by level 2, and possibly an information packet from level 3. 1 will use the convention of calling level 2 blocks frames and level 3 blocks *packets. The* functions performed by level 2 are

1. To establish the link connection to a level 2 at a remote site.
2. To transfer packets for level 3 securely, and in sequence.
3. To disconnect the link without loss of level 3 information.

To carry out these functions, the X. 25 level 2 uses three types of frame format. The uses of each format are shown in the next section, but first the fields in the frames are detailed

Flag field

This is a unique 8 bit pattern (01111110) which marks the beginning and end of each frame. The use of the flag as a delimiter presents a problem: to ensure that the end of the frame is correctly interpreted by the receiver, the flag pattern must not appear anywhere within the data in the frame. This means that the frame must be transparent to the hardware looking for a flag to mark the beginning or ending of a frame. The problem of transparency occurs in all link level protocols as they all use special bit patterns for synchronisation and for marking various parts of the frame. In X. 25 level 2 the flag is used as the level 1 synchronisation character (see chapter 2 on synchronous character frames). To ensure that the flag pattern does not occur within the frame, X.25 uses a technique called 'bit stuffing'. The bit stuffing technique involves the sender in inspecting the frame contents prior to transfer to level 1. Whenever a sequence of five Is occurs a 0 is inserted.

Notice that the 0 is inserted regardless of the value of the sixth bit. Bit stuffing in this way is easily implemented by hardware and only increases the length of the frame by 1 bit for every sequence of five Is. As the receiving hardware scans the incoming frame, a 0 following a sequence of five Is is removed. If the sequence of five Is is followed by a further 1, then the flag may have been found. The seventh bit is then inspected: if it is a 0 the flag has been found (01111110), whereas if the seventh bit is another 1 (01111111) then the frame is in error. Thus a sequence of seven Is is used to abort the frame.

There are other ways of providing transparency, such as using escape characters, or bit counts, but none is quite so efficient and flexible as bit stuffing.

Address field

This is really redundant in a point-to-point link. The intention in the HDLC protocol was to use this as an address for multipoint lines, but the present X. 25 recommendation does not include multipoint lines. However, X.25 uses the field as an additional check in the protocol, as well as having the field ready should multipoint lines be considered in the future. The addresses used in this field allow commands and responses to be separated. The level 2 link can be thought of as two separate channels.

Channel A for transferring data from the network (DCE) to the host (DTE) and

Channel B for transferring data from the host (DTE) to the network (DCE).

Any frames relating to information flow from the DCE to the DTE carry the address A (11000000) including any frames from the DTE to the DCE relating to information transfer from the network to the host; similarly for channel B (10000000). To help separate the channels, frames are divided into two classes: *commands* and *responses*, Commands always flow in the direction of information on a channel; responses flow in the opposite direction. Responses are obviously the receiver's replies to various commands.

Command field

This 8 bit pattern determines the type of the frame, as well as being used for sequence numbering and acknowledgement. The command field has a different meaning for the three types of frame (information, supervisory, unnumbered). A 0 in bit 1 indicates that this is an information frame. An information frame is the only type that carries a level 3 packet in the information field. Bits 2, 3 and 4 contain the sequence number of this frame, bits 6, 7 and 8 contain the acknowledgement number. The sequence number and acknowledgement number are used in the ARQ techniques explained in chapter 6 for error correction and flow control. Level 2 uses a stop-go flow control. Bit 5 is the poll/final (P/F) bit. This is set in a command frame as a poll bit and the receiver will set the final bit in any response frame that is a reply to a command frame with the poll bit set. The use of the poll/final bit enables the sender of a command to recognise the corresponding response frame. Bits 1 and 2 set to 10 indicate a supervisory frame. Bits 3 and 4 indicate which type of supervisory frame, Supervisory frames are not given sequence numbers as they do not contain any level 3 information, but they may be used to acknowledge information frames and so bits 6, 7 and 8 contain an acknowledgement number. Bit 5 is the poll/final bit which is the same as before.

The command field format for the *unnumbered frame,* so called because it contains neither sequence number nor acknowledgement number. Bits 1 and 2 set to 11 indicate an unnumbered frame and bit 5 is the poll/final bit. The remainder of the bits are used to indicate the type of unnumbered frame.

Information field

This field only occurs in information frames; it is the position in the frame where the whole level 3 packet is placed. The other level 2 fields provide an envelope for the level 3 packet during the level 2 transfer.

Frame check sequence

The FCS field is found by counting 16 bits back from the terminating flag. This is a 16 bit field to contain the CRC remainder used in error checking. The remainder is calculated using the CCITT recommended generating polynomial of $X^{16} + X^{12} + X^5 + 1$.

It is interesting to note that all the fields of the X.25 level 2 header and the CRC are multiples of 8 bits. This makes transmission easier, because the 8 bit byte is the lowest common multiple of most modern computer word sizes, as well as being the character frame size for synchronous transfer. However the information field and the CRC may be increased by bit stuffing for level 1 transmission.

Operation of X.25 level 2

This section describes the semantics of level 2, with the various commands and responses being explained in context. The level 2 at the DTE (host) end of the connection performs the protocol functions with the level 2 at the DCE, using the HDLC protocol over the level 1 physical connection.

Establishing the link connection

An earlier specification of the X.25 protocol included a lever 2 initialisation procedure called LAP (Link Access Protocol) This procedure has been superseded by a simpler *balanced* procedure called LAPB. The LAPB method of initialisation sets up both channels simultaneously.

Data transfer

Level 2 should provide a sequenced, error-free transport of lever 3 packers from the DTE to the DCE and vice versa. As only 3 bits are allowed for the sequence number and acknowledgement number in the C field, the maximum window size is 7. In X. 25 the link level window size is fixed when the subscriber first applies to use the network. The operation of the data transfer allows the use of limited buffers at the sender (no more than 7) and no requirement for extra buffers to handle out-of-sequence frames at the receiver. The cost of the small buffer requirement is extra channel capacity taken up with retransmission. The use of X.25 to connect hosts to networks would normally involve a fairly high-speed circuit between the DTE and DCE The limiting factor in performance is more likely to be the network and level 3, so a superefficient level 2 is not necessary; thus simpler techniques, such as Go-Back-N, can be used.

The transfer of sequenced frames of information is straightforward but what makes the operation complex (and this applies to every protocol) is the handling of exceptions and errors. There are two basic errors that can occur during data transfer.

1. The frame check sequence indicates an error in the packet.
2. The packet appears to contain no transmission errors but the contents of the A and C fields are not those expected.

In case 1 above the frame is thrown away and no further action is taken by the receiver. Obviously when a frame is discarded the next frame received is not the one expected. In case 2 there are a number of inconsistencies that can be classed as errors. The most common would be a sequence error where a previous packet had been lost or discarded. To ensure that the frame sequence is maintained at the receiver, any frame that does not contain a sequence number matching that of the next expected frame variable, V(R), is an error. If the sequence number of the error frame is within the window, the receiver returns an REJ response to indicate, in the N(R) field, the frame from which the sender should retransmit. If the frame sequence number is not within the window then the sequence numbers of the two ends have become unsynchronised. The only way to recover from a synchronisation problem is to reset the sender and receiver to a known state. The CMDR (command reject) frame initiates a reset which is completed by going through the link establishment exchange. After a reset, the two end-stations will be in a known, initial state. The reset procedure is used to recover from all errors other than the loss of an information frame. A reset may be caused by the receipt of a command or response that is not expected; for instance, a UA if the data transfer is in progress, or the setting of the P/F bit in a response when no command has been sent with that bit set.

The RNR (receiver not ready) frame tells the data sender that the receiver will ignore any further information frames (flow control stop). Once the receiver has returned an RNR response to an information frame, no more information frames are accepted, but the *N(R)* field in the header of any further information frames is inspected so that information frames in the opposite direction are properly acknowledged. The RNR response only stops information on one channel; the other channel is unaffected. When the receiver has more buffer space, an RR (receiver ready) frame is sent to inform the information sender on that channel that more information frames may be transmitted (flow control go), starting at *N(R)*. Note that both RNR and RR have acknowledgement numbers, *N(R)*. The RR frame has another use: if the receiving station does not have any information frames to be sent on the opposite channel, the acknowledgements cannot be piggybacked, and the RR frame is then used to acknowledge the information frames.

A receiver, especially a DCE (node), may not have enough buffers to take a full window for every level 2 link to which it is connected. Instead a statistical allocation could be used which assumes that not all links will be fully active at the same time and that the data is forwarded within a given time. When the network becomes busy this allocation means that a receiver may run out of buffers and need to use some technique to stop the flow of data from one or more links. Every frame, whether it is data or control, needs some buffer space for its receipt. If all the buffers are used up by one link then none of the other links will be able to continue transferring information. Also, if every buffer is allocated, there may be no more buffers to receive a control frame acknowledging a data frame and releasing buffer space! To avoid these problems, complex buffer allocation methods may be used. Normally, enough free buffers are always kept to receive at least one frame on each link so that control information can be exchanged even if data cannot. An information frame would be received, the control information used (for example *N(R)*), and then the frame discarded so that the buffer may be used again.

The loss of information frames as a result of buffer starvation means that information is lost not only because of errors in transmission, but also because of the internal operation of the nodes of a network, especially when the network becomes heavily loaded.

Link disconnection

The LAPB procedure for closing a link requires an exchange of a DISC command and a UA response. The poll/final bit is used to obtain synchronisation between the DCE and DTE.

X.25 level 3—the network level

The function of level 2 is to carry a level 3 packet across a link. The function of the network level is to carry a piece of information from one host (DTE) to another via intermediate network nodes. The transfer of the level 3 information will involve a number of level 2 links. The X. 25 specification only covers the link between the DTE and DCE, but we will assume a similar protocol is used between each node of the network as well. Each level 3 packet contains a certain amount of level 3 protocol information in a header, and possibly some user data (from the transport level). The major differences between levels 2 and 3 are the use of addresses and logical channel numbers. Most hosts will be connected to the network by one level 2 link. This link then has to be used to enable the host to communicate with several other hosts by multiplexing logical channels on to the one physical link. Level 3 is used to achieve this multiple connection via a single link. Using level 3 a host establishes a logical channel to another host by making a connection request using the full address of the remote host. When the connection is established it becomes a logical channel with a unique number, the logical channel number. The logical channel number is unique only for each link. Using the logical channel concept, packets for several calls may pass across the same level 2 link as they are all identified by the unique channel number. At the DCE the channel number is used to decide which route the packet will take. The logical channel is in fact a virtual circuit.

The network level has the same basic functions to perform as the link level.

1. Connection establishment.
2. Data transfer.
3. Connection disconnection.

The difference for the network level is that these functions are now carried out (apparently) between two hosts.

Packet format

The X.25 level 3 headers are used to contain a variety of information, so they are not of uniform size like the level 2 frame headers. The level 3 headers are different for every type of packet, which makes the format quite complex. The general format identifier (GFI) field indicates which format of level 3 header follows. The logical channel group number and logical channel number provide a 12 bit channel-numbering field. Splitting the field may allow subdivisions to be used for, say, different services. Call request and incoming call packets contain the address of the remote host (DTE). The addresses may contain fields indicating a particular process on a host as well as identifying a host. The address fields are of variable length, preceded by a byte count.

Connection establishment

To begin a call, a host uses the full address of the remote host in a call request packet sent from the DTE to the DCE. The DCE will respond with either a call accepted packet if the request was successful, or a clear indication packet if the call was refused.

At the remote host the DCE will send an incoming call packet to the host to indicate that a remote call has been requested. The DTE receiving an incoming call packet will inspect the header to decide if the call is to be established or not. If the call is accepted a call accept packet is sent to the DCE; if the call is rejected a clear request is sent to the DCE. The channel number chosen for a new outgoing call by the DTE is the lowest available number. The channel number for an incoming call is chosen by the DCE as the highest available number. If the DTE and DCE agree on the channel numbers, and the DCE will accept the call, all subsequent packets on that call will only use that channel number, not the full address. A call has been established to a remote

DTE when a host receives a call accepted packet having the same channel number as the call request packet. The call is established at the remote DTE when the call accepted packet is sent to the remote DCE.

Information transfer

Level 3 transfers data to the network in a sequenced stream using Go-Back-N ARQ. The techniques of sequence numbers, piggybacked acknowledgements, RNR, RR and REJ responses are the same as for level 2, but they control the data flow across the network and into the remote host for each, independent logical channel. The use of windows and sequence numbers was for error control in level 2 as the level 1 link was prone to errors. At level 3 the level 2 link is assumed to be error free so. the emphasis is different. The windows and sequence numbers are now used primarily for end-to-end flow control. The receipt of acknowledgements allows more information into the network, while the window limits the number of data packets in flight at any one time. Complete suspension of the data flow can be achieved by using a level 3 RNR, but the flow can be partially adjusted by the rate of acknowledgement.

Interrupt

An extra mechanism is used at level 3 to handle what is known as *out-of-band* transmission. Normal user data on an X.25 virtual call is kept in strict sequence; this is called *in band* transmission. However, a user application often requires a special signal which is not subject to the normal flow control. Such a signal is the abort character which a terminal user would type to stop a runaway program. X.25 level 3 uses an interrupt packet to carry this out-of-band signal. The interrupt is not subject to the normal information flow control, the idea being that the interrupt could overtake information packets already in the network. The interrupt packet contains a field to indicate the cause of the interrupt; it is up to the application to decide what to do both with the interrupt and any subsequent data. When the DTE sends an interrupt packet the DCE responds with an interrupt confirmation. The interrupt sequence is shown in figure 9.10. X.25 permits only one interrupt to be outstanding on a logical call at any one time.

Resets and restarts

In level 2 the reset was introduced as a mechanism for recovering from a protocol error where the two ends in the link became unsynchronised. The same thing can happen between the DTE and DCE at level 3, except that there are two areas where problems may occur.

The first problem is due to the information frames and sequence numbers becoming out of synchronisation on a single call. This may be detected by receiving a sequence number outside the window or an acknowledgement for a packet that was not sent. An error may also have been detected by a higher-level protocol, perhaps because of a network failure. In these cases only the one logical channel is affected so a *reset* is used. This sets the level 3 sequence numbers to 0 at the DTE and DCE. The reset will also be propagated to the remote DTE-DCE pair. The reset can be initiated from either the DTE or DCE and requires the usual request-confirmation exchange. A reset may cause the loss of any information packets within the network so a higher-level protocol will need to recover any lost data.

More drastic action is needed if the DTE and DCE become unsynchronised over global level 3 operation. An example is the choice of a channel number for a call request. If the DCE does not agree with the DTE over the chosen channel number (it should be the lowest free number) it means one of them thinks it has more logical calls opened than the other! The freeing of logical channel numbers correctly is the reason for the clear-request and clear-confirmation pair. When the whole level 3 needs resynchronisation a restart is initiated. This affects all the logical channels on the DTE-DCE link. A reset on the level 2 link is propagated as a restart at level 3.

Call disconnection

A DTE wishing to terminate a call issues a clear request packet, to which the DCE will respond with a clear confirmation packet when the call has been cleared in the DCE. This may involve waiting for the forwarding of any information packets still held there. When the clear confirmation is received the channel number is freed for further use. At the remote end the DCE wit send a clear indication packet indicating that the remote host has closed, and no more information packets will follow. The remote DTE will respond with a clear confirmation packet when all outstanding information packets have been acknowledged.

Data flow

The level 3 transport mechanism requires the data from the higher-level protocols to be broken into packets for transfer across the DTE-DCE interface. The X.25 recommendation specifies possible data lengths of 128 256, 512 and 1024 bytes, where 128 is the preferred maximum. It is probable that the PTT networks will guarantee 128 byte data packets. This means a user message must be broken into 128 byte sequences, the last one being perhaps less than 128 bytes. To enable the receiver to reassemble a message from multiple packets, level 3 uses a *more data bit* (M) in the information packet header to indicate that the current packet is not the last one of a message.

Just as the level 2 and level 3 need to include control information in the frames and packets as well as information from the next higher level, it is likely that a higher-level protocol would like to send control and data over level 3. The higher-level protocol may decide to add the control bits to the front of messages it passes to level 3. However, level 3 provides a mechanism that allows a higher-level protocol to multiplex data and control information on to the level 3 packet stream, thus maintaining the sequence of data and control across the network. This mechanism is the Q *bit*. The Q bit is set when the packet contains control information, and is clear when the packet contains data. Thus the higher-level protocol can quickly separate control and data information when receiving level 3 packets.

X.25 implementation

An advantage claimed for X.25 is that it only describes the host-to-node (DTE-to-DCE) interface. The network itself (internode) can use any convenient protocols, even completely different protocols, and the user would be unaware of them. In fact the proposed PTT networks are all planning to use X.25, or variations, within the networks for node-to-node transfer. The problem considered here is the implications of two methods of implementing an X.25 interface in a DCE that produce quite different results for the user. The discussion will show that even standards have complex problems of *meaning* (or semantics).

The two methods of implementation involve the mechanism for generating responses to various DTE packets at level 3. From the above description it can be seen that a command response sequence is used throughout level 3. The X.25 specification indicates quite clearly what responses are required, but leaves it up to the implementer to decide when, and under what criteria, the responses are made.

Consider the implementation that produces the DCE response as soon as the DTE's packet has been processed at the (local) DCE. This means the DCE's answer is sent to the DTE at the same time as the original request is forwarded across the network and well in advance of its arrival at the remote DTE. Such an implementation would give a very quick response to the user host. For instance, as data is passed to the DCE it is acknowledged immediately, even before it has crossed the network. The DCE-DTE flow control would ensure the DCE was not flooded with data, but large amounts could be in transit within the network before the call has been established at the remote end. This implementation would give the host the appearance of high throughput, as the DCE-DTE flow control would be the only restraint. If the DTE receives a level 3 acknowledgement for a data packet, does this mean that the remote DTE has received it, or only that the local DCE has? To be consistent in this implementation it would have to be the latter, so the DCE has taken on the responsibility for delivery of that data. A higher-level protocol would be needed, with its own flow control, to handle the host-to-host transfer.

This implementation has the effect, mentioned above, of apparently providing a fast throughput. A host may be able to open a call (to the local DCE), send data, and close the call, before the remote DTE has received any data. The network, however, will contain a large amount of unacknowledged packets as the DTE-DCE flow control will accept packets as fast as the DCE can forward them into the network. This makes end-to-end flow control in the network difficult and can quickly lead to congestion.

In the second implementation we only allow the DCE to respond to the DTE when the response from the remote DTE has been received by the local DCE. Data sent from the DTE is not acknowledged until the remote DTE has accepted the packet. This gives the host an impression of a long delay. In fact the delay is the round trip to the remote host, plus processing. This end-to-end use of the level 3 protocol reduces the amount of processing required from higher-level protocols. The sending DTE will only be able to have a window of packets outstanding which will represent the maximum number of data buffers which the whole network will need for the call. This makes the resource management within the network easier and is less likely to produce congestion. The cost is the lower performance seen by the user. Each packet takes longer to be acknowledged, thus reducing the throughput. There is also the problem of gaps which occurs when a window full of packets is sent rapidly, which is followed by a delay until the first acknowledgement comes back. This *bursty* mode of operation gives the network an uneven response and is difficult for both the host and DCE to manage.

Internet Management: SNMPv1 and SNMPv2

SNMPv1 AND MIB-II

In Internet, network management was done using the *Simple Gateway Monitoring Protocol* (SGMP). Then the *Simple Network Management Protocol* (SNMP) was defined for the management of networks and network devices. However, the syntax and semantics of SNMP are different from those of SGMP. The objects to be managed are defined in the *management information base* (MIB). These objects must follow a certain set of rules as mentioned in the *Structure of Management Information (SMI)* such that an object defined by the X group is compatible with the definition of the object by the Y group.

Objects in Internet and those in OSI are different. Internet objects are similar to attributes in OSI, and an Internet object group can best be described as analogous to an OSI managed object class. In Internet, an object is more like a variable found in programming languages; it has a syntax and semantics. Each object can have one or more object instances, each of which, in turn, has one or more values. In the following text, the terms *object* and *variable* are used interchangeably because of the closeness in the semantics of the two terms. The network management system consists of one or more *network management stations* (NMSs) and one or more *network elements* (NEs) with network management functions, management information, and management protocols. The concepts of manager and agent are relatively new in Internet network management. An NMS is analogous to a manager in concept, and the network management functions of NEs are rolled into agents. NMSs have the following primary functions:

- Retrieve values of objects in NEs using agents. This management operation is done by a Get.

- Change or alter the values of objects in NEs using agents. This can be done by a Set.

Network management functions are responsible for monitoring and controlling the managed nodes. SNMP provides the management protocol for network management in the Internet world. The application entities, which can be manager or agent, exchange management information. These application entities are known as SNMP application entities. NMS sends requests and receives responses from the agents. They can also receive notifications known as *traps.* A trap is an unsolicited message sent from an agent. Agents reside in NEs, which are also sometimes known as *managed nodes.* These managed nodes are devices such as hosts, routers, LAN adapters, modems, multiplexers, hubs, and printers. Agents have the following important functions:

- They are instrumented to retrieve management information from the objects, which represent the resources.
- They alter the values of objects.
- They receive responses and traps and send them, in turn, to network management stations.

SNMP is used to communicate management information between a management station and the agents. The management applications are built on the top of network management stations. Some key philosophies involved in the design of SNMP are as follows:

- The management protocol should be as simple as possible and must be provided at least cost. The management protocols should have bare-minimum operations.
- Network management must be robust and able to provide the services, even when the state of the network is not quite reliable or when there are too many errors. SNMP must be able to handle the worst-case scenarios.
- The standard MIB will have core objects defined, and new objects to cover managed devices or managed nodes should be added to the MIB as needed. This extensibility should be easy.
- In the workload distribution between the NMS and the agents in the managed nodes, the major workload will be off-loaded to the NMS, such that it will be easy to add new managed nodes to the network. This will also help the easy extensibility of the managed nodes supported.
- The transport used for carrying management protocols is connectionless UDP. It is not necessary to have the facilities provided by a connection-oriented transport, because they add complexity to the transport.

- The initial objective was to have easy migration to the OSI network management. Now, due to the popularity of SNMP, this objective is in question. Some proponents of SNMP support abandoning the ultimate migration to OSI and, instead, favor the independent growth of Internet network management.

Internet network management framework (SNMPv1)

The original network management framework consisted of RFC 1155, RFC 1157, and RFC 1212. This is known as SNMP Version 1 (SNMPv1). The syntax and semantics used for the definition of objects for network management are furnished in RFC 1155, and are known as the structure of management information (SMI). SMI primarily states how to define objects and how to access them. RFC 1157 furnishes the SNMP management protocol used for accessing the objects. This management protocol is used for monitoring and controlling objects. RFC 1212 furnishes guidelines for defining new MIB modules. RFC 1213 furnishes the definitions of a core set of objects known as MIB-II and which provide the base set for network management. SNMP needs the support of the transport and network layers below it. The transport layer provides multiplexing and demultiplexing of services. This can result in the many-to-many relationships that are possible between SNMP entities. Also, transport protocols provide for the end-to-end checksum, thus improving the reliability of data transfer.

The network layer provides for the routing capabilities between networks. Also, this layer shields the SNMP entities from differences in the media. In addition, the fragmentation and reassembly of packets of different sizes transmitted across the networks are provided by this layer. In some cases, it may not be necessary to use the transport and network layers. The network management functions may be provided directly over data link layers, as in the case of network management for point-to-point or out-of-band (OOB) management directly to the managed devices. In OOB, connections are sometimes made from management stations to the managed devices directly via dial-ups.

However, sometimes the network layer will be required. When management must be done over devices across networks, then it may be necessary to use the routing capabilities of the network layers. Skinny UDP/IP stacks may also be required in some cases. So, ultimately, these decisions must be made while designing management functions for networks.

Because much overhead is involved in maintaining one or more connections or establishing a connection and tearing it down for each SNMP entity operation on an object, a connectionless transport layer was preferred. This was one of the reasons for choosing UDP. UDP provides unreliable datagram service as a trade-off to keep the protocol simple. Every piece of management information is supposed to be carried in a single and independent transport datagram. With this, the complexity involved in assembling frames and the recovery for failures, such as frames not being received in order or lost frames being retransmitted, is avoided.

Internet network management operations are kept simple by limiting the operations to retrieve the value of a variable or set the value of a variable. Also, the traps sent from agents are very limited so as to reduce network traffic. Imperative commands, or commands which trigger some other action, are avoided. The Internet network management functions can be part of the network operations center (NOC). The NOC is usually a central location for monitoring the operation of a network and rectifying network problems. The exchange of management information between an NMS and an NE is done by SNMPs. Each NE has a set of objects also known as the SNMP MIB view. We will discuss the SNMP MIB in detail in a later section. When an SNMP AE in an agent is associated with a set of SNMP AEs in one or more managers, this pairing is known as a community. Each community has an identifier known as the community name. The data type of the community name is OCTET STRING of a size from 0 to 255 octets. Only printable ASCII characters are allowed. An SNMP message consists of a version identifier, an SNMP community name, and an SNMP PDU. The messages exchanged between an NMS and agents are independent of each other. Assume that we are keeping count of messages sent from an NMS to an agent. We have sent 15 messages, and message 16 is sent from the management station to the agent. Now, message 16 does not have any dependency on message 15. Also, in the SNMP implementation, it is recommended that message length not be more than 484 octets. The SNMP community authentication scheme, defined by a set of rules, determines whether the messages sent between AEs are authentic ones. One example is that of an SNMP agent. It is possible that this agent would not send a trap to one particular manager, in which case, checking whether the agent is really allowed to send the trap must be done by the authentication scheme.

Internet object

SNMP uses ASN.1 for defining objects and PDUs exchanged by the management protocol. However, all data types defined in OSI ASN.1 are not used. It was thought that by using a subset of data types, other data types could be constructed. ASN.1 data types used are INTEGER, OCTET STRING, OBJECT IDENTIFIER, NULL, SEQUENCE, and SEQUENCE OF. The data types not used in SNMP are BOOLEAN, OBJECT DESCRIPTOR, EXTERNAL, REAL, ENUMERATED, SET, and SET OF. Object types also must to be encoded be sent across a network. To keep the network management process simple, SNMP uses only a subset of the BER of OSI for transfer syntax. Definite length form and nonconstructor encodings are used.

SMI permits two kinds of constructor types:

- list has the following syntax:

  list ::= SEQUENCE { <type1>,..............<typeN>}

  "type 1" stands for one of the ASN.1 primitive types defined in SMI. DEFAULT and OPTIONAL clauses are not allowed within the SEQUENCE of a list. We can imagine "list" as being analogous to a one-dimensional row or a column.

- *table* is defined as

  table ::= sequence of <entry>

  Here "entry" corresponds to the list constructor. "table" is two-dimensional and has one or more rows, with each row having one or more columns.

RFC 1155 states how the objects are to be defined. The syntax of an object is as follows:

- *Object name:* Should consist of the textual name along with the OBJECT IDENTIFIER. The textual name is known as OBJECT DESCRIPTOR. An example is sysLocation {system 6}. Here sysLocation is the OBJECT DESCRIPTOR, and {system 6} is the OBJECT IDENTIFIER. In Internet, the naming conventions for naming objects are similar to the ones used in OSI; however, the object name must be unique and easily identifiable, and it must be a printable string. {system 6} states that sysLocation is a child under "system" and is the sixth node in the object registration hierarchy. Note here that the object registration hierarchy in Internet is similar to that in OSI.
- *Syntax:* Refers to the syntax used by the object type and should map to one of the permitted ASN.1 data types. sysLocation object type syntax is DisplayString (SIZE (0..255)), for example, DURHAM2154.
- *Definition:* Contains an unambiguous description of the object type. This description is useful for instantiating object types.
- *Access:* States how the object can be accessed by management operations, and it is the minimum level of support for an object type. The values are read-only, read-write, write-only, and not-accessible. With read-only we cannot change the value by the SNMPv1 operation, SetRequest. The operations that can be performed for read-only are GetRequest and GetNextRequest. The access right of write-only enables the SetRequest operation to be done on an object. With read-write, one can perform GetRequest, GetNextRequest, and SetRequest operations.
- *Status:* Refers to the implementation support to the object type. The values are mandatory, optional, or obsolete.

SMI standard RFC 1155 also defines the following object types:

- *Network address:* Presents options for stating addresses in different protocols. At present, only the Internet family of network addresses is allowed.
- *IP address:* Represents the 32-bit Internet address and is represented using OCTET STRING. For BER, only primitive encoding is allowed.
- *Counter:* A nonnegative integer value which increases from zero to the maximum value of 2121. After reaching the maximum value, the counter becomes 0 and increases in value. This is also known as *wrapping around*.

- *Gauge:* A nonnegative integer, which can increase or decrease in value. The maximum value allowed for gauge is 2 32 1. One difference between a counter and a gauge is that in a gauge no wrapping around is allowed.
- *TimeTicks:* A nonnegative integer, which represents elapsed time, in hundredths of a second, since a particular action. The description of the object type must clearly state the particular action, such as the last update of an object.
- *Opaque:* Permits an object to transmit any data as an OCTET STRING. It is similar to the ASN.1 EXTERNAL type. Note here that an NMS and agents must have previous knowledge of the data type to parse the data.

SMI Definitions

SMI document RFC 1155 covers the object information model and a set of generic types used to describe management information. As we have seen earlier, MACROs extend the ASN.1 grammar, and the OBJECT-TYPE MACRO is included in SMI definitions. RFC 1155 defines SMI as follows:

```
    RFC1155-SMI DEFINITIONS::= BEGIN

    EXPORTS -- EVERYTHING

    Internet, directory, mgmt, experimental, private, enterprises, OBJECT-TYPE,
ObjectName, ObjectSyntax, SimpleSyntax, ApplicationSyntax, NetworkAddress,
IpAddress, Counter, Gauge, TimeTicks, Opaque;

-- the path to the root

Internet        OBJECT IDENTIFIER::= {iso org(3) dod(6) 1}
directory       OBJECT IDENTIFIER::= {Internet 1}
mgmt            OBJECT IDENTIFIER::= {Internet 2}
experimental    OBJECT IDENTIFIER::= {Internet 3}
private         OBJECT IDENTIFIER::= {Internet 4}
enterprises     OBJECT IDENTIFIER::= {private 1}

-- definition of object types

    OBJECT-TYPE MACRO ::=

    BEGIN

   TYPE NOTATION::= "SYNTAX" type (TYPE ObjectSyntax)

           "ACCESS" Access

           "STATUS" Status

   VALUE NOTATION::= value (VALUE ObjectName)
```

```
Access ::=    "read-only"
              "read-write"
              "write-only"
              "not-accessible"
Status::=     "mandatory"
              "optional"
              "obsolete"
END
-- names of objects in the MIB
              ObjectName::= OBJECT IDENTIFIER
-- syntax of objects in the MIB
 ObjectSyntax ::=
CHOICE {
                        simple SimpleSyntax,
-- note that simple SEQUENCEs are not directly mentioned here to keep
-- things simple (i.e., prevent misuse). However, application-wide types
-- which are IMPLICITly encoded simple SEQUENCEs may appear in the
-- following CHOICE.
 application-wide ApplicationSyntax
}
SimpleSyntax
 CHOICE {
      number     INTEGER,
      string     OCTET STRING,
      object     OBJECT IDENTIFIER,
      empty      NULL
}
ApplicationSyntax ::=
      CHOICE {
      address    NetworkAddress,
```

counter	Counter,
gauge	Gauge,
ticks	TimeTicks,
arbitrary	Opaque

-- other application-wide types, as they are defined will be

-- added here.

ObjectSyntax

An object is defined using the OBJECT-TYPE macro. The data type of an object is ObjectSyntax. Though RFC 1155 does not have the simply constructed type, Marshall Rose (one of the original authors of RFC 1155), in *The Simple Book* also includes simply constructed in the ObjectSyntax.

SimpleSyntax is a CHOICE of one of the data types--INTEGER, OCTET STRING, OBJECT IDENTIFIER, or NULL. Application Syntax is again a CHOICE of the data types--NetworkAddress, Counter, Gauge, TimeTicks, or Opaque. We have already discussed the individual data types used in ApplicationSyntax.

Management information base (MIB-II)

In Internet, as with the OSI, the details of objects are stored in a database called the Management Information Base (MIB). MIB is an abstract concept applied to storing data. In the MIB, objects have the object type described by the OBJECT DESCRIPTOR along with OBJECT IDENTIFIER. MIBs are defined by different RFCs. The earlier MIB versions followed RFC 1065, Structure and Identification of Management Information for TCP/IP-based Internets, and RFC 1066, Management Information Base Network Management of TCP/IP-based Internets. RFC 1065 specified how the objects were to be defined and has been superseded by RFC 1155. RFC 1066 defined the objects, but was made obsolete by RFC 1156.

RFC 1155, Structure and Identification of Management Information for TCP/IP-based Internets, specified how the objects were to be defined. This RFC attempted to structure the definition of objects more like the OSI managed object class definitions. RFC 1156, known as MIB-I, contained the definition of objects. This became the Full Standard Protocol. Extensions were added to MIB-I in RFC 1158, and this version is known as MIB-II. This RFC added new objects to different groups and deprecated some objects. (Deprecated means that these objects will be removed in the next versions.) The idea behind these changes was to provide support for multiprotocol entities, as well as readability, clarity, and cleaning up.

RFC 1212, Concise MIB definitions, provided methods to clean up and remove the redundant object descriptions. RFC 1213, MIB-II for Network Management of TCP/IP-based Internets: MIB II, is yet another improvement over RFCs 1156 and 1158. It adds and refines objects defined in RFCs 1156 and 1158, and also makes use of RFC 212. However, readers should consult the latest IAB Official Protocol Standards, published often, for information about the current standardization maturity and requirement levels. Changes are frequently being made to accommodate new requirements and compatibility with OSI systems management.

Internet registration hierarchy

Objects must be uniquely identified for manipulation for management purposes, which is accomplished by using OBJECT IDENTIFIERs. OBJECT IDENTIFIERs are a series of identifiers derived by tagging the numbers attached to the nodes from the root in the registration hierarchy. These numbers are separated by periods.

At the starting point of registration tree, there has been three children with labels of ccitt(0), iso(l), and join-iso-ccitt(2). Here, ccitt stands for the textual description of the International Telegraph and Telephone Consultative Committee, and "0" stands for the position within the root. Similarly, iso(l) stands for the ISO, and the joint-iso-ccitt(2) indicates joint administration by ISO and ITU-T.

The administrative control of each of the subtrees for assigning the numbers below them is the responsibility of the nodes. However, this may be delegated as we go down the tree. Under iso(l), org(3) is assigned to national standards organizations. The two nodes below org(3) have been assigned to the U.S. National Institute of Standards and Technology (NIST). Of the two, one node, dod(6), has been assigned to the Department of Defense (DOD), U.S. Here, internet(l) is the child under dod(6).

There are four children under internet(l): directory(1), mgmt(2), experimental (3), and private(4). The child directory(1) is reserved for the future use of OSI directory services. The Internet MIB-II is defined as a first child under mgmt(2). The IAB has delegated the authority to assign numbers in this subtree to the Internet Assigned Numbers Authority. So the object identifier would be 1.3.6.1.2.1. Here, I is from iso; 3 is from org; 6 is from dod, 1 is from internet; 2 is from mgmt; and the final is from MIB-II.

The experimental(3) subtree is meant for objects used in Internet experiments. As an example, if an experimenter gets a number, 12, then the object identifier is 1.3.6.1.3.12. Here, except for the last two numbers, the registration numbers are the same. The next-to-last number, 3, is from the experimental node, and 12 is the number that has been assigned to the experimenter by the Internet Assigned Numbers Authority.

However, the private(4) subtree is used for numbering the objects registered by private bodies. For example, the ABCD Company may ask for a number for registering objects. If it receives a number of 100 from the Internet Assigned Numbers Authority, it will be under the private(4) subtree. The ABCD Company can define its own objects under this registration number of 100; for example, it may define an adapter for token ring as 25. Then the object identifier for token ring is 1.3.6.1.4.2.100.25. Here, the first four numbers are as explained earlier. The registration number of 4 indicates private, and 100 is the~ number for the ABCD Company. As already mentioned, the Internet, Assigned Numbers Authority assigns these private numbers.

Object instance identification

To know the value of an instance of an object, it is necessary to identify the instance. This is done using the OBJECT IDENTIFIER. The following conventions apply for identifying object instances:

- *Scalar objects:* These have only one instance associated with an object. An example of a scalar object is snmpInBadValues. The OBJECT IDENTIFIER for the snmp subtree is 1.3.6.1.2.1.11. By extending the snmp subtree, the snmpInBadValues OBJECT IDENTIFIER is 1.3.6.1.2.1.11.10 We have concatenated the subidentifier of 10 to the snmp subtree to get the OBJECT IDENTIFIER of snmpInBadValues. For each scalar object of snmpInBadValues, there is only one instance, and this instance is identified again by concatenating a value of 0 to the OBJECT IDENTIFIER of snmpInBadValues. So an instance identifier for the instance of snmpInBadValues is 1.3.6.1.2.1.11.10.0. The same procedure for deriving an instance identifier is shown as follows:

	OBJECT IDENTIFIER
snmp subtree	1.3.6.1.2.1.11
snmpInBadValues	1.3.6.1.2.1.11.10
An instance of snmpInBadValues	1.3.6.1.2.1.11.10.0

- *Columnar objects*: Only objects in a table, known as Columnar objects, can be manipulated by SNMP Tables in SNMP are two-dimensional. Instances of objects in tables are identified by the INDEX clause or the AUGMENTS clause. The INDEX clause refers to a row in a table. Note that the AUGMENTS clause is an addition in SNMPv2. Let us take the example of ipAdEntIfIndex in ipAddrTable and see how an instance identifier is formed. The OBJECT IDENTIFIER of the ip subtree is 1.3.6.1.2.1.4. The OBJECT IDENTIFIER of ipAddrEntry is obtained by concatenating subidentifiers 20.1 to the ip OBJECT IDENTIFIER. Hence, the OBJECT IDENTIFIER of ipAddrEntry is 1.3.6.1.2.1.4.20.1. The INDEX clause for ipAddrEntry has ipAdEntAddr (RFC 1213). The OBJECT IDENTIFIER of ipAdEntIfIndex is derived by concatenating the column number of 2 to the OBJECT IDENTIFIER of ipAddrEntry, which is 1.3.6.1.2.1.4.20.1.2. Now any row of ipAdEntIfIndex is indexed by the INDEX clause subidentifiers associated with ipAdEntAddr.

	OBJECT IDENTIFIER
ip subtree	1.3.6.1.2.1.4
ipAdEntIfIndex	1.3.6.1.2.1.4.20.1.2
Fifth instance of ipAdEntIfIndex row value of ipAdEntAddr)	1.3.6.1.2.1.4.10.1.2. (fifth

- *Conceptual rows and tables:* When the object types are just rows and tables, they are known as conceptual rows and conceptual tables. There are no instance identifiers associated with the conceptual tables. They are not accessible by SNMP operations.
- *Lexicographic ordering: Webster's New Collegiate Dictionary* defines *lexical* as "of or relating to words or the vocabulary of a language as distinguished from its grammar or construction." OBJECT IDENTIFIERs are arranged in increasing value in SNMP MIBs. Referring to the previous example of the ip subtree, the OBJECT IDENTIFIER of ipAdEntIfIndex is lexicographically greater than the OBJECT IDENTIFIER of ip. This lexicographic ordering is useful for traversing a table without a management station actually knowing the OBJECT IDENTIFIER of an entry. For example, to retrieve the fifth instance of ipAdEntIfIndex, four GetNextRequest PDUs will be enough to obtain the value of the fifth instance.

The following rules are used for instance identification using the INDEX clause:

- *Integer-valued:* Has a single-value subidentifier to identify an object instance. These are nonnegative integers. The value of ifIndex, which can take any value ranging from 1 to the value of ifNumber, is an example of an Integer-valued INDEX clause.
- *String-valued* (fixed-length strings): Has *n* octet length with n subidentifiers.
- *String-valued* (variable-length strings): Has *n*+1 octet length with *n* subidentifiers. The first octet has the value of *n,* which indicates the number of subidentifiers.
- *Object-identifier-valued:* Used with object identifiers. The first: value is the number *n* of subidentifiers used along with the *n* subidentifiers.
- *IpAddress valued:* Associated with four subidentifiers familiar in the IP address of the type a.b.c.d.
- *NsapAddress-valued:* Uses syntax similar to a fixed-length string with the length of the string as *n.*

Table manipulation

In MIB-II tables each object is represented by a column; the value of each object instance is represented in a row. The way to retrieve values from a table is somewhat nonintuitive. The length of each column is traversed in its entirety, and then one moves on to the next column. To add the value of an object instance, the value is entered in a row with a set operation. To delete an entry, again using the set operation, the value is set to invalid.

Whether or not to remove the invalid entries is left as an implementation option. It is better to remove invalid entries when storage is a constraint; traversing the table will be faster with fewer entries. But this involves extra work--now and then, some sort of "cleaning" of the table to remove invalid entries must be done. If it is decided to do this cleaning, then it must also be determined how frequently to remove the invalid entries. Ultimately, these decisions involve trade-offs that should be examined during the design stage.

MIB-II Details and Objects (RFC 1213)

It, is necessary to follow rules when defining new MIBs. Old object types are not deleted, but they may be deprecated. The semantics of old object types should not be changed between versions. However, if it is necessary to change the semantics, then new object types must be formed. Some of these rules are formulated for the coexistence of multiple versions of MIBs.

In MIB, only the essential objects are defined. This has been done to make the implementations simple. However, there is enough flexibility to define the implementation of specific objects. The guidelines for defining new objects are provided by SMI. New objects can be added under the experimental subtree or under the enterprises subtree. Also, new versions of MIB can be released for the new standard objects, by which the definition of objects is sufficiently flexible in Internet.

MIB-II has added the data type, DisplayString. DisplayString is defined as OCTET STRING, and is a printable ASCII character string of size ranging from 0 to 255 octets. Another data type of PhyAddress is again an OCTET STRING used to represent media addresses. As an example, a token-ring address can be represented in binary in six octets.

Objects in Internet are classified into different groups. These groups are under {mgmt 2}, and the classification into groups assists in easily assigning object identifiers to the groups. Also, the objects under these groups must be implemented as a group. For example, if the TCP group is implemented, then all objects under the TCP group, such as tcpRtoAlgorithm, and tcpRtoMin, must be implemented.

Conventions used in the figures on MIB-II object groups are:

- Each object group is shown in a separate figure. The object group name starts at the top.
- Some object groups have tables. Objects in these tables are shown in separate figures.
- The number after an object stands for the node within a group hierarchy. For example, sysDescr (1) stands for sysDescr {system 1}

In the explanations of the objects in MIB-II furnished subsequently, the syntax of the object type is supplied along with the object, in parentheses. For example, in sysDescr (DisplayString), sysDescr is the OBJECT IDENTIFIER, and DisplayString is the data type of the object. Also, in the following explanation, objects are mentioned. There are two types of objects: MIB-II objects and the object instance representing a resource, which is monitored by a network management system. This subtle difference between the two types of objects should be noted.

System group

The system group is mandatory. The objects in this group broadly explain the names and versions of hardware and software, the vendor's subsystem, the length of time the network management system portion was up and running, the contact person for this node, the node's domain name, the physical location, and the sum of services the node provides. Concerning different objects in the system group, RFC 1213 states, "if an agent is not configured to have a value For any of these variables, a string length of 0 is returned." The return value of zero should be avoided for stating that an object is not supported. This can be ambiguous in some cases. It is hard to distinguish whether the value is actually zero or an object is not supported. For Avoiding different interpretations during implementations, the unsupported cases should show theoretically impossible return codes instead of zero. This scenario is also well explained in implementations.

Most of the objects in the system group are useful for configuration management. Some of the objects, such as sysDescr, sysObjectID, and sysContact, are also useful for fault management.

- *sysDescr (DisplayString):* Includes details of the system such as hardware name, hardware version, and software details on the operating system, networking, and communication.
- *sysObjectID (OBJECT IDENTIFIER):* Uniquely identifies the network management subsystem (agent) in the naming subtree. The naming tree for the subsystem is under the SKI enterprises subtree {1.3.6.4.1}. This helps identify an object representing the subsystem for network management.
- *sysUpTime (TimeTicks):* Refers to the elapsed time in hundredths of a second since an agent has been reinitialized or come up.
- *sysContact (DisplayString):* Supplies detailed information on the contact person for the managed node being monitored.
- *sysName (DisplayString):* Furnishes the contact name of the person who is administratively responsible for the managed node.
- *sysLocation (DisplayString):* Contains information on the actual physical location of the managed node.
- *sysServices (INTEGER):* Is calculated as the sum of the services provided by the managed node. Each layer has a value such as the following: physical--1, datalink/

subnetwork--2, Internet--3, end-to-end--4, applications--7, OSI sessions--5, and OSI presentations --6. Then, for each layer a value of 2^{L-1} is calculated, where L stands for a layer value. For a managed node, the total of the services performed is calculated and reported in this object.

Interfaces group

The interfaces group is mandatory. Here, *interface* refers to the interface associated with a subnetwork. This group consists of details such as the number of interfaces, the list of each interface, the objects at the subnetwork, details about the interface's manufacturer, interface details of the physical and link layer protocols, the size of the largest datagrams that can be sent or received, the interface's bandwidth, the physical addresses if available, the status of interfaces, and the details of the packets received or transmitted.

- *ifNumber (INTEGER):* The number allocated to the network interfaces of a managed node.
- *ifTable (SEQUENCE OF IfEntry):* Furnishes a list of interface entries. The number of entries is equal to ifNumber.
- if*Entry (SEQUENCE):* Refers to the number of objects at and below the subnetwork layer.
- *IfIndex (INTEGER):* A unique value for an interface, which ranges from I to the value of ifNumber.
- *ifDescr (DisplayString):* Furnishes in textual string interface details such as the manufacturer's name, product name, and version of interface.
- *ifType (INTEGER):* Provides the value of the protocol below the network layer. MIB-II has 32 values provided for different protocols. For example, Frame Relay has a value of 32.
- *ifMTU (INTEGER):* Used for furnishing the largest datagram size in octets which can be handled by the interface.
- *ifSpeed (Gauge):* Provides bandwidth (transmission rate) in bits per second.
- if*PhysAddress (PhyAddress):* Has interface's address below the network layer. For example, in the LAN interface, the MAC address is the physical address. If there is no physical address, then an OCTET STRING of zero length must be used.
- *ifAdminStatus (INTEGER):* Describes the desired state of the interface. Values allowed are: up = 1, down = 2, and testing = 3.
- *ifOperStatus (INTEGER):* Describes the current operational status of the interface with values of up = 1, down = 2, and testing = 3.
- *ifLastChange (TimeTicks):* Refers to the elapsed time since the current operational

state has been reached. However, if an object has attained current operational status before an agent is initialized, then the value is zero.

- *ifInOctets (Counter):* Has the total number of octets received by the interface since last initialization.
- *iflnUcastPkts (Counter):* Provides the packets delivered to the next layer. It excludes the broadcast and multicast packets. Note that this granularity of packets into different types is useful for performance management, where we may be required to analyze different types of packets for meaningful performance tuning. This granularity is also useful in fault management to identify problems.
- *IfInNUcastPkts (Counter):* Takes account of the broadcast and multicast packets delivered to the next layer.
- *iflnDiscards (Counter):* The total of packets received at an interface which have not been delivered to upper layers. These packets were discarded even though there were no errors. One example furnished in RFC 1213 is the possibility of freeing up buffer space.
- *ifInErrors (Counter):* Provides the errors that have been noticed in the inbound packets. These packets have not been delivered to the upper layer. iflnErrors is useful for analyzing problems. If there are too many errors in the received packets, then reasons for the errors need to be identified. One drawback of SNMP is that there is no threshold data type. When a threshold value is reached, a trap should be sent indicating that action is required *now.*
- *iflnUnknownProtos (Counter):* Provides the number of PDUs A received and discarded because the protocols are unsupported or unknown.

So far we have described objects used to analyze the PDUs that have been received. Data can be sent through an interface, too. Thus, some of the objects described as follows relate to the measurements on the PDUs transmitted.

- *ifOutOctets (Counter):* Used for counting the total number of PDUs transmitted out of an interface.
- *ifOutUcastPkts (Counter):* Furnishes the total number of non-broadcast and nonmulticast PDUs, which were requested by the higher layers to transmit to an address. It includes those PDUs which have been discarded or not sent for different reasons.
- *ifOutNUcastPkts (Counter):* In ifOutUcastPkts, the broadcast and multicast PDUs transmitted were not counted. To compensate, in ifOutNUcastPkts, the PDUs requested by the upper layers to transmit via the interface to multicast and broadcast addresses are totaled. Here, too, we take into account those packets which were discarded or not sent.

- *ifOutDiscards (Counter):* Counts the PDUs that were discarded for reasons such as freeing up buffer space.
- *ifOutErrors (Counter):* Refers to the total number of PDUs which were discarded because of errors.
- *ifOutQLen (Gauge):* Refers to the length of the output queue. It i measured in terms of PDUs.
- *ifSpecific (OBJECT IDENTIFIER):* Refers to MIB definitions on media (Ethernet, token ring, and others) used at the interface. If this value is not present, then OBJECT IDENTIFIER {0 0} must be used.

Address translation group

The address translation group has been provided for compatibility with MIB-I, and will be removed in MIB-III. This group is mandatory for all systems. The address translation group has one table, atTable, for mapping network addresses such as the IP address to the physical address such as the MAC address. However, reverse mapping is also required in some cases. Hence, each network protocol group will have its own address translation table.

- *atTable (SEQUENCE of AtEntry):* This table has mapping of NetworkAddress such as an IP address to a physical address. If this table is empty, then it has zero entries.
- *atEntry (SEQUENCE):* This refers to a single entry in the address translation table.
- *atIfIndex (INTEGER):* This has the same value as that of ifIndex in the interfaces group.
- *atPhysAddress (PhysAddress):* This refers to the physical address, such as a MAC address. A string of zero length invalidates an entry in the address translation table.
- *atNetAddress (NetworkAddress):* This refers to a network address, such as an IP address.

IP group

The IP group is also mandatory. This furnishes information on whether the IP gateway functions or the IP host functions are used. Here, only IP gateways forward datagrams, and IP hosts forward datagrams using source routing through the hosts. This group mainly furnishes the details on the datagrams, such as datagrams forwarded and datagrams discarded. Note that the gateways referred to are the "routers" in the industry. The IP group has the following three tables:

- *ipAddrTable (SEQUENCE OF IpAddrEntry):* This has five columns and also has IP addresses. IpAddrEntry is a SEQUENCE of five entries, each representing a column in the ipAddrTable.

- *ipRouteTable (SEQUENCE OF IpRouteEntry):* This has 13 columns, and contains the routing information. Each row has one route to a particular destination. As seen in ipAddrTable, IpRouteEntry is a SEQUENCE of thirteen entries.
- *ipNetToMedia able (ipNetToMediaEntry):* This has mapping of an IP address to a physical address. This address mapping is done by ARP and proxy ARP. This table has five columns. Here, too, IpNetToMediaEntry is a SEQUENCE of four entries.

Referring to Figure, the explanations of IP group entries are:

- *ipForwarding (INTEGER):* Has two values: forwarding = 1 and: not-forwarding = 2. It primarily states whether or not a node acts as a gateway that forwards datagrams received.
- *ipDefaultTTL (INTEGER):* Contains default time-to-live value whenever this value is not supplied by the transport layer.
- *ipInReceives (Counter):* Refers to the total number of datagram received by the IP layer from lower layers, including those with errors.
- *ipInHdrErrors (Counter):* Helps identify the PDUs received with errors in the header. These datagrams, as is the common practice, are discarded.
- *ipInAddrErrors (Counter):* Here, the datagrams that have invalid IP addresses are counted. These include invalid addresses, addresses not supported, and addresses which are not local addresses in hosts.
- *ipForwDatagrams (Counter):* Used for counting datagrams which have been forwarded. These datagrams can refer to datagrams forwarded in gateways or source routing datagrams.
- *ipInUnknownProtos (Counter):* Refers to the count of datagrams discarded due to unsupported or unknown protocols.
- *ipInDiscards (Counter):* Includes the datagrams discarded for reasons such as lack of buffer space. However, this count excludes datagrams which were discarded during reassembly.
- *InDelivers (Counter):* Refers to the number of datagrams which were successfully delivered by the IP layer to the immediate upper layer. It also includes the number of ICMP datagrams.
- *ipOutRequests (Counter):* The datagrams which are transmitted to the lower layer by the IP layer, including ICMP datagrams. Note that this counter excludes the count of datagrams in ipForwDatagrams. ipOutRequests can be regarded as a counter for datagrams flowing in the opposite direction to that of the ipInDelivers counter.
- ip*OutDiscards (Counter):* Used to count the outbound datagrams which have been discarded for reasons such as lack of buffer space, and also includes datagrams counted under ipForwDatgrams.

- *ipOutNoRoutes (Counter):* Refers to the data discarded because no routes to the destination were available, and includes datagrams counted in ipForwDatagrams. It also includes datagrams discarded due to failures of gateways.
- *ipReasmTimeout (INTEGER):* Furnishes the maximum amount of time in seconds that a fragment had to wait for the reassembly of fragments to a datagram.
- *ipReasmReqds (Counter):* Refers to the total number of fragments which were reassembled in the IP layer.
- *ipReasmOKs (Counter):* Used to count the number of IP datagrams which were successfully reassembled in this IP layer.
- *ipReasmFails (Counter): A* count of the number of failures in reassembly for reasons such as time out or errors. Note that this number is not the same as the number of IP fragments discarded.
- *ipFragOKs (Counter):* Refers to the number of successful IP fragments formed in this IP layer.
- *ipFragFails (Counter):* Some datagrams cannot be fragmented into smaller frames, if the don't-fragment bit is set. This counter takes care of these counts.
- *ipFragCreates (Counter)*: Refers to the total number of fragments formed from IPdatagrams for onward transmission to the lower layer.

As previously mentioned, ipAddrTable has five columns:

- *ipAdEntAddr (IpAddress):* Has the IP address.
- *ipAdEntIflIndex (INTEGER):* Refers to the value for this interface and has the same value as that of ifIndex.
- *ipAdEntBcastAddr (INTEGER):* Refers to the least significant bit of the IP broadcast address.
- *ipAdEntReasmMaxSize (INTEGER):* Refers to the largest datagram size which can be formed by reassembling fragments. Values range from 0 to 65535.

The second table, ipRouteTable has thirteen columns. Note that the information in this table refers to the routing information. The columns are interpreted as follows:

- *ipRouteDest (IpAddress):* Has the destination IP address.
- *ipRouteIflndex (INTEGER):* The local interface number. Its value is the same as the value of ifIndex.
- *ipRouteMetric1(INTEGER):* Refers to the value used for the primary routing metric. The semantics are determined by the IPRouteProto value. The entry of IPRouteProto is explained after the next three entries. A value of -- 1 indicates that this entry is not used.

- *IpRouteMetric(2-4) (INTEGER):* Used to indicate the values of matrices of alternate routes.
- *IpRouteNextHop (IpAddress):* Refers to the next top IP address.
- *ipRouteType (INTEGER):* Corresponds to the values associated with a route. The values are: other = 1, invalid = 2, direct 3, and indirect = 4.
- *ipRouteProto (INTEGER):* Corresponds to the routing protocols used for learning the routes. The values are: other = 1, local = 2, netmgmt = 3, iemp = 4, egp = 5, ggp = 6, hello = 7, rip = 8, isis = 9, esis = 10, ciscoIgrp = 11, bbnSpfIgp = 12, ospf = 13, and bgp = 14. It is not necessary for the host to support these gateway protocols.
- *ipRouteAge (INTEGER):* Refers to the value in seconds since the route was last updated.
- *ipRouteMask (IpAddress):* Furnishses the subnet mask of a route.
- *ipRouteMetric5 (INTEGER):* Also provides the alternate routing metric in addition to the ones already seen.
- *ipRouteInfo (OBJECT IDENTIFIER):* Contains MIB definitions pertinent to a routing protocol. If this value is not there, then this value is set to OBJECT IDENTIFIER {0 0}

As already mentioned, the third table used by the IP group is the IP address translation table identified as ipNetToMediaTable. It has the following four columns:

- *ipNetToMediaIfIndex (INTEGER):* Contains the value associated with this interface and has the same value as the one used in I ifIndex for this interface.
- *ipNetToMediaPhyAddress (PhysAddress):* Refers to the physical address, such as the MAC address of the interface.
- *ipNetToMediaNetAddress (IpAddress):* Has the IP address.
- *ipNetToMedia TYpe (INTEGER):* Describes how the address translation is done. It has these values: other = 1, invalid = 2, dynamic 3, and static = 4. A value of 2 invalidates an entry.
- *ipRoutingDiscards (Counter):* Contains the number of valid routing entries which have been discarded for reasons such as freeing buffer space. Note that ipRoutingDiscards is not part of the address translation table.

ICMP group

The ICMP group implementation is mandatory. The ICMP group furnishes details on the ICMP messages, and basically has counters on different types and conditions of ICMP messages. These counters are useful for performance management. Objects used are:

- *icmpInMsgs (Counter):* Furnishes the total number of ICMP messages received, including those with errors.
- *icmpInErrors (Counter):* Refers to the ICMP messages which had errors for reasons such as bad checksurn or bad length.

The following ICMP objects count the different types of ICMP Messages received.

- *icmpInDestUnreachs (Counter):* Keeps count of the number of ICMP Destination Unreachable messages received.
- *icmPInTimeExcds (Counter):* Useful for keeping track of the number of ICMP Time Exceeded messages received.
- *icmpInParmProbs (Counter):* Refers to the total number of ICMP Parameter Problem messages received.
- *icmpInSrcQuenchs (Counter):* Keeps track of the ICMP Source Quench messages received.
- *icmpInRedirects (Counter):* Used for counting the total number of ICMP Redirect messages received.
- *icmpInEchos (Counter):* Refers to the number of ICMP Echo Request messages received.
- *icmpInEchoReps (Counter):* Used for totaling the number of ICMP Echo Reply messages received.
- *icmpInTimestamps (Counter):* Used for keeping track of ICMP Timestamp Request messages received.
- *icmpInTimestarnpReps (Counter):* Counts the total number of ICMP Timestamp Reply messages.
- *icmpInAddrMasks (Counter):* Furnishes the total number of ICMP Address Mask Request messages received.
- *icmpInAddrMaskReps (Counter):* Provides the total number of ICMP Address Mask Reply messages received.

In the ICMP group, "In" counters keep track of different ICMP messages received by a local IP entity. Similarly, there are corresponding "Out" counters, which furnish the counters of different ICMP mes~: sages sent from a local IP entity. There is no difference, except that one counter is for messages received, while the other one is for messages transmitted; hence, these "Out" counters and their explanations are not listed here.

TCP group

The TCP group is mandatory if TCP is implemented. Here, instances refer to the TCP connections, and their values are valid only during a connection. This group provides details on the conditions of connections, relevant connection addresses, retransmission timeout values, and details on segments transmitted and received. Like other groups, this group has objects which will be useful for gathering information on a TCP layer. Objects defined for the TCP group are:

- *tcpRtoAlgorithm (INTEGER):* Furnishes the algorithm used for calculating the timeout value for unacknowledged segments. Values are: other 1, which stands for none of the furnished algorithms; constant 2; rsre = 3, which refers to MIL-STD-1778; and vanj = 4, which refers to Van Jacobson's algorithm.
- *tcpRtoMin (INTEGER):* Provides minimum permitted value for a retransmission timeout.
- *tcpRtoMax (INTEGER)*: Refers to the maximum permitted value for a retransmission timeout.
- *tcpMaxConn (INTEGER)*: Furnishes the maximum number of connections allowed in a TCP module. If the connections are dynamic, then a value of - 1 is used.
- *tcpActiveOpens (Counter)*: Provides the number of active open coonnections. The transitions from the CLOSED state to the SYNSENT state are counted in the counter. Different TCP states are furnished in RFC 793.
- *tcpPassiveOpens (Counter)*: Refers to the number of passive opens. The transition from the LISTEN state to the SYN-RCVD state is considered for this counter.
- *tcpAttemptFails (Counter)*: Keeps track of the total number of TCP connections which have made the transition from the SYN-SENT or SYN-RCVD state to the CLOSED state, and those TCP connections which have made the transition from the SYN-RCVD state to the LISTEN state.
- *tcpEstabResets (Counter):* Furnishes the total number of connections which have been reset. A reset is identified by a transition to Ii. CLOSED state from either the ESTABLISHED state or the CLOSE-WAIT state.
- *tcpCurrEstab (Gauge):* Provides the total number of connections which are in the ESTABLISHED or CLOSE-WAIT states.
- *tcpInSegs (Counter):* Furnishes the total number of segments received on established connections by a TCP module. It also includes segments which are in error.
- *tcpOutSegs (Counter):* Provides the segments trans-mitted. However, this does not include segments which have been retransmitted.
- *tcpRetransSegs (Counter):* Keeps track of the segments that have been retransmitted from a TCP module. This is important data for performance analysis, because it indicates the state of the connections.

The TCP group contains tcpConnTable. This table has information pertinent to TCP connections, and has five columns:

- *tcpConnState (INTEGER)*: Refers to the state of a TCP connection with these values: closed = 1, listen 2, synSent 3, synReceived = 4, established = 5, finWait1 6, finWait2 7, closeWait = 8, lastAck = 9, closing = 10, timeWait = 11, and deleteTCB = 12. A management station (manager) may send only deleteTCB, which means the termination of a connection.
- *tcpConnLocalAddress JpAddress):* Refers to the local IP address associated with a TCP connection.
- *tcpConnLocalPort (INTEGER):* Has the local port number associated with a TCP connection.
- *tcpConnRemAddress (IpAddress):* Contains the remote IP address of a TCP connection.
- *tcpConiiRernPort (INTEGER):* Refers to the remote port number associated with a TCP connection.

The following additional TCP objects are also part of the TCP group:

- *tcpInErrors (Counter):* Refers to the total segments which have been received with errors. This data is useful for performance management. If errors exceed certain limits, it is worth the analysis. This may provide some useful information for rectifying the TCP connections and thus reduce the number of errors.
- *tcpOutRsts (Counter):* Contains the total number of TCP segments which were sent with the RST flag set.

UDP group

The UDP group is similar to the TCP group, and objects defined in this group are required if UDP is implemented' Here also, the UDP group furnishes details about UDP datagram and UDP endpoints on which a local application is accepting datagrams. UDP has the following objects:

- *udpInDatagrams (Counter):* Contains the total number of UDP, datagrams delivered to the user of a UDP module.
- *udpNoPorts (Counter):* Provides the number of UDP datagrams which could not be delivered because there was no application at the destination port.
- *udpInErrors (Counter):* Refers to the UDP datagrams which could not be delivered to the user. This excludes the number of UDP datagrams included in udpNoPorts.
- *udpOutDatagrarns (Counter):* Pertains to the UDP datagrams sent from the user of a UDP module.

UDP has one table: udpTable with two columns. This table has information on the UDP local endpoints on which an application is receiving datagrams. The entries are:

- *udpLocalAddress (IpAddress):* Has a local IP address associated with a UDP.

- *udpLocalPort (INTEGER):* Contains the local port number associated with a UDP.

EGP group

The EGP group objects must be implemented if EGP is used. EGP is the protocol used by routers and is explained in RFC 904. The EGP group provides details on EGP messages generated, messages not sent due to resource limitations in EGP, EGP messages received and their details, and conditions of EGP neighbors.

- *egpInMsgs (Counter):* Has the total number of EGP messages which have been received without errors.
- *egPInErrors (Counter):* When we exclude errors in egpInMsgs, it should be intuitively obvious that there should be a separate counter for the total number of EGP messages which have been received with errors. egpInErrors serves this purpose.
- *egpOutMsgs (Counter):* Contains the total number of EGP messages that have been generated by the EGP module. However, this does not cover messages which have errors.
- *egpOutErrors (Count):* Covers those EGP messages which have not been transmitted due to problems, such as resource limitations.
- egpNeighTable has information on the EGP neighbors and consists of the following 15 columns:
- *egpNeighState (INTEGER):* Has information on the state of the neighbor. The values used for describing the state are: idle = 1, acquisition = 2, down = 3, up = 4, and cease = 5.
- *egpNeighAddr (IpAddress):* Contains the IP address of the EGP neighbor.
- *egpNeighAs (INTEGER):* Refers to the autonomous system number of the remote EGP peer.
- *egpNeighInMsgs (Counter):* Has the number of EGP messages received from the EGP neighbor that did not contain errors.
- *egpNeighInErrs (Counter):* Refers to the number of EGP messages from the EGP neighbor with errors.
- *egpNeighOutMsgs (Counter):* Has the number of EGP messages generated by the local EGP module to this neighbor.
- *egpNeighOutErrs (Counter):* Pertains to the number of EGP messages which were not transmitted by a local EGP node to the neighbor due to errors.
- *egpNeighInErrMsgs (Counter):* Refers to the number of EGP messages received from an EGP neighbor which were in error.

- *egpNeighOutErrMsgs (Counter):* Contains the number of EGP messages which were in error, but were sent to an EGP neighbor.
- *egpNeighStateUps (Counter):* Refers to the number of state transitions to the UP state from this EGP neighbor.
- *egpNeighStateDowns (Counter):* Provides the number of state transitions from the UP state to any other state for the EGP neighbor.
- *egpNeighInterualHello (INTEGER):* Furnishes the time interval in hundredths of a second to send Hello messages.
- *egpNeighIntervalPoll (INTEGER):* Provides the time interval in hundredths of a second between poll messages.
- *egpNeighMode (INTEGER):* Furnishes the polling mode of the EGP neighbor. The value can be either passive or active.
- *egpNeighEventTrigger (INTEGER):* Used to provide the control variable to trigger Starts and Stops by operators.
- *egpAs (INTEGER):* Has the autonomous system number. Also note that this object is not part of egpNeighTable.

CMOT group

The objects required for CMOT are defined under {mib 9}. The subtree under cmot is labeled "oim." Because CMOT has been relegated to historical status, the chances of using these objects are remote.

Transmission group

The transmission group is meant for objects relating to the underlying transmission media. At first, they are included under the experimental category, but as they become mature, they are elevated to new object identifier under the transmission group.

SNMP group

The SNMP group defines the objects for one SNMP protocol entity. The implementation of the SNMP group is mandatory if., SNMPs are supported. Depending on the implementation, a node can be either an agent or a management station. So, in some cases, the objects in the following list will be zerovalued. The SNMP group has a number of objects defined to reflect the different SNMP protocol entity messages that are received or delivered to the underlying transport protocol.

- *snmpInPkts (Counter):* Contains the total number of SNMP messages received by the SNMP module from the transport layer below the SNMP (i.e., UDP).
- *snmpOutPkts (Counter):* Refers to the total number of SNMP messages delivered to the layer below the SNMP.

- *snmpInBad Versions (Counter):* Provides the total number of SNMP messages which could not be processed due to unsupported versions.
- *snmpInBadCommunityNames (Counter):* Pertains to the SNMP messages received with bad community names.
- *snmpInBadCommunity Uses (Counter):* Refers to the SNMP messages with bad community uses.
- *snmpInASNParseErrs (Counter):* Contains the total number of SNMP messages which had ASN. 1 or BER errors.
- *snmpInTooBigs (Counter):* Refers to the SNMP messages received with tooBig in the error status field.
- *snmpInNoSuchNarnes (Counter):* The total number of SNMP messages received with noSuchName in the error status field.
- *snmpInBadValues (Counter):* Provides the total number of SNMP messages received with badValues in the error status field.
- s*nmpInReadOnlys (Counter):* Can arise due to bad implementations of SNMP, This counter is similar to the earlier ones, and has the total number of SNMP messages received with readOnly in the error status field.
- *snmpInGenErrs (Counter):* Refers to the total number of SNMP messages which have genErr in the error status field
- *snmpInTotalReqVars (Counter):* Contains the total number of MIB objects retrieved successfully due to SNMP GetRequest and GetNextRequest PDUs.
- *srimpInTotalSetVars (Counter):* Provides the total number of MIB objects which have been altered successfully due to SNMP SetRequest PDUs.

The following objects are used to keep track of different SNMP PDUs that have been received and processed:

snmpInGetRequests (Counter)

snmpInGetNexts (Counter)

snmpInSetRequests (Counter)

snmpInGetResponses (Counter)

snmpInRaps (Counter)

The preceding lists indicated many objects which were used to count SNMP messages received with different values in the error status field. The following SNMP objects are used to keep track of messages sent out from an SNMP module. Those SNMP messages which contain "Out" are mirror images of those containing "In."

snmpOutTooBigs (Counter)

snmpOutNoSuchNames (Counter)

snmpOutBadValues (Counter)

snmpOutGenErrs (Counter)

snmpOutGetRequests (Counter)

snmpOutGetNexts (Counter)

snmpOutSetRequests (Counter)

snmpOutGetResponses (Counter)

snmpOutTraps (Counter)

snmpEnableAuthenTraps (INTEGER): Provides information about whether an SNMP agent is permitted to generate authentication failure taps. It has two values: enabled = 1 and disabled = 2.

The MIB-II objects explained here can be classified and folded into different network management applications such as configuration management, fault management, performance management, accounting management, and security management. These appli-cations can be made a part of the network management station. Leinwald and Fang provide a good breakdown of MIB-II into different network management functions.

Functioning of SNMPv1 PDUs

SNMP is used for carrying messages from one *protocol entity* (PE) to another. A PDU is constructed in ASN.1 form and is then sent to an authenticator, along with the community name and source and transport addresses. The authenticator checks whether the sending and receiving protocol entities can really exchange messages. The result of the check, which can be an authentication failure or an ASNA object, is sent back to the PE. If the message has passed the authenticator check, it is formatted using BER and sent by the transport mechanism to the receiving PE.

On the receiving side, receiving a PE parses the data received and checks for version numbers. If the PDU fails during this action, then the datagram is discarded. After this operation, user data, community name, and source and destination addresses go to the authenticator. The authenticator checks whether the receiving PE can actually receive data from the sending PE. The result can be authentication failure. In such a case, a trap may be generated and sent to the sending PE. However, sometimes this trap is just logged and a record is maintained for any remedial action to be taken. On the other hand, if the authenticator passes the authentication process, the receiving PE processes the message and takes the appropriate action and sends the response back to the sending PE.

Here we must note that some management applications may not need the security provided by authentication. In such implementations, the authentication steps may be skipped altogether for managernent applications. Also, in some cases, additional security steps may be needed, such as extra access control functions. Thus, the level of authentication required is guided by implementation considerations.

When SNMPv1 protocols are used, errors can be generated. The value of no Error is 0 and they progressively increase in value by 1. Thus, badValue has a value of 3. Let us examine the individual SNMPvl PDU function. When a GetRequest PDU is sent, the receiving PE checks whether the object name is correct. If the object name is not correct, then the error status is noSuchName. Afterwards, a check is made as to whether the object type is aggregate. Because SNMP does not allow aggregate object types, the error status of noSuchName is set for the aggregate object type cases.

SNMPv1 Protocol Errors

noError
tooBig
noSuchName
badValue
readOnly
genErr

A response for GetRequest must be within the capacity of the local PE. If it is not possible to generate responses, then the error status is set to tooBig. When processing a GetRequest, there may be errors. In such a case, the error status is set to genError. When there are no errors, the error status is set to noError. Responses in all cases are sent in the form of a GetResponse PDU.

GetNextRequest is similar to the GetRequest except that we retrieve the next value instead of the one furnished and the PDU type is different. Here the assumption is that MIB has object names arranged in a lexicographical order. However ' if a lexicographical successor is not available, then error status is set to genErr. In SetRequest, too, if a variable name is not available, then the error status is set to noSuchName. If the value of a variable whose value must be changed to the value furnished in SetRequest is not in conformity with ASN.1 language, type, length, or variable, the error status is set to badValue. The case of error status set to tooBig is similar to that explained earlier. If the value of a variable cannot be changed, then it is classified under genError. However, if the value of a variable is changed to the value mentioned in SetRequest, then the reply PDU of GetResponse has the error status set to noErr.

SNMPv1 Traps Generated

coldStart
warmStart
linkDown
linkUp
authenticationFailure
egpNeighborLoss
enterpriseSpecific

A trap is used to present problems or changes in Internet. A trap PDU consists of the object type generating the trap; the address of the object generating the trap, the generic trap type, the timestamp when the trap was generated, and any variable binding carrying relevant information. If the enterpriseSpecific trap is present, the specific trap field is present. Let us briefly review the meanings of different generic traps. The first trap is coldStart, which implies that an agent is reinitializing and the configuration and implementation details might have changed. Thus, the station receiving this trap will have to reset itself; whereas in the case of warmStart, there are no changes in the configuration and implementation details when reinitializing.

The traps linkDown and linkUp are used when the communication links used are affected, and the affected link name and value are furnished in variable bindings. When a protocol message fails authentication, then the authenticationFailure trap is generated. egpNeighborLoss is generated when an EGP neighbor is no longer available. When traps cannot be specifically classified into any one of these above traps, then the enterpriseSpecific trap comes in handy. This trap can also be used to convey any specific trap that may be implementation specific. This is carried in the specific trap field.

Proxy

The proxy concept is very popular. It is possible that a management station is not able to manage a device such as a modem, bridge, or router because it responds to proprietary commands. In such a case, a proxy agent is used. Between a management station and a proxy agent, standard protocols are used. However, between the proxy agent and the managed devices, proprietary protocols are used. The proxy assumes the role of an agent with respect to the manager and acts as a manager for managed devices. One of the main functions of a proxy agent is protocol conversion. As an example, the standard command from the management station is converted or mapped to the semantically equivalent proprietary command and sent to the managed devices. As mentioned earlier, managed devices understand these proprietary commands. Similarly, responses to the commands sent to managed devices are mapped back to standard responses in the proxy agent. The conversion from standard protocols to proprietary protocols can be done by two methods. One is the mapping or translation of each field of standard protocols to each field of proprietary protocols. However, in some cases, one-to-one mapping of fields may not be possible, because there may not be similar, functionally equivalent fields. In such cases, the best possible assumptions will have to be made.

Another method is by encapsulating the standard protocols within the data fields of the proprietary protocols. This information will have to be retrieved by the software or hardware in the managed devices, but the managed devices will have the added responsibility of interpreting standard protocol fields. In some cases, the information carried in standard protocols may prove to be redundant or may not be amenable for proper interpretation. In either case, it is possible that some information will be lost due to the inability to use one-to-one mapping or the inability to retrieve all the information. To overcome this, the proprietary protocols are normally continuously modified to keep abreast of the standards.

Furthermore, the introduction of a proxy agent adds complexity. The mapping of standard protocols to the proprietary protocol requires resources. Note that we are adding one more level to the communication between the management station and managed devices. Also, if the proxy is in a separate workstation, there are considerations such as additional backup in case of the failure of the backup. All these add to the complexity.

Also, a proxy agent provides the flexibility to enforce "under the cover" access policies. The SNMP MIBs do not have to bother about them. The access policy can be for managed devices represented as objects, and it will be between the proxy agent and the managed devices.

A proxy can also be used for selectively forwarding information to a, management station. It may log the information it receives from managed devices. It may maintain details of aggregate objects. Aggregate objects are defined for combining the details on more than one object. The management system may ask the proxy to send the details on aggregate objects. The aggregate objects may also be defined for summary statistics, configuration details, etc.

SNMP over different protocols

SNMPs over different popular protocols have been defined. Some of them are:

SNMP over IPX (RFC 1420)

SNMP over Ethernet (RFC 1089)

SNMP over AppleTalk (RFC 1419)

SNMP over OSI (RFC 1418)

SNMPv2

The original SNMPs did not have elaborate security arrangements. To overcome this major weakness, SNMP version 2, or SNMPv2, was released. Accordingly, the original SNMP is known as SNMP version 1, or SNMPv1. In SNMPv2, the following enhancements have been made to SNMPvl:

— In SNMPv1, security is a weak link. It is quite easy to learn the community name, which is as good as providing no security. To overcome this, the *digest authentication protocol* and *symmetric privacy protocol* have been added. Also, access control has been added.

— There have been major enhancements to the Structure of' Management Information of SNMPv1. MIB-II has been extended to include managed objects for SNMPv2. The syntax and semantics of managed objects have been refined. Also, textual conventions have been enhanced to extend the semantics of the standard object types defined in SMI.

— More operational PDUs have been added. GetBulkRequest has been added to retrieve a large amount of management information. InfomRequest has been added for communication between managers. InformRequest facilitates communication between managers in a distributed environment.

— Conformance statements have been added, and a strategy for the migration of SNMPv1 to SNMPv2 has been provided.

— The transport used for carrying SNMPv2 protocols has been made more flexible and defined for different environments.

The list of 12 RFCs, which constitute the SNMPv2 standards.

SNMPv2 architectural framework

Any set of network management functions can be broadly broken up into different frameworks or models. SNMPv2 can be architecturally subdivided into different frameworks. However, we must note that there are certain interdependencies between these frameworks, and rigid partitions into different frameworks sometimes lack practical value. The frameworks are:

- *Administrative framework:* Relates to the concepts of party, context, and security.
- *Information framework:* Pertains to how the management information can be structured. This broadly includes SMI and textual conventions.
- *Operational framework:* Here the management protocols, the transport protocols, and the migrational aspects from SNMPv1 to SNMPv2 enter the picture.
- *Conformance framework:* States the minimum requirements to cater to the standards and the capabilities provided. Conformance is very important for interoperability.

Marshall T. Rose, one of the authors of the SNMPv1 and SNMPv2 standards, has included the conformance function in the informational portion, and refers to these frameworks as models in *The Simple Book* . However, SNMPv2 RFCs describe the administrative framework, but do not refer to the other frameworks. So, in the following discussion, we refer to the administrative framework and have omitted the discussion on the basis of the classification of RFC documents in terms of the information, operational, and conformance frameworks.

SNMPv2 entity

Central to SNMPv2 is the concept of an SNMPv2 entity. In a generic sense, it is a process that performs network management operations. It generates SNMPv2 PDUs, such as GetRequest and GetNextRequest, and receives SNMPv2-Trap PDUs. It can concurrently communicate with many parties; thus, a process can have many threads at one time.

The SNMPv2 entity also interacts with a local database of access privileges of SNMPv2 parties, the list of all known SNMPv2 parties, and known resources. The SNMPv2 entity can take up the role of a manager, agent, or proxy, depending on the operations it performs. The role is dictated by the SNMPv2 protocol messages and traps. If management operations are initiated by SNMPv2 protocol messages or the receiving of traps, then the entity is in a manager role. ' On the other hand, when these management operations are performed as a result of the receipt of protocol messages or sending a trap, then the role is that of an agent.

There is a provision for proxy SNMPv2 entities to account for the difference in protocols and the versions such as SNMPv1. Basically, the proxy agent role of the SNMPv2 entity makes it behave like an agent for a manager and act like a manager for another remote entity. Note that a remote entity need not be another SNMPv2 entity.

SNMPv2 party

An SNMPv2 party is a conceptual execution environment. A subset of protocol operations which an SNMPv2 entity can perform can be done on a party.

```
SnmpParty:: = SEQUENCE       {
    partyIdentity              OBJECT IDENTIFIER
    partyTDomain               OBJECT IDENTIFIER
    partyTAddress              OCTET STRING
    partyMaxMessageSize        INTEGER
    partyAuthProtocol          OBJECT IDENTIFIER
    partyAuthClock             INTEGER
    partyAythPrivate           OCTET STRING
    partyAuthPublic            OCTET STRING
    partyAuthLifetime          INTEGER
```

partyPrivProtocol	OBJECT IDENTIFIER
partyPrivPrivate	OCTET STRING
partyPrivPublic	OCTET STRING}

Let us briefly examine each term. Note that some of the terms will be explained in more detail later. The terms are:

partyIdentity: An identifier to distinguish one party from another."

partyTDomain: A transport domain which indicates the type of transport used. For SNMPv2, the default is UDR

partyTAddress: Furnishes the transport addressing information on which network management traffic is received. For snmpUDPDomain, partyTAddress is formulated by concatenating the four-octet IP address and the two-octet port number. The default value is "0000 0000" H.

partyMaxMessageSize: Indicates the maximum size in octets of the messages that SNMPv2 is prepared to accept. As in earlier cases, this is tied to a party.

partyAuthProtocol: Specifies the authentication protocol used. If authentication is used, there is verification of origin and integrity. At present, two authentication protocols used are v2md5AuthProtocol and noAuth. If noAuth is used, then there is no authentication of origin and integrity.

partyAuthClock: Represents the authentication clock, which is a notion of current time of a party.

partyAuthPrivate: Has the private and secret key used for authentication. This value can be altered by a SetRequest operation, but the value cannot be retrieved by a management operation.

partyAuthPublic: Used to carry a public key used in an authentication protocol.

partyAuthLifetime: Indicates the maximum time allowed for message delays while using authentication.

partyPrivProtocol: Specifies the privacy protocol used. Privacy protocols are used for data confidentiality. At present, the privacy protocols used are noPriv and desPrivProtocol. noPriv indicates that no privacy protocols are used.

partyPrivPrivate: A party's private key used to support the privacy protocol. The value can be altered by a SetRequest management operation; however, it cannot be read by a management operation.

partyPrivPublic: Refers to a party's public key used by the privacy protocol.

An SNMPv2 entity is termed nonsecure if the authentication protocol is noAuth and the privacy protocol is noPriv.

RFC 1447 defines partyMIB as well as some new data types, including:

Party (OBJECT IDENTIFIER): Refers to the object identifier of an SNMPv2 party.

TAddress (OCTET *STRING):* Denotes a transport service address.

Clock (UIteger32): Refers to the nonnegative valued authentication clock. It is undefined for noAuth, and for v2md5AuthProtocol, it is incremented in value.

Context (OBJECT IDENTIFIER): Indicates the object identifier of an SNMPv2 context.

StorageType (INTEGER): Relates to the storage used for a conceptual row. It has the values: other = 1, volatile = 2, nonVolatile 3, and permanent = 4. The volatile value states that the values are lost while rebooting; nonVolatile indicates that the values are in stable storage, and permanent states that the values cannot be changed or deleted.

Under the subtree partyAdmin, the following subjects are defined

noAuth: States that the protocol does not have authentication.

noPriv: Indicates that no privacy protocols are supported.

desPrivProtocol: Stands for the DES privacy protocol support.

v2md5AuthProtocol: Indicates that the MD5 authentication protocol is supported.

Under the same subtree of partyAdmin, temporal-Domains is defined. temporalDomains is related to time and has the following objects:

currentTime (OBJECT IDENTIFIER): Refers to the management information at the current time.

restartTime (OBJECT IDENTIFIER): Relates to the management information at the next reinitialization of a managed device.

cacheTime (OBJECT IDENTIFIER): Indicates the management information that is cached in a managed device and is at most N seconds old.

In addition, partyAdmin has intialPartyId and initalContextId, which are primarily used for the initial configuration of devices with administrative policy information. RFC 1447 provides the initial party identifier, initial context identifiers, SNMPv2 context, access control policy, and MIB view information.

SNMPv2 party database group. The SNMPv2 party database group has one partyTable. This partyTable has information on all the parties known to an SNMPv2 entity. partyTable has one or more partyEntrys. Because most of these terms have been discussed earlier,they will not be repeated. The new objects in partyEntry are

partyLocal (TruthValue): Refers to whether an SNMPv2 listens to SNMPv2 messages at partyTAddress. A value of true(l) indicates that SNMPv2 will listen to the SNMPv2 messages, while a value of false(2) signifies that SNMPv2 will not listen to the SNMPv2 messages.

partyCloneFrom (Party): Indicates the identity of a party to clone authentication and privacy parameters.

partyStorageType (StorageType): Refers to the storage type associated with this conceptual row in partyTable

partyStatus (RowStatus): Represents a row status of a conceptual row. The data type, RowStatus.

SNMPv2 context

SNMPv2 context concept is tied in with objects which an SNMPv2 entity can access. These objects can be local or remote. if the context is local, the object resources represent the MIB view. In the case of a remote context, an SNMPv2 entity retrieves the management information from objects via a proxy. SNMPv2 context database group. The SNMPv2 context database group has information on the contexts known to an SNMPv2 entity. This group has one contextTable with one contextEntry for each instance of a context. The objects in this group are.

contextIdentity (Context): Identifies a context in an SNMPv2 entity.

contextIndex (INTEGER (l..65535)): Has a unique value for each SNMPv2 context.

contextLocal (RuthValue): Indicates whether this context is valid for this SNMPv2 entity.

contextViewIndex (INTEGER (0..65535)): Indicates whether the context refers to a MIB view or a proxy relationship. If the value is zero, then it represents a proxy relationship.

contextLocalEntity (OCTET STRING): Indicates a MIB view with local management information if it has a zero value, or a MIB view of some other local entity if it has a nonempty string.

contextLocalTime (OBJECT IDENTIFIER): Represents the temporal context of the management information. This value is relevant only if contextViewIndex is greater than zero.

contextProxyDstParty (Party): Has the value of the proxy SNMPv2 entity. This value is valid only if the value Of contextViewIndex is zero; otherwise, contextProxyDst-Party has a value of {0 0}.

contextProxySreParty (Party): Indicates the value of the source proxy in a proxy relationship. contextProxy-SrcParty behaves just like contextProxyDstParty.

contextProxyContext (OBJECT IDENTIFIER): Represents the context of a proxy relationship. As we have seen earlier, this value is valid for contextViewIndex with a value of zero; otherwise, it has a value of {00}.

contextStorageType (StorageType): Indicates the storage type used for storing the conceptual row in a contextTable. The default value is nonVolatile, which states that the data on context are not lost with rebooting.

contextStatus (RowStatus): Has the status of the conceptual row.

MIB view database group. Each SNMPv2 party can access a certain portion of the MIB. The MIB view is a subset of all the objects associated with an entity. Objects included in a MIB view are defined in the MIB view database group . This group has one table: viewTable. MIB has subtrees which are included or excluded from an SNMPv2 party, depending on the viewMask provided. We will investigate the role of viewMask later. The objects in this group are:

viewIndex (INTEGER (l..65535)): Has a unique value for each MIB view, which is the same as the contextViewIndex.

viewSubtree (OBJECT IDENTIFIER): Represents the object id tifier associated with a MIB subtree.

viewMask (OCTET STRING (0.. 16)): Determines whether or not subtree is included in a MIB view. The object identifier for the egp subtree is 1.3.6.1.2.1.8. By extending this to egpNeighAddr, the object identifier is 1.3.6.1.2.1.8.5.1.2. Using a viewMask of 101111, the obvious check of whether 1.3.6.1.2.1.8.5. 1.2 is part of 1.3.6.1.2.1.8, is made as follows:

egp subtree object identifier	1.3.6.1.2.1.8
viewMask1	1 0 1 1 1 1
Object identifier of egpNeighAddr	1.3.6.1.2.1.8.5.1.2
egp subtree object identifier	1.3.6.1.2.1.8
viewMask	1 0 1 1 1 1
Object identifier of udpLocalPort	1.3.6.1.2.1.7.5.1.2

In the preceding check, the second bit of 0 in viewMask is a wildcard match, and all the subidentifiers below it match. In viewMask, a bit value of I requires an exact match. In this example, notice that viewMask is shorter than the egp subtree identifier, so viewMask is extended with 1 1 1 1 to become 1 0 1 1 1 1 1 1 1 1. There is a match of egpNeighAddr; hence, egpNeighAddr is part of the egp subtree. However, in the second case of udpLocalPort, it is not included in the egp subtree, because there is a mismatch in the subidentifier place.

uiewType (INTEGER): Determines whether or not instances of viewSubtree and viewMask include a subtree of MIB view. Values are: included = 1 and excluded = 2. viewStorageType and viewStatus have the same significance as the corresponding entries previously defined.

SNMPv2 management communication

SNMPv2 management communication refers to the exchange of management information, such as SNMPv2 protocol messages between two parties, and is represented by an ASN. I value as follows:

```
SnmpMgmtCom:: = [21 IMPLICIT SEQUENCE{
      dstParty                  OBJECT IDENTIFIER,
      srcParty                  OBJECT IDENTIFIER,
      context                   OBJECT IDENTIFIER,
      pdu                       PDUs
      }
```

An SNMPv2 context is tied to a party for accessing management information. The management information has the following fields: destination party identifier, source party identifier, context used for accessing the management information, and SNMPv2 protocol operation such as GetRequest.

SNMPv2 authenticated management communication

The syntax of authenticated management communication in ASNA is as follows:

```
SnmpAuthMsg::= [1] IMPLICIT SEQUENCE {
      authInfo      ANY,  defined by authentication protocol
      authData      SnmpMgmtCom
      }
```

SNMPv2 private management communication

Private management communication is used for protecting authenticated management communication from disclosure. The syntax in ASN.1 is as follows:

```
SnmpPrivMsg::= [1] IMPLICIT SEQUENCE {
      privDst              OBJECT IDENTIFIER,
      privData             [1] IMPLICIT OCTET STRING
      }
```

It has the destination party to which the message is sent and possibly encryrpted data which must be guarded against disclosures such as eavesdropping.

SNMPv2 access control Policy

When a management operation is received, a check is made using aclTable as to whether the management operation can be done. aclTable has information on the source party, destination party, text, and the management operation allowed. The source party SNMPv2 party is known as a *subject,* and the destination par known as a *target.* aclTable has identifiers to distinguish the subjects and targets, the resources which are to be accessed, and the a privileges associated with management operations. ASNA.1 definitions for an SNMPv2 access control entry are:

```
AclEntry::= SEQUENCE I
            aclTarget       OBJECT IDENTIFIER,
            aclSubject      OBJECT IDENTIFIER,
```

aclResources OBJECT IDENTIFIER,
aclPrivileges INTEGER

SNMPv2 access privileges database group. The SNMPv2 access privileges database group is a database on the access privileges, which has one aclTable with one aclEntry for each subject of an SNMPv2 party and target SNMPv2 party for a particular context. The objects in this group are:

aelTarget (INTEGER (1..65535)): Identifies the target SNMPv2 party and has the same value as the partyIndex object.

aclSubject (INTEGER (l..65535)): Has a value for the source SNMPv2 party, and has the same value as the partyIndex object for the party

aelResources (INTEGER (l..65535)): Has the value of the SNMPv2 context and has the same value as the contextIndex object for the SNMPv2 context.

aclPrivileges (INTEGER (0..255)): The sum of values associated with each management operation. The values for management operations are Get = 1, GetNext = 2, Response = 4, Set = 8, GetBulk = 32, Inform = 64, and SNMPv2Trap = 128. For example, a value of 76 ls obtained by adding the values of Response, Set, and Inform management operations. Note that the value of 16 is unused.

aclStorageTYpe and *aclStatus* have the same signi-ficance as discussed earlier for corresponding objects in other groups.

SNMPv2 security

SNMPv2 has provided a secure environment by ensuring data integrity, data origin authentication, data confidentiality, and access control. Let us review what each term means

Data integrity: Means that data has not been altered in any manner. The data can be corrupted or errors can creep in due to transmission errors or hardware or software errors. Data can also be maliciously tampered with by unauthorized users. Checksum helps to detect such errors

Data origin authentication: Checks whether the originator Of data is the one claimed in a message. In other words, this ensures that the originator is the one who is authorized to send the message.

Data confidentiality: Only the sender and receiver must know the details of the message, and any other user is expected not to know the contents of the message.

Data integrity and data origin authentication are provided by digest authentication protocol, according to which a secret known only to a sender and receiver is prefixed to the message ensures data origin authentication.

For supporting data integrity, a 128bit digest is calculated over designated portion of the SNMPv2 message, which also includes a secret value. This message digest becomes part of the SNMPv2 message which is sent by the sender. For calculating this message digest refer to Rivest. Source and destination time-stamp values are also part of each message generated. The source timestamp value is the authentication clock value of a message's source, and the destination timestamp value is set to the authentication clock value of the message's intended receiver. The timestamp values help to make sure that the message is a recent one. However, for the digest authentication protocol, clocks must be synchronized between the originator and receiver. There are many ways to synchronize clocks; one method is presented in RFC 1446.

It is required that the digest authentication protocol be used by the originator and receiver only if both of them use it. If one of them does not use this protocol, it should not be used at all. Because it is preferable not to proliferate these algorithms in nonsecure environments, this requirement is sound and reasonable. The symmetric privacy protocol is used for data confidentiality. Here messages are encrypted using keys known only to the originator and receiver of the messages. The Data Encryption Standard (DES) has been chosen. The mode of operation recommended is *cipher block chaining.* These standards have, been published by the National Institute of Standards and" Technology (NIST) and the American National Standards Institute (ANSI). However, there is a caveat with RFC 1446. It does not specific recommend which of the algorithms be used for message digest encryption. Thus these algorithms are termed "acceptably secure under present circumstances. SNMPv2 security assumes that secret values must be shared~, between the parties. These have to be changed often so that security measures are not compromised. For clock synchroni-zation and sharing of key values, there is a need for at least one management station to perform these tasks.

SNMPv2 partyMIB conformance

SNMPv2 conformance objects are used to check the compliance of the implementations. All the objects in this group are required to support snmpMIBGroup, noAuth, and noPriv protocols. The objects in the partyMIB Conformance group are:

unSecurableCompliance: Provides the compliance state-ments for SNMPv2 entities which implement partyMIB. At this level of compliance, no support is provided for authentication and privacy protocols.

partyNoPrivacyCompliance: Indicates the support for v2md5AuthProtocol for authentication and no support for privacy protocols.

partyPrivacyCompliance: States that v2md5AuthProtocol is supported, but there is only partial support for privacy protocols, which indicates that the security parameter can access parameters such as creating and maintaining parties.

fullPrivacyCompliance: Indicates the availability of v2md5AuthProtocol and desPrivProtocol.

SNMPv2 Structure of management information (SMI)

Structure of Management Information for the SNMPv2 (RFC 1442) describes rules for defining modules, objects, and traps. Note that a module is a collection of related objects. SMI provides the following definitions:

- *Module definitions:* The ASN.1 macro, MODULE-IDENTITY, is used to provide the syntax and semantics when defining a module.
- *Object definitions*: The ASNA macro, OBJECT-TYPE, provides the syntax and semantics to define an object.
- Notification definitions: The ASNA macro, NOTIFICATION-TYPE, is used to describe a notification. Notification is unsolicited management information within either an SNMPv2-Trap-PDU or an InformRequest-PDU.

SMI definitions

SNMPv2 SMI definitions furnished in RFC 1442 are:

```
SNMPv2-SMI DEFINITIONS::= BEGIN

path to the root

internet          OBJECT IDENTIFIER::= {iso 3 6 1}
directory         OBJECT IDENTIFIER::= {internet 1}
mgmt              OBJECT IDENTIFIER::= {internet 2}
experimental      OBJECT IDENTIFIER::= {internet 3}
private           OBJECT IDENTIFIER::= {internet 4}
enterprises       OBJECT IDENTIFIER::= {private 1}
security          OBJECT IDENTIFIER::= {internet 5}
snmpV2            OBJECT IDENTIFIER::= {internet 6}
—transport domains
snmpDomains       OBJECT IDENTIFIER::= {snmpV2 1}
—transport proxies
snmpProxys        OBJECT IDENTIFIER::= {snmpV2 2}
—module Identities
snmpModules       OBJECT IDENTIFIER::= {snmpV2 3}

—definitions for information modules

MODULE-IDENTITY MACRO::=
BEGIN

  TYPE NOTATION::=
                  "LAST-UPDATED" value(Update UTCTIME) "ORGANIZATION" Text
```

```
                    "CONTACT-INFO" Text "DESCRIPTION" Text RevisionPart
  VALUE NOTATION::=
                    Value(VALUE OBJECT IDENTIFIER)
  RevisionPart
                        Revisions
                        | empty
  Revisions::=
                        Revision
                        | Revisions Revision
  Revision::=
                    "REVISION" value(Update UTCTime)
                    "DESCRIPTION" Text
  Text::= """" string """"       — uses the NVT ASCII
character set
END
OBJECT-IDENTITY MACRO::=
BEGIN
  TYPE NOTATION::=
                        "STATUS" Status
                        "DESCRIPTION" Text
                                     ReferPart
  VALUE NOTATION::=
                        value(VALUE OBJECT IDENTIFIER)
  Status::=             "current"
                        | "obsolete"
  ReferPart:: = "REFERENCE" Text
                        | empty
    Text::=       """" string """"
END
— name of objects
  ObjectName::=  OBJECT IDENTIFIER
— syntax of objects
    ObjectSyntax
    CHOICE {
                        simpleSimpleSyntax,
                        — note thatSEQUENCEs for conceptual tables
                        — and rows are not mentioned here.
                        applicationwide ApplicationSyntax
```

```
— builtin ASN. 1 types
      SimpleSyntax :: =
            CHOICE {
   integervalue          INTEGER (-2147483648..2147483647),
   string-value          OCTET STRING,
   object-IDvalue        OBJECT IDENTIFIER,
   bit-value             BIT STRING
   }
— indistinguishable from INTEGER, but never needs more than 32 bits for
— a twos complement representation.
     Integer32 :: = [UNIVERSAL 2] IMPLICIT INTEGER
     (-2147483648..2147483647)
— application-wide types
     ApplicationSyntax::=
      CHOICE {
     ipAddress-value          IpAddress,
     countervalue             Counter32,
     gaugevalue               Gauge32,
     timeticksvalue           TimeTicks,
     arbitraryvalue           Opaque,
     nsapAddressvalue         NsapAddress,
     bigcountervalue          Counter64,
     unsignedintegervalue     UInteger32
— in network-byte order (this is tagged type for historical reasons)
   IpAddress[APPLICATION 0] IMPLICIT OCTET STRING (SIZE (4))
—this wraps
   Counter32 ::= [APPLICATION 1] IMPLICIT  INTEGER
   (0..4294967295)
—this does not wrap
   Gauge32 ::= [APPLICATION 2] IMPLICIT INTEGER
   (0..4294967295)
—hundredths of seconds since an epoch
   TimeTicks :: = [APPLICATION 31 IMPLICIT INTEGER
   (0..4294967295)
—for backward compatibility only
   Opaque :: =    [APPLICATION 41 IMPLICIT OCTET STRING
—for OSI NSAP addresses
   (this is tagged type for historical reasons)
   NsapAddress :: =
```

```
  [APPLICATION 5] IMPLICIT OCTET STRING (SIZE (114..21)
—for counters that wrap in less than one hour with only 32 bits
    Counter64 :: =
     [APPLICATION 61 IMPLICIT INTEGER
 (018446744073709551615)
—an unsigned 32-bit quantity
    Ulnteger32:: = [APPLICATION 7] IMPLICIT INTEGER                    (04294967295)
—definition for objects
OBJECTTYPE MACRO::=
BEGIN
  TYPE NOTATION::=
                     "SYNTAX" type(Syntax)
                     UnitsPart
                     "MAXACCESS" Access
                     "STATUS" Status
                     "DESCRIPTION" Text
                     ReferPart
                     IndexPart
                     DefValPart
VALUE NOTATION::=  value (VALUE ObjectName)
  UnitsPart::=       "UNITS" Text
                     | empty
  Access::=          "not-accessible"
                     | "read-only"
                     | "read-write"
                     | "read-create"
  Status::=           "current"
                     | "deprecated"
                     | "obsolete"
  ReferPart::=       "REFERENCE" Text
                     | empty
  Indexpart::=       "INDEX" 'T' {"Index Types "}"
                     | "AUGMENTS" "{" Entry"}"
                     | empty
  IndexTypes::=      IndexType
  IndexType::=       | Index Type","Index Type
  IndexType          "IMPLIED" Index
                     | Index
—use the SYNTAX value of the correspondent OBJECT-TYPE invocation
```

```
      Index::=   value(Indexobject ObjectName)
--use the INDEX value of the correspondent OBJECT-TYPE invocation.
      Entry:: =          value(Entryobject ObjectName)
      DefValPart         "DEFVAL""{"value(Defval Syntax) "}"
                         | empty
      --uses the NVT ASCII character set
      Text::=""""string""""
END
--definitions for notifications
NOT1FICATIONTYPE MACRO::=
BEGIN
      TYPE NOTATION::=

                         ObjectsPart
                         "STATUS" Status
                         "DESCRIPTION" Text
                         ReferPart
VALUE NOTATION::= value(VALUE OBJECT IDENTIFIER)
ObjectsPart::=      "OBJECTS" "{" Objects "}"
                    | empty
Objects::=          Object
                    | Objects "," Object
Object::=           value(Name ObjectName)
Status::=           "current"
                    | "deprecated"
                    | "obsolete"
ReferPart::=        "REFERENCE" Text
                    | empty
--uses the NVT ASCII character set
Text::= """"string""""
END
END
```

Information module

An information module is an ASN.1 module and provides information for network management. In SMI definitions, the term MODULE-IDENTITY was used. An information module is identified by a MODULE-IDENTITY macro. It provides the contact and revision history of the information module. There are three kinds of information modules:

MIB modules: Contain information on related objects.

Compliance statements: Provide compliance requirements for MIB modules:

Capability statements: Have the capabilities of the agent implementations.

An information module need not have all three modules; instead, it can contain just one or more of them.

Many terms have been used in SMI definitions for SNMPv1. Some of the new terms which need explanation are:

BIT STRING: Used for enumerations, and starts from a value of zero.

NsapAddress: A variable-length string used to represent the OSI address. The first octet provides the length of the OSI address and can be from three to twenty octets in length. A single octet with a value of 0 represents the default NSAP address.

Counter64: A wraparound counter with a maximum value of 2^{64}—1.

UNITS: Has textual definition of the units of measurements, such as hours and minutes, associated with an object.

MAX-ACCESS: Relates to the maximum level of access allowed for an object. Note the distinction between the access rights of read-write and read-create. read-write is the maximum level of access allowed. With the read-write access right, an object instance can be created in addition to the read-write permission.

INDEX. Used for object instance identification in a conceptual row. A new keyword, IMPLIED, is used for objects with variable-length syntax.

AUGMENTS: An alternative to an INDEX clause, it extends the conceptual row with reference to a base conceptual row provided by an INDEX clause.

Naming of objects

The snmp V2 object subtree is contained in the internet subtree. Under the snmpV2 subtree are snmpDomains(l), snmpProxys(2), and snmpModules(3). snmpDomains is used for transport mapping, snmpProxys is for transport proxies, and snmpModules is for module identities.

RFC 1443 defines a base set of textual conventions which use the conventions of the TEXTUAL-CONVENTION ASN. 1 macro, and they are:

DisplayString (OCTET STRING (SIZE(O..255))): Represents the textual convention using the ASCII character set. It is used for easy readability. The length of DisplayString should not exceed 255 octets.

PhysAddress (OCTET STRING): Used to indicate the media address.

TruthValue (INTEGER): Provides a means to indicate a Boolean value, with *true* being 1 and *false* being 2.

TestAndIncr (INTEGER (0..2147483647)): Tests first whether a value provided using a management protocol matches the value of the object instance. If the value matches, then the value of the object instance is increased by one. If the value of an object instance is the maximum value of 2147483647, then the object instance value wraps to zero. However, a mismatch between the value provided and the value of the object instance results in an *inconsistent value* error.

Autonomous Type (OBJECT IDENTIFIER): Can be used to extend objects with a distinct identifier. Here the key is "autonomous," and the extension must be easily distinguishable. This textual convention can be useful for defining additions to hardware and protocols.

InstancePointer (OBJECT IDENTIFIER): Refers to the name of an instance of the first columnar object in a row. As explained earlier, row is an abstract concept used for manipulating tables.

MacAddress (OCTET STRING (SIZE(6))): Represents the MAC address as defined by IEEE 802.1 with the least significant bit transmitted first.

RowStatus (INTEGER):, Used to manipulate the creation and deletion of managed objects in conceptual rows. RowStatus has the values of active, notInService, notReady, createAndGo, createAndWait, and destroy.

TimeStamp (Time Ticks): The same as sysUpTime, which is the value in TimeTicks when an agent was last reinitialized.

TimeInterval (INTEGER (0..2147483647)): Represents the interval in units of 0.01 s between two time periods.

DateAndTime (OCTET STRING (SIZE 8111)): Used to indicate the date and time. The length of DateAndTime can be 8 or 11 octets.

SNMPv2 MIB

There are some changes between SNMPv2 and SNMPv1 MIBs. The IMPORT statement refers to MIBs used in SNMPv2, and they are to be used. Under the snmpModules subtree, there are subtrees snmpMIB(l), snmpM2M(2), and partyMIB(3). snmpMIB has snmpMIBObjects and snmpMIBConformance subtrees. Again, below the snmpMIBObJects, there are snmpStats(l), snmpVl(2), snmpOR(3), snmpTtap(4), snmpTraps(5), and snmpSet(6).

snmpStats group

The snmpStats group objects are provided for collecting statistics of an SNMPv2 entity. It has objects such as snmpStatsPackets, which is used for counting the total number of packets received by an SNMPv2 entity from the underlying transport service. Most of the these objects can be used for performance and security management. The objects in this group are:

snmpStatsPackets (Counter32): Refers to the total number of packets received from the transport service by the SNMPv2 entity.

snmpStats30Something (Counter32): Contains the total number of packets with a hexadecimal value of 30 in the initial octet received by the SNMPv2 entity. These packets are misdirected SNMPv1 messages.

snmpStatsEncodingErrors (Counter32): Refers to the total number of packets received by the SNMPv2 entity which had encoding errors.

snmpStatsUnknownDstParties (Counter32): Has the total number of snmpPrivMsgs which had unrecognizable privDst field. This data can be used by the security management function.

The following statistics pertain to the total number of wrong SnmpPrivMsgs that result from different fields being bad. The reasons for bad SnmpPrivMsgs are furnished along with the explanation of each object. These counters are useful for the security management function.

snmpStatsDstPartyMismatches (Counter32): Has the number of SnmpPrivMsgs, for which there was a mismatch between the authData.dstParty and privDst fields.

SnmpStatsUnknownSrcParties (Counter32): Refers to the number of SnmpAutbMsgs which had unknown authData.srcParty.

snmpStatsBadAuths (Counter32): Contains the number of privData.authInfo fields incompatible with the source party authentication protocol.

snmpStatsNotInLifetimes (Counter32): Used to count the messages when authlnfo.authSreTimestamp is less than the sum of the source party's clock and lifetime.

snmpStatsWrongDigestValues (Counter32): Like its predecessors, it furnishes data on wrong SnmpAuthMsgs. Here a SnmpAuthMsg is treated as wrong when authInfo.authDigest field is not equal to the expected digest value.

snmpStatsUnknownContexts (Counter32): Refers to the total number of SnmpMgmtComs with unknown context fields.

snmpStatsBadOperations (Counter32): Refers to the number of messages due to PDU types not being allowed in aclTable

snmpStatsSilentDrops (Counter32): Counts the management operational PDUs which have inappropriate sizes. The criterion for inappropriate size is that the size of the Response-PDU with an empty variable-bindings field for management operations such as GetRequest-PDU is greater than the limitations on the size of a message.

snmpV1 group

Some SNMPv2 entities may also implement SNMPv1. The objects in this subtree are used to collect statistics of the SNMPv1 portion of the entity. This is mainly limited to the usage of community in the SNMPv1. These statistics are useful for security management. The objects in this group are:

snmpVIBadCommunityNames (Counter32): Has the number of SNMPv1 messages which had community names unknown to an SNMPv2 entity.

snmpBadCommunity Uses (Counter32): Refers to the total number of SNMPv1 messages which had operation not allowed for the community specified in a message.

snmpOR group

Objects in the object resource group are used by SNMPv2 entities which are acting in an agent role. These objects must be capable of being dynamically configurable, and are useful for configuration management. In this group there is one table: snmpORTable. In this table, each object has an instance identified by snmpOREntry with columns snmpORIndex, snmpORID, and snmpORDescr. Objects in the snmpOR group are:

snmpORLastChange (TmeStamp): Has the most recent change, provided by sysUpTime, in snmpORID.

snmpORIndex (Integer32): Is an identifier for identifying object instances in snmpORTable.

snmpORID (OBJECT IDENTIFIER): Refers to the identifier used for identifying a resource in an SNMPv2 entity, and is similar to the sysObjectID object in MIB-II.

snmpORDescr (DisplayString): Provides the description of the object resource in an SNMPv2 entity.

snmpTrap group

snmpTrap group objects are used by SNMPv2 entities in the agent role to generate SNMPv2-Trap PDUs. Objects in this group are useful for fault management. In this group, there is one table, snmpTrapTable, which has one entry, snmpTrapNumbers. Objects in the snmpTrap group are:

snmpTrapOID (OBJECT IDENTIFIER): Refers to the unique identifier of a trap.

snmpRapNumbers (Counter32): Has the total number of traps sent to an SNMPv2 entity. The benchmark for measurement is the most recent initialization or creation time of an SNMPv2 entity.

snmpRapEnterprise (OBJECT IDENTIFIER): Has the authoritative identification of the enterprise associated with a trap.

snmp V2EnableAuthen Raps (TruthValue): Indicates whether an SNMPv2 entity can be disabled from generating an authenticationFailure trap. This object must be stored in nonvolatile storage.

snmpTraps group

The snmpTraps group refers to the wellknown SNMPv2 traps. We have seen these traps in SNMPv1. *These traps* are useful for fault management.

snmpSet group

The snmpSet group has one object and is used by SNMPv2 *entities acting* in a manager role to coordinate the use of an SNMPv2 set operation. This object can be used by *performance man*agement. One *object in* this group is:

snmpSetSerialNo (TestAndIncr): Refers to the lock for coordinating the use of a set operation by a group of cooperating SNMPv2 entities.

snmpMIBConformance group

The snmpMIBConformance group provides the compliance *statements for* SNMPv2 *entities* implementing SNMPv2 MIB. The compliance statements are provided by the snmpMIBCompliance. snmpVIGroup is mandatory for SNMPv2 entities implementing SNMPv1. snmpMIBGroups refer to the compliance statements for the collection of *objects for* each of the SNMPv2 MIB groups we examined earlier.

Conformance statements

Conformance *statements define* the acceptable level of implementation. An implementation can compare the actual functions provided with the benchmark provided in conformance *statements to* check whether the implementation satisfies the requirements. There are two types of notations used in SNMPv2, and they are defined in RFC 1447. The conformance notations are:

Compliance statements: Refer to the requirements imposed on the objects in agents. This compliance is checked with the ASNA.1 MODULE-COMPLIANCE macro.

Capability statements: Capabilities provide the actual functions provided by *objects in* an agent and the ASN.1 AGENT-CAPABILITIES macro.

The *objects used* for conformance are combined to form a group, and the ASNA macro OBJECT-GROUP is used to provide the syntax and semantics for this group.

Let us examine each of the macros used in compliance and capabilities statements. SNMPv2 conformance macros are defined in RFC 1444, and they are:

```
SNMPv2-CONF DEFINITIONS::= BEGIN
—definitions for conformance groups
OBJECT-GROUP MACRO::=
BEGIN
      TYPE NOTATION::=
                    objects part
                    "STATUS"Status
```

```
                    "DESCRIPTION" Text
                    ReferPart
VALUE NOTATION::=
                    value(VALUE OBJECT IDENTIFIER)
ObjectsPart::=      "OBJECTS" "{" Objects "}"
Objects::=          Object
                    | Objects","Object
Object::=           value(Name ObjectName)
Status::=           "current"
                    | "obsolete"
ReferPart::=        "REFERENCE"Text
                    | empty
—uses the NVT ASCII character set
Text::=""""string""""
END
—definitions for compliance statements
MODULE-COMPLIANCE MACRO::=
BEGIN
  TYPE NOTATION::=
                    STATUS" Status
                    "DESCRIPTION" Text
                    ReferPart
                    ModulePart
  VALUE NOTATION::=
                    Value(VALUE OBJECT IDENTIFIER)
Status::=           "current"
                    | "obsolete"
ReferPart::=        "REFERENCE" Text
                    | empty
ModulePart::=       Modules
                    | empty
Modules::=          Module
                    | Modules Module
Module::=           "MODULE" ModuleName—name of
module
                    MandatoryPart
                    CompliancePart
ModuleName::=       Modulereference Moduleldentifier -- must
not be empty unless contained  in MIB                                    Module.
```

```
                    | empty
ModuleIdentifier::= | value(ModuleID OBJECT IDENTIFIER)
                    | empty
MandatoryPart::=    "MANDATORY-GROUPS" "{"Groups "}"
                    | empty
Groups::=           Group
                    | Groups "," Group
Group::=            value(Group OBJECT IDENTIFIER)
CompliancePart::=   Compliances
                    | empty
Compliances::=      Compliance
                    | Compliances Compliance
Compliance::=       ComplianceGroup
                    | Object
ComplianceGroup::=
                    "GROUP" value(Name OBJECT IDENTIFIER
                    "DESCRIPTION" Text
Object::=           "OBJECT" value(Name ObjectName)
                    SyntaxPart
                    WriteSyntaxPart
                    AccessPart
                    "DESCRIPTION" Text
—must be a refinement for object's SYNTAX clause
SyntaxPart ::=      "SYNTAX"type(SYNTAX)
                    | empty
—must be a refinement for object's SYNTAX clause
WriteSyntaxPart::=  "WRITE-SYNTAX"type(WriteSYNTAX)
                    | empty
AccessPart::=       "MIN-ACCESS" Access
                    | empty
Access::=           "not-accessible"
                    | "read-only"
                    | "read-write"
                    | "read-create"
—uses the NVT ASCII character set
Text::= """" string """"
END
—definitions for capabilities statements
AGENT-CAPABILITIES MACRO::=
```

```
BEGIN
TYPE NOTATION::=
                    "PRODUCT-RELEASE" Text
                    "STATUS" Status
                    "DESCRIPTION" Text
                    ReferPart
                    ModulePart
VALUE NOTATION::=
                    Value (VALUE OBJECT IDENTIFIER)--
                    agents'sysObjectID [3] or snmpORID [4]
Status::=           "current"
                    | "obsolete"
ReferPart::=        "REFERENCE" Text
                    | empty
ModulePart::=       Modules
                    | empty
Modules::=          Module
                    | Modules Module
Module::=           "SUPPORTS" ModuleName—name of
module
                    "INCLUDES" "{" Groups "}"
                    VariationPart
ModuleName::=       identifier ModuleIdentifier
ModuleIdentifier::=value(ModuleID OBJECT IDENTIFIER)
                    | empty
Groups::=           Group
                    | Groups "," Group
Group               value(Name OBJECT IDENTIFIER)
VariationPart::=    Variations
                    | empty
Variations::=       Variation
                    | Variations Variation
Variation::=        "VARIATION" value(Name ObjectName)
                    SyntaxPart
                    WriteSyntaxPart
                    AccessPart
                    CreationPart
                    DefValPart
                    "DESCRIPTION" Text
```

```
—must be a refinement for object's SYNTAX clause
SyntaxPart::=       "SYNTAX" type(SYNTAX)
                    | empty
—must be a refinement for object's SYNTAX clause
WriteSyntaxPart::="WRITE-SYNTAX" type(WriteSYNTAX)
                    | empty
AccessPart::=       "ACCESS" Access
                    | empty
Access::=           "not-implemented"
                    "read-only"
                    "read-write"
                    "read-create"
                    write-only—for backward compatibility.
CreationPart::=     "CREATION-REQUIRES" "{" Cells "}"
                    | empty
Cells::=            Cell
                    | Cells "," Cell
Cell::=             value(Cell ObjectName)
DefValPart::=       "DEFVAL" "{" value(Defval ObjectSyntax)
"}"
                    | empty
—uses the NVT ASCII character set
Text::=  """" string """"
END
END
```

SNMPv2 PDUs

SNMPv2 PDU definitions

SNMPv2 PDUs are defined in RFC 1448.

```
SNMPv2-PDU DEFINITIONS::=
BEGIN
IMPORTS
            ObjectName, ObjectSyntax, Integer32 from
SNMPv2-SMI
—protocol data units
PDUs::=
CHOICE{
        get-request                 GetRequest-PDU,
        get-next-request            GetNextRequest-PDU,
        get-bulk-request            GetBulkRequest-PDU,
```

```
        response                    Response-PDU,
        set-request                 SetRequest-PDU,
        inform-request              InformRequest-PDU,
        snmpV2-trap                 SNMPv2-Trap-PDU
--PDUs
    GetRequest-PDU::=               [0] IMPLICIT PDU
    GetNextRequest-PDU::=           [1] IMPLICIT PDU
    Response-PDU::=                 [2] IMPLICIT PDU
    SetRequest-PDU::=               [3] IMPLICIT PDU
    -- [4] is obsolete
    GetBulkRequestPDU::=            [51 IMPLICIT PDU
    InformRequestPDU ::=            [61 IMPLICIT PDU
    SNMPv2T~apPDU::=                [71 IMPLICIT PDU
max-bindings
INTEGER::= 2147483647
PDU ::=
 SEQUENCE{
                request-id    Integer32,
                error-status -- sometinies ignored
                        INTEGER{
                            noError(0),
                            tooBig(l),
                            noSuchName(2),  -- for proxy
                            —compatibility
                            badValue(3), -- for proxy
                            —compatibility
                            readOnly(4), -- for proxy
                            —compatibility
                            genErr(5),
                            noAccess(6),
                            wrongType(7),
                            wrongLength(8),
                            wrongEncoding(9),
                            wrongValue(10),
                            noCreation(11),
                            inconsistentValue(12),
                            resourceUnavailable(13),
                            commitFailed(14),
                            undoFailed(15),
                            authorizationError(16),
```

```
                                        notWritable(17),
                                        inconsistentName(18)
                                        }
                                        error-index INTEGER(0..max bindings),—
                                          —sometimes
                                          —ignored
variable-bindings                        VarBindList
                                      — values are
                                      — sometimes
                                      — ignored
}
— BulkPDU must be identical in structure to PDU
BulkPDU :: = —must be identical in structure to PDU
SEQUENCE{
     request-id              Integer32,
      non-repeaters          INTEGER (0..max-bindings),
      max-repetitionsI       NTEGER (0..max-bindings),
     variable-bindings       VarBindList --values are ignored
}
—variable binding
VarBind::=
       SEQUENCE{
              name              ObjectName,
              CHOICE {
                     value        ObjectSyntax,
                     unSpecified  NULL -- in retrieval requests
                                        -- exceptions in responses
                     noSuchObject[0]          IMPLICIT NULL,
                     noSuchInstance[1]        IMPLICIT NULL,
                     endOfMibView[2]          IMPLICIT NULL
    }
}
—variable-binding list
VarBindList :: =
       SEQUENCE (SIZE (0..max-bindings)) OF VarBind
END
```

SNMPv2 protocol messages

SNMPv2 uses slightly different protocol messages *for* communicating management information than does SNMPv1. The format of SNMPv2 PDUs, such as GetRequest, GetNextRequest, SetRequest, SNMPv2Trap, Response, and InformRequest, are Similar to those shown in Figure 8.23; however, there are some minor differences, as follows:

- A trap PDU of SNMPv1 is no longer there, and the PDU type of 4 used for the SNMPv1 trap is obsolete. The new value of the PDU type for SNMPv2Trap is 7.
- The GetResponse of SNMPv1 is now known as the response PDU in SNMPv2.
- The GetBulkRequest PDU has been added. Note also that InformRequest is a new PDU.
- A brief explanation of the SNMPv2 PDUs is as follows:
- *GetRequest:* When an application requests an SNMPv2 entity, this is generated by the entity and sent to an agent. This message is similar to the SNMPv1 GetRequest message. On the receiving end, this message is analyzed to check whether the request is a proper one. If it is a proper one, then the error status field is set to noError and the error index field is set to zero in the response and sent to the manager.
- *GetNextRequest:* This message is similar to the GetNextRequest in SNMPv1 messages and is based on the tabular concept of the SNMP MIB. If there are no errors, then the response has the next instance of a variable which has been sent in the request. If there are any errors, then the error status and error index fields correspond to the errors observed.
- *SetRequest:* This is a slightly trickier one. There are two steps involved: a validation phase and, if this succeeds, changes are made. During the validation step, a check is made of whether change on a variable can be made. If this is not possible, then the error status and error index fields are set accordingly in the response PDU. However, if the validation step is successful, then the value of the variable is set to the value mentioned in the SetRequest PDU. If the variable is not there, it is created and its value is set. In this case, in the response PDU, the error status field shows noError, and the error-index field is zero.
- *GetBulkRequest:* This is primarily used for retrieving a large amount of table data from the MIB, unlike GetRequest and GetNextRequest PDUs. Here also, if there are errors noticed in the receiving end, the error status and error index fields are set. If no errors are noticed, data is sent in the response PDU.
- *InformRequest:* This is a protocol message for conveying MIB information from one SNMPv2 entity to another SNMPv2 entity, both acting in the manager role. This is primarily meant for manager-to-manager communication. The receiving SNMPv2 checks to see if there are any errors. If errors are noticed while processing this PDU, the response PDU has the corresponding error status and error index fields set. If there are no errors, the MIB information is passed on to the application using the receiving SNMPv2 entity and generates a response to the sending SNMPv2.
- *Response:* This PDU is generated for GetRequest, GetNextRequest, SetRequest, and GetBulkRequest PDUs sent from a sender SNMPv2 entity. The sender SNMPv2

entity is the manager. The receiving SNMPv2 entity is the agent, and it prepares the response PDU and sends it back to the sending SNMPv2 entity. The sender SNMPv2 must be able to handle the errors generated and pass on the response PDU to the application using the sender SNMPv2 entity.

- *SNMPv2-Trap:* When an exceptional situation occurs in an SNMPv2 entity acting in an agent role, then a trap is generated and sent to the SNMPv2 entity consulting aclTable. The access privileges for SNMPv2 are maintained in the SNMPv2 access privileges database. The trap numbers in SNMPv2Trap indicate the reasons why a trap has occurred. The SNMP traps as mentioned in SNMPv1 are used here, too.

Functioning of SNMPv2 protocols

The flow of how an SNMPv2 PDU is generated is shown in Figure. Basically, an originator SNMPv2 entity generates a management protocol PDU such as GetRequest. At first, an SNMPv2 management communication (SnmpMgmtCom) is constructed. This has originator and receiver parties. This also has the context and SNMPv2 PDU fields. A local database is consulted for the context and the authentication protocol to be used.

From the SNMPv2 management communication (SnmpMgmtCom), SNMPv2 authenticated management communication (Snmp AuthMsg) is constructed. This is derived by prefixing authentication information to the SNMPv2 management communication data. Here, if the authentication protocol is not used for a party, then the authentication protocol for the party is noAuth. In this case, the autholnfo field corresponds to an OCTET STRING value of zero length.

If partyAuthProtocol is 2md5AuthProtocol, then authentication protocol provides data origin identification and data integrity. snmpAuthMsg is supplied as an input to MD-5 message-digest algorithm. The output from the message-digest algorithm is a 16-octet string known as digest. This digest goes in the authDigest field. From SNMPv2 SnmpAuthMsg, SNMPv2 private management communication is (SnmpPrivMsg) constructed by prefixing the privacy destination field. Here, if the privacy protocol of the destination is noPriv, then the SnmpAuthMsg field is not encrypted. Otherwise, this field is encrypted, and it is formed using the privacy protocol.

The message to be sent to the destination party is SnmpPrivMsg. This has a privDst, which refers to the destination party. The intended message and private data are meant for the destination party. The private data field is possibly in the form of encrypted data. This private data is SNMPv2 authenticated management communication (SnmpAuthMsg). Then the SNMPv2 SnmpAuth-Msg is converted to BER and sent to the destination party using the transport protocol and transport address of the receiving SNMPv2 party.

First, a check is made of whether the format of the message received is of the proper type. If the check is successful, then the destination is checked using the local database. From this, the ASNA string is recreated using decryption with the help of the privacy protocol. The authentication and context checking are also done on the receiving side, then access privileges are checked for management operations to be done. A check is also necessary to know whether the SNMPv2 context refers to the local object resources or remote object resources. In all this checking, the local database is consulted whenever required.

One of the key aspects of processing security protocols is that the originator is not sent any response indicating the reasons for the failure of the request. The primary reason for this action is that any unauthorized user need not be alerted that the request has been discarded. On the receiving side, the request is simply discarded.

Manager-to-manager communication

When there is a large network, it is difficult to centralize all network management activities in one place. The same is true of many networks internetworked to one another. In such situations, it is better to distribute the network management functions in different portions of the networks. This way each portion of the network can have a manager. For manager-to-manager communication, the InformRequest PDU and the manager-to-manager MIB have been created. These are explained in RFC 1451.

Manager A sends the InformRequest PDU and, in response, Manager B sends the Response PDU, which has the management information requested from B. However, to check whether the managers are functioning, polling is done frequently.

Some of the key concepts in manager-to-manager MIB, are:

- *snmpAlarm:* This is a specific condition detected when a management variable falls outside a configured range. The checking for a configured range, such as crossing a threshold value, is done periodically by sampling. Only variables with the data type of INTEGER (Integer32, Counter32, Gauge32, TimeTicks, Counter64, and Ulnteger32) can be monitored for an alarm condition.
- *snmpEvent:* This triggers one or more notifications when an alarm condition is reached. These notifications are packaged in InformRequest PDUs.

Manager-to-manager MIB. The manage to manager MIB group has the following three tables:

- *snmpAlarmTable*: Has the details on the variable to be monitored, such as sampling interval, threshold values, and the manner in which these threshold values are crossed. contextIdentity provides the context to be queried, and each context may have zero or more snmpAlarmEntrys associated with it.
- *snmpEventTable*: Furnishes details on the events generated by an SNMPv2 entity acting in a dual role of manager and agent. These events can be generated by alarm conditions associated with snmpAlarmTable or due to conditions defined in the NOTIFICATION-TYPE macro.

- *snmpEventNotifyTable*: Defines the destination' and the type of notifications to be sent by an entity in a manager, role on a even

The objects in the snmpAlarm group are:

- *snmpAlarmIndex (INTEGER (1. 65535)):* Uniquely identifies an entry in the snmpAlarmTable.
- *snmpAlarmVariable (InstancePointer):* Refers to the object'~ instance being sampled.
- *snmpAlarmInterval (Integer32):* Indicates the time interval for sampling, in seconds.
- *snmpAlarmSample Type (INTEGER):* Specifies how sampling must be done. This object has two values: absoluteValue = 1 and deltaValue = 2. For absolute-Value, the sampled value of a variable at the end of the sampling interval is compared with the

snmpAlarmRisingThreshold and snmpAlarmFalling-Threshold values. For deltaValue, the delta value is first derived by subtracting the value at the end of a sampling interval of the predecessor from the sampling value at the end of the sampling interval. This deltaValue is compared with the snmpAlarmRisingThreshold and snmpAlarmFallingThreshold values.

snmpAlarmValue (Integer32): Refers to the last sampled value

snmpAlarmStartupAlarm (INTEGER): Indicates the alarm that may be sent when the first sample is compared with the threshold. This alarm has three values: risingAlarm = 1, fallingAlarm = 2, and risingOrFallingAlarm = 3.

snmpAlarmRisingThreshold (Integer32): Furnishes the upper threshold limit.

snmpAlarmFailingThreshold (Integer32): Indicates the lower threshold limit. Note that an event is generated when a sampled value crosses s FallingThreshold.

snmpAlarmR1singEventIndex (INTEGER (0..65535)): Indicates the entry in the snmpEventTable when the sampled value exceeds the value of snmpAlarmRisingThreshold.

snmpAlarmFallingEuentIndex (INTEGER (0..65535)): Associated with snmpAlarmFallingThreshold.

snmpAlarmUnavialableEuentIndex (INTEGER (0..65535)): Corresponds to a row in snmpEventTable. This row is used to generate an event when a variable being sampled is no longer available.

snmpRisingAlarm, snmpFallingAlarm, and *snmpObject-UnavilableAlarm,* defined by NOTIFICATION-TYPE macros, present the events generated when similar conditions to those seen in snmpEventTable are met.

An object in the snmpEvent group is:

- snmpEventNextIndex (INTEGER (0..65535): Refers to the next, available row for creating an instance of an event.

The following six objects are associated with snmpEventTable"

- snmpEventIndex (INTEGER (0..65535)): Identifies a conceptual row and is associated with notification to be sent for an invocation of a NOTIFICATIONTYPE macro.
- *snmpEventID (OBJECT IDENTIFIER):* Refers to the unique identifier of the event entry.
- *snmpEventDescription (DisplayString (SIZE (0 ..127))):* Describes the event entry.
- *snmpEventEvents (Counter32):* Furnishes the number of events generated till now.
- *snmpEventLastTimeSent (TimeStamp):* Relates to sysUpTime, when an event was last generated. If this value is zero then no event has been generated.
- *snmpEuentStatus (RowStatus):* Provides the status of the snmpEvent entry.

We return to the explanation of the remaining objects in the snmpEvent group.

- *snmpEuentNotifyMinInterual (Integer32):* Provides the time interval for retransmitting InformRequest PDU.
- *snmpEuentNotifyMaxRetransmissions (Integer32):* Represents the maximum number of InformRequest PDUs that will be sent.

snmpEventNotifyTable has the following managed objects:

- *snmpEventNotifyIntervalRequested (Integer32):* Furnishes the time interval for retransmitting an InformRequest PDU.
- *snmpEventNotifyRetransmissionsRequested (Integer32):* Has the lesser value of the actual retransmissions of InformRequest or snmpEventNotifyMaxRetrans-missions.
- *snmpEventNotifyLifetime (Integer32):* Represents the number of seconds the entry in snmpEventNotifyTable will remain active. After the expiry of the time, the snmpEventNotify status is set to "destroyed."
- *snmpEventNotifyStatus (RowStatus):* Used for representing the status of snmpEventNotifyEntry.

snmpM2MConformance objects present the description and configuration of the alarm and event group objects.

Transport mapping for SNMPv2

SNMPv2 management protocols must be associated with a transport service for transferring the management information. However, there are different types of transport services that can be used for SNMPv2. The term snmpDomains stands for the association of the SNMPv2 management protocols with a transport service. As we have seen, the SNMPv2 PDUs are serialized using BER. The following types of transport service for SNMPv2 have been defined:

- *snmpUDPDomain:* SNMPv2 over UDP is the preferred manner to transfer management information.
- *snmpCLNSDomain:* SNMPv2 over OSI's Connectionless-mode Transport Service (CLTS) is an alternative. Connectionless transport service works over the Connectionless Network Service.
- *snmpCONSDomain:* Here, SNMPv2 is transferred using the Connection-oriented Network Service (CONS). Here, connection less-mode transport service runs over the Connection-oriented network service.
- *snmpDDPDomain:* SNMPv2 uses the AppleTalk@ DDP for the transport service.
- *snmpIPXDomain:* SNMPv2 uses the NetWare@ IPX for the transport service.

Migration from SNMPvl to SNMPv2

For migration, proxy has been suggested. In a proxy approach, an SNMPv2 entity may be acting as a manager; the SNMPv1 entity can be in an agent role. However, in this case, the SNMPv2 proxy agent will have to convert the GetBulkRequest PDU to GetNextRequest PDU and set nonrepeaters and max-repetitions fields to zero. Traps will have to be modified in the proxy agent. In a bilingual approach, a manager functions as a proxy when dealing, with an SNMPv1 agent. Here a manager maps SNMPv2 PDUs to, SNMPvl PDUs. Some of the strategies for migration are to:

- Upgrade management stations to SNMPv2. If this is done, it is easy to support SNMPv2 agents as they become available.
- Upgrade and acquire if required, new SNMPv2 agents. Once the management stations can handle SNMPv2, it is easy to add new SNMPv2 agents.
- Handle the existing SNMPv1 agents, the proxy approach provides easy coexistence.

Device-dependent objects

In addition to the objects defined in MIBII and other SNMPv1 and SNMPv2 documents, objects are defined for different media types. These are useful, and they can be incorporated in agents. Some of the device-specific objects defined in different RFCs. However, while implementing these objects, consult the latest *Internet Official Protocol Standards* on the requirement and maturity levels of these RFCs.

Advantages of SNMP

SNMP is a simple protocol, and it is easy to add this protocol to the agents. Many applications using SNMP protocols have been implemented. It is easy to get and modify SNMP code. Because Internet is quite popular, it has a large base, which itself is causing SNMP to be accepted as a de facto standard worldwide.

RFCs for managed objects for devices

RFC number	*Description of the RFC*	
1749	IEEE 802.5 Station Source Routing MIB Using SMIv2	
1696	Modem Management Information Base (MIB) Using	SMIv2
1695	Managed Objects for ATM Management Version 8.0	Using SMIv2
1694	Managed Objects for SMDS Interfaces Using SMIv2	
1643	Managed Objects for the Ethernet-like Interface	Types
1604	Managed Objects for Frame Relay Service	
1595	Managed Objects for the SONET/SDH Interface Type	
1525	Managed Objects for Source Routing Bridges	
1516	Managed Objects for IEEE 802.3 Repeater Devices	
1515	Managed Objects for IEEE 802.3 Medium Attachment	Units (MAUs)
1512	An FDDI Management Information Base	
1493	Managed Objects for Bridges	
1407	Managed Objects for the DS/E3 Interface Type	
1406	Managed Objects for the DS1 and El Interface Types	
1317	Managed Objects for RS-232-like Hardware Devices	
1315	Management Information Base for Frame Relay DTEs	
1304	Managed Objects for the SIP Interface Type	
1239	Reassignment of Experimental MIBs to Standard	MIBs

Also, it is easy to add objects required for specific implementations. This can done by adding object extension to the MIB. Continuous improvements and extensions are being added to the protocol with implementation experiences.

Limitations of SNMP

When SNMP was designed, the idea was to keep the management protocol simple. This has its own drawbacks. The network management has a whole range of functions in addition to the SNMP protocols defined. A framework for management functions such as OSI may be useful. Also, as distributed computing becomes popular, there are issues such as how different subnetwork managers behave, how the replication of management operational data collected by network management functions is done, and how the management operational data collected is archived. These aspects need to be standardized. Otherwise, there are possibilities of different vendors interpreting and implementing in different ways. This will also raise the problems of interoperability of network management systems.

As we move into a client-server environment with a large number of networks, management domains and communications between them will assume a significant role. Management domains are also important for distributed network management.

Incidentally, there is much work to be done in this arena in the Internet Network Management Framework.

A manager must enforce access control and authentication to ensure that important data are not compromised by intruders. This becomes critical when concepts of distributed systems are extended to Internet, and it still leaves a hole in SNMP security.

It is also necessary to define objects for the different network management functions, such as configuration management, fault management, security management, performance management, and accounting management. These may be borrowed from OSI. This is required as an interim measure, because the convergence of network management of OSI and Internet may take a while.

In configuration and fault management, relationships between different monitored objects are very important in tracing the origins of faults. Thus, relationships and attributes must be defined and standardized.

In configuration management, aggregation objects need to be defined. In some cases, the status of an object may be the aggregation of objects below a subtree. In such cases, the status will have to be combined by either simple or weighted aggregation. Also, the configuration may be a combination of objects; for example, a network may be a combination of an IP network, an OSIbased network, and an SNA network. To show the whole network, it is necessary to define aggregate objects. The health or status of a network may be represented by different colors.

The Internet group is focused on protocols used by the Internet community, and it expects a certain lowerlayer stack. It also assumes certain physicallayer interfaces. So, the emphasis is on the TCP/IP protocol suite and on Ethernet LANs, while the other type of LANs based on token-ring protocols are also popular. As a result, the Internet stack gets priority while standardizing. This may be regarded as a strength as well as a weakness. It is a strength in that problems facing the Internet community get immediate attention, while others may have to wait longer for standardization.

Therefore objects may have to be specifically defined and extensions added to the MIB for many resources. This may result in defining the same resources in different manners, which can create problems for the interoperability of network management functions.

The definition of objects in OSI allows the use of inheritance and polymorphism. This makes possible the reuse of attributes; hence, the implementations becomes simpler with this approach. We have already explained polymorphism. Polymorphism helps in the migration and coexistence of different versions of the same applications.

We have seen that in OSI, managed objects have attributes, operations, notifications, and behaviors. In SNMP, object definitions are less powerful and have only attributes and operations. As a result, they carry less information. The advantages of having notifications in the definitions of managed objects in OSI are flexibility and more power. To compensate for the absence of notifications in SNMP, traps and trap-directed polling are used. However, simplicity was one of the main considerations in the definition of SNMP, and lack of notification has not hindered many SNMP implementations.

As a final consideration, interoperability will be a problem TCP/IP is not globally accepted. Otherwise, the integration of OS protocols in some nations and Internet protocols in some other nations may lead to problems at a later date. Because the ultimate objective of Internet is to migrate to OSI standards, this may not be major obstacle in the long run.

Interoperability with OSI

For interoperation between OSI and TCP/IP protocols, RFC 1006 is recommended. RFC 1006 mimics the transport layer on top of TCP. By this, layers such as the session, presentation, and application layers can run on top of TCP/IP protocols. This enables applications such as systems management and mail services to operate on TCP/IP. Some of the salient features of RFC 11006 are:

- *ISO transport Class 0 is supported.* Class 0 provides the most simple basic Connection-oriented support during connection establishment and connection release phases. It does not provide a mechanism to detect protocol errors. Quality of service (QOS), which classifies transport services in terms of Class 0, Class 1, Class 2, Class 3, and Class 4, is not supported.
- *Some departures from Class 0 are made.* Initial data may be exchanged during the connection establishment phase; expedited data service is supported; and much larger Transport Protocol Data Unit (TPDU) size is supported. For performance reasons, a default TPDU size of 65531 is taken. However, smaller TPDU sizes are allowed, but they must be negotiated.
- Network service is provided by the TCP
- *TPDU is encapsulated within each packet designed specifically for this RFC.* This packet consists of a packet header and the TPDU. The packet header has 8 bits for version, 8 bits of reserved field, and 16 bits of length field.

Systems management functions for TCP/IP

Having discussed SNMPvl, MIB, RMON, and SNMPv2, it is appropriate to peek into network management in Internet. In TCP/IP, there are no clear-cut rules regarding how to partition MIBII objects into different systems management functional areas. Unless there is standardization in this direction, the partitioning of MIBII objects will not be uniform in implementations from different vendors.

These MIBII objects will be in agents. The data on the MIBII objects will be collected by the respective systems management functional areas. In addition, each of the device and protocol-specific objects should be partitioned to different systems management functional areas. In some cases, such as that of a router, all MIBII objects may not be supported; therefore, we should take the MIBs defined for a router. Similarly, an agent may not have device-specific objects. At the same time, we should remember that we may have to use proxy agents to incorporate the proprietary protocols and proprietary objects.

Implementation of TCP/IP

TCP/IP protocol suite RFCs, including those of network management, change quite frequently to meet new requirements. Before implementing any RFC, one must ensure that it is the latest and is not superseded by a more recent RFC. To do so, the first document to consult is the *RFCINDEX,* which is an up-to-date index of the RFCs that have been released. The next document to consult during design and implementation is the RFC on IAB *Official Protocol Standards,* which furnishes the requirement and maturity levels of RFCs. These two documents are regularly updated.

3

Smart System Support

The principal technologies that impinge upon smart systems implementations are: (1) rule-based expert systems, (2) neural networks, and, (3) data structures. Expert systems contribute to the infusion of intelligence into systems by encasing previously acquired knowledge into modules that can react to external stimuli in a way that an expert would. Neural systems integrate the stimuli into a pattern, and thereby interpret these results based upon their total integrated affects, classifications, or characteristics. Data structures, on the other hand, contribute to intelligence by the way they organize, store, and retrieve data associated with the intelligence functions. Each of these contributing technologies will be discussed briefly below.

Expert systems have experienced a tremendous growth over the past few years. Between 1986 and 1988, the number of expert systems developed and used in commercial or government applications in the United States increased 215 percent from 475 to 1025. Between 1988 and 1990 the number of systems available jumped again by another 147 percent to 1510 Even today, most expert systems development and delivery are executed on PCs using development tools costing less than $1000. Expert systems support practically all facets of network management, such as maintenance planning, and operations.

Neural networks are an attempt to model and simulate the neural architecture and functioning of the brain. In particular, such models are an attempt to emulate the processing and interpretation of the various sensory modalities of the mammalian central nervous system. This seemingly huge task is accomplished through the use of simplified models of neural processing, as conducted by neurons that are arranged in interconnecting patterns. These patterns are, in turn, exercised by external stimuli to yield the correct responses to problems presented to them. Neural network models can be developed on conventional computers from simple PCs to parallel processors, and super-computers using special software developed for such purposes. In addition neurochips have been developed embodying the capabilities to perform neural network simulations. Finally, application specific integrated circuits (ASICs) have been developed for individual situations that have the ability to execute and analyze a specific neural net problem.

What is a neural net problem? A neural net problem is one for which there are no set of formal or articulated rules. A neural network problem is, therefore, one that is solved by trial and error using a training paradigm that is exercised until it yields the right set of outputs given the inputs presented. Thus, because neural nets are trained rather than programmed, they are especially suited for classification and pattern recognition problems. Examples of applications to which neural network could be applied include diagnostics, machine vision, modeling and theory development, pattern recognition and classifi-cation, signal processing, speech recognition and classification, and robotics. For network management systems and applications, neural networks have widespread possibilities. Neural network inputs that might be equated to different features of an operational network can be routed and applied to the first layer of a typical neural network. The subsequent processing can generate a pattern, the output of which can be used for reference, or to modify the neural network so that it attains a reference point. This pattern now becomes one of the comparison elements, against which pattern alterations can be judged.

Data structures and file management: While not usually thought of as an essential ingredient of AI, data structures and file management facilities contribute greatly to the infusion of intelligent features into systems because they provide the facilities to speedily locate or properly associate data items of interest with each other, and with the subject. A good case in point is the subject of list processing. An AI program known as LISP, short for list processing, was developed to facilitate the association of objects and their attributes with each other. List processing is a file structure facility where lists and taxonomies of different categories of items are organized for later recall, sorting, and reorganization, as directed by the LISP commands.

Cited below are some of the most important features of data structures and file management technology.

Data searching: Data searching is the process of accessing a particular piece of information. Many times this search process will entail the use of a key value that is best defined as the argument of the search. Search techniques can be identified as being either linear or nonlinear. There are several varieties of linear search techniques that may be applied to finding one item out of many. For the most part these linear search techniques require on-the-order-of (O) N searches or $N/2$ searches to find the item of choice, where N is the number of total items from which to choose. On-the-order-of is roughly analogous to rough order of magnitude.

Nonlinear approaches can have fewer steps than the $O(N/2)$ steps required by linear techniques. One of these nonlinear techniques is the binary search technique that has the smallest number of required steps. This approach requires $O(\log_2 N)$, and can be used to search either records or smaller entities, such as data fields.

Another series of search techniques is involved in file management where the data are arranged in records. In such situations, searching can be accomplished by the use of addressing mechanisms that utilize keys. The three principal methods of searching using these methods are direct mapping, directory look-up, and calculation. All of these can be thought of as a lock and key combination, where the key is the name of the item of interest and the lock is the manipulation that allows the address of the item of interest to be identified. Direct mapping is a search technique in which the key of the data item to be located is, in fact, the address of that data item. In such a case, there is no mapping or translation of the key per se. For directory lookup, the key will point to some location in a separate directory where the address will be found somewhat like the use of a telephone directory. The final type of search technique is also called "hashing," or calculation, after the meal that contains many ingredients. The hash technique takes the key and transforms it into the address using any number of different algorithms. The algorithms do not have to make logical sense if they accomplish the required task. One of the hash techniques used is called division remainder. In this technique, the key is divided by some appropriate number, the remainder of which becomes the relative address of the record or data item sought.

Sorting: Sorting is important for database systems involved in network management because it directly supports the storage of parameter values associated with factual data, and the searching techniques that perform access operations to retrieve that stored data. The normal method of storing data is to assign a storage entity, or record, for each parameter of interest. These records may be either sorted or unsorted as they are stored in the database system, If the records are sorted, then searching is greatly speeded up. Sorting is sometimes categorized as either being internal or external, depending upon whether the sort routine can be performed in existing memory or whether auxiliary memory is required for the operation. External sorts depend for speed on two major features of the system, one being the read and write times of the hardware and software support system, and the other being the speed of the sort algorithm itself. There are families of sort algorithms associated with data arrangement, these being selection sorts, insertion sorts, and exchange sorts.

The selection sort consists of surveying a set of keys and selecting each key in turn in either ascending or descending value. Such a sort is said to require $O(N^2)$ comparisons for completion. The insertion sort is a technique in which an unsorted list is again subjected to scanning, and each key is taken from the unsorted list and placed into a sorted list such that each key is inserted into its proper position in the sorted list as it is selected. The class known as exchange sorts offers the best results in terms of efficiency in the sorting process and consists of such sorts as the bubble sort, quick sort, heap sort, and tournament sort, to name a few.

The tournament sort is probably the most popular of all sorts today. It was first described in 1956 by E. H. Friend, a noted mathematician. It is used today by many database vendors in their file-sorting software packages. The tournament sort operates much as the tournament elimination process in sports would operate except that we can sort in either a descending or ascending order.

For an ascending ordered list, the process begins with a raw list of values and the first four values, divided into two pairs, are initially selected for comparison. These two pairs of values are compared for minimum values in each pair. The smaller of each comparison is selected and again compared to the "winner" of the first comparison. The smaller of this comparison is placed in a holding position. The value ultimately selected is replaced by the next unsorted key in the raw list, and the process is repeated. This activity continues until all raw keys are processed. At some point in the sort process a new raw key is selected that has a value that is smaller than the last key output to the processed list. In this event, the new raw key is placed in the sort tree but eliminated from consideration unless and until all the branches of the tree are filled with keys smaller than the last key output to the processed list.

At this point the process is repeated to generate a new list that has ascending ordered keys. There are now two lists, one being the processed list and the other being the keys remaining in the comparison slots. These two lists can now be compared and merged as previously discussed.

Updating

Updating is a process of periodically reorganizing and reconstituting information sets. It consists of two phases, one being the handling of overflows and the other the actual update itself. Database systems utilize several techniques for data updating, all of which are a function of the overflow techniques used, and these are explained below. Overflow techniques go by such names as progressive overflow, count-key progressive overflow, chained progressive overflow, and separate overflow area. Basically, the problem in data storage is to accommodate data items for which there is no current space available in the primary storage area. In other words, primary storage can only accommodate so much data, and after this is used up, temporary storage must be allocated so that the database transactions can continue unabated until some stopping point is reached, at which time the data records can be reorganized into their proper order.

The actual update process may be solved in different ways. In the case of a sequential file, one in which records are stored one after the other in some ordered form, the update may require the following: all current records and new records to be added, as well as requests for certain records to be deleted, are reordered by sorting and merging, similar to the tournament sort and merge procedures described above. Updating of more complex systems may require elaborate methods, such as various storage-splitting reorganizations. In these types of updating processes, the storage space is based upon a series of keys that are associated with addresses. Thus, no predefined space need be allocated.

When limits are reached for storage, overflow temporarily accommodates this component until the update can be performed. In some cases, the update can be performed on the fly. What this entails is that the number of keys at each storage location, which have reached their maximum, are physically split such that two groups of keys are made from one and the groups are linked by the use of pointers. Techniques such as this one in various forms, are used in balanced tree, B tree, and other database design approaches.

Sensor Technology

A sensor can be roughly described as any reportable data source, but more often is described as any device that gathers data. A data source could contain performance, configuration, or accounting information that might be correlated with other time critical data to arrive at the system status. Sensors consist of two basic ingredients, namely the data collection function and the data assimilation function. In a satellite operations environ-ment, the data collection function packages the collected data and relays it to the ground control center where the assimilation is performed through status updates, report collation, report trend assembly, etc. The assimilation may often suggest further analysis and subsequent interpretation.

Most of the time, however, sensors are thought of as analog devices that either collect data, convert it to digital form, and transmit it to some monitoring station, or convey it in its original analog form. There is, however, no requirement, per se, that a sensor device be analog with add on capability to convert the data to digital form for relay. The sensor may also be digital in its collection mode of operation. As a matter of fact, the sensor may actually be part of the functioning component being sampled. Lastly, the sensor may be a processor that analyzes and evaluates the data collected for subsequent disposition.

There is no question that sensor technology is increasing in importance, mostly due to the use of sampled data in the analysis and control of new and better-equipped instruments for human benefit. This increased need for sampled data is also partially due to its use in expert systems. Obviously, there are many types of sensors that must be brought to bear on the system at hand. Sensors in the sense intended here means the monitoring of certain components where either analog or digital processes are involved. Intelligent, integrated systems require that sensors be an integral part of such systems. These systems are seeing the development of sensors as intelligent peripherals to the main processing system that can be programmed and accessed by more than one system processor. There are four phases to the evolution of the integrated sensor, these being the expansion of the micro-structured types and varieties of sensors available, the expansion of the functionality of the sensor, e.g., the filtering and compensation; self-diagnosis and calibration capabilities of the sensors, and finally the intelligent peripheral state of the sensor that makes it a reliable and valid partner in the system operation.

Types of sensors

Sensor systems must be thought of as integral to the realization of complete automated systems both currently under development and slated for development in the future. Digital, bus-capable sensor interfaces are one of the solutions foreseen for future applications of sensor technology that will support integrated sensor and operational functions. These interfaces can best be accomplished through the definition of an open sensor interface that offers the flexibility to exchange the equipment of different manufacturers. Multipoint sensors are important to the effective management and tracking of connectivity within a system.

Digital sensors

sensing in digital systems is normally accomplished by one of several methods, one being to convert analog signals to digital format and then incorporate that data into messages that are transmitted between the affected equipment and the network management system. Another method is to monitor the direct digital sequences generated by the target equipment and to incorporate that information into status messages for transmission to the network management system. This all assumes, of course, that the transmission system itself, which carries the status messages, is intact. If it is not, the digital sensor paradigm fails because the transport medium itself is missing. The transmission medium over which the status messages as well as the operational messages travel is clearly the weak link in the overall process. One way around the problem of having to use a common transport medium is to make use of a wireless or a radiofrequency (RF) link between sensor and monitoring point. Thus, the sensor, no matter bow implemented, can provide reliable backup communications for monitoring and control purposes via a separate RF link that interfaces with the sensor unit. A second and more common method of assuring reliable status communi-cations between equipment and network management systems is to provide redundant circuits, one of which is used for the status transmissions. Short of complete failure, the transmission medium provides the communications link(s) between the sensors and their reporting points. Digital sensor interfaces are implemented via one of two methods, i.e., message passing and rendezvous techniques between target units and their monitoring stations. Message passing is the process of conveying a message between a unit and its higher-level monitor. The message rendezvous process is the technique of conveying a message between unit and supervisor via some intermediary such as an electronic mail box or storage point.

The fact that digital sensors are operating on discrete data at irregular intervals makes it difficult to treat them in the same way as analog sensors. One of the ways to rationalize digital sensor data is to view digital sensor output as a continuum tracing the movement of events as if they were readings that had been subjected to an analog-to-digital (A/D) conversion. Another way is to view the digital output as a time series trend analysis.

Analog sensors

Analog sensors have been around for many years and are found in almost all large-scale processes, partly because the modeling and simulation of big operations has been almost impossible until the advent of high speed, and large-capacity memory computers, thus making the data collection needed for large scale systems design a function of direct measurements Additionally, until more economical and inferential measurements could be made, analog sensors have been necessary and useful in the monitoring of operational processes that benefited from any such monitoring.

Implementation of sensor functions

Sensor messages are of two principal types, these being status and diagnostic. The status messages alert the control station to potential congestion problems, their locations within the system, and their nature. Diagnostic messages alert the control station of different types of failure within the network element. These two types of messages are the result either of data collection by the sensor within the unit itself, with subsequent formatting and conveyance to the control station, or of status and diagnostic messages generated by the unit itself with subsequent conveyance to the control station. Sensory functions acting internal to the equipment are a different concept that deserves some attention. Such a process could be accomplished by a software module residing within the equipment or by a hardware/firmware device interfacing with the control station across the input/output (I/O) port(s) of the equipment item. One very pertinent question that might be asked is, "How can these sensors be implemented within a typical equipment environment?" Potentially, there are four ways that this can be done and each is discussed briefly below.

(1) The network element itself can act as the sensor by collecting and periodically reporting status informa-tion about its processes.

This can be manifested as a hardwired capability without direct computer control, or it can be implemented under software control integrated with the basic system. An example here might be a signal repeater. The repeater receives incoming signals, boosts their power levels, and repeats these boosted signals on the output side. Thus, the repeater is a means of relaying a signal at some minimum level. Its status can be determined by its continuing functional performance at specified levels of acceptance, and not require further monitoring.

(2) A separate software sensor module can be implanted within the equipment software environment as a nonintegrated element of the processing capability.

This entity can continually monitor and periodically measure the telecommunications subsystem's readiness and its status. There are two principal modes of operation for the software sensor, one being the *error-trapping mode,* where an error initiates a message through the communications interface to the monitoring system, and the second being the *status report mode,* where periodic reports are sent to the monitoring system by the sensor module. Such a device could be implemented either with or without memory. A memory component would facilitate its ability to analyze data within the unit, to develop trends, and to report status at infrequent intervals.

(3) A hardware device can be attached to the network element to monitor, collect, and transmit status and health information about the component to a central information control platform.

A very good illustration of this approach was suggested by IBM. The cabling could be either a databus or local area network (LAN) configuration where the various devices to be monitored are controlled by a host computer, or some other device, such as a server or controller. Each sensor interface card consists of a specialized network attachment interface that varies with the communications protocol employed. After that, the components are similar in that the same functions must be performed in order to sample, receive, judge, and format each piece of data examined.

Each sensor interface has its own hardware device acquisition subsection that would possibly be analog at the interface, an analog-to-digital conversion for those inputs that were analog, a controller that strobes the data reports into the random access memory (RAM) memory, its own read-only memory (ROM) instruction repository that determines the rates of data acquisition, and another interface to the specific network protocol in use, e.g., Ethernet.

(4) A hardware device can be used to interface several network elements at a time so that sensory information can be handled at some centralized point.

This scenario involves the direction of sensory messages to one or a series of intermediate collection points where they are filtered and forwarded in an efficient and timely fashion.

Sensor failure modes

There are two major types of sensor failure which, not surprisingly, are referred to as hard failures and soft failures. When a system element fails to respond totally to the requests of a sensor module, or when it fails to acknowledge a sensor module request, a hard failure has occurred. This is synonymous to a light switch or binary event. A soft failure encompasses that whole area of circumstances between total failure and complete operational availability. Soft failures occur when inappropriate or unfounded responses are sent from the equipment to the sensor. Such responses might result in garbled data, in undefined data sequences, or in illogical responses. Soft failures are also the hardest types of failures to resolve because their manifestations may be intermittent or based upon component failures that are difficult to trace because they still allow data flow between sensor and system element.

Data fusion technology

Data fusion is not a thing or technology per se, but rather it is a way of thinking about the data collection problem. In this respect, it is an application-specific procedure that is implemented through a combination of software, hardware, and human-orchestrated procedures. Data fusion can be thought of as the bringing together of two or more sensor reports from the same type of sensors or dissimilar sensors for the purpose of verifying and tracking conditions or events. The issue of data fusion stresses the importance of time, thereby provoking a series of reports closely spaced in time to speed up the analysis and association of events, and therefore the decision-making process. A series of reports from the same sensor may well generate the same answers to the questions at hand, but time and independent verification will be sacrificed, leading to decreased confidence or confusion at the decision point.

The utilization of several reports that cover multiple sources of interest is of much more value than a single report, simply because one reporting source does not convey as much meaning as do a group of such sources. This can easily be appreciated by considering what multiple source information imparts to the viewer.

The data fusion model

As one might imagine, the data fusion problem is of major concern in a military environment and the basis for effective action in many engagement situations. The network management environment provides many similar parallels. There are several groups in the defense arena that have spent many years of effort to investigate and describe how data fusion can be implemented at the Department of Defense (DoD) level. The data fusion process has been described as having three levels of activity. Each of these levels is identified and briefly described below.

(1) *Level 1*: The position and identification of the fault or undesired condition is made here. Data fusion techniques are used to eliminate any ambiguity involved in resolving the point at issue. Isolating the point of a problem is a difficult task. The number and location of sensors directly affects the isolation of a problem down to some acceptable level of ambiguity.

(2) *Level 2*: The assessment of the situation is made at this point using techniques to determine the extent and magnitude of the technical problem. The situation assessment usually applies to the physical and functional attributes of the system. Specifically, the situation assessment evaluates the extent of the problem upon the elements of the system.

(3) *Level 3*: The threat or impact assessment is carried out here. This level has to do with the operational impacts of system or subsystem capabilities that may be compromised as a result of one or more component problems. In other words the object here is to determine what operational capabilities are impaired or stalled.

Decision support and executive information systems

Any hardware/software system that provides information about its operation to the user of that system is a *decision support system.* The term has grown to be somewhat more selective through restriction of its meaning to systems that provide some intelligence to, or analysis of, the raw data collected, so that informed decisions can be made about and actions taken concerning that system. The collection, organization, and even decision-oriented analysis of information pertinent to network management operations is of little value unless human concurrence and control can be exercised over that information. Decision support systems provide this human-oriented capability using highly interactive design tools. Decision support systems were first developed and implemented in numerous ways and places within the military environment over the past 50 years. More recently, the concepts involved have been migrated to the commercial world for use in finance, manufacturing, service provisioning, and distribution arenas, and have begun to be known as executive information systems.

The decision support systems are not a substitute nor alternative for network management facilities, but rather they support the specific five functions defined by the OSI model for the total network management problem. These functions are: (1) fault monitoring; (2) performance monitoring; (3) configuration manage-ment; (4) accounting management; and, (5) security management.

Decision support, however, targets the three main issues within the realm of network management, these being planning, performance, and maintenance. Fault and operational data analysis feed the fault evaluation module. This information is used to update the system configuration module. The system configuration status and the operational data analysis modules feed performance evaluation that in turn provides input to the control implementation module that provides instructions to the system for re-configuration. Meanwhile, the periodic updating of the system configuration module activates the planning evaluation module which also contains the system goals. The network configuration files contain connection routing tables, equipment inventory, network topology, and element capabilities.

The external environment supplies the raw data needed for analysis. Trends and historical arrays of these data are stored in the database and available for manipulation through the use of the database management system. The model base provides a replication of reality as seen from the user's point of view. The model is a set of rules that expresses how the system should function, and how its operation is affected when it doesn't function properly.

External stimuli arriving at the input to the system are examined for correlation with the current status of the model as driven by the data items in the database. The decision support interface assembles the most appropriate view of the situation along with options to design or redesign a solution. To determine exactly what is appropriate is the challenge for the decision support interface. Presumably, there is a need to provide enough information in a short period of time and to package it in as meaningful a form as possible for the user to digest and react to. It is interesting to note that the technology is and has been available for many years to supply sophisticated decision support systems. Unifortunately, the pressure has not been there to force the development of these tools until recent years, partly due to the lack of competitive influences, or lack of complete understanding as to how these tools relate to a company's success. Now that the stimulus is present, there are several problems with which the decision support designer must grapple.

These problems are briefly outlined below:

(1) *Technology*: The technology systems needed or desired to solve the network management problem are many and varied. The technology problem usually revolves around the questions of speed, capacity, reliability, Physical and functional connectivity, and access to data.

(2) *Behaviour*: Decision and general psychological theory are areas of investigation that bear directly upon the decision support system and its utility. Decision theory is implemented in several ways, some of which rely on such classical approaches as Bayesian statistics and others that rely on expert systems approaches, such as rule-based methods that attempt to emulate human logic.

(3) *Computer-based systems*: Picking and using the right set of tools is the subject of this component of decision support systems. The computer instruments that are part of the decision system must have the capacity to provide the most natural and unthreatening view and control access to the operation. This includes the presentation, and switch control and other activation methodologies.

(4) *Tasking analysis*: Specific problems are subjected to an analysis of their situation and specific tasks are determined based upon these analyses. The task may be related to an outage report, overload or planning need, all of which result in some task definition that awaits human review and sometimes approval. The elements of each task may be carried out by diverse elements within the system, such as a computer system, expert system, human, or switching element.

The decision support system is just another step in a long line of technologies developed since World War 11 to cope with the needs and volume of data generated from and necessary for the technology revolution that spawned the information age. First, there was the electronic data processing (EDP) era that saw the collection of data about processes. Next, there was the management information system (MIS) era. During this period, a certain amount of intelligence was created by organizing the output of EDP into specific reports for management usage. Following this ' there was the time when great emphasis was placed upon management science and operations research (MS/OR) to assist management in making choices out of the volumes of MIS reports.

MS/OR helps one make decisions from highly structured information. Finally, there is now the era of decision support systems (DSSs). This is a set of technologies that allows the user to design his or her own solutions based upon incomplete information.

The expert system

Expert systems are a major element of decision support systems because they provide the intelligence needed for the decisions reached. They can be roughly equated to the model used internally to aid the decision process.

(1) *The inference engine*: The inference engine is that software program that uses the production rules to work out the logic of a particular problem. This is done mainly through sophisticated sequential searching and comparisons using lists supplemented with external facts. Additionally, the conclusions drawn are weighted by probabilities of success or correctness. Thus, facts are collected, hypotheses accessed, probabilistic judgments developed, and conclusions drawn that fit the initial facts.

(2) The rulebase: The rulebase is that segment of the database that contains the rules upon which the inference engine operates to resolve the problem at hand. The rule base is essentially a model of the system in which resides a representation of the system's structure, status, and history. The rulebase can be invoked to reveal the rulebase's formal logic, and its and parameter assignments.

(3) *The factbase*: The factbase is that portion of the database that provides the basic facts or data used by the inference engine to evaluate the rules, and therefore, to reach a conclusion. This information usually comes from external means, such as from attached or remote sensors, or from organized sources reached over communications channels, The structure of the factbase is extremely important to the effective use of the data available.

Expert maintenance systems were probably the first expert systems to be developed with computer technology and the decision support interfaces for such systems were and are, needless to say, important as well. The terms maintenance, fault control, and failure monitoring are sometimes used interchangeably to imply the same thing, i.e., that the maintenance system has the capacity to detect, identify, and resolve system problems. The decision support application that interfaces with the maintenance system has several requirements to satisfy in order to make it appropriate for the job at hand, and these requirements are summarized as follows:

(1) *identification of the problem*: The DSS must have access to the data necessary to determine that a problem has occurred. This determination many times surfaces as a result of several indicators as opposed to a single occurrence. Problem identification may come in many forms, such as failure of a parametric test, or a logic test.

(2) *Isolation of the problem*: Determining where the problem exists is many times not an easy task. The location may be masked by several other conditions or situations that make this step a difficult one. Testing for a specific location is sometimes an effective tool.

(3) *Association of the problem*: The exposure of the problem immediately stimulates a search of the previous times or situations during which the problem may have occurred. If no such circumstances have occurred, association can be established by reference to an operational model of the system. Such events and references provide a starting point for problem attack.

(4) *Implications of the problem*: The association of the problem with its place in the system often provides information that might implicate the problem with other system elements that the current problem may infect. The current problem may also imply or implicate other processes that are more pertinent to the malfunction or bottleneck situation.

(5) *Visualization of the problem*: A conceptualization of the problem as something that a human can appreciate is important in any system, expert or otherwise. Such a concept presentation can be provided as a graphical display or even a functioning picture of the system. The problem visualization is executed by simulation of the system functionality or processes and as a result will often suggest one or more solutions to the problem at hand.

(6) *Options for solving the problem*: The system simulation, isolation and association are the principal vehicles for enumerating the options for problem resolution. These processes provide a list of possible options that can be implemented. In addition, the options may carry a list of caveats and degrees of difficulty that may be encountered as a result of exercising each of these options.

The performance management system likewise has several uses for decision support. Such systems monitor operational traffic and, using decision support capabilities can anticipate bottlenecks, isolate operational trouble areas, and correlate fault messages with operational conditions. Examples of performance management systems implemented include NEMESYS and XTRAC. NEMESYS is an AT&T tool developed to assist in fighting congestion in the inter-exchange carrier business. It is based upon techniques to optimize performance during overload or outage emergencies. Information on the number of and reasons for call blockages is collected and used to derive suggestions for call rerouting. XTRAC is a system that also reallocates resources based upon priority considerations. Performance measurement and problem resolution based upon performance problems, are both associated with the types of performance problems incurred within the network whether they be location specific or time based. These types of problems can be categorized as follows:

Routine capacity overload

This is the most common problem handled by a performance management system. It occurs as a result of some cable or transmission route becoming undersized for the load placed upon it as traffic increases over that route with time. In this type of situation, the route experiences periodic durations of overload at an increasing frequency and for an increasing duration per overload period as the general loading becomes greater.

Focused overload

The focused overload results from sudden increases in local demand due to some type of emergency either man-made or natural. Examples might include severe weather or a nuclear power plant problem. The focused overload becomes most troublesome when the facility needed to complete the circuit itself is the object of the overload, such as the telephone end office, because in this case, there is little or no rerouting possible around the problem.

General overload

In this type of overload situation, the overload is not localized as with the focused overload. It is ubiquitous throughout the network. An example of a general overload situation would be Mother's Day or Christmas. During a general overload period, there is little rerouting and few alternatives available to resolve the problem. The problem will usually go away in a few hours. Recent catastrophes, however, have shown that general overload may not go away in a few hours. Certain local problems such as that in New York City that affected the entire air traffic system and the software bugs that affected new telephone switches around the country are problems that may be harbingers of more dire situations in the future.

Facility failure

Facility failure is a situation where there may be a failure of a trunk group as a result of weather problems. Here the situation resembles a focused failure except that the capacity has been reduced due to equipment failure as opposed to an increase in demand. In many such cases, the problem can be circumvented by use of spare components or switching around the problem.

Planning management systems

The typical planning function occurs either to support cost, schedule, or technical performance objectives. One example of a planning management system is one which operates as an expert assistant in designing networks. It is called *DESIGNET* and acts as a configuration tool for boards, racks ' cables, interfaces, etc., at each site in a network environment. The DESIGNET module provides the user with many different views of the network configuration and performs sensitivity analyses by answering why and what-if questions for the operator. Another such planning system was developed at GTE Laboratories and is known as *MARVEL.*

As the technology becomes ever more capable of supporting sophisticated information needs, the possibilities for commercial decision support systems, referred to as executive information systems, approach ever more rapidly. The Frito-Lay company is one such example of effective technology transfer from military battlefields to commercial battlefield. Frito-Lay has developed a distributed, layered executive information system that provides this snack company food for action as well as thought. The system is available in at least two flavors for both the upper and management teams so that they can track, plan, and execute their operations more effectively. The main objective of this executive information system is to carve up the massive array of constant data flowing to the operation into small enough pieces that can be digested by even the most modest of the desktop systems at the levels indicated. Each targeted display station also receives the data in a form that is concise and focused upon the concerns of that particular station user.

The company started at the bottom of the management strata and built the information system upward. The system has two types of information, that pertaining to the Frito-Lay products and that pertaining to competitors' products. The basic information gathered is obtained from the field supply trucks that collect and enter into portable computers the inventory levels at each store and order information. The systems also have the capability to print invoices for product delivered at each stop on a route. At the end of a day the portable computer is interfaced to a larger computer at a regional distribution center to which the invoices are copied, and from which pricing and promotional information is received for use on the next day's route. The timely volume of data now flowing into the company allowed the upper management to be in closer touch with current operations, thus providing them with the means to avert problems as they started. The information now available to upper management, in graphical and pictorial chart form, included reports on regional status, product status, sales status, production, and delivery status. Information on competitors is also available to company executives and is updated weekly. Direct and indirect expenses are also tracked and available for evaluation. For product promotion, the company developed a trade development system that allows sales representatives to show store managers how combinations of Frito-Lay products with other non-Frito products could stimulate sales. Finally, the system also collects information about competitors, using the same portable computers that the delivery drivers use to track inventory and generate invoices from placed orders. Such information includes competitor pricing and presentations and is used to evaluate how the company is doing versus its competitors.

Integration of data into meaningful and useful information are referred to in the aerospace-defense sector as decision support systems (DSSs), or executive information systems (EISs), as they are known in civilian-commercial environments. DSS/EIS is viewed in some contexts as a simulation dealing with "what if' questions. Also, EIS may be construed as a means of tracking resource usage, while DSS may be interpreted as a means of requesting direction. By varying the input parameter values, or the model, the consequences can be determined, and a family of answers can be developed. Multi-variate changes can also be evaluated in many cases using the simulation approach. Whether or not DSS/EIS is classified as a simulation or an on-line control, it functions to provide the user some degree of oversight with regard to the telecommunications system, and in that regard, it is a valuable network management tool. As such a tool, the DSS/EIS can be used in the background to play out scenarios about the functioning of the network, and the various faults that may befall the system.

The idea behind the DSS is to provide the observer with the best view of the situation, resources, actions, and options available to him or her that can be constructed. In this regard, DSSs are not a substitute or alternative for network management facilities, but rather they support the specific five functions defined by the OSI model for the total network management problem. These functions are: (1) fault monitoring (2) performance monitoring; (3) configuration management; (4) accounting management; and, (5) security management.

Decision support, however, targets the three main issues within the realm of network management, these being planning, performance, and maintenance. Fault and operational data analysis feed the fault evaluation module. This information is used to update the system configuration module. The system configuration status and the operational data analysis modules feed performance evaluation that in turn provides input to the control implementation module that provides instructions to the system for reconfiguration. Meanwhile, the periodic updating of the system configuration module activates the planning evaluation module, which also contains the system goals. The network configuration files contain connection routing tables, equipment inventory, network topology, and element capabilities.

DSS/EIS is not intended to be an entirely simulation-style tool, as will be seen at the end of this chapter. Often, in the early stages of DSS/ElS development, the capability is concerned with tying together remote locations via communications links. Additionally, the objective is to provide users with the accesses to multiple databases. And lastly, the system is completed by supplying report generators. Report generators may undergo a lengthy or even indefinite development period where the generator progresses from data presentation, to data transformation into parameters of value, to simulations, and finally to intelligent applications. Such applications may use rules, heuristics, or any of a number of references to generate suggestions, or decision-action situations. In this chapter we look at the use of DSS/EIS to perform information assessment and plan generation, evaluation, and execution. The tools required to perform these tasks include the system architecture, the user interfaces needed, and the various analysis aids. All of these tasks involved and the tools needed will be addressed here. The next few sections will discuss briefly some of the distinctions associated with decision or executive information support.

The assessment of, and recommendations for present and future actions associated with a particular subject are the domain of the decision support or EIS system. Present action analysis and decision making involves the assimilation of current data received into the system. Such data is can be received in real-time or via some other slower methods, such as telephone relay, hardcopy, manual collection, etc. Future action analysis and decision making involves the use of simulation tools to reach conclusions based upon current trends, and projected outcomes.

The buildup of DSS/EIS systems in a decision-oriented environment requires the use of modular concepts. The use of building blocks is usually necessary due to the complexity of the processes involved and also to provide incremental features for the user. Finally, it is critical that the DSS provide the right vehicle for decisions. It is a given here that decision support will not replace decision makers in human form, but it can be a powerful assistant to the human decision maker.

Distinctions between DSS and other decision aids

MIS, as a toot set, is one of the closest such tools to DSS, and therefore a source of confusion for someone involved in this area. MIS appears to be more concerned with the efficiency than the effectiveness of the measures derived. MIS takes reported data and distills it down to needed measures of operation. Additionally, MIS appears to be more occupied with current, and past data sets than developing future or predictive models.

Another type of decision aid is simulation. Simulation is a generic term applied to any procedure that utilizes probabilities, obtained from current or past performances, that are applied to projections of future performance. Simulation has reached significant heights of sophistication with graphic representations, interfaces to other programs, and artificial intelligence features. Simulation tools are very sophisticated these days, and provide some of the valuable features of DSS capabilities.

The decision support cycle

The decision process is the culmination of several steps aimed at affecting an outcome of some objective. The utility of developing an effective DSS lies in the results it creates, i.e., its validity, the time it takes to generate an answer, and its consistency, i.e., reliability of its results. If the results are within an acceptable range of error, the system is considered to meet a certain set of expectations, sometimes known as specifications. If the system turns out the same set of results time-after-time, it is demonstrating an agreement with functional requirements. And, if it meets response time constraints, it is meeting both specifications and functional requirements. The first part of the process involves data observation (sensors), and data collection (fusion) of events within the environment.

The steps following the decision action are part of the executive function, i.e., the translation of decision into a command structure, communication of orders to the command, the execution of orders, and the responses elicited by the execution of orders upon the environment. The communications infrastructure is usually the object of initial interest. In real-life implementations, such as those cited at the end of this book, many such DSSs started with ad hoc communications systems implemented to satisfy increased communications requirements between functional and/or geographical units. At some point later, DSS/EIS capabilities were conceived and developed separately.

First, the decision support system must be able to receive data relevant to the decision environment. The selection and use of the right input data sets, is critical to the effective generation of decision alternatives. Second, the key to the success and evaluation of the DSS is its ability to measure the impact of previous decisions from responses obtained from the environment. Third, some form of communications medium is needed to put the decisions into action. No DSS worthy of the name can be effective without a collection facility, feedback capability, and a means to put the decision into effect.

Architectures

Generic requirements

The challenge for DSSs is not that they must keep pace with the increasing influx of data, but rather that they must do a better job of making sense of the data that is collected. The typical DSS will have a series of attributes associated with it, some of which are:

(1) timeliness

(2) filtering

(3) user aids

(4) interfaces to other systems

(5) intelligence

The degree to which values and ranges are assigned to these attributes, will determine their utility in the decision part of DSS. The variety of attributes available for analysis will dictate the support part of the DSS, and the breadth of sensors providing input will give meaning to the system part of the DSS expression.

Some brief definition of these attributes is provided below.

Timeliness

Timeliness, as an attribute, means that the incoming data must bear some resemblance to other incoming data sets in order for proper evaluations to be made. The timing of inputs often provides valuable clues as to the relationships between reports, the validity of reports, or their reliability.

Filtering

Filtering is the ability of the DSS to make selective judgments about information, and/or minor decisions, the object being to separate information from what is crucial to the decision process. 'Many times, the distinction between necessary and unnecessary information helps draw lines about the credibility of the process or the results obtained.

For instance, the value of an operation may be its safety impact as opposed to cost control or revenue impact. The latter measures may, therefore, be somewhat unnecessary or irrelevant when evaluating the basic value of the system. Reports about such issues may, therefore, be filtered out so that the system can evaluate reports of interest to the user.

User aids

User aids are the tools by which the user can distill and clarify information into something meaningful, and therefore, something of importance to the mission of the DSS. User aids give the system a certain utility so that the intended user can exercise the system effectively. These aids include the presentation formats, user interfaces, the analysis tools, correlation capabilities with other data, and interfaces to other systems.

Interfaces

Interfaces to other systems are the connectivity issues, both physical and functional, that allow data and decisions to be conveyed to other systems, and that make reception of data possible into the system. The ability of the system to interface to other systems also gives it additional power to draw upon resources not part of its basic make-up. This interfacing, again, requires communication means such that the sharing of data lends increased power to each unit, redundancy within the network, and access to databases not possible with isolated units.

Intelligence

Intelligence is the internal composition of the DSS that allows it to exercise some degree of problem solving, and range of action. Intelligence is usually equated to such features as artificial intelligence, machine vision, and robotics.

Types of DSSs

The various types of decision support systems are described and delineated here. One such type, the MIS system, was mentioned above. It was one of the first organized decision structures to be developed in the early era of computerized data manipulation. Since then, more sophisticated means of decision support have been developed, but MIS systems still exist in most companies as decision aids.

(1) Report generator systems (similar to MIS)

(2) Data analysis systems

(3) Analysis information systems

(4) Accounting models

(5) Representational models

(6) Optimization models
(7) Suggestion models

Report generator systems

The first and primary information need is access to data items. MIS was developed to meet this need. Implicit in this delivery is the immediacy of the data item availability. Thus, MIS stresses on-line accesses to the supporting databases, with rather basic user interfaces to bridge the databases and the report generation.

Data analysis systems

Such systems are developed to perform very specific analyses. Users could manipulate the data to generate very specific reports. The range of analyses is limited to the applications software of the system.

Analysis information systems

This type of system utilizes relational databases and modeling capabilities to create the data measures required. Such systems have some latitude as to the nature and form of measures created.

Accounting models

Accounting models use definitional procedures to calculate the outcomes of particular circumstances. These systems are used to calculate the consequences of possible financial decisions.

Representational models

Modeling used in this type of system is directed at attributes and items that are not necessarily accounting-oriented in nature. In such systems accounting terms are derived as opposed to being entered as parameters, as would be the case with accounting packages.

Optimization models

These systems provide the ability to profile situations mathematically that provide the best answers among the modelled circumstances. Examples of such capabilities are the required price and inventory points necessary to achieve customer demands.

Suggestion models

Suggestion models offer recommended courses of action as opposed to offering the tradeoffs that are part of optimization models. This is an outcome approach as opposed to an evaluation-based approach to modelling.

The basic configuration for any DSS/EIS includes the following elements:

Interface to the outside world

This feature can involve environmental or process sampling, database interfaces, and interfaces to other computational systems. External interfaces for network management systems usually involves an array of sensory inputs provided via communications services, e.g., private line, packet network, and dial-up facilities.

Buffering and storage

The data stream from the external interfaces must usually have a temporary repository while it is waiting for processing. Such temporary storage is provided by the buffer/storage control and memory area of the computer. At this point, some preprocessing is also performed on the incoming data sets to eliminate such problems as duplicate and unreliable data.

Algorithmic manipulation

The main DSS/EIS activity is concerned with the procedural control and transformation of the external data stream. This process may range from summary data reporting, solutions of equations and subsequent reporting, multiple solutions to equations used to generate graphical representations with the help of graphics generators, simulation systems to allow projections and to play what-if games, and rule-based derivations to isolate likely solutions.

Human-machine interface

This element has already been discussed to a large extent. In summary, the human action is directed at assuring that the required input data is available, the appropriate processing is performed, the parameters and answers obtained are reasonable, and that the proper output or results are reported. Such a set of activities can either be labor intensive, or with the help of expert systems technology, human judgment can sometimes be replicated and substituted effectively.

Generalized architectures

The external environment supplies the raw data needed for analysis. Trends and historical arrays of these data are stored in the database and available for manipulation through the use of the database management system. The model base provides a replication of reality as seen from the user's point of view. The model is a set of rules that expresses how the system should function, and how its operation is affected when it doesn't function property.

External stimuli arriving at the input to the system are examined for correlation with the current status of the model as driven by the data items in the database. The decision support interface assembles the most appropriate view of the situation along with options to design or redesign a solution. To determine exactly what is appropriate is the challenge for the decision support interface. Presumably, there is a need to provide enough information in a short period of time and to package it in as meaningful a form as possible for the user to digest and react to.

It is interesting to note that the technology is and has been available for many years to supply sophisticated decision support systems. Unfortunately, the pressure has not been there to force the development of these tools until recent years partly due to the lack of competitive influences or lack of complete understanding as to how these tools relate to a company's success. Now, however, that the stimulus is present, there are several problems with which the decision support designer must grapple. These problems are briefly outlined below:

The technology systems needed or desired to solve the network management problem are many and varied. The technology problem usually revolves around the questions of speed, capacity, reliability, physical and functional connectivity, and access to data.

Decision and general psychological theory are areas of investigation that bear directly upon the DSS and its utility. Decision theory is implemented in several ways some of which rely on such classical approaches as Bayesian statistics and others of which rely on expert systems approaches, such as rule-based methods that attempt to emulate human logic.

Picking and using the right set of tools is the subject of this component of DSSs. The computer instruments that are part of the decision system must have the capacity to provide the most natural and unthreatening view and control access to the operation. This includes the presentation, and switch control and other activation methodologies.

Specific problems are subjected to an analysis of their situation and specific tasks are determined based upon these analyses. The task may be related to an outage report, overload or planning need, all of which result in some task definition that awaits human review and sometimes approval. The elements of each task may be carried out by diverse elements within the system, such as a computer system, expert system, human, or switching element. The DSS is just another step in a long line of technologies developed since World War 11 to cope with the needs and volume of data generated from different collection devices. The decision support systems that followed became the stimuli for the technology revolution that spawned the information age. First, there was the *electronic data processing* (EDP) era that saw the collection of vast amounts of data about processes, from financial to scientific. Next, there was the *management information system* (MIS) era. During this period, a certain amount of intelligence was created by organizing the output of EDP into specific reports for management usage. The term, intelligence, may be misused, because the results were little more than reports segmented to provide insights into specific areas of the operation. Following this, there was the time when great emphasis was placed upon *management science and operations research* (MS/OR) to assist management in making choices out of the volumes of MIS reports. MS/OR helps one make decisions from highly structured information.

Finally, there is now the era of DSS. This is a set of technologies that allows the user to design his or her own solutions based upon incomplete information. This thrust provides a very fertile ground from which to implement many forms of smart systems technologies. The initial attempts at DSSs have been far from what was envisioned, but the potential is there for this evolutionary progress.

Expert systems are a major element of DSSs because they provide the intelligence needed for the decisions reached. They can be roughly equated to the model(s) used internally to aid the decision process. They are:

The inference engine

That software program that uses the production rules to work out the logic of a particular problem. This is done mainly through sophisticated sequential searching and comparisons using lists supplemented with external facts.

The rule base

That database segment that contains the rules upon which the inference engine operates to resolve the problem at hand. The rule base is essentially a model base in which resides a representation of someone's version of reality, and reveals the rule base's form of logic.

The fact base

That portion of the database that provides the basic facts or data used by the inference engine to evaluate the rules, and therefore, to reach a conclusion. This information usually comes from external means, such as from attached or remote sensors, or from organized sources reached over communications channels.

Expert maintenance systems

Expert maintenance systems were probably the first expert systems to be developed with computer technology, and the decision support interfaces for such systems were and are, needless to say, important as well. The terms maintenance, fault control, and failure monitoring are sometimes used interchangeably to imply about the same thing, i.e., that the maintenance system has the capacity to detect, identify, and resolve system problems. The decision support application that interfaces with the maintenance system has several requirements to satisfy in order to make it appropriate for the job at hand, and these requirements are summarized as follows

Identification of the problem

The DSS must have access to the data necessary to determine that a problem has occurred. This determination many times surfaces as a result of several indicators as opposed to a single occurrence. Problem identification may come in many forms, such as failure of a parametric test, or a logic test.

Isolation of the problem

Determining where the problem exists is many times not an easy task. The location may be masked by several other conditions or situations that make this step a difficult one. Testing for a specific location is sometimes an effective tool.

Association of the problem

The exposure of the problem immediately stimulates a search of the previous times or situations during which the problem may have occurred. If no such circumstances have occurred, association can be established by reference to an operational model of the system. Such events and references provide a starting point for problem attack.

Implications of the problem

The association of the problem with its place in the system often provides information that might implicate the problem with other system elements that the current problem may infect. The current problem may also imply or implicate other processes that are more pertinent to the malfunction or bottleneck situation.

Visualization of the problem

A conceptualization of the problem as something that a human can appreciate is important in any system, expert or otherwise. Such a concept presentation can be provided as a graphical display or even a functioning picture of the system. The problem visualization is executed by simulation of the system functionality or processes and as a result will often suggest one or more solutions to the problem at hand.

Options for solving the problem

The system simulation, isolation and association are the principal vehicles for enumerating the options for problem resolution. These processes provide a list of possible options that can be implemented. In addition, the options may carry a list of caveats and degrees of difficulty that may be encountered as a result of exercising each of these options.

Performance management systems

The performance management system likewise has several uses for decision support. Such systems monitor operational traffic and, using decision support capabilities can anticipate bottlenecks, isolate operational trouble areas, and correlate fault messages with operational conditions. Examples of performance management systems implemented include NEMESYS and XTRAC. NEMESYS is an AT&T tool developed to assist in fighting congestion in the inter-exchange carrier business. It is based upon techniques to optimize performance during overload or outage emergencies. Information on the number of and reasons for call blockages is collected and used to derive suggestions for call rerouting, XTRAC is a system that also reallocates resources based upon priority considerations.

Performance measurement and problem resolution based upon performance problems are both associated with the types of performance problems incurred within the network whether they be location specific or time based. These types of problems can be categorized as follows:

Routine capacity overload

This is the most common problem handled by a performance management system. It occurs as a result of some cable or transmission route becoming undersized for the load placed upon it as traffic increases over that route with time. In this type of situation, the route experiences periodic durations of overload at an increasing frequency and for an increasing duration per overload period as the general loading becomes greater.

The focused overload results from sudden increases in local demand due to some type of emergency either manmade or natural. Examples might include severe weather or a nuclear power plant problem. The focused overload becomes most troublesome when the facility needed to complete the circuit itself is the object of the overload, such as the telephone end office, because in this case, there is little or no rerouting possible to get around the problem. In this type of overload situation, the overload is not localized as with the focused overload. It is ubiquitous throughout the network. An example of a general overload situation would be Mother's Day or Christmas. During a general overload period, there is little rerouting and few alternatives available to resolve the problem. The problem will usually go away in a few hours. Recent catastrophes, however, have shown that general overload may not go away in a few hours. Certain local problems such as the one in New York City that affected the entire air traffic system and the software bugs that affected new telephone switches around the country are problems that may be harbingers of more dire situations in the future.

Facility failure is a situation where there may be a failure of a trunk group as a result of weather problems. Here the situation resembles a focused failure except that the capacity has been reduced due to equipment failure as opposed to an increase in demand. In many such cases, the problem can be gotten around by use of spare components or switching around the problem.

The typical planning function occurs either to support cost, schedule, or technical performance objectives. One example of a planning management system is one which operates as an expert assistant in designing networks. It is called *Designet* and acts as a configuration tool for boards, racks, cables, interfaces, etc. at each site in a network environment. The DESIGNET module provides the user with many different views of the network configuration and performs sensitivity analyses by answering why and whatif questions for the operator. Another such planning system was developed at GTE Laboratories and is known as MARVEL.

The history of human interface with computers begins with human interaction with machinery. Early computational systems used switches and hand fed tape to operate and program such machinery. Soon, the user interface developed some more complex relationships that will be discussed further below. The progression of computer input interfacing ranges from keyboard mechanical inputs to touch screens. Output interfacing has progressed from scrolling tabular presentations to three dimensional illustrations of output information. Interfaces are divided into three categories, namely formal, natural language, and graphic interface dialogues. These various dialogues are discussed below.

Formal dialogue

As mentioned above, early computers were programmed and operated by switches, supplemented with tapes to input a large amount of data, Later typewriter-style keyboards were introduced to facilitate the operator's use of dedicated and time-share system.

Natural language dialogue

Input specifications have developed from the point where computer control required a strict protocol in order to have the user's desires obeyed by the computer. This progression has been greatly enhanced through the use of the icon, or graphic representation, to substitute for the laborious and error-prone typed input.

Graphics interface dialogue

Icons have become the graphics tools of choice for human-machine interface. They assume the attributes of most of the previously typed file information, security, and movement specifications. Currently, icons are controlled by any of the formal dialogue methods. In the future they are likely to be controlled by touch screen or even brainwave methods. The formal dialogue, natural language, and graphics interfaces are all involved on the input side of the system. The output side is characterized by increasingly sophisticated displays and interactions of these display buffers with external systems and databases, as well as with special display modes, such as color, scanned displays, and hardcopy generators. Input devices range from scanners to biomechanic body-sensing devices to voice activators.

While the variety of input devices is almost unlimited, the corresponding output is limited to three-dimensional and time-related imagery coupled with some form of sound accompaniment.

Planning

The development of a plan suitable for a particular DSS/EIS application begins with a rigorous elaboration of the requirements. In some cases the requirements are simply to integrate the information flow. More elaborate plans call not only for the integration of the information flow but also the ability to make unstructured requests for information and/or analyses to which the system can respond using built in intelligence, drawing from all data resources available.

At the low end, the DSS/EIS is supported by some type of data communications capability with, at the very least, some type of E-mail facility. The high end DSS/EIS is equipped with a distributed data processing facility, fully capable of sophisticated AI-based decision support. Within a short time asynchronous transfer mode (ATM), a broadband packet-based switching and transport technology will become available on a wide scale. With this capability, the developer will have almost unlimited capacity to specify different combinations of distributed, multimedia data for the target user population. Even the low end developer and users have plenty of decisions to make regarding their communications commitments to technologies and equipments. As the user becomes more comfortable with the communications capabilities, the next major hurdle is that of accessing the various databases and the protocol differences that invariably plague the melding of disparate data sources for access by single applications programs. The third challenge is that of managing this diverse network in terms of geography, database management, security and privileges, and communications capacity for each locale. The development of nonintelligent report generators is next and is no small task even for the dedicated systems engineer. The types and varieties of such reports can be staggering, if the commitment to DSS/EIS is really there.

The final step is that of infusing smart systems technologies into the design and implementation. For now, however, it can be said that expert systems, for example, will be pervasive in the decision maker's office of the 1990s. Some companies, such as Mrs. Field's Cookies, have taken a very aggressive position relative to DSS/EIS by setting up a "lights out" business operation that essentially makes all operational decisions with only veto power on the part of the human overseer. The current market for decision support is estimated to be about $600 million during the decade of the 1990s. The current vendors of EIS include IBM and Software Publishing, with possible likely entrants to be Borland, Lotus, and Microsoft.

Tools

The strategy being applied by most vendors in the emerging EIS marketplace is one that emphasizes connectivity first, integrated reporting facilities second, and freestyle query/response capabilities third. This approach is best exemplified by the architecture posed by IBM, which is the basic architecture being put forth by other vendors as well. In this approach the host, or hosts, are the central repositories for all incoming data or file transfers from other locations, internal or external alike. The host computers distribute requested data to their destinations that, in the case of the IBM product, call for routing via LU 6.2, IBM's communications interface for external PC/LAN configurations, 3270 terminals via their controllers, and via direct connection to DOS and OS/2 environments. The LU 6.2 interface also provides connection to various environments on the LAN, such as OS/2, DOS, and eventually Windows, UNIX, and Macintosh.

Other EIS vendors, such as Holistic Systems, have moved ahead insofar as the current wave of EIS direction is concerned. The first concentration of EIS offerings was in the area of graphically oriented, navigation interfaces that provided the user with ability to move into increasingly deeper levels of data using pre-defined penetration schema. These interfaces are supported by generalized as well as specialized algorithmic engines to do a lot of the preprocessing and parameter calculations. The newer wave of EIS offerings will aim at greater distributed sources and destinations and will increasingly emphasize DSS/EIS tasking at the desktop and greater simplification of the query/response process.

Smart systems can be categorized to a variety of expert and neural systems applications, usually implemented in software, ranging from maintenance advisors, to decision support modules, to pattern understanding, and sometimes including natural language interfaces for the human operators. The characteristics of a processing entity, that qualifies it as being an intelligent, or smart, system are summarized below. Network management systems, for which smart capabilities are contemplated, should be examined for compatibility with these characteristics. The whole thrust of technological innovation from the industrial revolution onward has been to extend and improve upon the capacities and capabilities of the human operator. Intelligent systems, to be referred to here as smart systems, are merely another step in that logical extension of human abilities in the telecommunications arena. To be more exact, smart systems are aimed at the extension of our ability to reason and learn. In order to emulate the human abilities for reasoning, associating, discriminating, and interpreting, one must turn to the model from which the conclusions are drawn, i.e., the human brain. Many such references are made to the brain in several places in this book. Smart systems are viewed as subsets of the total apparatus of the system that oversee some purposeful mission, in this case the telecommunications network operation and support. These systems have the capability to draw conclusions and implement or recommend decisions based upon the inference of and reference to facts available to those systems. They, of necessity, must be able to generate, transmit, receive, and interpret communications between themselves and the controlling elements of the system, these controlling elements, many times, being human. In addition, they must be capable of some form of reasoning or logic process that allows them to reach their inferences or their recommended reference points. And, finally, smart systems must have access to real-time or external information sources and the reasoning framework, called by such names as rule base, frame base, etc., necessary to act upon these external data sources. The importance of smart systems with regard to telecommunications technology developments, and in particular network management, cannot be over-emphasized. In today's competitive environments, coupled with differing communications options available to the buyer, such as wireless, broadband, etc., the availability of the telecommunications platforms their services is critical for ongoing customer satisfaction. This availability can only be realized through effective network management systems implemented using smart systems tools.

The system's knowledge should be *coherent*, i.e., it should be capable of being shared among all the modules within the system, be commonly available to these modules, and adhere to a common formatting structure, taxonomy, and lexicon. In conventional processing programs, information is segmented and parsed so as to be available to only one or a few processing modules. Distributed database systems, in a far-flung and complex network management system, provide this coherent knowledge reservoir by providing a consistency and accessibility of data.

All data available to the system should be accessible to all the intelligent modules regardless of the potential variety of data structures and access methods used in the individual database systems servicing the system. Conventional programs are usually constrained to interface with one database system because the interface driver software is designed for only one database system. Integrated access provides the capability to reformat and translate data files from one system environment to another. Thus, the subnetwork managers must be supported with data translators, so that access to needed data can be had. Integrated access also requires that a security system be established so as to provide appropriate levels of access privileges.

To some greater or lesser extent, the reasoning and understanding used by the system should be made available to the user on demand through the use of informal-style questions that the user can pose to the system for resolution, or as part of a more lengthy dialogue with the system. In conventional software, the algorithms used by the program are seldom made known to the user during module execution. At a minimum, these algorithms should be made available to the user, the logic used should be published, on demand, to the user, and decision criteria should be made available as required. This facility enhances the network manager and gives its decisions or recommendations credibility.

The execution of decisions either reached by or supported through smart systems, is a more far-reaching proposition that will entail further research and incremental development work in this area. However, as this time arrives, the affects of intelligent systems can be hypothesized. Intelligent submodules should, eventually, be able to initiate appropriate actions on their own as conditions warrant. Execution of these modules depends upon external stimuli as opposed to user initiation. These smart sensors can also be integrated into a data *fusion* module so that filtering and data integration can make decision support more accurate and timely. The topic of *data fusion* will be discussed in more detail in the next section.

The intelligent modules should be able to extend the expertise of the overall system and to identify inconsistencies. Because these programs are dealing with a view of the entire system, they are in a position to determine the limits and extent of the system's capabilities as well as identify analytical inconsistencies. Knowledge is currently acquired through information input by way of rules, or through references to desired results. In such circumstances, the rules involved are updated from outside sources as well. Research and some limited development efforts to date have attempted to train systems to acquire and use acquired knowledge to reach new conclusions. These systems are known as neural networks, and are based upon a human-interpreted emulation of the operation of the vertebrate brain. The acquisition and use of knowledge in network management, such as that provided through neural networks, makes the operation more stable, and system reports more believable and accurate.

Further down the product development road yet is the ability for the smart system to solve problems outside the realm of the intended application. This is known as non-domain-specific problem solving. The intelligent system should be capable of solving problems not anticipated by the developer. Sometimes the smart system leads to a point of departure not anticipated by the developer by identifying a condition that requires further investigation. These requirements are best handled through a system capable of learning on its own, such as neural networks. The technologies of network management are constantly crossing into areas not anticipated by the developers. This tool, if properly implemented, could be a great time saver and problem solver for the system administrator.

Data sorting

Here we will begin to survey and explore the various elements of the network management system that can be implemented with smart features. To begin with, there are several areas in the network system into which smart systems technology can begin to be infused, as a result of architectural design. These areas include front-end monitoring, and data fusion, which is closely aligned with the overall data collection process. *Data fusion* is the physical and logical integration of temporally and spatially dispersed reports. Data fusion, although not always explicitly stated in discussions on network management, is also an integral task in any network management system even though it may not be implemented to any detailed level. The first area is the front-end monitoring of system components. Sensors monitor, evaluate, and report on component performance, and status. Sensors, as a general category of performance monitoring, have been around since the advent of electronics. Up until recent times, they have been relegated to the position of reporting on such problems as framing errors, transmission errors, and the like. Since the system sensors, as we will characterize them, are operating as elements within the network components in locations remote from the monitoring and control points, we would like for them to be somewhat autonomous in their roles and actions. The various functioning components and elements of the telecommunications network are usually the sources of status information about the network that is needed for the assessment of the total system. Each is a sensor of sorts that collects and reports on the status of its environment.

The second area into which smart systems technology can be infused into the network is that point at which the sensor data are brought together, and typed, sorted, and categorized. This is the data fusion function, and comes in two varieties, these being direct fusion and indirect fusion. Direct fusion is an integration of sensor data in a local environment, e.g., among the various equipments within a communications node. Here certain problems of distance, communications relay, and so forth, are minimized or negated due to the localization involved. Indirect fusion is the integration of widely dispersed sensor data collected in, and through, many nodes and transmission paths. Information flowing into these areas must be continually evaluated both individually and in relation to other data in order to track the status and performance of the system. It is interesting to note that the very act of data integration has an impact upon the conclusions of system and subsystem health, and when added to the fact that synergistic data can be derived from multiple inputs and/or confirmations, the whole issue of data fusion becomes even more powerful. Unfortunately, data fusion requires additional effort to implement and even more effort to take full advantage of it. Thus, like everything else, there is a trade-off to be considered when considering its relative advantages versus its disadvantages.

There are six main tasks associated with data fusion. Association is especially critical, since it is the point at which reports from seemingly divergent areas, but concerned with the same objects, are matched. Correlation is then invoked to determine the extent to which these initially matched reports are actually related. These data fusion tasks are:

Collection: This task is performed by the sensors at the collection sites specifically, or as part of the relay process of data from the collection sites to the fusion site(s). The collection process is critical for the data fusion activity, because the data reports have to be separable and definable for later correlation and collation. The number of incoming reports can be staggering, so a network management system must be provided that meets these data rate needs. The collection task can help mitigate the number of incoming reports by examining reports for redundancies, duplications and repeats, and eliminating such reports.

Alignment: This is the point at which filtering occurs. Filtering consists of clearing up ambiguity, as much as possible, about the individual incoming reports. Additionally, alignment means to assign credibility to individual reports, so that such reports can be given even more confidence as the data fusion process continues to the next steps.

Association: This task involves updating and composition of report states. The task of associating reports, either the same reports over multiple time periods, or different reports relating to the same circumstances is handled in this task. The object here is to match different reports with the same object or event, and to single out redundant and/or unnecessary reports, either from the same or different sources

Correlation: This is the point at which ambiguity resolution occurs when the association process cannot resolve ambiguous reports. Correlation is of its nature a chance situation; thus, techniques suitable to the specific network management situations must be employed to minimize the probabilities of errors.

Classification: This task is directed at the identification of a class of problems from which more specific elemental identification can be made later. The integration of several sensors is usually involved accompanied by some form of decision process to specify class I.D. and confidence level. In a network management environment, classification may involve categorizing reports into different levels of alarm, different levels of maintenance attention, different levels of operational alerts and so on. Thus, a multi-level, multi-category set of needs arise.

Control: This task is involved in the allocation of direct sensor systems, their optimization, and their prioriti-zation. Control encompasses a range of tasks and functions too vast to address here. In essence, the control subject involves the acts of delivering the right information to the right point at the right time. Decision support/ executive information systems are all about the problem of control and its ongoing resolution. Because of the increasing complexities of equipment, functions, and sizes of networks, the various smart systems technologies to be addressed here are critical to the effective control of telecommunications networks.

Data fusion is a more complex subject than it may appear. The network data involved are many times from vastly different environments and from different vendor equipment arrays. The formats vary from each other and the correct interpretation of data contents can be very different. Data fusion is also the point in the data collection and analysis functions which the confidence of incoming status data is confirmed or calculated. As a at matter of fact, the major reason for implementing data fusion is to verify network status indicators, and to assess confidence in the ensemble of incoming data elements.

Data fission is the opposite of data fusion. Data fission is the process of finding an object of interest in an array of previously collected objects. Data fusion involves the act of sorting individual objects, locating, then labeling them for future fission operations at which point they are split out for usage. Clearly these two processes are mutually dependent, because the efficacy of the fused data makes searching very dependent upon the time element which in turn determines the usefulness of the total process. The last area of smart systems infusion into the network management scheme is the point of decision making. This point is often referred to, in the defense sector, as decision support, and, in the commercial sector, as the executive information support function. Decision support involves the use of categorized and sorted data from the data fusion function, coupled with decision criteria, frames of reference, decision criteria, and the decision maker's preferences, to arrive at a rational course of action.

Each of these topics will be briefly addressed and associated with each other before a more thorough examination is made in the ensuing chapters. The smart system concept is broken down into three main segments, namely, sensors, data fusion and decision support. The primary operational segments of the communications system, its data converters and transmitters, its switches and relays, and its monitoring and control units are each roughly equated to each of the smart systems segments, e.g., sensors are associated with the data converters and transmitters, and so forth.

The selection of an architecture that provides the system coverage, responsiveness, and diagnosis capabilities is always difficult, partly because no two telecommunications systems are the same, and partly because these systems lack homogeneity. The typical approach has been to integrate individual network management subsystems using an additional network manager that recognizes the attributes and characteristics of each of those subsystems with which it interfaces. Another approach is to bypass the subsystem network managers, and to route each of the equipment elements to a single network manager. Yet another approach has been to utilize the existing performance characteristics of the subsystems and to infer the maintenance and performance of each equipment on the basis of these characteristics. Smart systems greatly enhance this latter approach. The intelligent features of each of these segments is infused into these segments via the main avenues defined, i.e., sensors, fusion, and decision support. Thus, the sensors associated with the data converters and transmitters are designed and implemented so as to incorporate Artificial Intelligence (AI) features and autonomous operational capabilities. Similarly, data fusion is associated with the switching and relay elements of the typical system, and its features are designed to incorporate expert systems capabilities. Likewise, the decision support function is akin to the monitoring and control elements, where their functions are incorporated into the design of decision support capabilities that reflect AI features.

The overall network management scheme is to monitor operating units for status and health, and to take action when and where necessary to continue the communications traffic flow. From such collected data, there is an assumption that all other needed information can be derived. This information is periodically or continuously relayed to a point where it is analyzed or in some way organized. From there it is evaluated and decisions are made based upon the logic used for such decisions, the criteria established for decisions, and the efficacy and accuracy of the data categorization.

Until now, the thinking was that the various data organizational and evaluation parameters would be found or derived in the data fusion and decision support functions. Now, however, processing power makes it possible for these capabilities to be off loaded into the sensor function. Hence, intelligent systems technology can possibly be imparted to the front end of the system using very high scale integrated circuits (VHSIC) or very large scale integrated (VLSI) circuits. These technologies provide sizing, memory, and software advantages and capabilities to execute expert tasks at high speeds while performing normal sensor tasks, such as collecting and reporting the data. At the back-end or control point, these technologies can also be of some use, due primarily to the fact that wireless and/or mobile monitoring and control facilities will be of importance to the network manager of the future. Wireless and mobile monitoring channels can now provide access to equipment operations in environments where conventional transport is inconvenient or too expensive. These channel connections are made through wireless transmitters and receivers, and digital interfaces made to the sensor components.

4

Processing Systems

Integration of data into meaningful and useful information are referred to in the aerospace-defense sector as decision support systems (DSSs), or executive information systems (EISs), as they are known in civilian-commercial environments. DSS/EIS is viewed in some contexts as a simulation dealing with "what if' questions. Also, EIS may be construed as a means of tracking resource usage, while DSS may be interpreted as a means of requesting direction. By varying the input parameter values, or the model, the consequences can be determined, and a family of answers can be developed. Multi-variate changes can also be evaluated in many cases using the simulation approach. Whether or not DSS/EIS is classified as a simulation or an on-line control, it functions to provide the user some degree of oversight with regard to the telecommunications system, and in that regard, it is a valuable network management tool. As such a tool, the DSS/EIS can be used in the background to play out scenarios about the functioning of the network, and the various faults that may befall the system.

The idea behind the DSS is to provide the observer with the best view of the situation, resources, actions, and options available to him or her that can be constructed. In this regard, DSSs are not a substitute or alternative for network management facilities, but rather they support the specific five functions defined by the OSI model for the total network management problem. These functions are: (1) fault monitoring (2) performance monitoring; (3) configuration management; (4) accounting management; and, (5) security management.

Decision support, however, targets the three main issues within the realm of network management, these being planning, performance, and maintenance. Fault and operational data analysis feed the fault evaluation module. This information is used to update the system configuration module. The system configuration status and the operational data analysis modules feed performance evaluation that in turn provides input to the control implementation module that provides instructions to the system for reconfiguration. Meanwhile, the periodic updating of the system configuration module activates the planning evaluation module, which also contains the system goals. The network configuration files contain connection routing tables, equipment inventory, network topology, and element capabilities.

DSS/EIS is not intended to be an entirely simulation-style tool, as will be seen at the end of this chapter. Often, in the early stages of DSS/EIS development, the capability is concerned with tying together remote locations via communications links. Additionally, the objective is to provide users with the accesses to multiple databases. And lastly, the system is completed by supplying report generators. Report generators may undergo a lengthy or even indefinite development period where the generator progresses from data presentation, to data transformation into parameters of value, to simulations, and finally to intelligent applications. Such applications may use rules, heuristics, or any of a number of references to generate suggestions, or decision-action situations. In this chapter we look at the use of DSS/EIS to perform information assessment and plan generation, evaluation, and execution. The tools required to perform these tasks include the system architecture, the user interfaces needed, and the various analysis aids. All of these tasks involved and the tools needed will be addressed here. The next few sections will discuss briefly some of the distinctions associated with decision or executive information support.

The assessment of, and recommendations for present and future actions associated with a particular subject are the domain of the decision support or EIS system. Present action analysis and decision making involves the assimilation of current data received into the system. Such data is can be received in real-time or via some other slower methods, such as telephone relay, hardcopy, manual collection, etc. Future action analysis and decision making involves the use of simulation tools to reach conclusions based upon current trends, and projected outcomes.

The buildup of DSS/EIS systems in a decision-oriented environment requires the use of modular concepts. The use of building blocks is usually necessary due to the complexity of the processes involved and also to provide incremental features for the user. Finally, it is critical that the DSS provide the right vehicle for decisions. It is a given here that decision support will not replace decision makers in human form, but it can be a powerful assistant to the human decision maker.

Distinctions between DSS and other decision aids

MIS, as a toot set, is one of the closest such tools to DSS, and therefore a source of confusion for someone involved in this area. MIS appears to be more concerned with the efficiency than the effectiveness of the measures derived. MIS takes reported data and distills it down to needed measures of operation. Additionally, MIS appears to be more occupied with current, and past data sets than developing future or predictive models.

Another type of decision aid is simulation. Simulation is a generic term applied to any procedure that utilizes probabilities, obtained from current or past performances, that are applied to projections of future performance. Simulation has reached significant heights of sophistication with graphic representations, interfaces to other programs, and artificial intelligence features. Simulation tools are very sophisticated these days, and provide some of the valuable features of DSS capabilities.

The decision support cycle

The decision process is the culmination of several steps aimed at affecting an outcome of some objective. The utility of developing an effective DSS lies in the results it creates, i.e., its validity, the time it takes to generate an answer, and its consistency, i.e., reliability of its results. If the results are within an acceptable range of error, the system is considered to meet a certain set of expectations, sometimes known as specifications. If the system turns out the same set of results time-after-time, it is demonstrating an agreement with functional requirements. And, if it meets response time constraints, it is meeting both specifications and functional requirements. The first part of the process involves data observation (sensors), and data collection (fusion) of events within the environment.

The steps following the decision action are part of the executive function, i.e., the translation of decision into a command structure, communication of orders to the command, the execution of orders, and the responses elicited by the execution of orders upon the environment. The communications infrastructure is usually the object of initial interest. In real-life implementations, such as those cited at the end of this book, many such DSSs started with ad hoc communications systems implemented to satisfy increased communications requirements between functional and/or geographical units. At some point later, DSS/EIS capabilities were conceived and developed separately.

First, the decision support system must be able to receive data relevant to the decision environment. The selection and use of the right input data sets, is critical to the effective generation of decision alternatives. Second, the key to the success and evaluation of the DSS is its ability to measure the impact of previous decisions from responses obtained from the environment. Third, some form of communications medium is needed to put the decisions into action. No DSS worthy of the name can be effective without a collection facility, feedback capability, and a means to put the decision into effect.

Architectures

Generic requirements

The challenge for DSSs is not that they must keep pace with the increasing influx of data, but rather that they must do a better job of making sense of the data that is collected. The typical DSS will have a series of attributes associated with it, some of which are:

(1) timeliness

(2) filtering

(3) user aids

(4) interfaces to other systems

(5) intelligence

The degree to which values and ranges are assigned to these attributes, will determine their utility in the decision part of DSS. The variety of attributes available for analysis will dictate the support part of the DSS, and the breadth of sensors providing input will give meaning to the system part of the DSS expression.

Some brief definition of these attributes is provided below.

Timeliness

Timeliness, as an attribute, means that the incoming data must bear some resemblance to other incoming data sets in order for proper evaluations to be made. The timing of inputs often provides valuable clues as to the relationships between reports, the validity of reports, or their reliability.

Filtering

Filtering is the ability of the DSS to make selective judgments about information, and/ or minor decisions, the object being to separate information from what is crucial to the decision process. 'Many times, the distinction between necessary and unnecessary information helps draw lines about the credibility of the process or the results obtained.

For instance, the value of an operation may be its safety impact as opposed to cost control or revenue impact. The latter measures may, therefore, be somewhat unnecessary or irrelevant when evaluating the basic value of the system. Reports about such issues may, therefore, be filtered out so that the system can evaluate reports of interest to the user.

User aids

User aids are the tools by which the user can distill and clarify information into something meaningful, and therefore, something of importance to the mission of the DSS. User aids give the system a certain utility so that the intended user can exercise the system effectively. These aids include the presentation formats, user interfaces, the analysis tools, correlation capabilities with other data, and interfaces to other systems.

Interfaces

Interfaces to other systems are the connectivity issues, both physical and functional, that allow data and decisions to be conveyed to other systems, and that make reception of data possible into the system. The ability of the system to interface to other systems also gives it additional power to draw upon resources not part of its basic make-up. This interfacing, again, requires communication means such that the sharing of data lends increased power to each unit, redundancy within the network, and access to databases not possible with isolated units.

Intelligence

Intelligence is the internal composition of the DSS that allows it to exercise some degree of problem solving, and range of action. Intelligence is usually equated to such features as artificial intelligence, machine vision, and robotics.

Types of DSSs

The various types of decision support systems are described and delineated here. One such type, the MIS system, was mentioned above. It was one of the first organized decision structures to be developed in the early era of computerized data manipulation. Since then, more sophisticated means of decision support have been developed, but MIS systems still exist in most companies as decision aids.

(1) Report generator systems (similar to MIS)
(2) Data analysis systems
(3) Analysis information systems
(4) Accounting models
(5) Representational models
(6) Optimization models
(7) Suggestion models

Report generator systems

The first and primary information need is access to data items. MIS was developed to meet this need. Implicit in this delivery is the immediacy of the data item availability. Thus, MIS stresses on-line accesses to the supporting databases, with rather basic user interfaces to bridge the databases and the report generation.

Data analysis systems

Such systems are developed to perform very specific analyses. Users could manipulate the data to generate very specific reports. The range of analyses is limited to the applications software of the system.

Analysis information systems

This type of system utilizes relational databases and modeling capabilities to create the data measures required. Such systems have some latitude as to the nature and form of measures created.

Accounting models

Accounting models use definitional procedures to calculate the outcomes of particular circumstances. These systems are used to calculate the consequences of possible financial decisions.

Representational models

Modeling used in this type of system is directed at attributes and items that are not necessarily accounting-oriented in nature. In such systems accounting terms are derived as opposed to being entered as parameters, as would be the case with accounting packages.

Optimization models

These systems provide the ability to profile situations mathematically that provide the best answers among the modelled circumstances. Examples of such capabilities are the required price and inventory points necessary to achieve customer demands.

Suggestion models

Suggestion models offer recommended courses of action as opposed to offering the tradeoffs that are part of optimization models. This is an outcome approach as opposed to an evaluation-based approach to modelling.

The basic configuration for any DSS/ElS includes the following elements:

Interface to the outside world

This feature can involve environmental or process sampling, database interfaces, and interfaces to other computational systems. External interfaces for network management systems usually involves an array of sensory inputs provided via communications services, e.g., private line, packet network, and dial-up facilities.

Buffering and storage

The data stream from the external interfaces must usually have a temporary repository while it is waiting for processing. Such temporary storage is provided by the buffer/ storage control and memory area of the computer. At this point, some preprocessing is also performed on the incoming data sets to eliminate such problems as duplicate and unreliable data.

Algorithmic manipulation

The main DSS/EIS activity is concerned with the procedural control and transformation of the external data stream. This process may range from summary data reporting, solutions of equations and subsequent reporting, multiple solutions to equations used to generate graphical representations with the help of graphics generators, simulation systems to allow projections and to play what-if games, and rule-based derivations to isolate likely solutions.

Human-machine interface

This element has already been discussed to a large extent. In summary, the human action is directed at assuring that the required input data is available, the appropriate processing is performed, the parameters and answers obtained are reasonable, and that the proper output or results are reported. Such a set of activities can either be labor intensive, or with the help of expert systems technology, human judgment can sometimes be replicated and substituted effectively.

Generalized architectures

The external environment supplies the raw data needed for analysis. Trends and historical arrays of these data are stored in the database and available for manipulation through the use of the database management system. The model base provides a replication of reality as seen from the user's point of view. The model is a set of rules that expresses how the system should function, and how its operation is affected when it doesn't function property.

External stimuli arriving at the input to the system are examined for correlation with the current status of the model as driven by the data items in the database. The decision support interface assembles the most appropriate view of the situation along with options to design or redesign a solution. To determine exactly what is appropriate is the challenge for the decision support interface. Presumably, there is a need to provide enough information in a short period of time and to package it in as meaningful a form as possible for the user to digest and react to.

It is interesting to note that the technology is and has been available for many years to supply sophisticated decision support systems. Unfortunately, the pressure has not been there to force the development of these tools until recent years partly due to the lack of competitive influences or lack of complete understanding as to how these tools relate to a company's success. Now, however, that the stimulus is present, there are several problems with which the decision support designer must grapple. These problems are briefly outlined below:

The technology systems needed or desired to solve the network management problem are many and varied. The technology problem usually revolves around the questions of speed, capacity, reliability, physical and functional connectivity, and access to data.

Decision and general psychological theory are areas of investigation that bear directly upon the DSS and its utility. Decision theory is implemented in several ways some of which rely on such classical approaches as Bayesian statistics and others of which rely on expert systems approaches, such as rule-based methods that attempt to emulate human logic.

Picking and using the right set of tools is the subject of this component of DSSs. The computer instruments that are part of the decision system must have the capacity to provide the most natural and unthreatening view and control access to the operation. This includes the presentation, and switch control and other activation methodologies.

Specific problems are subjected to an analysis of their situation and specific tasks are determined based upon these analyses. The task may be related to an outage report, overload or planning need, all of which result in some task definition that awaits human review and sometimes approval. The elements of each task may be carried out by diverse elements within the system, such as a computer system, expert system, human, or switching element. The DSS is just another step in a long line of technologies developed since World War 11 to cope with the needs and volume of data generated from different collection devices. The decision support systems that followed became the stimuli for the technology revolution that spawned the information age. First, there was the *electronic data processing* (EDP) era that saw the collection of vast amounts of data about processes, from financial to scientific. Next, there was the *management information system* (MIS) era. During this period, a certain amount of intelligence was created by organizing the output of EDP into specific reports for management usage. The term, intelligence, may be misused, because the results were little more than reports segmented to provide insights into specific areas of the operation. Following this, there was the time when great emphasis was placed upon *management science and operations research* (MS/OR) to assist management in making choices out of the volumes of MIS reports. MS/OR helps one make decisions from highly structured information.

Finally, there is now the era of DSS. This is a set of technologies that allows the user to design his or her own solutions based upon incomplete information. This thrust provides a very fertile ground from which to implement many forms of smart systems technologies. The initial attempts at DSSs have been far from what was envisioned, but the potential is there for this evolutionary progress.

Expert systems are a major element of DSSs because they provide the intelligence needed for the decisions reached. They can be roughly equated to the model(s) used internally to aid the decision process. They are:

The inference engine

That software program that uses the production rules to work out the logic of a particular problem. This is done mainly through sophisticated sequential searching and comparisons using lists supplemented with external facts.

The rule base

That database segment that contains the rules upon which the inference engine operates to resolve the problem at hand. The rule base is essentially a model base in which resides a representation of someone's version of reality, and reveals the rule base's form of logic.

The fact base

That portion of the database that provides the basic facts or data used by the inference engine to evaluate the rules, and therefore, to reach a conclusion. This information usually comes from external means, such as from attached or remote sensors, or from organized sources reached over communications channels.

Expert maintenance systems

Expert maintenance systems were probably the first expert systems to be developed with computer technology, and the decision support interfaces for such systems were and are, needless to say, important as well. The terms maintenance, fault control, and failure monitoring are sometimes used interchangeably to imply about the same thing, i.e., that the maintenance system has the capacity to detect, identify, and resolve system problems. The decision support application that interfaces with the maintenance system has several requirements to satisfy in order to make it appropriate for the job at hand, and these requirements are summarized as follows

Identification of the problem

The DSS must have access to the data necessary to determine that a problem has occurred. This determination many times surfaces as a result of several indicators as opposed to a single occurrence. Problem identification may come in many forms, such as failure of a parametric test, or a logic test.

Isolation of the problem

Determining where the problem exists is many times not an easy task. The location may be masked by several other conditions or situations that make this step a difficult one. Testing for a specific location is sometimes an effective tool.

Association of the problem

The exposure of the problem immediately stimulates a search of the previous times or situations during which the problem may have occurred. If no such circumstances have occurred, association can be established by reference to an operational model of the system. Such events and references provide a starting point for problem attack.

Implications of the problem

The association of the problem with its place in the system often provides information that might implicate the problem with other system elements that the current problem may infect. The current problem may also imply or implicate other processes that are more pertinent to the malfunction or bottleneck situation.

Visualization of the problem

A conceptualization of the problem as something that a human can appreciate is important in any system, expert or otherwise. Such a concept presentation can be provided as a graphical display or even a functioning picture of the system. The problem visualization is executed by simulation of the system functionality or processes and as a result will often suggest one or more solutions to the problem at hand.

Options for solving the problem

The system simulation, isolation and association are the principal vehicles for enumerating the options for problem resolution. These processes provide a list of possible options that can be implemented. In addition, the options may carry a list of caveats and degrees of difficulty that may be encountered as a result of exercising each of these options.

Performance management systems

The performance management system likewise has several uses for decision support. Such systems monitor operational traffic and, using decision support capabilities can anticipate bottlenecks, isolate operational trouble areas, and correlate fault messages with operational conditions. Examples of performance management systems implemented include NEMESYS and XTRAC. NEMESYS is an AT&T tool developed to assist in fighting congestion in the inter-exchange carrier business. It is based upon techniques to optimize performance during overload or outage emergencies. Information on the number of and reasons for call blockages is collected and used to derive suggestions for call rerouting, XTRAC is a system that also reallocates resources based upon priority considerations.

Performance measurement and problem resolution based upon performance problems are both associated with the types of performance problems incurred within the network whether they be location specific or time based. These types of problems can be categorized as follows:

Routine capacity overload

This is the most common problem handled by a performance management system. It occurs as a result of some cable or transmission route becoming undersized for the load placed upon it as traffic increases over that route with time. In this type of situation, the route experiences periodic durations of overload at an increasing frequency and for an increasing duration per overload period as the general loading becomes greater.

The focused overload results from sudden increases in local demand due to some type of emergency either manmade or natural. Examples might include severe weather or a nuclear power plant problem. The focused overload becomes most troublesome when the facility needed to complete the circuit itself is the object of the overload, such as the telephone end office, because in this case, there is little or no rerouting possible to get around the problem. In this type of overload situation, the overload is not localized as with the focused overload. It is ubiquitous throughout the network. An example of a general overload situation would be Mother's Day or Christmas. During a general overload period, there is little rerouting and few alternatives available to resolve the problem. The problem will usually go away in a few hours. Recent catastrophes, however, have shown that general overload may not go away in a few hours. Certain local problems such as the one in New York City that affected the entire air traffic system and the software bugs that affected new telephone switches around the country are problems that may be harbingers of more dire situations in the future.

Facility failure is a situation where there may be a failure of a trunk group as a result of weather problems. Here the situation resembles a focused failure except that the capacity has been reduced due to equipment failure as opposed to an increase in demand. In many such cases, the problem can be gotten around by use of spare components or switching around the problem.

The typical planning function occurs either to support cost, schedule, or technical performance objectives. One example of a planning management system is one which operates as an expert assistant in designing networks. It is called *Designet* and acts as a configuration tool for boards, racks, cables, interfaces, etc. at each site in a network environment. The DESIGNET module provides the user with many different views of the network configuration and performs sensitivity analyses by answering why and whatif questions for the operator. Another such planning system was developed at GTE Laboratories and is known as MARVEL.

The history of human interface with computers begins with human interaction with machinery. Early computational systems used switches and hand fed tape to operate and program such machinery. Soon, the user interface developed some more complex relationships that will be discussed further below. The progression of computer input interfacing ranges from keyboard mechanical inputs to touch screens. Output interfacing has progressed from scrolling tabular presentations to three dimensional illustrations of output information. Interfaces are divided into three categories, namely formal, natural language, and graphic interface dialogues. These various dialogues are discussed below.

Formal dialogue

As mentioned above, early computers were programmed and operated by switches, supplemented with tapes to input a large amount of data, Later typewriter-style keyboards were introduced to facilitate the operator's use of dedicated and time-share system.

Natural language dialogue

Input specifications have developed from the point where computer control required a strict protocol in order to have the user's desires obeyed by the computer. This progression has been greatly enhanced through the use of the icon, or graphic representation, to substitute for the laborious and error-prone typed input.

Graphics interface dialogue

Icons have become the graphics tools of choice for human-machine interface. They assume the attributes of most of the previously typed file information, security, and movement specifications. Currently, icons are controlled by any of the formal dialogue methods. In the future they are likely to be controlled by touch screen or even brainwave methods. The formal dialogue, natural language, and graphics interfaces are all involved on the input side of the system. The output side is characterized by increasingly sophisticated displays and interactions of these display buffers with external systems and databases, as well as with special display modes, such as color, scanned displays, and hardcopy generators. Input devices range from scanners to biomechanic body-sensing devices to voice activators.

While the variety of input devices is almost unlimited, the corresponding output is limited to three-dimensional and time-related imagery coupled with some form of sound accompaniment.

Planning

The development of a plan suitable for a particular DSS/EIS application begins with a rigorous elaboration of the requirements. In some cases the requirements are simply to integrate the information flow. More elaborate plans call not only for the integration of the information flow but also the ability to make unstructured requests for information and/or analyses to which the system can respond using built in intelligence, drawing from all data resources available.

At the low end, the DSS/EIS is supported by some type of data communications capability with, at the very least, some type of E-mail facility. The high end DSS/EIS is equipped with a distributed data processing facility, fully capable of sophisticated AI-based decision support. Within a short time asynchronous transfer mode (ATM), a broadband packet-based switching and transport technology will become available on a wide scale. With this capability, the developer will have almost unlimited capacity to specify different combinations of distributed, multimedia data for the target user population. Even the low end developer and users have plenty of decisions to make regarding their communications commitments to technologies and equipments. As the user becomes more comfortable with the communications capabilities, the next major hurdle is that of accessing the various databases and the protocol differences that invariably plague the melding of disparate data sources for access by single applications programs. The third challenge is that of managing this diverse network in terms of geography, database management, security and privileges, and communications capacity for each locale. The development of nonintelligent report generators is next and is no small task even for the dedicated systems engineer. The types and varieties of such reports can be staggering, if the commitment to DSS/EIS is really there.

The final step is that of infusing smart systems technologies into the design and implementation. For now, however, it can be said that expert systems, for example, will be pervasive in the decision maker's office of the 1990s. Some companies, such as Mrs. Field's Cookies, have taken a very aggressive position relative to DSS/EIS by setting up a "lights out" business operation that essentially makes all operational decisions with only veto power on the part of the human overseer. The current market for decision support is estimated to be about $600 million during the decade of the 1990s. The current vendors of EIS include IBM and Software Publishing, with possible likely entrants to be Borland, Lotus, and Microsoft.

Tools

The strategy being applied by most vendors in the emerging EIS marketplace is one that emphasizes connectivity first, integrated reporting facilities second, and freestyle query/response capabilities third. This approach is best exemplified by the architecture posed by IBM, which is the basic architecture being put forth by other vendors as well. In this approach the host, or hosts, are the central repositories for all incoming data or file transfers from other locations, internal or external alike. The host computers distribute requested data to their destinations that, in the case of the IBM product, call for routing via LU 6.2, IBM's communications interface for external PC/LAN configurations, 3270 terminals via their controllers, and via direct connection to DOS and OS/2 environments. The LU 6.2 interface also provides connection to various environments on the LAN, such as OS/2, DOS, and eventually Windows, UNIX, and Macintosh.

Other EIS vendors, such as Holistic Systems, have moved ahead insofar as the current wave of EIS direction is concerned. The first concentration of EIS offerings was in the area of graphically oriented, navigation interfaces that provided the user with ability to move into increasingly deeper levels of data using pre-defined penetration schema. These interfaces are supported by generalized as well as specialized algorithmic engines to do a lot of the preprocessing and parameter calculations. The newer wave of EIS offerings will aim at greater distributed sources and destinations and will increasingly emphasize DSS/EIS tasking at the desktop and greater simplification of the query/response process.

5
Network Monitoring

Network monitors, also known as network analyzers or probes, are quite useful for network management. They basically collect and analyze the packets going through them. These data may be statistics, such as packet sizes, number of collisions, and number of packets per second. In relation to management stations, these network monitors are remote; hence, they are known as *remote network monitors* (RMON). These network monitors, by using the RMON MIB, can be extended to collect data for network management and to communicate with management stations. Note that the RMON MIB extends MIB-II RFC 1271 defined MIB objects primarily for the Ethernet protocol. RFC 1513 is an extension of RFC 1271 and defines the MIB objects required for monitoring networks running on token-ring protocols. RFC 1757 makes RFC 1271 obsolete. RFC 1757 is basically the same as RFC 1271, except it corrects and clarifies some of the terms, such as channel and captureBuffer, used in RFC 1271. Management data collected by a network monitor is sent to management stations. This can be on an exception basis, that is, when changes happen. The location of the network monitors is implementation-dependent. One network monitor can be placed per segment, per subnetwork, or per token-ring network.

As an example, in which there is one network monitor for each subnetwork. FDDI rings have management stations M1 and M2. Remote network monitors are placed in RMON agents Al, A2, A3, and A4, which provide functions such as protocol support for communication with management stations and error recovery for the remote network monitors. RMON agents act as intermediaries between remote network monitors and management stations. For transfer of data to management stations, these RMON agents can use SNMPvl or SNMPv2 protocols. However, if RMON agents are to be implemented, SNMPv2 is preferable because SNMPvl agents must ultimately migrate to SNMPv2 agents. We have made the assumption that RMON agents communicate with only one management station. It is not necessary to have this restriction; an RMON agent carrying a remote network monitor may send data to one or more management stations. Also, these RMON agents can be placed in hosts, routers, and bridges, and there are no set rules prescribed in RFC 1757 or RFC 1513 on the placement of remote network monitors.

This particular approach of having a network monitor exclusively for the purpose of network management has its own advantages. The network monitor can continuously collect data and selectively send it to the management stations. Also, when thresholds are crossed, events may be formed and alarms can be sent to the management stations. This action can help reduce network traffic, because the data collected is logged in agents with network monitors instead of transmitting every piece of data to the management stations. When the management stations need further details, they can access and collect the information required from the agents with remote network monitors.

RFC 1757 covers some of the scenarios where remote networking monitoring may be used. These include:

Offline operation: Primarily relates to cases in which the network monitor operates as a stand-alone monitoring device. These cases can arise due to communication failure between the remote network monitor and a management station, or due to selective collection of data by a management station. Because a remote network monitor can operate independently of the management station, it can continue to perform its operation of continuously collecting and storing data. The management station, in turn, can retrieve these data stored whenever required.

Communication with management stations on an exception basis: Because the remote network monitor can function independently of management stations, it can collect data on the network and log data for analysis at a later time. When problems are observed in the network due to crossing thresholds or failures, notifications can be sent to management stations. Management stations can retrieve the logged data for problem analysis and diagnostics.

Relevant data collection: A monitor can also concentrate on the hosts in its portion of the network that have maximum traffic or errors and can log the data required for management stations. This will help in zeroing in on a portion of the network, as well as with the collection of data on the critical hosts in a network.

Multiple management stations: Management stations may be organized on the basis of actions performed. Under these circumstances, it may be necessary to concurrently deal with more than one management station to which a network monitor is reporting. Also, a breakdown by function, such as accounting, will help reduce the workload in management stations and makes it easy to focus on each of the functions. This can help to centralize the data required for certain network management functions such as configuration management. In many cases, configuration management activities need to be centralized in one management station. Similarly, under certain circumstances, it may be necessary to have centralized fault management, including monitoring, in another management station. So, a scenario where a remote network monitor may have to communicate with more than one management station becomes quite common, especially in large networks with thousands of workstations.

RMON for Ethernet (RFC 1757)

Objects defined in the remote network monitoring MIB are primarily for the Ethernet protocol. They can be expanded to cover token-ring and FDDI protocols. RMON objects are defined using the guidelines furnished in SMI (RFC 1155). However, in addition to the ASN.1 data types mentioned in SMI, RMON defines the following two data types:

OwnerString (DisplayString): Contains information such as IP address, management station name, network manager's name, location, and phone number. This data type is used for identifying the owner of a resource, and helps in resolving conflicts when more than one management station is the owner of a resource. For example, if an instance of a resource is to be deleted by a management station, then there is the possibility that one management station may delete the instance created by another management station. But, by identifying the owner, a rule may be made that only the management station that created an object instance can delete that object instance. Thus, the data type OwnerString is useful when resources are shared by more than one management station.

EntryStatus (INTEGER): Useful when a resource is shared by more than one owner. Suppose that an object instance is created by,, one owner. At the same time or later, another management station' creates an object instance with conflicting values to the one that has been already created. In such a case, there can be major problems regarding the validity of values. The major question is which are the correct values? Under such circumstances, EntryStatus is quite useful because it helps to determine whether an object instance exists.

EntryStatus has these values: valid = 1, createRequest = 2, underCreation = 3, and invalid = 4. As we have seen previously, creating an object instance is equivalent to creating a row entry in a MIB table. So, when an object instance is created, we have the value createRequest. Creating an instance may lead to supplementary actions such as creation of more objects by an agent. During this operation, the value is set to underCreation. When this operation is completed, the value is set to valid, abort, or invalid, depending on the results of the object creation operation. Another management station that wants to create the same entry will get a result of error. Thus, it is prudent for a management station to check whether an object instance has already been created by checking EntryStatus.

After examining the new data types OwnerString and OwnerStatus, we can conclude that their primary objective is for facilitating resource sharing. This is due to the fact that network monitors can send monitored data to more than one management station, which is one of the salient points of RMON. These objects are transmitted across the wires using the BER, which was discussed in earlier chapters.

Under the subtree {mib-2 16}, new groups for RMON are defined. Nine main groups are defined in RFC 1757. The tokenRing group, {rmon 10}, has been added in RFC 1513 specifically for monitoring networks working with the token-ring protocol.

Ethernet statistics group

Objects in the statistics group are used to collect statistics on each of the monitored devices. The statistics group has one table, etherStatsTable, which is formed as shown in Figure 9.5. etherStatsTable will have a row for each Ethernet interface. Thus, there are etherStatsEntryl to etherStatsEntryN in the etherStatsTable, and each etherStatsEntry has columns from etherStatsIndex and etherStatsDataSource up to etherStatsStatus. This procedure is followed in forming some of the tables in RMON and is similar to the ones used in MIB-II.

Data types for the statistics group are mainly counters, and they are created with a value of zero. In the statistics group, objects are:

etherStatsIndex (INTEGER): Provides the row position in the etherStatsTable.

etherStatsDataSource (OBJECT IDENTIFIER): Relates to the Ethernet interface from which a remote network monitor is receiving the data.

etherStatsDropEuents (Counter): Provides the number of times packets were dropped in network monitors for limitations of resources, such as lack of storage space.

etherStatsOctets (Counter): Provides the total number of octets received on the network monitor from an Ethernet interface. This includes the total number of data octets and FCS octets. However, these octets do not include the framing bits.

etherStatsPkts (Counter): Includes the total number of packets received, including those packets which had errors.

etherStatsBroadcastPkts (Counter): Furnishes the total number of good broadcast packets received in an Ethernet interface.

etherStatsMulticastPkts (Counter): While in etherStats-BroadcastPkts, the concern is good broadcast packets; in etherStatsMulticastPkts, a count of good multicast packets is kept.

etherStatsCRCAlignErrors (Counter): Provides the number of packets which were between length 64 and 1518 octets or had FCS errors. While counting the length, the FCS octets are included but the framing bits are excluded.

etherStatsUndersizePkts (Counter): Relates to the total number of good packets which had lengths less than 64 octets.

etherStatsOversizePkts (Counter): Refers to the well-formed packets which had lengths greater than 1518 octets.

etherStatsFragments (Counter): Provides data on packets which had bad lengths or FCS errors, and were of lengths less than 64 octets.

etherStatsJabbers (Counter): etherStatsFragments provides details on the bad packets which are of lengths less than 64 octets. We need to have data on bad packets which are over the Ethernet length limit of 1518 octets. etherStatsJabbers provides this data.

etherStatsCollisions (Counter): Provides the number of collisions in a subnetwork.

etherStatsPkts64Octets through *etherStatsPkts1024to-1518Octets:* Provide granularity for counters by breaking them into different counters for lengths of packets ranging from 64 to 1518 octets. Note that these packets also include the error packets.

etherStatsOwner (OwnerString): Identifies the owner that created this row in the etherStatsTable. As we have seen earlier, OwnerString furnishes many details.

etherStatsStatus (EntryStatus): Provides the status of the etherStats entry.

Objects in the statistics group are basically very useful for performance management, but some of them, such as etherStatsDropEvents, etherStatsCRCAlignErrors, and etherStatsUndersizePkts, will be useful for fault management, too. If corrective action is to be taken before a failure occurs, then it may be useful to have thresholds set for objects such as etherStatsDropEvents, etherStatsCRCAlignErrors, and etherStatsCollisions.

History group

In the history group, samples at fixed time intervals are collected and stored. This data can be used for analysis in fault and performance management. As is apparent from the figure, there are two tables: historyControl Table and etherHistoryTable. historyControlTable provides information on how data are to be collected. Corresponding to a row in the historyControlTable there are one or more rows of data in etherHistoryTable. etherHistoryTable has the actual data which is useful for analysis purposes. This pattern is followed by some tables in RMON MIB. RFC 1757 recommends that while collecting data, it is better to start data collection at the beginning of the next hour of the day. If data is collected for different stations in a network uniformly at the same time, data will be useful and meaningful for comparison purposes. Objects of the historyControlTable are:

historyControlIndex (INTEGER): A unique identifier of an entry in the historyControlTable. Each entry defines a set of entries in the etherHistoryTable on an Ethernet interface.

historyControlDataSource (OBJECT IDENTIFIER): Relates to the Ethernet interface on which a remote network monitor is collecting data.

historyControlBuckersRequested (INTEGER) : Porovides the requested number of sampling intervals.

historyControlBucketsGranted (INTEGER): In a network monitor there may be limitations on resources, so naturally, a network monitor cannot always provide the numbers of sampling intervals as requested in historyControlBucketsRequested. As a result, history-ControlBucketsGranted furnishes the feasible number of sampling intervals, and, as is obvious, the historyControl BucketsGranted value is kept as close to the value requested by historyControlBucketsRequested.

historyControlInterval (INTEGER): Refers to the sampling interval in seconds for each bucket. The value can be set from 1 to 3600 seconds.

historyControlOwner (OwnerString): Identifies the owner which created this row in the historyControlTable. Because management stations will be using the data collected, history Control Owner refers to a management station.

historyControlStatus (EntryStatus): Provides the status of historyControlEntry.

etherHistoryTable has the data which have been collected over an Ethernet interface. Parameters for data collection are guided by historyControlEntry. The columns in etherHistoryTable starting from etherHistoryDropEvents up to etherHistoryCollisions are similar to those in the etherStatsTable, and mean almost the same thing, therefore, we will discuss those objects which are unique to the etherHistoryTable. These objects are:

etherHistoryIndex (INTEGER): Has the same value as historyControlIndex. This entry links the historyControl-Table and etherHistoryTable.

etherHistorySampleIndex (INTEGER): Each etherHistory-Index has one or more entries for etherHistorySample Index. This entry starts from 1, and each sample has a unique value increasing by 1.

etherHistoryIntervalStart (YYrnencks): Refers to the sysUpTime when data collection was started.

etherHistory Utilization (INTEGER): Provides the best estimate of the mean physical layer network utilization in percentage over the time interval during which data collection was done etherHistoryUtilization refers to the utilization over one Ethernet interface.

Alarm group

Implementation of the alarm group is optional. If it is implemented, then the event group must also be implemented because they are interrelated. In the alarm group periodic samples are collected and then compared with the threshold values. If the value of a monitored variable crosses the threshold, then an event is generated. Objects in this group are useful for performance management. Events generated are useful for fault management. The alarm group uses an alarmTable which has entries stating how samples are to be taken and how the alarms are to be generated. The objects in the alarmTable are:

alarmIndex (INTEGER): A unique identifier which identifies a row in the alarmTable.

alarmIndex refers to a sample for an object at a particular interval of time.

alarmInterval (INTEGER): States the time interval during which samples are taken from an object being observed.

alarmVariable (OBJECT IDENTIFIER): Refers to the identifier of the object being sampled. The object being sampled should have a data type of INTEGER, Counter, Gauge, or TimeTicks.

alarmSampleType (INTEGER): States how sample values are interpreted. It has two values: absoluteValue = 1 and deltaValue= 2. If the sample value is the absoluteValue, then it is compared against the threshold value for generating alarms. However, if it is a deltaValue, then the previous sample value is subtracted from the current value and this difference is compared with the threshold values.

alarmValue (INTEGER): Provides the last valid sample value. A sample value is complete and available only at the end of a sampling period.

alarmStartupAlarm (INTEGER): Has three values: rising-Alarm 1, fallingAlarm = 2, and risingOrFalling-Alarm = 3. This states what type of alarm will be generated. When a sample value is greater than or equal to alarmRisingThreshold, and, alarmStartupAlarm is equal to risingAlarm or risingOrFalling Alarm, then a single rising alarm will be generated. Similarly, when a sample value is less than or equal to alarm. FallingThreshold and the alarmStartupAlarm is equal to fallingAlarm or risingOrFallingAlarm, then a falling alarm will be generated. These conditions can result in events being generated and sent to network monitors or management stations.

alarmRisingThreshold (INTEGER): Represents a threshold value for a monitored object. A rising event can be generated when the sample value of a monitored object is greater than or equal to alarmRisingThreshold. The previous value should not have crossed the alarmRisingThreshold value. A rising event can also be generated if the first value of this entry is greater than or equal to the alarmRisingThreshold value and the associated alarmStartupAlarm is equal to risingAlarm or risingOrFallingAlarm.

alarmFallingThreshold (INTEGER): Similar to the alarmRisingThreshold, but it represents a threshold value in the opposite direction. When a sampled value is less than or equal to this alarmFallingThreshold and when the value of the previous sampling interval was greater than the alarmFallingThreshold, a falling event is generated. A falling event is also generated if the value of the first entry is less than or equal to this threshold value and the associated alarmStartupAlarm is equal to fallingAlarm or risingOrFallingAlarm.

alarmRisingEventIndex (INTEGER): Used to identify the event generated when a rising threshold is crossed. The value in this entry corresponds to the eventIndex in an eventTable. If there is n corresponding entry in eventIndex, then there is no relationship this alarm entry with the event entry in eventTable. If this value zero, then there is no valid entry in eventTable.

alarmFallingEuentIndex (INTEGER): While alarmRising-EventIndex is used when crossing rising thresholds, alarmFallingEventlndex is used when a falling thresholds is crossed.

alarmOwner (OwnerString): Refers to one or more management stations which configured this entry in alarmTable.

alarmStatus (EntryStatus): Refers to the status of the entry in alarmTable.

Host group

The host group contains statistics on each of the hosts discovered in the network. These are derived by noting good packets received on the network. Each host is identified by the MAC address.

hostControl Table: The entries in this table determine how the statistics on hosts are to be maintained. Based on the parameters' of this table, data is collected and entered in hostTable and hostTimeTable.

hostTable: Has entries on each host based on the MAC addresses. These MAC addresses are used to index into hostTable.

hostimeTable: The rows in this table are arranged in order of hostTimeCreationOrder. The hostTimeCreationOrder column of the table starts from 1, and this is used for indexing into hostTimeTable. There is a subtle difference between hostTable and hostTimeTable. In hostTable, we index into the table using MAC addresses, while in hostTimeTable, we index into the table using hostTimeCreationOrder. The format of the data collected is the same for both tables. By indexing in the order in which the entries are created in hostTimeTable, it is easier to download these tables by means of management stations using SNMP. Also, it is easy to break the packets into manageable SNMP PDUs. The other advantage is that to get details of new hosts added after a download of data from hostTimeTable, entries must be downloaded after a particular value of *N* instead of downloading hostTimeTable all over again.

The entries in hostTable and hostTimeTable are useful for configuration, performance, and fault management. Knowing the addresses of hosts in a network by frequently downloading the entries in hostTimeTable helps in keeping track of the active hosts in the network. When entries are deleted from hostTimeTable, the configuration of the network on the hosts can be accordingly modified. The different objects of the host group are:

hostControlIndex (INTEGER): Each discovered host in a network has an entry in hostControlTable. hostControlIndex is a unique identifier for a row and a host.

hostControlDataSource (OBJECT IDENTIFIER): Identifies t source for data. This source can be any interface on a host and h a corresponding entry in ifIndex.

hostControlTableSize (INTEGER): Corresponds to the number of entries in hostTable for a host. As the entries in hostTable and hostTimeTable have one-to-one correspondence, this number also refers to the number of entries in hostTimeTable.

hostControlLastDeleteTime (TimeTicks): Relates to the time when an entry was last deleted from hostTable. A zero value indicates that no deletions were made in hostTable.

hostControlOwner and *hostControlStatus* have the same significance as described earlier in other RMON MIB groups. In both hostTable and hostTimeTable, only the objects which need explanation will be examined, and we will avoid discussing those objects which are similar in meaning to the ones already explained. Some of the objects which need explanation are:

hostAddress (OCTET STRING): Refers to the MAC address of the host.

hostCreationOrder (INTEGER): A number from I to *N* and having a corresponding row in hostControlEntry. The numbers in hostCreationOrder are increased by one as a new entry is created.

hostIndex (INTEGER): The value in this column is the same as the value in hostControlIndex.

hostInPkts (Counter): Provides the number of good packets received through this host address, furnished by hostAddress, after adding this host to hostTable.

hostOutPkts (Counter): Identifies the total number of packets transmitted by the host, including the error packets.

hostInOctets (Counter): Contains the total number of octets received by this host after it was added to hostTable. hostInOctets does not include error octets and framing bits.

hostOutOctets (Counter): Furnishes the total number of octets transmitted by this host. It includes error octets, but does not include framing bits in the count of octets.

hostOutErrors (Counter): Relates to the number of error packets transmitted by a host after being added to the host table. This object is very useful for performance and fault management. hostOutErrors along with hostOutOctets can furnish solid information on how a host is behaving.

hostOutBroadcastPkts (Counter): A counter for the number of good broadcast packets transmitted by this host after this entry was added to hostTable.

hostOutMulticastPkts (Counter): Counter contains only the packets transmitted to multicast addresses after being added to the host table. Because the distinction has been made between multicast and broadcast, this counter naturally does not include the number of packets broadcast by this host.

The entries in hostTimeTable are:

hostTimeAddress (OCTET STRING): Pertains to the MAC address of the host.

hostTime Creation Order (INTEGER): The index used for hostTimeTable. The entries are arranged sequentially from one to N. This entry has the same value as hostControlTableSize of hostControlTable.

hostTimeIndex (INTEGER): Has the same value as hostControlIndex of hostControlTable.

In hostTimeTable, other entries, from *hostInPkts* up to and including *hostOutMulticastPkts,* have the same significance as described in hostTable.

HostTopN group

The HostTopN group can be used to report the statistics on a group of hosts over a period of time. These statistics on selected hosts over a sampling interval is known as a *report* and is sent to one or more management stations. These statistics are derived from the host group. The interval for collecting data and start and stop times from the host group is determined by management stations. Once the data is collected in hostTopNTable, then it is available for management stations. The implementation of the HostTopN group is optional. However, if this group is implemented, then the Host group must also be implemented. Data collected from the HostTopN group are useful for performance and fault management. The objects in the HostTopN group are:

hostToPNControlIndex (INTEGER): A unique entry which identifies a top *N* report for one interface.

hostTopNHostIndex (INTEGER): The value of this entry and the value of hostIndex in hostTable are the same.

hostTopNRateBase (INTEGER): Identifies an object in hostTable on which data is collected. The values of the objects in hostTopNRateBase are: hostTopNInPkts = 1, hostTopNOutPkts = 2, hostTopNInOctets = 3, hostTopN-OutOctets = 4, hostTopNOutErrors = 5, hostTopNOut-BroadcastPkts = 6, and hostTopNOutMulticastPkts = 7. The significance of these variables is as explained in the host group.

hostTopTimeRemaining (INTEGER): Provides the time remaining in the sampling interval to complete the data collection for hostTopNTable. Only when the value becomes zero will hostTopNEntry be available. If the value is nonzero, then host top N entries cannot be retrieved.

hostTopNDuration (INTEGER): Provides information on the sampling interval in seconds for the previous report, or, if the data is being collected, then this furnishes elapsed time since data collection started. The value of hostTopNDuration is set along with the value of hostTopNTimeRemaining.

hostTopNRequestedSize (INTEGER): Identifies the maximum number of hosts requested for hostTopNTable. Here, the default value is 10.

hostTopNGrantedSize (INTEGER): Furnishes the number of hosts on which data can be collected in hostTopNTable. Because there can be limitations on resources, sometimes this value cannot be equal to the value of hostTopNRequestedSize. This value should be set as close to hostTopNRequestedSize as possible.

hostTopNStartTime (TimeTicks): Provides sysUpTime at which hostTopNReport was started.

hostTopNOwner and *hostTopNStatus* have the same meaning as described previously for corresponding entries in other RMON groups. HostTopN group also has hostTopNTable, which includes the following objects:

hostTopNReport (INTEGER): Identifies a report. Its value is the same as the value of hostToPNControlIndex.

hostTopNIndex (INTEGER): Identifies a row in the hostTopNTable. hostTopNIndex starts from 1 and increases by a value of 1.

hostToPNAddress (OCTET STRING): Refers to the MAC address of a host.

hostTopNRate (INTEGER): Provides the amount of change in the selected object, which is selected by hostTopNRateBase.

Matrix group

In the Matrix group the statistics on conversations between two sets of MAC addresses are maintained in two tables: matrixSDTable and matrixDSTable. Entries in these tables are controlled by the objects in matrixControlTable. In all these tables, when there are shortages of resources, the least recently used entries are deleted. Implementation of the matrix group is optional. matrixSDTable is primarily indexed on the basis of source and destination addresses. However, in matrixDSTable, the statistics on a conversation are indexed on the basis of destination and source addresses. So the major difference between these two tables is in the manner in which the tables are accessed for processing. These tables are useful for configuration, performance, and fault management. In configuration management, granularity may be depicted to the conversation levels, in which case, it is easy to collect data on active conversations from the matrix group. The explanations of objects in the matrix group are:

matrixControlIndex (INTEGER): Uniquely identifies an entry in matrixControlTable. For each matrixControlIndex entry, statistics are stored in matrixSDTable and matrixDSTable.

matrixControlDataSource (OBJECT IDENTIFIER): Represents the identifier of the source device on which conversation statistics are collected.

Other objects, from *matrixControlTableSize* through *matrixControl Status,* have the same meaning as corresponding objects in other *groups.*

matrixSDSourceAddress (OCTET STRING): Refers to the source MAC address for the conversation on which statistics are being collected. Note that the MAC address identifies a host.

matrixSDDestAddress (OCTET STRING): Refers to the destination MAC address.

matrixSDIndex (INTEGER): Has the same value as matrixControlIndex in matrixControlEntry. This entry helps to associate matrixControlEntry with a row in matrixSDTable.

matrixSDPkts (Counter): Provides the total number of packets transmitted from a source to the destination. It also includes error packets.

matrixSDOctets (Counter): Refers to the total number of good octets transmitted from a source to the destination address. It does not include framing bits but does include error octets.

matrixSDErrors (Counter): Includes error packets trans-mitted from a source to the destination address. By subtracting matrixSDErrors from matrixSDPkts, statistics on the number of,: good packets can be recovered.

The objects of matrixDSTable have similar meaning to those in matrixSDTable.

Filter group

The filter group helps in matching the conditions for capturing data or generating events. The concept of channels is used here. Input data is subjected to a set of filter rules stated in different variables in the filter group. Filter rules are applied to packet data and packet status. From the filter operation, a channel is obtained. The channel data can be stored with the aid of captureBufferTable. Note that *channel is* a technical concept and not a physical component. If the channel is enabled, then *events* are generated. An event can also enable the channel on or off. From a channel, we can generate SNMP trap messages and log the events.

The filter group has two tables: filterTable and channelTable. The objects provided are:

filterIndex (INTEGER): A unique index which identifies an entry in filterTable.

filterChannelIndex (INTEGER): Identifies a channel and matches the channelIndex in channelTable.

filterPktData Offset (INTEGER): Points to the starting point in data after which a filter will be applied. The offset is measured after framing bits in a physical layer frame.

filterPktData (OCTET STRING): Provides the data for filtering. It is used along with filterPktDataMask and filterPktDataNotMask.

filterPktDataMask (OCTET STRING): Bits with Is are relevant. filterPktDataMask is extended with Is if it is shorter than filterPktData.

filterktDataNotMask (OCTET STRING): The inverse of the filterPktDataMask. If the filterPktDataNotMask is shorter than the filterPktData, then this mask is extended with 0s.

filterPktStatus (INTEGER): Matched with the input packet, and the input bits relevant here are those corresponding to Is in the filterPktStatusMask.

filterPktStatusMask (INTEGER): Applied to the filterPktStatus, and only those bits which have Is are relevant. Here, as with filterPktDataMask, if filterPktStatus is shorter than the filterPktStatusMask, then filterPktStatus is extended by adding Is.

filterPktStatusNotMask (INTEGER): Operates inversely to filterPktStatusMask.

filterOwner and *filterStatus* have the same meanings as described for corresponding objects in other groups.

The objects in the channelTable are:

channelIndex (INTEGER): Identifies a unique entry in the channel table.

channelIfIndex (INTEGER): Uniquely identifies an interface on the RMON device (just like IfIndex).

channelAcceptType (INTEGER): Controls the actions of the filters associated with the channel. It has values of acceptMatched = 1 and acceptFailed = 2. In accept-Matched, packets will be accepted if there is a match of packet data and packet status. In acceptFailed, for a packet to be accepted, the packet data match or packet status match must fail.

channelDataControl (INTEGER): Controls the flow of data, status, and events through the channel. It has two values: on = 1 an~ off = 2. If the value is on, then data, status, and events can flow through the channel. If the status is off, then data, status, and events do not pass through the channel.

channel TurnOnEventIndex (INTEGER): Controls the generation of events. If an event is generated, then this value has a corresponding value in the eventIndex entry in eventTable.

channelTurnOffEventIndex (INTEGER): Will turn channel-DataControl to off from on, after an event is generated. It also has an entry in the eventIndex entry in eventTable.

channelEventIndex (INTEGER): Will identify the event to be generated when there is a packet match and channelDataControl is on.

channelEventStatus (INTEGER): Used for controlling the flow of events. It has three values: eventReady = 1, eventFired = 2, and eventAlwaysReady = 3. When this object is set to eventReady, an event will be generated and the object will change to the eventFired state. The eventAlwaysReady state will disable flow control, and events will be generated freely.

channelMatches (Counter): States the number of times there has been a packet match, including those cases where channelDataControl is off.

channelDescription (DisplayString): Describes the channel.

channelOwner and *channelStatus* have the same significance as described for corresponding objects in other groups.

Packet capture group

On the basis of filters, packets are captured and stored in, captureBufferTable of the packet capture group tables. A channel is associated with captureBufferTable. bufferControlTable determines how filtered data are stored in captureBufferTable. One row of captureBuffer-Table is used to store data on packets from a channel. The implementation of the packet capture group is optional. If the Filter group is implemented, then this group must be implemented. The objects in the packet capture group are:

bufferControlIndex (INTEGER): A unique index that identifies a entry in bufferControlTable.

bufferControlChannelIndex (INTEGER): Identifies the channel Its value is the same as the value in channelIndex.

bufferControlFullStatus (INTEGER): Shows the status of the buffer which is used to store data received from filters. It has two values: spaceAvailable = 1 and full = 2.

bufferControlFullAction (INTEGER): Will indicate the action to be taken when the buffer becomes full. It has two values: lockWhenFull = 1 and wrapWhenFull = 2.

bufferControlCaptureSliceSize (INTEGER): Furnishes the maximum number of octets of each packet which will be stored in the capture buffer. If it is set to zero, then as many octets as possible will be saved in the capture buffer.

bufferControlDownloadSliceSize (INTEGER): States the maximum number of octets that will be retrieved from a management station by an SNMP GetRequest or GetNextRequest PDUs. The default value is 100 octets.

bufferControlDownloadOffset (INTEGER): States the offset after which data in the buffer will be retrieved by a management station with an SNMP GetRequest or GetNextRequest PDU. The default offset value is 0.

bufferControlMaxOctetsRequested (INTEGER): Furnishes the maximum number of octets which a management station desires a capture buffer to save. *A* default value of -1 indicates that the request by the management station to the monitoring device is to save as many octets as possible.

bufferControlMaxOctetsGranted (INTEGER): We have noted earlier that a monitoring device may have resource limitations. Under those circumstances, it is not possible to furnish the buffer space requested by a management station. bufferControlMaxOctets Granted supplies the actual number of octets that can be saved, and if the default value is 1, then the capture buffer" will save as many octets as possible.

bufferControlCapturedPackets (INTEGER): Furnishes the nu ber of packets actually stored at present in a capture buffer.

bufferControlTurnOnTime (INTEGER): Provides sysUpTime when the capture buffer started functioning.

bufferControlOwner and *bufferControlStatus* have the same significance described for corresponding objects in other groups.

The captureBufferTable has the following entries:

captureBufferControlIndex (INTEGER) Provides the index of an entry in captureBufferTable.

captureBufferIndex (INTEGER): Increases in value by 1 from 1, and uniquely identifies an entry in captureBufferTable.

captureBufferPakcetID (INTEGER): An index, in ascending order, describing the order of the packets received on an interface. These packets may be stored in one or more capture buffers, hence aiding in identifying the packets.

Concepts of filter, channel, capture and events

captureBufferPacketData (OCTET STRING): Contains the captured data of a packet.

capture BufferPacketLength (INTEGER): Furnishes the length of the captured packet and includes the FCS octets.

captureBufferPacketnme (INTEGER): Furnishes the relative time in milliseconds when a packet was captured since the capture buffer was turned on.

captureBufferPacketStatus (INTEGER): Provides the error status of a packet. The values defined are: packet length greater than 1518 octets = 0, packet length less than 64 octets = 1, packet had CRC or alignment error = 2, first packet in the capture buffer after an error was discovered = 3 and packet's order in buffer is only approximate = 4. The fourth bit definition is an addition in RFC 1757.

Event group

The event group helps in the generation and notification of events. These events might have been generated due to conditions elsewhere in the MIB. It may be determined that when a certain threshold is reached an event is generated. Parameters of events are described in eventTable. When an event is generated, it may be necessary to log the event. Events are logged in logTable. Here an SNMP trap may be generated and used to notify a managing station. The objects are:

eventIndex (INTEGER): Identifies an entry in eventTable.

eventDescription (DisplayString): Provides the description of the event.

eventType (INTEGER): Describes the type of event. The values are: none = 1, log = 2, snmp-trap = 3, and log-and-trap = 4. If an event is logged, then a value of 3 is used and there is a corresponding entry in logTable. If an SNMP trap is sent to one or more management stations, then the value is 3. When the SNMP trap is logged the value is 4. *euentCommunity (OCTET STRING):* Names the SNMP community to which the SNMP trap must be sent.

eventLastTimeSent (TimeTicks): Furnishes sysUpTime when an event was last generated. If it is set to 0, then no event was generated.

eventOwner and *eventStatus* have the same signi-ficance as described for corresponding entries in other groups.

logEventIndex (INTEGER): Has the value of eventIndex for which a log was generated.

logIndex (INTEGER): Identifies an entry in the log table.

logTime(TimeTicks): Furnishes sysUpTime when an event that has been logged in logTable was created.

logDescription (DisplayString): Presents the description of the event.

RMON for Token Ring (RFC 1513)

RFC 1513 extends the RMON MIB for the tokenring protocol by adding a new group for tokenRing under RMON.

We discuss RFC 1513 separately, because it neatly describes extensions for the tokenring protocol. Because RFC 1271 is specifically tailored for collecting data on Ethernet protocols, new groups are exclusively added to statistics and history groups for the tokenring protocol. Error counters in a hostEntry for token ring will be incremented for isolating errors such as LineErrors, BurstErrors, ACErrors, InternalErrors, and AbortErrors. In token ring, matrix group error counters are not incremented. For bit mask interpretations for the filter group, refer to RFC 1513. The following new object groups have been added to the token-ring protocol:

Token-ring station
Token-ring station order
Token-ring station configuration
Source routing statistics

New data types in RFC 1513 are:

MacAddress (OCTET STRING (SIZE (6)): Defines the MAC address used in IEEE Standard 802. 1. When MacAddress is used, the source routing bit is stripped off.

TimeInterval (INTEGER): Refers to a period of time, and is measured in intervals of 0.01 seconds.

Token-ring MAC-layer statistics group

The token-ring MAC-layer statistics group consists of one table: tokenRingMLStatsTable. This table has statistics on the MAC layer for one token-ring interface, so the objects defined have significance to the MAC layer. We will discuss only those objects which are unique to this group and will not repeat the explanations of those objects which are similar to the ones we discussed with RFC 1757. As we have seen with RFC 1757, these statistics are useful for performance and fault management. In the following discussion, ML stands for MAC layer. The objects in the group are:

tokenRingMLStatsMacPkts (Counter): Refers to the total number of octets in good MAC packets received. It does not include the packets which had errors. A good frame refers to a token-ring frame defined by IEEE 802.5 standards.

tokenRingMLStatsRingPurgeEvents (Counter): Specifies the number of times the ring purge state has been reached from a normal state. In token ring, data is received when a station is in a *normal repeat mode.* In this mode, a station will receive a frame and transmit it. A ring purge MAC frame must be sent before an active monitor originates a new token. When a ring purge frame is received, timers in stations are reset, and stations enter the normal repeat mode.

tokenRingMLStatsRingPurgePkts (Counter): Refers to the total number of ring purge MAC packets.

tokenRingMLStatsBeaconEvents (Counter): Refers to the number of times a beacon state has been entered. To understand this counter, the concept of *beacoming* must be understood. In token ring, a ring can become nonoperational due to faults in stations, which are known as *hard errors.* A hard error in a station is usually detected by its immediate downstream neighbor. On receiving this frame, the downstream neighbor sends a *beacon frame,* which contains the address of its upstream neighbor and the information on the type of error. By knowing the address of the upstream neighbor, the ring station that has a failure can be pinpointed.

tokenRingMLStatsBeaconTime (TimeInterval): Furnishes the duration of the beaconing state.

tokenRingMLStatsBeaconPkts (Counter): Provides the total number of MAC beacon packets.

tokenRingMLStatsClaimTokenEvents (Counter): Separates the entry to the claim token state into three states: from the normal ring state, from the ring purge state, and from the beacon state. In this counter, only the first two cases are taken, and the total number of times a token enters the claim token state is furnished. Note that the claim token process is done to elect a new active monitor.

tokenRingMLStatsClaimTokenPkts (Counter): Refers to the total number of claim token MAC packets.

tokenRingMLStatsNAUNChanges (Counter): Has the total number of *nearest active upstream neighbor* (NAUN) changes. Note that when an active monitor broadcasts an active monitor present MAC frame, the first ring station that receives this frame saves the source address of the active monitor present frame as the NAUN address. These NAUN addresses are useful for isolating errors in a segment.

tokenRingMLStatsLineErrors (Counter): Provides the total number of line errors.

tokenRingMLStatsInternalErrors (Counter): Refers to the total number of adapter internal errors.

tokenRingMLStatsBurstErrors (Counter): Provides the total number of burst errors.

tokenRingMLStatsACErrors (Counter): Refers to the total number of address copied errors.

tokenRingMLStatsAbortErrors (Counter): A counter of the total number of abort delimiters in error-reporting packets.

tokenRingMLStatsLostFrameErrors (Counter): Refers to the total number of lost frames.

tokenRingMLStatsCongestionErrors (Counter): Provides the total number of receive congestion errors.

tokenRingMLStatsFrameCopiedErrors (Counter): For counting frame copied errors.

tokenRingMLStatsFrequencyErrors (Counter): Provides the total number of frequency errors.

tokenRingMLStatsTokenErrors (Counter): For counting the total number of token errors.

tokenRingMLStatsSoftErrorReports (Counter): Refers to the total number of *soft error* frames. Soft errors mean errors which temporarily make the rings nonoperational, although it is possible to recover from them. These soft errors can pose major problems if there are too many of them.

tokenRingMLStatsRingPollEvents (Counter): Relates to the total number of ring polls initiated by an active monitor.

The other group in the token ring statistics group is the token ring promiscuous statistics group. According to *Webster's New Collegiate Dictionary,* one meaning of *promiscuous is* "composed of all sorts of persons or things." In the MAC layer statistics group' data was collected on just the MAC layer. It is necessary to know data about the physical and link layers too. Hence, there is the tokenring promiscuous statistics group. Data on this group is also useful for performance and fault management. The objects in this group are similar to the data collected in etherStatsTable, thus, we will not discuss each of the objects in the group. Because there is no Ethernet restriction that the packets must be between 64 and 1518 octets, the range of packet length in token ring is greater.

Token-ring history group

Similar to the statistics group, the token-ring history group extends the history group described for RFC 1271. Here, too, history on a token-ring interface is collected and data are saved in tokenRingMLHistoryTable for the MAC layer and in tokenRingPHistoryTable for the non-MAC layer data. Data collected in these tables is useful for performance and fault management. The implementation of the token-ring history group is optional, but it requires the implementation of history groups mentioned in RFC 1757. The meanings of objects are similar to the corresponding ones in RFC 1757 and the token-ring statistics group, so we will not provide individual explanations.

Token-ring ring station group

The token-ring ring station group contains the statistics and status of each station attached to a token-ring network. When there are resource limitations on the network monitor, the resources which have been inactive for the longest time must be freed. The implementation of this group is also optional. The data collected for, this station are useful for configuration, performance, and fault management. RingStationControlEntry has parameters for collecting data on stations in the ring which have been discovered. ringStationEntry has the actual data on the stations. For this group, we will discus those objects that have new meanings.

ringStationControlActiveStations (INTEGER): Furnishes the number of active ringStationEntry in the ringStation-Table.

ringStationControlRingState (INTEGER): Presents the current status of the ring. The values are: normalOperation = 1, ringPurgeState = 2, claimToken-State = 3, beaconFrameStreamingState = 4, beaconBit-StreamingState = 5, beaconRing SignalLossState = 6, and beaconSetRecoveryModeState = 7. These status values can be useful for depicting status in appropriate colors, while showing the configuration and status of the token-ring network.

ringStationControlOrderChanges (Counter): Contains the number of add and delete events in ringStationOrderTable.

ringStationControlBeaconSender, ringStationControl-BeaconNAUN, and ringStationControlActiveMonitor refer to the address of the sender of the beacon frame, the address of the NAUN in the beacon frame, and the address of the active monitor, respectively.

ringStationTable furnishes statistics on a particular station in the ring. Here, ringStationStationStatus, which can have values of active = 1, inactive = 2, and forcedRemoval = 3, respectively, is very useful for depicting the status of a station in a ring in configuration management. These states of a station may be represented by different colors. In addition, ringStationLastEnterTime and ringStationLastExitTime indicate when a station entered and exited a ring and are also useful for configuration management. The value unknown, indicated by a value of 0 in these variables, can be shown by a specific color when depicting these stations in a ring.

Tokenring ring station order group

The token-ring ring station order group has ringStationOrderTable, in which stations are identified from the station on which the network monitor is placed. The order of a station relative to the station with the network monitor is furnished by ringStationOrder-Orderlndex, and the address of the station is furnished by ringStationOrderMacAddress.

Token-ring ring station config group

The token-ring ring station config group manages token-ring nodes. Another popular term to describe managing token-ring nodes is the *configuration of nodes.* The following describes the nonobvious objects in ringStationConfigControlTable:

ringStationConfigControlRemove (INTEGER): Has two values: stable = I and removing = 2. When RMON agents set the value of this variable to removing, it results in the remove station MAC frame. After this frame is processed, the RMON agent sets this variable to stable.

ringStationConfigControlUpdateStats (INTEGER): Also has two values: stable = I and updating = 2. The behavior of this object is similar to the behavior of ringStationConfigControlRemove. When this object is set to updating, then the configuration information associated with this entry is updated. After this update is over, the RMON agent will set this object to stable.

ringStationConfigTable provides the configuration, entries after a query by the ringStationConfig-ControlUpdateStats',, variable. These data are also useful for configuration management. Some of the associated variables needing explanations are:

ringStationConfigLocation (OCTET STRING(SIZEW): Refers to the actual physical location of the station.

ringStationConfigMicrocode (OCTET STRING(SIZE(10)): Indicates the microcode level of the station.

ringStationConfigGroupAddress (OCTET STRING (SIZE (4)): Pertains to the low-order four octets of the group address recognized by the station.

Token-ring source routing group

The implementation of the token-ring source routing group is optional. Data in this group are collected in source routing bridges and are valid in source routing environments. In transparent bridging or mixed source and transparent bridge environments, the data are not accurate. sourceRoutingStatsTable provides a list of entries with statistics on source routing for tokenring interfaces. Some of the variables in this group are:

sourceRoutingStatsRingNumber (INTEGER): In an internetwork, there may be many rings, which are assigned numbers by management stations. It is this ring number that is entered here.

sourceRoutingStatsInFrames (Counter): Provides the total number of frames sent to a token-ring station from another ring.

sourceRoutingStatsOutFrames (Counter): Refers to the number of frames sent out from a ring.

sourceRoutingStatsThroughFrames (Counter): Provides the total number of frames which went through a ring. Here, frames are received by a ring and they are transmitted to the next ring.

sourceRoutingStatsAllRoutesBroadcastFrames (Counter): Refers to the total number of good all routes broadcast frames that were received.

sourceRoutingStatsSingleRouteBroadcastFrames (Counter): Has the count of good frames received which had single route broad, cast.

sourceRoutingStatsInOctets, sourceRoutingStatsOut-Octets, sourceRoutingStats Through Octets, sourceRouting-StatsAllRoutesBroadcastOctets, and *sourceRoutingSingle-RoutesBroadcastOctets* have counts of octets instead of frames, which we saw earlier. The counts refer to good octets only.

sourceRoutingStatsLocalLLCFrames (Counter): Provides the total number of frames received which had no RIF field. All route broadcast frames are not counted here.

sourceRoutingStats1HopFrames through *sourceRouting-StatsMore Than8HopsFrames* provide the frames for the hops mentioned. The all route broadcast frames are not counted. The source and destination stations are expected to be in the same ring.

In the Internet community, the TCP/IP protocol suite is used extensively for computer networking. TCP/IP is very popular because of the simplicity and openness of the protocols. There is a difference between "capital I" Internet and small i" internet. The former is a global network formed by loosely organized and autonomous interconnected networks. It uses Internet Standards such as TCP/IP. Previously, it was called the National Science Foundation (NSF) backbone net. The TCP/IP protocol suite is also known as Internet. The scope of Internet Standards covers TCP/IP protocol suite and protocols, procedures, and conventions used in the Internet context. On the other hand, internet (lower-class) refers to a collection of networks not connected to the Internet, but using Internet Standards. TCP is a stream-oriented protocol and does not bother about record boundaries. It deals with bytes instead of records, as in some other protocols such as SNA. Also in TCP/IP, all computers are generically referred to as *hosts.* Notice that *host* in TCP/IP is a very generic term, which can mean a workstation, a personal computer, or even a mainframe. In the mainframe world, a mainframe is generally referred to as a host, unlike in the Internet arena. Devices which connect networks and forward Internet Protocol (IP) packets are known as *gateways,* which has here a broader meaning and scope than the gateways referred to in the LAN arena. TCP/IP gateways are similar to routers in the LAN arena. Currently, gateways may also be known as IP *routers.* The first layer is the *network interface* (NI) layer. Internet does not have any standards defined for this layer. This layer can have Ethernet, X.25, or token rings. The NI layer corresponds to the physical and link layers of the OSI seven-layer architecture as shown in Figure. Access the ports is achieved in the physical layer. In the link layer, one of MAC layer protocols is used.

The layer above the NI is the IP layer. This is a connectionless layer. Above this layer can be connection-oriented TCP or the connectionless *User Datagram Protocol* (UDP). On top of these layers are applications such as the *File Transfer Protocol* (FTP), *Simple Transfer Protocol* (SMTP), *TELNET,* and *Simple Net Management Protocol* (SNMP). A *message* or *stream of d* transferred from the application layer to the TCP/UDP layer. When transferred to the lower IP layer along with the TCP/UDP header, this message is called a *packet.* This packet, in turn, is wrapped proper IP headers and becomes an IP *datagram,* which is passe the NI. In the NI layer, the IP datagram is again packaged with the appropriate NI headers; this is known as a *frame.* This frame is transmitted over the network. Internet uses SNMP for network management. In the first version SNMP, security was a weak link. To overcome some of the weaknesses of SNMP, it has been modified. The earlier SNMP is known now as SNMPv1 or SNMP version 1; the new modified protocol known as SNMPv2 or SNMP version 2.

The main objective of this chapter is to introduce to readers the important lower-level protocols used in Internet network management, assuming SNMPs as the higher-layer application protocols. To understand SNMP, important concepts of the lower-layer protocols ",are required. Because this book deals with network management, only an overview of the lower-layer TCP/IP protocol suite is provided.

Internet addressing

In IP, transmission of data and headers is done as shown in Figure. Octet I is transmitted 'first, then octet 2, and so on. An IP address has two parts: network number and host number. The IP layer recognizes the IP address only. IP address classes are Class A, Class B, Class C, Class D, and Class E. The main distinction among Class A, Class B, and Class C is in the division between network number and host number, also referred to as the *rest field.* In Class D, the first four bits are 1110, and the remaining 28 bits are known as the *multicast address.* When IP packets have to be sent to a group of stations, this is known as multicasting. *Broadcasting* is an extension of multicasting, in which all the stations in a subnet receive the IP packet. In Class E, the first four bits are 1111. Class E addresses are reserved for future uses.

The main advantage of these classes is flexibility for arranging the networks. For example, a large number of workstations may need to be connected to form a network. In such a case, the Class A addressing scheme is convenient. If a relatively small number of workstations are to be connected to form a LAN, Class C may be appropriate.

The 32 bits of IP address are divided into four eight-bit fields. The IP addresses in *Dotted Decimal Notation* are formed by decimal numbers obtained from each of the eight-bit fields, and they are separated by periods. As an example, 183.127.2.35, a class B address, is shown in Figure. The network numbers are assigned by the Network Information Center (NIC). At the time this manuscript was written, work on IP version 6 was ongoing. In IP version 6, an IP address will be 16 octets (128 bits). This will solve the present problem of a shortage of IP addresses.

A process in the application layer chooses the transport it requires. It decides whether it wants to use a connection-oriented service such as TCP or a connectionless service such as UDR The next layer (TCP/UDP) wraps its own header to the data it received from the process in the application layer. The action of wrapping a header on the data received from an upper layer is known as *encapsulation.* The internet layer, in turn, adds its own header and sends the data to the local NI. The local NI maps the IP address to the local network address. If a packet is to be transmitted from one host in a network to a host in another network, then the local gateway address must be found and the packet must be transmitted to the right gateway. The gateway maps the IP address to the local network address and routes the packet to the destination host or another gateway in the path of the destination host. A packet may be delivered to a destination host by more than one path. To avoid such a situation, the gateways have algorithms to calculate the right path.

Internet protocol(IP)

he IP is a connectionless best-effort packet delivery service. In this protocol, there is no end-to-end guaranteed delivery, acknowledgment, flow control, retransmission, or error recovery. This protocol tries its best to deliver packets to the destination. The frames are discarded as a last resort. If connection-oriented support is required, then it must be provided by the upper layers. The IP layer deals with four-octet IP addresses.

The IP datagram is as shown in Figure, consisting of the IP header and the data portion. The first field in the IP header is the *version* of IP, which version is provided to furnish details of the IP software. Like any technology, changes do occur to account for advances. The present version is 4. The version field alerts the system to these changes and facilitates compatibility. The IP header length is in multiples of 32 bits. The *length* field extends from the version field to the beginning of the data portion. Total length is inclusive of the IP header and data, and is measured in octets. Because the length field is 16 bits, it can accommodate up to 65,535 octets. However, there is also a restriction that hosts must be able to accept IP datagrams larger than 576 octets.

Though IP imposes an upper limit of 65,535, protocols used in the lower levels impose their own restrictions. For example, Ethernet has its minimum of 64 octets and maximum of 1518 octet frame length limitations. So the length of datagrams sent in networks will be guided by limitations other than the ones imposed by the IP layer. The *type of service* (TOS) field is one octet long. The first three bits indicate *precedence,* for which different levels are defined. High-precedence traffic is regarded as more important than low-precedence traffic.

Bits 6 and 7 of the TOS field are reserved for future use, and they are set to zero. However, RFC 1349 redefines the TOS field. Here the TOS field is taken as four bits; the last bit is labeled Must Be Zero (MBZ), and this bit is unused. TOS values mentioned in Table are the values which will be tried. If the network cannot provide the TOS requested, then values used will be those of the network.

When a datagram is larger than the size that can be handled by a network, then a gateway converts the datagram into smaller-size fragments which are multiples of eight. As an example, the IP datagram shown in Figure can be converted to smaller datagrams as shown. This action of forming smaller datagrams out of a large one is known as *fragmentation,* also sometimes known as segmentation. However, these fragments are reassembled only in the destination host and not in the intermediate gateways.

The *identification* field is 16 bits in length. It has three bits of the *flag* field and 13 bits of *fragment offset.* In the flag field, the fist bit (bit 0) is set to 0. Bit I has two options. If it is set to 0, then it indicates that the datagram may be fragmented. If it is set to 1, then the datagram cannot be fragmented. Bit 2 of flag again has two options. When fragmentation is done, this bit in the last fragment is set to 0. However, in other fragments, this bit is 1, indicating that there are more fragments of the datagram. The other IP field, *fragment offset,* furnishes the offset of the datagram, which is in units of eight octets. The first fragment has a fragment offset of 0. The next IP header field, known as the *time to live* (TTL) field, is eight bits long and has time in seconds. TTL specifies how long a datagram remains in a system. Because a gateway is able to process a packet in less than a second, the TTL count is reduced by one. In such a case, the TTL counter becomes a maximum allowable count of hops for a packet to reach the destination host. When the TTL becomes zero, then a datagram destroys itself. This process is also known as *self-destruction* and prevents a datagram from making unnecessary cycles in the network.

The *protocol* field has the protocol number of the upper layer. For example, ICMP has a protocol number of 1, and the protocol number for TCP is 6. Assigned numbers of higher-layer protocols are furnished in Reference. The *header checksum* field provides the checksum of the IP header field only, and does not include the checksum of the data portion. It is obtained by adding the ones complement of different fields and then taking the ones complement of the sum. The source and destination IP addresses are the addresses of the sender and receiver. The destination IP address does not refer to the addresses of intermediate gateways.

The *options* field must be implemented in all hosts and gateways, but it is optional in datagrams. There are two types of options field, Case 1 and Case 2, as shown in Figure. In Case 1, the *option type* field is one octet long. Case 2 has a one-octet option type, one octet of *option length,* and the option data. The option length octet includes the length of the option data and two octets that include one octet of option type and one octet of option length fields. The option field has one bit of flag, two bits of option class, and five bits of option number.

One bit of flag indicates whether the option field is copied into fragments on fragmentation. If it is zero, then the option field is not copied and if it is set to one, then the option field is copied into all the fragments. The option field is quite useful for adding a variety of features, but options cannot be used unless they are accepted by the general Internet community. The *padding* field is used to ensure that the IP header aligns on a 32-bit boundary.

Internet control message protocol(ICMP)

ICMP is used for communicating error or control messages from one host to another host or from routers (gateways) to the host. ICMP is required in every IP layer. The ICMP message occupies the data portion of the IP. It has a header of its own and data. For an ICMP message, the protocol field in the IP header is set to 1. The ICMP message is formed as shown in Figure. For ICMP, TOS is always set to 0000. The source address refers to the host address or router address which generated the ICMP message. The destination address is the address of the host or router to which the ICMP message must be sent.

The ICMP field always has an ICMP type field, which distinguishes different ICMP messages. There is also a code field, which gives more details about messages, and the checksum field, which furnishes the checksum for the ICMP message portion only.

The IP header and first 64 bits of the original datagram refer to the header and the data of the layer above ICMP. The layer above can be either TCP or UDP. The first 64 bits of data are used for matching processes which may use the ICMP message. The ICMP message is quite useful for discovering hosts and routers. The Packet InterNet Groper (PING) is used for checking the connectivity of a host with a remote host and getting the details of a host. It is also quite useful for network management. PING is an echo request and echo reply, and is useful for gathering data on hosts and routers. The ICMP message for an echo request and echo reply is shown in Figure. When an echo request is to be sent, the ICMP type is 8. The destination address is the address of the router or host IP which must send an echo of the message back to the sender. For the echo reply, which has same message sent in the echo request, the ICMP type is 0.

Identifier and sequence numbers are used for identifying and matching a message and its replies. If code is 0, then both identifier and sequence number may be 0. As we have seen earlier, echo request and echo reply can be used to gather data and statistics on the network and hosts and routers. They are also useful for debugging purposes.

Transmission control protocol (TCP)

TCP is a connection-oriented, reliable, packet-switching protocol used for communication between processes in host computers. These host computers are distinct and are part of a communication network. The data transfer is full-duplex, which means that the sender sends data in one direction and can simultaneously receive data from the opposite direction. One of the strengths of the TCP protocol is its flexibility. It does not specifically mandate any protocol for the layer above it or the layer below. Usually, in Internet, the lower-layer protocol is IP. TCP is a stream-oriented protocol, and the combination of TCP layer data and headers is known as a *segment*.

An important concept in TCP is that of a connection. TCP provides for a set of addresses or *ports* within each host. Many processes can be associated with a port. The IP address and port number identify a *socket.* A pair of sockets identify a *connection.* Before communication can take place, a connection must be established between processes. This connection is referred to as a *virtual circuit*, which is analogous to a telephone connection being formed before the start of a conversation.

In a network, segments of data may be damaged or corrupted, lost, duplicated, or delivered out of order. To account for this, there is provision for acknowledgment and retransmission. When data is sent by a sender, the sequence number of the first octet of data in the segment is also sent. At the same time, the sender starts a timer. The receiving end sends an acknowledgment number. This acknowledgment refers to the sequence number of the next expected data octet to be sent by the sender. However, if the acknowledgment is not received before the timer runs out, then the sender retransmits the segment. There is also provision for a checksum of the data to identify whether the data has been corrupted. We have seen earlier that IP does not provide a checksum of the data; it provides for a checksum of the IP header only. So TCP takes account of this fact to provide a reliable communication mechanism.

Flow control is achieved by means of a variable window that can be sent along with an acknowledgment by a receiver. If the receiver does not have much buffer space left, then it sends a smaller window. Conversely, where the receiver is willing to accept and process data at a faster rate, it adjusts the window to a larger number than the existing one. The destination IP address identifies the destination host, and the source IP address identifies the source host address. In this figure, SA1 is the source host IP address, and DA1 is the destination host IP address. The applications Al, A2, and A3 are the source ports. It is assumed that they want to communicate with destination ports B1, B2, and B3, respectively. The process in Host 1, where applications are combined, is analogous to multiplexing, and the process in Host 2, where they are directed to the respective ports, is similar to demultiplexing seen in the data transmissions across a transmission medium.

A TCP segment has a TCP header part and a data part. The TCP header has the following fields:

Source port number: A 16-bit field, containing a source port number.

Destination port number: Also a 16-bit field, with a destination port number where a data segment must be sent.

Sequence number: The sequence number of a data octet of a segment that is being sent from a sender. In the case of synchronization or when the SYN bit is set, it is the *initial sequence number* (ISN). The first octet of data starts from ISN + 1. Here note that the ISN need not always start with 0, or the first octet sequence number need not always start with 1. The sequence number is a 32-bit field.

Acknowledgment number: A 32-bit field, always sent once a connection has been established. This is the number of the first data octet which a receiver expects to receive next. For example, if a receiver has received data up to 100 octets, the receiver puts the acknowledgment number as 101. The receiver next expects a segment in which the data octet starts with 101.

Data offset: A four-bit field. A TCP header is a multiple of 32 bits. This field contains the length of the TCP header measured in terms of 32 bits. In a segment, data offset indicates where the data starts.

Reserved: Intended for future use and set to 0. It is six bits in length. It is a good idea to provide for a reserved field in any protocol. When technology changes or new technologies are incorporated, these reserved bits can be used.

The first six fields in the following list are all one-bit fields.

URG: Urgent pointer significant field. TCP has provided for sending out-of-band urgent data. When this bit is set, the receiver is expected to process this segment first, interrupting all other activities. When the URG bit is set, the urgent pointer field has relevance..

ACK. Acknowledgment significant field. When this field is set, an acknowledgment number is sent.

PSH: Push function field. When this field is set, the sender is expected to send whatever data is available in the buffer instead of waiting for the send buffer to be filled up.

RST. Used for resetting a connection. When this bit is set, depending on the states of sender and receiver, actions are taken. For example, reset is sent when a segment for another connection is received.

SYN: For synchronizing sequence numbers. This is used in the beginning to establish a connection by means of a three-way handshake.

FIN: Used for closing a connection.

Window: A 16-bit field. Because the data in IP segments are in terms of octets, window states the number of octets which a receiver is willing to receive, starting from one.

Checksum: A 16-bit field. The checksum is calculated and includes a TCP pseudo header and TCP segment. The TCP pseudo header has source and destination addresses, eight bits set to 0, the protocol, and TCP length. The pseudo header is used for computing the checksum and is not transmitted while transmitting data. That is the reason for naming it a pseudo header. Here, TCP length is the sum of the TCP header and TCP data. This TCP length does not, however, include 12 octets of the TCP pseudo header. For checksum, header and text octets must be even. To make these even, sometimes the last octet is padded with 0. To form the checksum, the ones complement of the TCP header is taken, then the ones complement of the result is taken.

Urgent pointer: Provides positive offset from the sequence number in a segment. This points to data offset following urgent data. As mentioned earlier, this field is taken into consideration only if the URG bit is set. This is a 16-bit field.

Options: A variable-length field, with length in multiples of eight bits. Here, too, there are two options:

- Case 1: Has one octet of option.
- Case 2: Has one octet of option, one octet of option length, and variable-length options data. Here, as in the IP, length includes two octets due to the option and option length.

User datagram protocol (UDP)

SNMP, Internet Name Server, and Trivial File Transfer use the UDP protocol. This is a connectionless datagram service. UDP, in turn, depends upon the connectionless IP layer. As a result, there is no guarantee that data will be delivered; there may be duplicate frames sent, or data may be received in an order different from the order in which they were sent. Also, there is no acknowledgment that data has been delivered. However, if an application wishes to provide services that are available in a connection oriented service, it is the responsibility of the application to incorporate them in upper-layer software. In UDP, an application that wants to transmit data to another application uses a scheme similar to TCP The data of the application are initially enveloped with a UDP header. Then, at the IP layer, the IP header is appended. In the NI layer, the network header is appended to the IP frame. This frame is transmitted over the Internet to the other end. On the receiving end, the NI layer removes the network layer header, and the IP layer strips off the IP header. The UDP layer, in turn, removes the UDP header and routes data to the appropriate application. If there is a mismatch or the proper frame is not received, the ICMP message can be sent to the original application with causes for the error.

The UDP datagram is as shown in Figure. It has 16 bits each of source port and destination numbers. The length field contains the number of octets of the UDP frame and includes the length of the UDP frame headers. The next field in the UDP header is the checksum field, which is an optional field. If it is not used, then this field has zeros; however, if the checksum field is used, it contains the ones complement of the checksum derived from a pseudo header.

The UDP pseudo header is similar to the TCP pseudo header. The UDP pseudo header has four octets each of source IP address and destination IP address, zero padding, protocol, and UDP length. One octet of zero padding is done to make the UDP frame a multiple of two. One octet protocol field is 17 for IP, and the two-byte UDP length field is the length of the UDP datagram in octets. However ' the UDP length field does not include the length of the pseudo header. Thus, an application that wants to send data needs to know the IP addresses of source and destination beforehand in the UDP layer itself.

The use of checksum is mostly guided by the application. Note here that IP uses only the header checksum; it does not use the checksum over the IP data portion. Hence, if some validation of whether the UDP frame is the correct one is required, then the checksum in UDP is required. In some cases, we may not want to have the overhead of computing the checksum., since the loss of some UDP frames may not matter much. One such case is that of monitoring the performance of a resource, where the loss of a UDP datagram may not mean much. Also, in some cases, a network may be very reliable, without the risk of losing frames. In other cases, the application may be critical and the loss of a frame may lead to problems. In such cases, it is better to use checksum. Also, when a network is unreliable, it is appropriate to use the cheeksum to make sure that the data delivered is correct.

Address resolution protocol (ARP)

We have seen that Internet knows only the IP address. Let us investigate how an IP packet is sent to the other end. An IP packet has a destination IP address. Then the local host looks at the ARP table and checks where the destination is. An ARP table is a sort of lookup table which has a mapping between an IP address and its corresponding physical address. Then the NI layer inserts the actual physical address of the destination host. The Ethernet or token-ring frame has this destination physical address. On the destination side, this Ethernet frame is stripped of its physical address and routed to the right IP layer. When this happens, the destination is in the same network. However, it is possible that the destination could be another network, in which case, instead of the physical address of the destination host, the physical address of the IP router is appended in the Ethernet frame. In the IP router, a check is again made with a routing table to see where the destination IP address is. If there are many hops or steps required before a destination can be reached, then the physical addresses of the IP routers are successively inserted. In the last IP router, the destination host physical address is retrieved from the destination IP address to route the IP packet to the correct destination.

The next issue is how to build an ARP table. This is done by broadcasting an ARP request packet, which has a source IP address, source physical address, and destination IP address. When this packet is broadcast, each host examines the IP address and looks whether it matches its own IP address. If it matches, the host puts its IP address and physical address in the source. The earlier source IP and physical addresses are transferred to the destination IP address and the destination physical address, and the response is sent back.

In the original host that sent the ARP request packet, the ARP table now has the mapping of the destination IP address and physical address. It is possible that no host has a matching IP address when an ARP request packet is sent. In such a case, the IP address is not, known.

The manner in which the IP packet handles cases in which mapping between the IP address and physical address is not known is, implementation dependent. In some cases, when the mapping is not there, the IP packet is queued and an ARP request packet is sent. When the destination physical address becomes known, the ARP request packet is received. The IP packet is dequeued and sent to the destination. If the address is not known, the IP layer discards the packets. In some cases, these IP packets may not be queued. If the IP packets are not delivered, the upper layers are alerted by *timeouts*.

Reverse address resolution protocol(RARP)

RARP is the reverse process of ARP, in which mapping is from a physical address to the IP address. A station may have its physical address; it sends a RARP to a server giving its IP address, and the server maps the IP address and sends back the physical address.

Subnet addressing

A network that uses a single access protocol under the control of a single administrative domain is known as a *subnetwork.* As a corollary to this definition, a subnetwork can be a collection of smaller networks. The IP address consists of a network number part and a host number part. The network number part is used for routing from network to network. This provides the first level of routing. The technique of partitioning a network address to cover multiple networks is known as *subnet addressing*. Here, a host number is further divided into a subnet number part and a host number part, which enables one more level of partitioning of networks, and also helps in forming further routing levels.

In subnet addressing, to recover the network number part, a 32-bit subnet mask, which has all 1s in the network number and subnet number part, is used. The subnet mask has zeros in the rest of the mask. So when data is to be sent from station A, it goes to the appropriate router. The router uses the subnet number part to send it to the proper subnet or network; then the host number is used to deliver the data to the right destination host. If all the networks are not using subnet addressing, routers use proxy ARP. According to this, for an ARP on a station address, the router answers by giving its hardware address for the address of a station. This is analogous to saying: I know station B's address; you can send frames meant for it to me. So when station A has to send the frame, it sends it to the correct router. The router, in turn, interprets the address and sends it to the right station.

A computer network is basically a bunch of computers hooked together somehow. In concept, it's sort of like a radio or TV network that connects a bunch of radio or TV stations so that they can share the latest episode of "The X-Files." Don't take the analogy too far. TV networks send the same information to all the stations at the same time (it's called broadcast networking); in computer networks, each particular message is usually routed to a particular computer.

Unlike TV networks, computer networks are invariably two-way, so that when computer A sends a message to computer B, B can send a reply back to A. Some computer networks consist of a central computer and a bunch of remote stations that report to it (a central airline-reservation computer, for example, with thousands of screens and keyboards in airports and travel agencies). Others, including the Internet, are more egalitarian and permit any computer on the network to communicate with any other. The Internet isn't really a network it's a network of networks, all freely exchanging information.' The networks range from the big and formal (such as the corporate networks at AT&T Digital Equipment, and Hewlett-Packard) to the small and informal (such as the one in John's back bedroom, with a couple of old PCs bought through the Want Advertiser) and everything in between. With networks, size counts for a great deal because the larger a network is, the more stuff it has to offer. Because the Internet is the world's largest computer network, it has an amazing array of information to offer.

The Internet is new communications technology that is affecting our lives a scale as significant as the telephone and television. Some people believe that when it comes to disseminating information, the Internet is the most significant invention since the printing press. If you use a telephone, write letters, read a newspaper or magazine, or do business or any kind of research, the Internet can radically alter your entire world view. When people talk about the Internet today, they're usually talking about what they can do and whom they have met. The Internet's capabilities are so expansive that we don't have room to give a complete list here (indeed, would fill several books larger than this one), but here's a quick summary:

Electronic mail (e-mail):

This service is certainly the most widely used-you can exchange e-mail with millions of people all over the world. People use e-mail for anything they might use paper mail or the telephone for: gossip, recipes, rumors, love letters-you name it. (We hear that some people even use it for stuff related to work.) Electronic mailing lists enable you to join in group discussions with people who have similar interests and meet people over the Net. Mail servers (programs that respond to e-mail messages automatically) let you retrieve all sorts of information.

The World Wide Web

When people talk these days about surfing the Net, they often mean checking out sites on this (buzzword alert) multimedia hyperlinked database that spans the globe. The Web, unlike earlier Net services, combines text, pictures, sound, and even animation, and it lets you move around with a click of your computer mouse. New Web sites are growing faster than you can say "Big Mac with cheese," with new sites appearing every minute. In 1993 when we wrote the first edition of this book, the Internet had 130 Web sites. Today it has more than 600,000 and statistics indicate that the number is doubling every two months. The software used to navigate the Web is known as a browser. The most popular browsers today are Netscape Navigator and Microsoft Internet. Explorer.

Information retrieval

Many computers have files of information that are free the taking. The files range from U.S. Supreme Court decisions and library card catalogs to the text of old books, digitized pictures (nearly all of them suitable for family audiences), and an enormous variety of software, from games to operating systems. Special tools known as search engines, directories, and indices help you find information on the Net. Lots of people are trying to make the fastest, smartest search engine and the most complete Net index. We tell you about two of the most useful, Alta Vista and Yahoo! so that you get the picture. As mentioned in the introduction to this book, you see a Web icon here and there; it points to resources you can retrieve from the Net yourself.

Electronic commerce

This term is just a fancy word for buying and selling stuff over the Net. It seems that everybody's doing it, and now the software is available to make sending your credit card number over the Net safe and secure. You can buy anything from books to stock in microbreweries.

Newsgroups

A system called *Usenet* is an enormous, distributed, online bulletin board with about 700 million characters of messages in more than 20,000 different topic groups flowing daily. Online bulletin boards date from the 1970s-they're systems set up for people of like interests for discussion via e-mail, message areas, and real-time chat. Although most independent, non-Internet-connected bulletin board systems have been replaced by the Internet, the boffo bulletin board of all time, Usenet, is alive and well and is integral to the Internet. Topics range from nerdy computer stuff to hobbies such as cycling and knitting to endless political arguments to just plain silliness. The most widely read Usenet newsgroup is one that features selected jokes, most of which are pretty funny.

Intranets

Wouldn't ya know? Businesses have figured out that this Internet stuff is really useful. They're using e-mail and Web technologies on their own internal networks and calling them intranets.

Games and gossip

A game called MUD (Multi-User-Dimension or Multi-User Dungeon) can easily absorb all you waking hours. In it, you can challenge other players who can be anywhere in the world. Internet Relay Chat (IRC) is a party line over which you can have more or less interesting conversations with other people all over the place Although Irc seems to be frequented primarily by bored college students, you never know whom you will encounter. Many Internet providers have facilities for "chatting" that enable you to have online conversations with a bunch of people at the same time. In the 1960s scientists in USA started experimenting on direct connection of remote computers. The government decided to finance the project and use it for military purposes. During cold war time the US military wanted to come up with a system that would be reliable even in war time. Three mainframe computers in California and one in Utah were interconnected forming the DARPANET (later known as ARPANET). In this Arpanet model, communication always occurs between a source an ' the destination computers assuming that the network itself is unreliable (typical military philosophy). Hence the communication must occur with minimum information from server/client computers. The message data is put into an envelope (called IP packet) and addressed correctly. This was the original thought while the Internet Protocol (mutually agreed upon method of communication between parties) was designed. Although the Organization for International Standards (ISO) was spending years designing ultimate communication standards, the computing community could not wait! The IP protocol became de-facto and people started implementing it on different platforms.

This grew exponentially and later down the time even the universities were also allowed to hook up to this net. The volume of work grew so fast that the military traffic had to be shifted to a separate network called MILNET. Procedures were set up to regulate the allocation of addresses and to create voluntary standards for the network. Some non-IP based local area networks became more pervasive and many hosts became gateways to local networks. Thus non-IP based networks also became Internet users. A network layer to allow the interoperation of these networks was developed through Internet Protocol (IP). Over the time other groups created long haul IP based networks (NASA, NSF, states ...) These nets, too, interoperate because of Internet protocols. The collection of all of these interoperating networks is the Internet. The commercial use of the Internet was also permitted before some time. In India it started from August 1995. And as of today, anyone (with a desire to communicate and as little as Rs. 5000 or Rs. 500 for students) can be on the Internet! The organization structure of Internet is as complex as the rest of it! The ultimate authority of Internet is the Internet Society (ISOC). The ISOC is a voluntary membership organization whose purpose is to promote global information exchange through Internet. It appoints a council of elder members called Internet Architecture Board IAB) which is responsible for technical management. Thanks to Iab the Internet is not Vendor specific or Platform stuck. Another voluntary organization that is less technical in nature is the Internet Engineering Task Force IETF). Internet is a network of networks. From a tiny number of 4 mainframes in 1960 the number has (out) grown to more than 40,000 networks, 200 countries and 100 million users. With the growth rate of 6000% p.a. it surely is, as Bill Gates quotes, "The Road Ahead".

A few groups provide much of the information services on the Internet. Information Sciences Institute ISI) does much of the standardization and allocation work of the Internet acting as the Internet Assigned Numbers Authority (IANA). Sri International provides the principle Information services for the Internet by operating the Network Information Center (NIC). Today's Internet is a network having PCs, Minis, Mainframes and Super-computers sharing information with each other.

The touch of Internet could be felt in a variety of flavors which can be broadly classified into three classes. Access through Gateway type connection is the poormen's connection to the Internet. It's like access to the Internet without being on it. Imagine a small network or BBS that has nothing to do with Internet as such. But as one of the computers on this network gets the Internet access, all the remaining computers on the network get hooked up to it. Thus this intersection point computer provides a gateway to Internet access for the rest of the network.

The' advantages of this gateway style connectivity are:

- The low cost of access as the cost is shared by the whole network.

- Even the existing non-IP based networks can be easily connected.

The disadvantages are:

- You are not really on the Internet. Means the network depends on the facilities provided by the gateway.

AOL (America On-Line), CompuServe, Prodigy and even VSNL GIAS are examples of gateway connectivity. Many of the gateways provide access to only E-mail service of the Internet. Some others provide many other services as well. Currently in India, VSNL Gateway is providing E-mail, FTP, Telnet, Chat, Kermit, Zmodem upload/ download and UNIX prompt facilities to its subscribers. Remote Access Connectivity is achieved through a dial up terminal connection. The mainframe on the Internet is used as a host using a dial up connection. The host carries out commands typed at terminal. This is the most widely used type of Internet connectivity. The problem associated with this level is that only the programs present at the host can be executed. Loading a new program or client does not provide the ability to execute it. Similarly downloading a file from any site becomes a two step process. Downloading from the site to host and then transferring from host to local terminal.

This highest and most expensive type of connectivity is achieved by high speed lines to go online on the Internet. Internet is available round the clock. It is usually opted with heavy load and a number of users using a mainframe computer. A new class of connectivity that is now coming into existence is the On-Demand Direct connectivity. The direct connection is provided on demand by the service providers based on Point to Point Protocol (PPP) or the Serial Line Internet Protocol (SLIP). It costs very less and still gives the power of direct connection. But Direct connectivity and Remote access connectivity are too expensive to be discussed here. Besides, it is most unlikely that you might come across anything except gateway connectivity, so we shall stick to it.

E-mail Connectivity

From 15th August 1995 onwards Gateway Internet access is possible in India through VSNL. Yes this is true in a broader sense but then India is a big country! Hundreds of cities of India and other countries do not have local connectivity and probably will have to wait for years before they have it. With e-mail company here not having put up a good show, it is least likely anybody will go in for investment to provide Internet access for a long time. Similar is the case in most small cities. Does this mean millions of geographically unlucky people in these cities will have to be deprived of such a wonderful magic link. Presenting a virtual kind of Internet connectivity for which you require only E-mail and a little knowledge. The section of this book "Internet Access by e-mail" describes how you can access almost any resource using E-mail as your only weapon. You can Access WWW, Gopher, Ftp, Usenet, Archie and much more if you have E-mail at your disposal.

This is not only useful for these geo-unlucky people who cannot get hooked to Internet but also for those who are already hooked-on because when you go online your meter starts ticking. A TCP/IP account today costs hourly Rs. 30 for individuals to Rs.50, for companies (plus STD or INET charges if you are geo-unlucky). The line conditions in India leave you trapped in statue pOSItion for unbearable time making it not only boring but also costly to access resources. These simple tricks can help you surf offline and save money, your time and connectivity time.

You can arrange a talk "in real time" with your client in Tokyo (Japan) and two of his financiers one in Boston (US) and other in Kingston (Australia); read a book from Drexel University library (Philadelphia, US) and then go to Singapore to book a room in a hotel on the Orchid street and send a small video clip of your new pet dog (Jimmy) to your uncle living some 300 km away from your house; conduct an interview of a head of the business house of Sri Lanka asking him how tough are business conditions in his country and listen to some latest soundtracks released in Africa last weekend and all this in a matter of some 45 minutes and not at the cost of a fortune. Your house is locked and every one is gone for a tour. A visitor comes home and pushes the doorbell button! Ting-Tong. The doorbell is connected to your desktop which, by Internet, is connected to you. You are in a taxi heading for a business meeting in other country. The cellular phone rings and your laptop picks it up for you. You talk to the visitor. Oh! you had a date. Damn it you forgot.

Anyway now let her In. So you press that access code and the door of your house unlocks and then you put on the TV change channel to 4. talk to her (mainly saying sorry you see I had ....) and as she leaves lock the door turn the TV off and.... well the only thing which is unusual about this fiction is that it isn't! This is a reality that's not too far away.

A survey in January 1996 shows that the number of host computers (a computer which has it's own numerical Internet address, the doted quard) has Zoomed up to 9,472,000 exhibiting an annual growth rate of 85%. The growth of domain names surpasses the growth of hosts putting the number to 2,40,000.

The country wise breakup of host computers is as under:

Germany (de)	4,52,997	Netherlands (nl)	1,74,888
UK (uk)	4,51,750	Sweden (se)	1,49,87 7
Canada (ca)	3,72,891	France (fr)	1,37,217
Australia (au)	3,09,562	US (us)	2,33,912
Japan (jp)	2,69,327	Finland (fi)	2,08,502

Israel witnessed a phenomenal growth in claiming its Internet presence during the later half of the 1995. Other countries that had a similar trend of growth were Singapore, Italy, France, Japan and Taiwan. More than 35 countries got hooked up to the Internet by registering a host for the first time during the same period. Today there are more than 40,000 networks, 200 countries and 100 million total users on the net and the number is growing at 10% every month! Macs, IBM PCs, Minis, Mainframes and super computers' running all different operating systems.

The biggest problem one is likely to face when first using the 'net is similar to being lost in a new city. You don't know where to find things. Even the experienced internauts find themselves surprised when they discover a new possibility they'd never known even existed.

A basic difference between the postal service and E-mail is that E-mail gives you a feeling that it's not merely your message that reaches the destination but you who reaches out. It is rightly called the DEATH OF DISTANCE.

Reaching where you want to go can often be one of the most difficult aspects of using any networks.

Each country also has its own top-level domain. For example, the U.S. domain includes each of the fifty states belonging to the USA. Other countries represented with domains include:.

au	Australia
jp	Japan
ca	Canada
se	Sweden
fr	France
fi	Finland
in	India
sg	Singapore
su	Soviet Union (one place where it still exists)
uk	The United Kingdom.

These also have sub-domains of things like 'ac.uk' for academic sites and 'co.uk' for commercial ones.

The internet numbering system

Every single machine on the Internet has a unique address, called its Internet number or IP Address. It's actually a 32-bit number, but is most commonly represented as four numbers joined by periods C.'), like 202.54.1.18. This is also called a dotted quad; there are literally thousands of different possible dotted quads. The ARPAnet 9the mother of today's Internet) originally only had the capacity to have up to 256 systems on it because of the way each system was addressed. In the early eighties, it became clear that things would fast outgrow such a small limit; the 32-bit addressing method was born, feeling thousands of host numbers.

Each piece of an Internet address (like 202) is called an "octet," representing one of four sets of eight bits. The first two or three pieces (e.g. 202.54.1) represent the network that a system is on, called its subnet. For example, all of the computers for Wesleyan University are in the subnet 129.133. They can have numbers like 129.133.10.10, 129.133.230.19, up to 65 thousand possible combinations (possible computers). Fortunately enough the IP addresses and domain names aren't assigned arbitrarily-that would lead to unbelievable confusion.

To number or to names

Ok, computers can be referred to by either their Fully Qualified Domain Names (FQDN) or their Internet address. Fortunately No. The Internet is designed so that one can use either method. Since humans find it much more natural to deal with words than numbers in most cases, the FQDN for each host is mapped to its Internet number. Each domain is served by a computer within that domain, which provides all of the necessary information to go from a domain name to an IP address, and vice-versa. For example, when someone refers to giasbm0l. vsnl.net. in starting from right we get.in means it's in India, VSNL stands for Videsh Sanchar Nigam Limited and GIAS for Gateway Internet Access Service, BM for Mumbai server. So referring to giasbm0l. vsnl.net in tells the computer that we are looking for GIAS of VSNL at Mumbai in India. Going by the numbers it would have been 202.54.1.18. All of this boring stuff happens where it should, behind the scenes.

Seventh-grade students in San Diego use the Internet to exchange letters and stories with kids in Israel. Partly it's just for fun and to make friends in a foreign country, but a sober academic study reported that when kids have a real audience for their stuff, they write better. In some parts of the world, the Internet is the fastest and most reliable way to move information. During the 1991 Soviet coup, a tiny Internet provider called RELCOM, which had a link to Finland and through there to the rest of the Internet world, found itself as the only reliable path to get reports in and out of Moscow because telephones were shut off and newspapers weren't being published. RELCOM members sent out stories that would have been in newspapers, statements from Boris Yeltsin, and their personal observations from downtown Moscow.

Medical researchers around the world use the Internet to maintain databases of rapidly changing data. People with medical conditions use the Internet to communicate with each other in support groups and to compare experiences. The Internet is its own best source of software. Whenever we hear about a new service, it usually takes only a few minutes to find software for our computers (various computers running various versions of Windows and a Macintosh Power PC), download it, and start it up. Nearly all the software available on the Internet is free.

The Internet has local and regional parts as well. When John wanted to sell a trusty but tired minivan, a note on the Internet in a local for-sale area found a buyer within two days. Margy's husband sold his used computer within half an hour of posting a message on the relevant Usenet newsgroup.

The Internet is unlike all the other communications media we have ever encountered. People of all ages, colors, creeds, and countries freely share ideas, stories, data, opinions and products.

Anybody can access it

One great thing about the Internet is that it's probably the most open network in the world. Thousands of computers provide facilities that area available to anyone who has Net access. This situation is unusual-most networks are very restrictive in what they allow users to do and require specific arrangements and passwords for each service. Although pay services exist (and more are added every day), many Internet services are free for the taking. If you don't already have access to the Internet through your company, your school, or a friend's attic, you probably have to pay for access by using one of the Internet access providers.

Another great thing about the Internet is that it is what one might call "socially unstratified." That is, one computer is no better than any other, and no person is any better that any other. Who you are on the Internet depends solely on how you present yourself through your keyboard. If what you say makes you sound like an intelligent, interesting person, that's who you are. It doesn't matter how old you are or what you look like or whether you're a student, a business executive, or a construct ' ion worker. Physical disabilities don't matter-we correspond with people who are blind or deaf. If they hadn't felt like telling us, we never would have known. People become famous in the Net community, some favorably and some unfavourably, but they get that way through their own efforts.

Here are some of the things people use the Internet for:

Finding people: If you have lost track of your childhood sweetheart, now's your chance to find him or her anywhere in the country. You can use one of the directory services to search the phone books of the entire United States.

Finding businesses, products, and services: New Yellow Page directory services enable you to search by the type of company you're looking for. You can indicate area code or zip code to help specify the location. People are shopping for that hard-to-find special gift item. A friend told us of her search for a bear pendant that took her to a company in Alaska that had just what she was looking for.

Research: Law firms are finding that a great deal of information they formerly paid $600 an hour to find from commercial services can be found for close to nothing when they go directly to the Net. Real estate appraisers use demographic data available on the Net, including unemployment statistics, to help assess property values. Genetics researchers and other scientists download up-to-date research results from around the world. Businesses and potential businesses research their competition over the Net.

Education: School teachers coordinate projects with classroom all over the globe. College students and their families exchange e-mail to facilitate letter writing and keep the cost of phone calls down. Students do research from their home computer. The latest encyclopedias are online.

Travel: Cities, towns, states, and countries are using the Web to put up tourist and event information. Travelers find weather information, maps, transportation schedules, and museum hours online.

Marketing and sales: Software companies are selling software and providing updates via the Net. (The folks making money from the manufacture of floppy disks are looking for new products. Aside from the large pile of AOL disks we now use as coasters, most software distribution is migrating to the Net.) Companies are selling products over the Net. Online bookstores and music stores allow people to browse online, choose titles, and pay for stuff over the Net.

Love: People are finding romance on the Net. Singles ads and match making sites vie for users. Contrary to Internet lore, the Net community is no longer just a bunch of socially challenged white men under 25.

Healing: Patients and doctors keep up-to-date with the latest medical findings, share treatment experience, and give one another support around medical problems. We even know of some exceptional practitioners who exchange e-mail directly with their patients.

Investing: People buy stock and invest money. Some companies are online and trade their own shares. Investors are finding new ventures, and new ventures are finding capital.

Organizing events: Conference and trade-show organizers are finding that the best way to disseminate information, call for papers, and do registration is to do it on the Web. Information can be updated regularly, and paper and shipping costs are dramatically reduced. Registering online saves on-site registration staff and on-site registration lines.

Nonprofits: Churches, synagogues, and other community organizations put up pages telling about themselves and inviting new people.

The earth-shattering, startling new idea of how to buy things over the Net lies buried in the inner meaning of the following phrase: "Enter your credit card number." We're not saying that you shouldn't exercise caution, but our experience of buying stuff over the Net in the past year tells us that you have no great cause for alarm. What have we bought? Books, Cds, clothing, encyclopedia subscriptions, and matchmaking subscri-ption. Here's what you need to know. Some folks seem particularly wary of sending their credit card number over the Net. If you use a credit card at all, remember that the credit card companies are even more concerned than you are about the idea of any kind of credit card fraud, on or off the Net. All cards have a limit on the amount of fraudulent use for which you're liable with many credit cards, you're not responsible for any charges resulting from your card or card number being stolen-and the most they can hold you responsible for, if you're a U.S. resident, is $50. Any fraud higher than that amount is the card company's problem, not yours.

Despite all the foofaraw (a technical term) about the risks of online credit card use, we haven't found one single case of a card number being stolen in transit over the Internet. On the other hand, every day we hand our actual physical cards with our handwritten signature to gas station attendants wearing distinctive outfits in bright colors not found in nature, to servers at restaurants, and to clerks at all sorts of stores. Do you know what they do with the card before they give it, back to you? Do you worry about it? We don't.

The point is, if you're comfortable using a credit card at all, you needn't get really scared about using it over the Net just because it seems new.

To avoid the possibility of bad guys or gals electronically listening to the bits of your private information whirring across the Net, stripping them off, and redirecting them to purchase their dream vacation, schemes have been invented to encode info sent over the Net so that even if the villains intercept the info, it won't do them any good-it gets all mixed up and hidden in such a way that only the legitimate recipient can decode it. The software that processes this information safely, hiding everything from possible perverse perusal, is known as a secure server. Many Web browsers have secure servers built right in. If you're the least bit antsy about sending your card number over the Net, stick to secure servers. Software that takes your credit card number (or any other information) over the Net without encoding it is known as an insecure server. Insecure servers are perfectly adequate for many transactions and shouldn't be shunned automatically. Think about the information that's being requested and whether you think that the risk of fraud is a problem. If you do, hold out for a secure server or find another way (such as using the phone) to carry out the business you need to do.

The Internet's funny place. In some ways it's completely anonymous and in others not at all. In the good olde days, people usually had Internet user names that bore some resemblance to their true identity-their name or initials or some combination in conjunction with their university or corporation gave a fairly traceable route to an actual person. Today, with the phenomenon of screen names (courtesy of America Online) and lengthy strings of numbers (courtesy of CompuServe), revealing your identity is, at best, optional.

Depending on who you are and what you want to do on the Net, you might, in fact, want different names and different accounts. Here are some legitimate reasons for wanting them: You're a professional-a physician, for example and you want to participate in a mailing list or newsgroup without being asked for your professional opinion.

You want help with an area of concern that you feel is private and would not want your problem known to people close to you who might find out if your name were associated with it.

You do business on the Net, and you socialize on the Net as well. You might want to keep those activities separate.

Safety first

The whole anonymous nature of the Internet has its downside as well. Although it's relatively rare, horrible things have happened to a few people who have taken their Internet encounters into real life. Many wonderful things have happened too. We have met some of our best friends over the Net, and some people have met and gotten married-no kidding! We just want to encourage you to use common sense when you set up a meeting with a Net friend. Here are a few tips:

Talk to the person on the phone before you agree to meet. If you don't like the sound of the person's voice or something makes you feel nervous, don't do it.

Depending on the context, try to check the person out a little. If you have met in a newsgroup or chat room, ask someone else you know whether they know this person. (Women, ask another woman before meeting a man.) Meet in a well-lit public place. Let someone else know where you're going.

If you're a kid, take a parent with you. If you're not a kid but you're a little nervous, bring along a friend. The Net is a wonderful place, and meeting new people and making new friends is one of its big attractions. We just want to make sure that you're being careful.

In the United States, people grown up with certain ' attitudes about freedom and privacy, many of which we take for granted. They tend to feel that who they are, where they go, and what they do is their own business as long as they don't bother anyone else. Well, it would seem that a whole bunch of people are very interested in who they are, where they go (on the Net, at least), and, most especially, what they buy. All this interest is being sanctioned in the name of that ever-so-altruistic-keeping-only-our-best-interests-in-mind holy being Marketing. We tell you this in case you're sensitive about data being collected about your personal Net habits. The next two sections tell you what's happening. To enhance your online experience, the makers of Web browsers, such as Navigator and Internet Explorer, have invented a type of special message that lets a Web site keep track of when you have visited that site. They thoughtfully store this info, called a *cookie,* on your very own machine to make your next visit to the same site smoother.

This info can in fact make your next transaction smoother, but it can also cause you some problems. Many cookies are quite handy. When you're using an airline-reservation site, for example, the site uses cookies to keep the flights you're reserving separate from the ones other users might be reserving at the same time. On the other hand, suppose that you use your credit card to purchase something on a Web site and the site uses a cookie to remember your credit card number. Suppose that you did this from a computer at work and the next person to visit that site used the same computer. They could, possible, make purchases on your credit card.

If may be true that cookies can make your life more convenient. You have to be the judge of that. Every Web server can offer you cookies. You need to know that this kind of software exists so that if you are concerned about your privacy, you can take steps to protect it.

Cookie files usually have the name cookie associated with them-cookies.txt and Magic Cookie, for example. You can delete your cookie files-your browsers will create a new, empty one. Modern browsers can tell you about cookies and ask you whether to accept them as servers offer them to you. When Carol checked her Macintosh, she found two cookie files-one from Navigator and one from Internet Explorer. If she hadn't been looking for them, she never would have known that they were there. Cookie files cannot get other information from your hard disk. They only collect information that the browser tells them about. As a general rule, we all need to be on the lookout for programs we install that do a little more than advertised. Internet Explorer keeps, in addition to the cookie file, a history file of where you have been on the Web. (Look in your Internet Explorer folder for something called History.html.) If anyone other than you uses your computer, you might want to delete this file after your use, unless you don't care who sees if. Courts have ruled, by the way, that companies own their computers and their contents. You have no "right to privacy" at work, even though most of us find the idea creepy. Companies can eavesdrop on phone calls, read you e-mail (going and coming) and read anything that's on your computer, including a history file detailing where you have searched. We find this tasteless and disturbing, so we think we ought to warn you.

Encryption and pretty good privacy

The Internet is not so private a place as you might think. While we're sitting in our homes typing on a keyboard, we hardly get the sense that someone could be watching our every move. Yet information gets relayed from machine to machine, and along the way, if someone really cares, she or he might be able to take a look at what comes across the wire. Whether you're sending your credit card number or sending e-mail, you might feel more comfortable if the absolute secure nature of the transmission were guaranteed.

You can guarantee security using encryption. Encryption is high-tech-ese for encoding-just like with a secret decoder ring. You know-codes, spies, secret messages.

Software exists that helps you package up your message and send it in a way that nobody can read it except the intended recipient. Some folks say that sending e-mail that's not encrypted is equivalent to sending your message on a postcard. Encryption is the virtual envelope that defies prying eyes. In practice, we rarely encrypt e-mail, though we're happy to know that the option exists. One reason we don't is that at this point it's too darned cumbersome. When e-mail software comes with encryption built-in, many more people will choose to use it. In the meantime, if you feel that you need it, you can learn about PGP, which stands for Pretty Good Privacy. Because it's complicated enough to require pages of explanation, we don't have room in this book to go into the details. New, easier-to-use versions of PGP come out every month or two, so by the time you read this chapter, a PGP add-in may well be available for your favorite mail program.

The ancestor of the Internet was the ARPANET, a project funded by the Department of Defense (DOD) in 1969, both as an experiments in reliable networking and to link DOD and military research contractors, including the large number of universities doing military funded research. (ARPA stands for Advanced Research Projects Administration, the branch of Defense in charge of handing out grant money. For enhanced confusion, the agency is now known as DARPA-the added D is for Defense, in case there was any doubt where the money was coming from.) The ARPANET started small, connecting three computers in California with one in Utah, but it quickly grew to span the continent.

The reliable networking part involved *dynamic routing*. If one of the network links became disrupted by enemy attack, the traffic on it could be rerouted automatically to other links. Fortunately, the Net rarely has come under enemy attack. Cutting a cable during road construction (known in the biz as *backhoe fade) is* just as much of a threat, however, so it's important for the Net to be backhoe resistant.

Because the ARPANET was wildly successful, every university in the country wanted to sign up. This success meant that the ARPANET began getting difficult to manage, particularly with the large and growing number of university sites on it. It was broken into two parts:

- MILNET, which had the military sites
- The new, smaller ARPANET which had the nonmilitary sites

The two networks remained connected, however, thanks to a technical scheme called IP (Internet Protocol), which enabled traffic to be routed from one network to another as necessary. Because all the networks connected in the Internet speak IP, they all can exchange messages. Although there were only two networks at that time, IP was designed to allow for tens of thousands of networks. An unusual fact about the IP design is that every computer on an IP network is, in principle, just as capable as any other, so any machine can communicate with any other machine.

Beginning around 1980, university computing was moving from a small number of large timesharing machine, each of which served hundreds of simultaneous users, to a large number of smaller desktop workstations for individual users. Because users had gotten used to the advantages of timesharing systems, such as shared directories of files and e-mail, they wanted to keep those same facilities on their workstations. (They were perfectly happy to leave behind the disadvantages of time-shared systems. A sage once said, "The best thing about a workstation is that it's no faster in the middle of the night.")

Most of the new workstations ran a variety of UNIX, a popular (and, for many versions, free or close to it) type of operating software that had been developed at AT&T and the University of California at Berkeley. The people at Berkeley had a government contract to improve computer networking, so their version of UNIX included all the software necessary to hook up to a network. Because workstation manufacturers also began to include the necessary network hardware, all you had to do to get a working network was to string the cable to connect the workstation, something that universities could do for cheap because they usually could get students to do it.

Then, rather than have one or two computers to attach to the ARPANET, a site would have hundreds. What's more, because each workstation was considerably faster than an entire 1970s multiuser system, one workstation could generate enough network traffic to swamp the ARPANET, which was getting creakier by the minute.

The next event was that the National Science Foundation (NSF) decided to set up five supercomputer centers for research use. The NSF figured that it would fund a few supercomputers, let researchers from all over the country use the ARPANET to send their programs to be "super computed," and then send back the results.

The plan to use the ARPANET didn't work out for a variety of reasons some technical, some political. So the NSF, never shy about establishing a new political empire, built its own, much faster' network to connect the supercomputing centers: the NSFNET. Then it arranged to set up a bunch of regional networks to connect the users in each region, with the NSFNET connecting all the regional networks.

The NSFNET worked like a charm. By 1990, if fact, so much business had moved from them ARPANET to the NSFNET that, after nearly 20 years, the ARPANET had outlived its usefulness and was shut down. The super computer centers the NSFNET was supposed to support turned out to be a fizzle: Some of the supercomputers didn't work, and the ones that did were so expensive to use that most potential customers decided that a few high performance workstations would do just as well. Fortunately, by the time the supercomputers were on their way out, the NSFNET had become so entrenched in the Internet that it lived on without its original purpose. By 1994, several large, commercial Internet networks had grown up within the Internet, some run by large, familiar organizations such as IBM and Sprint and others run by such specialist Internet companies as PSI and Alternet. The NSFNET has been wound down, with its traffic taken over by commercial networks.

Although the NSFNET permitted traffic related only to research and education, the independent, commercial IP network services can be used for any legal purpose. The commercial networks connect to the regional networks just as the NSFNET did, and they provide direct connections for customers.

Outside the United States, IP networks have appeared in many countries, either sponsored by the local telephone company (which is usually also the local post office) or run by independent national or regional providers. The first international connections were in 1973 with England and Norway. Nearly all countries are connected directly or indirectly to some U.S. network meaning that they all can exchange traffic with each other. The term Internet first appeared in 1982 with the DARPA launch of the Internet Protocol UP).

Internet service provider

To connect to the Internet, you have two major choices-or three, if you're lucky:

- *Sign up with an online service, such as America Online or CompuServe.* Online services tend to be easier to use, and they provide information in a more organized way. They usually don't give you the full range of Internet services, however. Unless services have a flat rate for unlimited use, they can be expensive if you use them for more than a few hours a month. Because the demand is growing faster than some providers are able to support, access is sometimes slow.
- *Sign up with an Internet provider for, an Internet account.* These days, most providers provide you with a PPP or SLIP account. Most still also provide that we will explain them again in a few paragraphs). Most still also provide UNIX shell accounts or both shell and PPP accounts. You need PPP or SLIP to use all the cool, new programs, such as Netscape Navigator, Microsoft Internet Explorer, and Eudora.
- *Sign up for, cable access.* We say "if you're lucky" because cable access is not widely available yet. It it is, however, all you have to do is call your cable company and arrange for them to come and install a network card in your computer and some cable to your home (if you don't already have cable TV). If you choose this option, you can skip the rest of this chapter and the next two chapters and just gloat. You don't need a phone, you don't need a modem, and you don't need a TV.

We had better explain what PPP and SLIP are. Here are the three incomprehensible acronyms you need to know:

- PPP (Point-to-Point Protocol): Enables your PC to connect to the Internet not as a terminal but as a full-fledged member of the Net, at least while your computer is on the phone to its Internet provider

- SLIP (Serial Line Internet Protocol): An older version of the same thing
- CSLIP (Compressed SLIP): A faster version of SLIP

Because these three protocols are identical for our purposes, we refer to them all as PPP. All three are versions of IP (Internet Protocol), the underlying part of TCP/IP (Transmission Control Protocol/Internet Protocol), which is they way that all computers on the Internet communicate with each other. All three are cool because many network operations are much simpler when your own computer is on the Net instead of acting as a terminal to someone else's big computer-programs running on your own computer can do much nicer sound, graphics, and animation than a terminal can.

To use a PP account, you need two types of programs:

- *A program to get you connected to the account:* The technical term for this type of program is a TCP/IP stack, although normal mortal human beings usually call it something like an Internet dialer program. If you use Windows, your Internet dialer program comes with a file called WINSOCK.DLL. Macintoshes have the basic TCP/IP stuff, called MacTCP, built in as of System 7. You also need MacPPP, MacSLIP, or InterSLIP to handle the telephone-dialing stuff. (New Macintoshes come with it already installed.)
- Programs to use various Internet services: These programs give you access to e-mail, the Web, and information over the Internet. They're known as client programs because they're part of a two-part strategy-part of the programs run on your computer; the other part, the server programs, run on your provider's computer.

You want an e-mail program to read and send e-mail,, a Web browser to surf the Web, and a newsreader program to read Usenet newsgroups. Or you can get a program that does all three, such as Netscape. If you use Windows, you can use any Winsock-compatible program (any program that works with the WINSOCK.DLL file that's part of your Internet dialer program). If you use a Mac, you can use any MacTCP-compatible program. All the cool Internet programs you have heard about are either WinSock-or MacTCP-compatible, and many work on both Windows and Macs.

PPP connections are easy enough to use, but they can be tricky to set up. In fact, connecting can be the hardest part of your Internet experience. Installing and setting up TCP/IP software requires entering lots of scary-looking numeric Internet addresses, host names, communications ports-you name it. Make sure that your provider is helpful and available, or choose another provider. If you have a friend or relative whom you can bribe or coerce into helping you, do so. Because each provider is just a tad different from the next, we can't go into exact step-by-step directions for everyone. We give the usual steps, help you understand the terms, and coax you through. If you find this process totally impossible and have no one you can press into service or just don't like the thought of doing this, don't despair. If you're Windows 95 user, in which we tell you where you can find detailed, step-by-step instructions. If you're not, consider using America Online or CompuServe to get started.

Hardware-wise, here's what you need to cruise the Net:

- *A modem that connects your computer to a phone line:* The faster the modem, the better. Try to get a modem that talks at 14.4 Kbps (bits per second), 28.8 Kbps, or even 33Kbps. Otherwise, things will be sluggish.
- *A phone line (you* probably guessed that): Make sure that your phone line doesn't have call waiting. If it does, you have to type 70 or 1170 at company to turn off call waiting for this phone call.
- *A computer capable or running Winsock-or MacTCP-compatible programs:* Any computer that can run Windows 3.1 or Windows 95 or any Macintosh will do fine. Note, however, that the World Wide Web is full of pictures that take up a large amount of hard disk space. To get the full effect, you probably want more than the minimal amount of memory that came with older machines, and you may need more disk space. Before you upgrade an older machine, look at the brand spanking new ones-they have changed a great deal in the past couple of years, and now may be the time to trade yours in.

To get your Windows PC set up for PPP, follow these steps:

1. Arrange for a PPP account from a local provider.

   In the following section, we give you ideas about how to choose one.

2. Get the basic TCP/IP software loaded into your computer somehow, either from a disk or over the phone.

   Use the software your PPP provider gives you, if any, or get a friend to download it from the Internet for you and give it to you on a floppy disk. Some providers mail you a disk. Others start you off with a UNIX shell accounts that they tell you over the phone how to set up and then provide a program to download the rest of the software you need.

   Later in this chapter are sections about TCP/IP and dialer software for Windows 95, Windows 3.1, and Macs.

3. Type about a thousand setup parameters, if you're not lucky.

   Your Internet provider (if it provided the software) or the software vendor should have given you instructions for when to type what. If you're lucky, your software has an automatic configuration program to set most or all of the setup parameters.

In the section "Many mysterious numbers," later in this chapter, we tell you as much as we know about the parameters you might encounter.

4. Crank up your TCP/IP program, and fiddle with it until it works.

Hey, sometimes it works the first time. If it doesn't call and ask your provider to help you. You may find it difficult and frustrating if you have only one phone line, and you have to hand up to call your provider. We can only sympathize and tell you that, yes, it's a real pain, it shouldn't be this difficult, and one day it won't be. For now, it is.

When you use a menu-driven application (such as gopher) to find information, you are guided through the complexities of the Internet in an orderly way. At every step, a menu provides a neat picture of your current location and your choices for further action. Many people find the "tree" metaphor useful for understanding menu-based systems: your search begins at the "root" menu and moves through various levels of branches until you finally arrive at the "leaf' level of the menu tree where you find the information you're after. If the information you retrieve through a menu-based system is incomplete, or if it raises new questions, you'll go back to the root menu and search through the menu tree again looking for something that addresses these new issues. In a conventional menu-based system, every search ends at the leaf level: the files to which the menus lead don't point to other resources that might be useful.

In the Internet community there are visionaries promoting a different way of organizing information, and this alternative view has become the fastest growing application on the Internet and a mainstream phenomenon. In place of a tree-shaped menu structure, imagine a "web," in which there are as few "dead ends" as possible. In this vision of how to structure information, even the files and documents you retrieve should be capable of pointing beyond themselves to other useful or related resources. The application that implements this vision on the Internet is the World Wide Web (also known as W3 WWW, or the Web).

W3 was developed at CERN (European Centre for Nuclear Research), an institution for high-energy physics research in Geneva, Switzerland. Its original purpose was to promote the sharing of research materials and collaboration between physicists at many different locations. W3 quickly developed an eager following outside the High-Energy Physics (Hep) community, and there are now more than 310OW3 servers worldwide. This count and some other statistics about W3's growth were done by Matthew Gray of Mit (mkgray@mit.edu). W3 is very strongly represented in Europe, and has recently caught on in North America. The Web has also begun to attract an audience outside the academic world. You'll find Web Servers for the Encyclopedia Britannica, the city of Palo Alto, Ca and the 1998 Winter Olympics. CERN has very generously made W3 available to this larger audience and continues to encourage the proliferation of servers.

W3 is a client/server application that is similar to gopher in many respects. Like gopher, W3 lets you retrieve information without having to know where on the Internet that information is stored. When you first use W3, it will probably seem a lot like gopher. At every step of the way, you'll have clearly identified choices presented to you in menus. Like gopher, W3 provides an interface to other Internet applications such as gopher, ftp, or WAIS (Wide Area Information Search). However, W3 has included a subject catalog from the outset, and even though the catalog is incomplete, it is a tremendous help in guiding the curious to resources of interest. W3 is also the only Internet application that is hypertext-based. Hypertext is what gives W3 its weblike character.

Hypertext is a word first coined in the midsixties by Ted Nelson, the founder of the Xanadu Project, to describe texts that offer alternatives to sequential reading. Today hypertext has come to signify electronically annotated documents that are linked to other documents (and potentially to graphics or to recorded sounds) than may help interpret or clarify the parent document. Imagine reading something and finding a word whose meaning you don't know. If you're reading plain text, you set it aside and look up the word in a dictionary. If you're reading hypertext, you select the unknown word to find any explanations that are lined to it. The explanation may in turn have links to other documents as well. Pursuing the links from document to document can lead to topics and ideas that might not have occurred to you just from reading the original document.

There is nothing about hypertext that forces it to be graphically sophisticated, and some of the hypertext resources you'll encounter on the Internet will be simple text files that happen to have links. You'll also encounter hypertext documents that are masterpieces of graphic design, and these give W3 its reputation as an application that is best enjoyed from a graphical interface. The trail of hyperlinks isn't limited to documents alone. It can also lead to pictures or audio recordings. The word "hypermedia" has been coined to describe these annotated mixedmedia presentations. If your computer has graphics and sound capabilities (and if you're using the right W3 client), you'll get all the sights and sounds that have been programmed into W3 resources. If you system doesn't support these media, the Web will deliver its resources to you as text only.

Creating hypertext is labour-intensive. Ideally every word in a document could have links to other sources of information, and links between documents don't just happen. They are made ("built") using a hypertext editor that encodes text in a language capable of expressing the text's links to other documents. Some of the resources you'll encounter on W3 will be plain hypertext, and even the hypertext documents may not be as heavily linked as you would like. The influence of hypertext is apparent throughout W3 , however. The underlying protocol used by W3 is the Hypertext transfer protocol (HTTP), and the Hypertext Markup Language (HTML) is used to produce and link documents. Working with W3, you'll see that the distinction between menus and documents or files becomes fuzzy, W3 menus tend to be wordy because they are actually documents. Documents, because they have links that lead to other resources, begin to take on a menu-like appearance.

It's possible to build a collection of hypertext documents that don't use a network at all. In that case, all the linked documents must reside on the same computer. The Web successfully combines hypertext with clients/server architecture. The startling thing about W3 is that it is a hypertext system in which the links from a document can point anywhere on the Internet.

The interaction between W3 clients and servers resembles the gopher client/server dialog. The client connects to a server long enough to submit one request and receive a reply. In W3, client requests take the form of URLs, Uniform Resource Locators. At first glance, Urls may look like gibberish. However, with a little practice at identifying fully qualified domain names and email addresses, you can learn to read URLs without much effort. URLs looks like this:

http://info.cern.ch/hypertext/WWW/TheProject.html

URLs consist of a resource type (http in this case), the name in FQDN format of the computer (info.cern.ch) that contains the resource, and optional port number for connecting to the computer just named, and a pathname for the resource itself (hypertext/WWW/The Project.html). Other information can be added to the URL as well, but file-type, machine-name, port number, and pathname are the essential fields.

When you browse through a W3 document, the hyperlinks pointing to other documents all represent URLs. When you select a hyperlink, your W3 client will read the attached URL and send a request to the appropriate server for the linked document. Most of the time this happens behind your back, and you don't need to be particularly conscious of URLs to use of the Web. However, many browsers will also allow you to steer through the Web by entering URLs manually, and occasionally, this is just what you'll want to do.

Choosing a Browser

The client software you use to look at hypertext is called a browser. Browsers give you a clear view of where the links are in hypertext document and a way of following links from one document to another. W3 browsers are also client programs: they interact with a server to retrieve documents; and of course, the W3 server must work with browsers in all sorts of display environments. Among W3 clients, you'll find ASCII line-mode browsers, several full-screen browsers for use with ASCII terminals, and browsers for graphical user interfaces (GUIs) such as Xwindows, Microsoft Windows, and the Macintosh. If your Internet access is via a conventional dialup connection, you'll need either a full-screen browser like Lynx or the line-mode browser www.

If your computer has a graphical user interface and you access the Internet via a protocol dialup connection, there are a number of GUI browsers available. You can reach W3 resources with any kind of browser, but GUI browsers can use your computer's audio and visual capabilities to make Web browsing more enjoyable. The examples in this chapter will use either the line-mode browser or Cello Browser for Windows. Cello is available from the Legal Information Institute at Cornell University. Another popular browser that is available for Windows, X Windows, and Macintosh is the Mosaic browser from the National Center for Super-computing Activity (NCSA) at the University of Illinois, Urbana-Champaign.

The line-mode browser is the most primitive, but it has the great advantage that you can use it with almost any display terminal and with any kind of connection to the Internet. To start the line-mode browser, log into your Internet access provider's computer, type www, and press J. If your www command results in a "www: Command not found" message, try again using the full pathname: /usr/ local/bin/ www. If this also returns a "Command not found" message, the line-mode browser is probably not installed on the machine you use for Internet access. If you don't have local access to the line-mode browser, you can still access W3 by using telnet to connect to info.cern.ch. (CERN is the home of W3.) The line-mode browser will start as soon as the telnet connection is made.

Full-screen browsers are a step up. They show you W3 documents a screen at a time and use the display capability of your terminal (highlighting, reverse video, or underlining) and cursor-movement keys. You can use a full-screen browser over any kind of Internet connection, but if you're working on a UNIX system, you'll have to tell it what kind of terminal you're using. There are several browsers available. The Lynx browser was developed at the University of Kansas, and offers a good selection of features. It allows you to search through the current document for strings. This is particularly useful if the document contains more than a few links. It also supports bookmarks. If you'd like to test the Lynx browser, telnet to ukanaix.cc.ukans.edu and log in as www. Another full-screen browser is www. To use this browser, telnet to www. njit.edu and log in as www. Instructions for retrieving these browsers via ftp appear in the sidebar above.

Neither line-mode nor full-screen browsers will be able to display graphics or play sounds for you; for that, you'll need a GUI browser. For example, W3 can lead you to the catalog for an exhibit of medieval art and historical documents from the Vatican. With a line-mode browser, you can read the modern commentary from the catalog, but with a Gui browser, you'll be able to see the pictures and view facsimiles of the documents from the comfort of your own computer.

Some GUI browsers will allow you to look at several documents at once in different windows. The drawback to GUI browsers is that they are very resource-intensive. Running a GUI browser on a slow modem, a slow computer, or a computer that has only a modest amount of memory installed can tax your patience. Running a GUI browser on a fast modem with a fast machine and lots of memory will remind you why you invested in the fancy hardware in the first place.

Using a browser

When you first start any W3 client, you'll see the browser's "home page," a page of information that contains links to other documents. When you first start the Cello browser, it, too, loads its home page from a local file. In line-mode browsers, links to other documents are shown as bracketed numbers following the keyboard or phrase to which the link is made. At the bottom of the screen there is a prompt that gives you the range of links from which you can choose and a selection of the browser's built in commands. To follow any link in the current document you type the number of the link. For help with the browser's commands, type h or help. All the browser's commands are triggered by pressing J. Pressing j without first entering a command advances the display to the next screenful of the current document. A description of the most important line-mode browser commands appears in the following sidebar.

GUI browsers mark the words or phrases that have hyperlinks attached in a way that doesn't disturb the document's on-screen format. Cello browser's home page is loaded from a file (default .htm) in the directory where the Cello browser is installed. Words that have links to other documents are underlined. To retrieve the contents of a hyperlink, you simply click on the link. This page contains hyperlinks for the top-level document at CERN that we'll look at below. To get to these documents, scroll down in the home page (using the mouse or the PgDn key) to the hyperlink for CERN. Click on this and Cello will retrieve the Overview document from CERN.

GUI browsers typically provide a number of menu commands that can be used to manage your W3 sessions. In addition to navigation from document to document, the Cello browser includes a jump feature for moving directly to different documents or even starting other Internet applications without going through intervening menus or documents. (Cello can also be used as a gopher client, for example.) Cello also maintain a history list of URLs visited in the current sessions and a bookmark list.

As with gopher, the W3 browser commands don't begin to describe what you can do with W3. Fortunately the Web has been set up with a few key documents that serve as navigation tools to help you get and stay oriented. These tools are:

- the CUI W3 Catalog
- the W3 Virtual Library (a Subject Catalog of W3 resources)
- the W3 List of Servers
- the W3 Classification of Resources by Type

The CUI Catalog deserves special mention: it is a searchable index of W3 resources that provide for the Web the same kind of service that archie and veronica provide for other Internet applications. The CUI W3 Catalog is a relatively new addition to the W3 tool kit from the Centre Universitaire d'Informatique at the Universtiy of Geneva in Switzerland. The great advantage of this catalog is that you can submit keyword queries to find resources you're interested in. The response to your query will come back as a hypertext document with descriptive text for each resource and a hyperlink to take you to its full text. This catalog hasn't yet found its way to the CERN overview page. It is so important a resource, however, that it's worth learning the relatively simple URLs that lead to it and setting a bookmark that will get you to this catalog easily.

http://cui www.unige.ch/w3catalog

http://cui www.unige.ch/cgi-bin/hygrep/file =W3 catalog/ isindex.html

There are two URLs because the catalog has two interfaces. The main interface for the CUI catalog is set up for newer W3 Clients that support query by forms. (The NCSA Mosaic browsers for X Windows, Windows, and Macintosh have this feature.) The second URL is for clients (like the line-mode and Cello browsers) that don't yet support query by forms. If you're using the line-mode browser, you can use the URL above with the go command. From the Cello browser, choose the Jump menu button and the URL option from the pulldown menu that follows it. This will bring up a dialog box into which you can type the URL above. The Cello browser's view of the CUI catalog, a query for entries containing the phrase world cup has returned several hits. Items that satisfy a query are returned in chronological order, with the most recent item first. The world cup query returned several items, among them a pointer to the W3 server for Palo Alto, CA.

As this example shows, the CUI W3 Catalog is particularly adept at finding W3 resources that might slip through the cracks* of a subject oriented index. The Palo Alto Web server is just the sort of thing that might otherwise be missed. The W3 Virtual Library is a subject catalog of resources that can be reached from W3. The subject index covers everything from Aeronautics to Sports. Cataloging resources systematically by subject is not widely done on the Internet. (An effort is underway to classify gopher resources by subject, but it is far from complete.) It is a refreshing change to be able to think about the subject matter you want to investigate instead of guessing at likely names for files that might have something to do with the area of interest.

As you page down the list of subjects, you'll encounter the "Music" category. When you select this category, you'll be led to a list of W3 resources devoted to various forms of music. Near the bottom of this document is an entry point for the Digital Tradition Database. (If you're using the line-mode browser, you'll notice that the prompt has changed to include the word FIND. In the Cello browser, a separate dialog box will prompt you for keywords.) To search for songs in this database that refer to the town of Carlow, you simply enter Carlow and press Return. The CERN

Overview document contains a hyperlink that leads to a classification of Internet resources by application type (that is, gopher, ftp, WAIS, WWW). When you jump to this listing, your browser will bring up a W3 document that is gateway to other Internet applications. From this single page in W3you can branch to approximately two dozen Internet applications or sources of information. Some of these services (archie, ftp, gopher, and teinet) may already be familiar to you. You'll even find a hypertext version of Scott Yanoffs Internet Services List, containing links that take you directly to many of resources it contains. Other services may still be unfamiliar to you. You can get to them all from this menu. When you use W' as a gateway to other applications, the user interface will resemble W3s.

The W3 Gateway to archie and ftp

You can also use W3 to perform archie queries and retrieve files via ftp. From the Web Overview document, follow the link to the "By Type" document. Then select "full hypertext archie gateway," and you'll see the menu. From this screen you can select any of several kinds of archie query and specify the keywords to be used in searching the archie database. As with the CUI W3 Catalog, there are different selections for browsers that support form-based queries and browsers that do not. W3 also provides a choice of archie hypertext servers for you to use. The databases at these sites vary somewhat, and a query that returns no results from one of these databases may find items on another.

In this example, the keyword tomato is entered. The results of the query are displayed as a page of hypertext that provides hypertext links for the filename that matched the keyword, the directory that contains that file, and the site that maintains the ftp archive in which the file was found. Selecting any of these links will open an ftp session to the host selected. Selecting the file link retrieves the file and displays it on the you screen. Selecting the directory link provides a menu of all the files in that directory. Selecting the host link opens an ftp sessions starting at the topmost ftp directory on that host.

Another Internet institution is the FAQ, a compilation of Frequently Asked Questions about some topic. FAQ documents exist for hundreds of topics discussed on the Internet, and they're a very helpful form of documentation if you can find them. Many FAQs are posted to Usenet newsgroups regularly, but finding the right newsgroup can sometimes be difficult.

W3 simplifies this dramatically by collecting links to more than 300 FAQs (about all sorts of topics) in a single hypertext document. In the By Type document, move to the Network News item. In the short description that accompanies this item there is a hypertext,link to a list of FAQs. Once you've jumped to this list, retrieving an FAQ requires only that you select a link from this list.

Finally, if you want to get an overview of the World of W3 servers, W3 itself is one of the resources in the classification of services by type. When you select the WWW Servers item from the Services By Type document, a menu of available W3 servers will be displayed. You can connect to any of the servers listed by simply selecting its link from this document. From the list of W3 servers there is a link to an automatically collected list of "home pages" for various servers. This is a particularly useful list if you are working with either a fullscreen or a Gui browser that supports bookmarks. W3 is an application in transition. It is breaking out of its traditional role as a medium for academic communications, and being used for publishing all sorts of information in a visually exciting way to Internet audiences. For new users of the Internet, W3 provides a uniform interface for network applications. The Web's phenomenal growth continues as it provides an easy way to take advantage of multimedia.

Internet documentation: RFCs

The Internet community has developed its own conventions for documentation. Topics that are of general interest to Internet users are documented in RFCs (Request for Comments). RFC authors submit their documents to an RFC editor, who reviews the document, assigns it a number, and makes the document available on-line. Once an RFC has been published and the requested comments start to arrive, if changes are required,. new RFC is generated that renders its predecessor obsolete. Both RFCs remain in circulation, however.

Many, but by no means all, RFCs address technical topics. Some RFCs are identified as For Your Information (FYI) documents discussing issues the entire Internet community needs to be aware of. Another subset of RFCs contribute to the definition of standards, and these are known as STDs. The RFCs themselves (and an index listing RFCs by number and title) are available from many ftp sites, including ftp.nisc.sri.com once connected, cd to the rfc directory) and nis.nsf.net (ed to internet/documents/rfc).

Following is a selection of introductory RFCs:

RFC 1118 Hitchhiker's guide to the Internet.

RFC 1175 FYI on where to start: A bibliography of internetworking information.

RFC 1206 FYI on Questions and Answers: Answers to commonly asked "new Internet user" questions.

RFC 1207 Fyi on questions and Answers: Answers to commonly asked "experienced Internet user" questions.

RFC 1150 FYI on FYI: Introducing to the FYI notes.

RFC 1208 Glossary of networking terms.

RFC 1087 Ethics and the Internet.

Logging In

If your connection to the Internet is via a local UNIX network at your business or educational institution, you've probably already learned the login procedure, and you can skip. If not, read on... When you connect to the Internet via phone you'll have to log in to your Internet access provider's computer. Internet access providers use all sorts of computers, but it's very likely that your Internet access will be via a computer running the UNIX operating system. Before you can log in to a UNIX system, you must have arranged with you Internet access provider for a login account. Your access provider will give you the login name and password for your account. Whether you have a conventional dialup connection or a protocol dialup connection, you'll have to log in to begin work.

Logging In tells the computer who you are. Your login name (or user name) is your on-line identity. It determines what files, directories, and programs you can work with. Any files or directories you create will be stamped with this identity, so that you can control access to them. All login names should also be protected by a password known only to the authorized user of the login account.

Many UNIX systems have a bare-bones login Prompt that looks like this:

login:

The prompt may be embellished with a brief message that identifies the computer or gives you any special login instructions for that system. In response to the login prompt, enter your login name exactly as it was assigned by your Internet access provider. UNIX systems are case-sensitive, so be careful about capitalization. The characters you type in response to the login prompt are echoed on the screen as you type them. If you make a mistake, you can back over the letters you've already typed one at a time by pressing the Delete key. On some systems, you may find that the Delete key doesn't backspace over mistyped entries. If this happens, you can try using the Backspace key or simply press J at both the login: and Password: prompts. Your login attempt will fail and return you to the login prompt where you can try again. When you've entered the login name correctly, press j the key.

You should almost immediately be prompted for your password:

Password:

Enter your password. At this prompt, characters you type are not echoed on the screen. This is intentional: maintaining the privacy of your password protects your login account, the computer, and the network from unauthorized use. Even if you aren't concerned about your own account, carelessly publicizing your password could compromise the security of other users or the network itself. When you choose a password, you should avoid words (your name, for example) that are easy to guess. You should also avoid words that might occur in common word lists (like the word list used by the UNIX spelling checker). It's a good practice to mix upper-and lowercase in your password and to include at least one number. Change your password frequently. You can correct typing mistakes in your password entry by using the Delete key carefully to backspace over the mistyped letters. If you've entered your login name and password correctly, you'll be admitted to the system. What happens next depends on how the computer is configured.

After you've logged in successfully, the system may need some additional information to set up your session correctly. The most common piece of information asked for is your terminal type. Be prepared for something like this:

Term? (vt 100)

This prompt asks you to enter the type of terminal you're using (for users connecting to the UNIX system from another computer, this means the type of terminal your communication software is emulating). The prompt above proposes vt 100 as a default. Vt 100 terminals were built by the Digital Equipment Company (DEC); but. many terminals behave like vt 100s, and vt 100 is a common terminal emulation.

The selection of a terminal type affects the way things look on your screen. UNIX has a database of features for common terminal types, and some of the programs/you run on the UNIX computer will check the terminal type you set and try to use features of that terminal. They do this by sending control codes the terminal recognizes. If the terminal type is set correctly, these control codes will do things like clear the screen, pOSItion the cursor, or turn special video attributes on or off. If the terminal type is not set correctly, your display may be difficult to read, and programs that try to control the screen may be difficult, to work with.

If you know what sort of terminal you're emulating, enter an identifier for that terminal. Unfortunately, there is no university appropriate response to the question about terminal type. On many systems the names "dumb" or "dialup" can be used to select a minimally featured terminal type that can be used safely. Once you're past the login procedure and have specified a terminal type, you will receive a prompt from the UNIX command interpreter (or "shell"). Exactly what the shell prompt is depends on which UNIX shell you use and how it is configured. The shell prompt can be something simple like $ (the default prompt for the Bourne Shell) or a % (the default prompt for the C Shell). Some Internet access providers use programs other than the standard command-line interpreters for a shell program.

Terminal servers

In some cases, the first piece of equipment you interact with may be a terminal server and not an Internet host. A terminal server is a special-purpose computer that does nothing but manage connections between terminals or modems and the computers on a local network. When you connect to a terminal server you should see a message identifying the terminal server and brief instructions. Typically the first prompt to which you must respond is a request for a user name. In the example below, the user name for the terminal server is the same as the Unix login name. For some systems the' name you use for the terminal server may be different from your UNIX login name.

Connect 9600

Welcome to the Xyplex Terminal Server.

Enter username> bennett

Xyrmt7> c optimise

Xyplex 010 Session 1 to Optimism established

SunOS Unix (optimise)

login: bennett

Password:

Last login: Fri Sep 3 10:37:44 from yoda

Terminal servers are not usually protected with a password. After you've entered a username the terminal server will start a session for you, and you can issue commands to the terminal server to start a login session with a host. You'll need to know the name of the host that you're authorized to log into. in the' example above, the host was named "optimism," and the command c optimism made a connection to that computer so the user bennett could log in. Terminal servers recognize only a few commands. Most terminal servers include a help command that you can execute by typing help, h, or ?. There are only a few ways the login procedure can misfire. By far the most common is that the login name or password is entered incorrectly. When this happens, you'll see a "Login incorrect" message and be returned to the login prompt to begin again. Different systems respond to login failures in different ways, and you should read carefully any messages or instructions that are displayed after a login attempts fails. At any point you can interrupt the login procedure and start again by typing Ctrl-D

Occasionally during' the login procedure, the computer may decide that you're on a terminal that can't distinguish between uppercase and lowercase. When this happens, everything displayed by the computer will be uppercase, and letters that ought to be capitalized will be accompanied by a "\". Here'a an example of this type of login sequence:

Ibm Aix Version 3 for Rise System/6000

(C) Copyrights by Ibm and by others 1982, 1991.

Login: Bennett

3004-030 You Logged in using all uppercase characters.

If your workstation also supports lowercase characters, log off, then log in again using lowercase characters.

\B\E\N\N\E\T\T'S\ Password:

3004-007\you entered an invalid login name or password.

In this situation, the system may have difficulty recognizing your login name or password. You can use Ctrl-D to recycle the login procedure and start again. On some systems you may be able to log in successfully even when the login program thinks you're on an uppercase-only terminal. When this happens, the system will continue to display everything in uppercase, using a '"\"' to introduce characters that really are capitalized. Once past the login procedure you can recover from this. In response to a shell prompt, type the command:

% Stty- Lcase

This lets the system know that your terminal can handle upperand lowercase characters, and mixed case will be used from that point on.

So many of the computers on the Internet are UNIX systems that it is a real boon to be familiar with some of the basics of UNIX, even if the computer you work with directly is not a Unix system (for example, if your Internet access is through a dialup service that uses UNIX computers). UNIX is a multiuser, multitasking operating system developed twenty-five years ago at Bell Laboratories. Many of the design features of the original UNIX systems are still present in today's versions. The elements of UNIX that most affect users are its file system (a collection of files and directories organized in a treelike structure) and its operating environment.

The UNIX File System

The UNIX directory hierarchy is a tree-shaped structure that allows users to refer to any directory or file& on any disk without having to know which disk contains the directory or file. (Many other operating systems, including DOS, organize their file systems into this sort of directory hierarchy.) The entire file system is a series of directory paths that branch, off from a "root" directory. Directories can contain files or other directories, and the names of directories can be strung together to form path names. To refer to the root directory in a command, use a slash character (/) by itself. If the/occurs at the beginning of a path name, it is a reference to the root directory, and path names that begin with/are called absolute path names. The/ character is also used in path names as a separator for directory or file names. Here are some sample absolute path names:

The root directory

/usr A subdirectory of the root, named usr.

/usr/bin A subdirectory of /usr, named bin.

/usr/bin/finger The full pathname for the finger program in /usr/bin.

While you're logged in to a UNIX system, your login session has a current or working directory. By default, this is the home directory that the 'system administrator (whether for your local UNIX network or for your access provider) has allocated for your login name. During a login session you can change the working directory, but you'll always be in one directory or another throughout the session. Path names that don't begin with "/" are relative path names: they are interpreted in relation to your current working directory. When you're compOSIng a relative pathname, you can use a period 0 to refer to the current directory and a double-period (..) to refer to the parent directory of the current directory. UNIX provides many commands to manipulate files and directories. The commands you'll use most often are is (list a directory's contents), cd (change directory), and pwd (print working directory). There are more detailed explanations of these commands.

The UNIX command environment

When you log in to a UNIX system, you'll work with a command interpreter or shell program that accepts commands, executes programs for you, and manages the environment of you login session. There are three common shell programs in use on UNIX systems today: the Bourne Shell, the Korn Shell, and the C Shell. The Bourne and Korn shells are similar. The default prompt for them is $. The C Shell is different, particularly in its commands for managing the shell environment. The default C Shell prompt is %. Regardless of which shell you use, your login session's environment will consist of variables whose values control your access to commands and how the system behaves. By resetting these variables, you can customize your login session. Common items in the UNIX shell environment are

HOME Full pathname for your home directory.

LOGNAME Your login name

MAIL Full pathname to the file that is your system mailbox.

PATH A list of directories that the system will search to find commands you execute.

SHELL The default command interpreter for your login account.

TERM The terminal type you're using.

TERMCAP Either a description of your terminal's capabilities or a full pathname to the file containing the terminal capabilities database.

The environment variables that have the most dramatic effect on how your login session behaves are PATH and TERM. If the TERM variables is not set correctly, you may have difficulty using programs (such as terminal-based client programs for gopher or W3) that try to manipulate your screen. The Path variable controls the list of directories that will be searched when the shell needs to look up a command for you. If you know what directory a program is stored in, you can always execute the program by typing its full pathname. For example, if the finger program is in /usr/bin, you can execute finger by typing:

%/usr/bin/finger resebodywell.sf.ca.us

However, if the PATH variable in your environment includes the directory /usr/bin. you can execute finger by just typing its name:

% finger resebodywell.sf.ca.us

On most UNIX systems, you can have access to everything you need with only few directories in your path: /bin, /usr/bin, /usr/local/bin. You may also want to add /usr/etc and, if your system has it, /usr/ ucb. If you're working with a commercial Internet access provider, you should not have to figure out for yourself what directories should be included in your PATH.

On some systems, your current directory won't be included in the PATH by default. This can be very frustrating when you try to execute a program in the current directory. The is command shows that the program is there, but attempts to execute it by name fail with a "Command not found" message. You can execute the program by full path name, execute it by relative path name (/programname)), or add the current directory to your PATH. Some application programs can be configured with environment variables as well. For example, if you want the World Wide Web line-mode browser to start up with a different home page, you can set the WWW_Home environment variable to indicate which page should be used.

How you set environment variables depends on which shell program you use. The Bourne and Korn shells use the same syntax to set variables. For example, this is how to set the PATH variable using either of these shells:

$ Path:/bin:/usr/bin:/usr/local/bin::

$ export Path

The variable is set in the first command. The export command makes the variable available to any programs you start from the session in which the variable was set. To do the same thing in the C Shell, use the setenv command:

% setenv Path :/bin/usr/bin/local/bin:

When you're entering directory names for the PATH variable, use a colon to separate the names. If the list of directories begins with this character, your working directory will be searched first. Directories are searched in the order they appear in the PATH variable. If you want to place your current directory elsewhere in the PATH variable, use... at the proper location. For example, Bourne shell users can put the current directory at the end of the PATH with this command:

$ Path: /bin:/usr/bin:/usr/1oca1/bin...

$ export Path

With the Bourne or Korn shells, the set command can be used to display all the variables in your environment. C shell users should use the command printenv. To examine the value of only one variable, use the echo command. For example, this command displays the current PATH setting:

$ echo $Path :/usr/local/bin:/usr/ucb:/bin:/usr/bin:

When a variable name is preceded by a "$", UNIX substitutes the current value of the variable. The same convention is used for all the shells. UNIX systems offer a number of programs for editing files. (Among Internet tools, you'll need to edit fliles when sending mail or posting to USENET newsgroups.) One of the most convenient editors on UNIX systems is named vi.

From the UNIX command line, you can start the vi editor by typing its name and pressing J. If you want to edit a file that already exists, include the filename on the vi command line. Some mailers and news readers will start the vi editor automatically when you need to edit a mail message or news posting. When VI starts, the screen clears and the first screenful of the file you're editing is displayed. If you're editing a new file, vi will clear the screen and mark each line with a "" Screen lines marked with "" are not part of your file, and you can't move the cursor into this portion of the screen. The vi editor has a rich command set, but you only need to know a couple of commands to use it for brief messages. vi is a "modal" editor, and it is always in one or three modes: insert mode, cursor movement mode, or command mode. Vi starts in "cursor movement" mode. You can move the cursor around using four keys: h (left), j (down), k (up), and i (right), When the cursor is pOSItioned where you want to enter text, you can enter "insert" mode by typing i. In insert mode anything you type will be inserted into the document. Vi does not break lines automatically. You'll have to press J at the end of each line. While you're in insert mode, you can backspace over characters, but vi's cursor movement commands won't work. When you're finished entering text, press the Escape key. This turns off insert mode and returns, you to "cursor movement" mode. To save your work and quit the editor, first enter command mode by typing a colon(:). The colon will be displayed on the bottom line of the screen. Next type wq and press j to write your changes and quit the editor. (If you just want to exit the editor, type q! instead of wq.).

By design, UNIX systems use a large number of single-purpose commands. Here are brief summaries of sixteen of the most commonly used UNIX utilities. Some of the following commands require file names or directory names on the command line. (Anything following the name of a UNIX command on the command line is called a command line "argument.") For may UNIX commands, arguments are optional. In the commands that follow, optional arguments appear in square brackets, with an indication of what sort of argument is expected. For example, an optional filename argument is shows as [filename].

cat filename

Display the named file on the screen. Similar to the DOS TYPE command.

cd [pathname]

Change the working directory to the named directory or to the user's home directory if pathname is omitted.

Compress filename

or

Compress -d filename

Compress (or, with the d option, decompress) the named file. The compressed file is named filename.Z. Compress appends a ".Z" suffix to the name of the input file, even if the input filename already had a suffix. Compressing inet.services.txt, for example, would produce a file named inet. services. txt. z. The compressed file will be one-third to one-half the size of the source file. Compressed files are binary and should be passed through uuencode before being dent via mail. The decompress option looks for filename.Z, decompresses it, and strips off the Z suffix creating a destination file that has the same name and the same size as the source file.

cp filename newname.

Make a copy of a file. If newname is a directory, a copy of the file will be placed in that directory.

grep pattern filename

Display any lines in the named file that contain the specified pattern

head filename

Display the first few lines of a file.

Is [pathname]

List the contents of the named directory or the current directory if pathname is omitted

mkdir dirname

Create a directory with the specified name.

mv oldname newname

Rename a file, or if newname is a directory, move the file to that directory.

passwd

Change your password.

pwd

Print the name of the current working directory,

rm filename

Remove the named file. Be careful, there is no way to "undo" the effects of rm.

rmdir dirname

Remove the named directory, which must be empty.

tail filename

Display the last few lines of a file.

uudecode filename.uue

Convert ASCII-encoded files to binary. Binary files can be converted to ASCII for e-mail or news posting with the command uuencode filename < filename > filename.uue

who

List currently logged-in users.

For a full explanation of these commands, use the Unix on-line.. manual. For example, to see the on-line article about the is command, s type man Is.

OSI systems management

We start this chapter with a brief discussion of some of the important OSI concepts, followed by the topic of OSI systems management. It is appropriate to add a cautionary note here. We must be very careful when implementing OSI standards. The OSI furnishes broad guidelines for the definition of managed object classes and management operations, but it does not go into specific implementation details. While implementing standards, modifications may be made, and definitions and guidelines may be expanded to suit individual cases. Also, in some cases, the definitions are in place, but the details are still being worked out. In such cases, individual implementations need to be formulated.

Important OSI cncepts

We will present a brief overview of OSI concepts; however, because it is beyond the scope of this book, we will not go into much detail on OSI layers below the application layer. For interested readers, there are many good books and OSI standard documents. Some commonly used OSI terms are:

- *Reference model:* This is the popular OSI seven-layer architecture and is used as the basis for the OSI standardization effort.
- *Service definition:* This is an abstract concept, and it includes a set of functions provided to the user of a layer. However, in the case of the application layer, the user is an application process. The service definition defines the capabilities that can be provided to a service user.
- *Protocol specification:* This furnishes a set of concrete rules which govern the interaction between two service providers and provides implementation guidelines. As conformance requirements and testing relate to the implementation of protocols, they apply to protocol specification only. Most of the OSI layers have service definition and protocol specification documents.

Concepts of the service access point (SAP)

In data communications, we often hear the term *entity.* Basically, an entity is an abstract concept. An entity is that which provides services. These services can include error recovery, segmentation, and assembly. These entities provide the services of the *service access point* (SAP). The SAP is an addressing concept. It is a conceptual intersection between two layers and is referenced as the address by an upper layer that wants to access the services of lower layers. So an (N)-layer is accessed by the (N+1)-layer using the intersection point address. In this (N+ 1) address AddrB is important and is subject to OSI standardization. As far as AddrA is concerned, it is a local matter, and it is not within the purview of OSI standardization.

Primitives furnish further details on a state. There are four primitives: request, indication, response, and confirmation. When a request is sent, the sender may wait for a reply. In this case, the request is known as a *confirmed* request. In some cases, the sender may not bother for a reply to come from the responder. In such a case, the request is known as an *unconfirmed* request. These requests and responses sent between a manager and an agent have their own distinct names: request, indication, response, and confirmation. When a requestor sends a message asking for a certain service to be performed by the responder, the requestor sends it in the form of a *request.* On the responder side, correspondingly, the responder receives a message asking the responder to perform a service. This becomes an *indication* on the side of the responder. When a responder has to send some message, it sends it in the form of a *response.* On the receiving side, the requestor sees the message as a *confirmation.*

In the preceding explanations, the broad term *message* is used to avoid the confusion that might arise if we referred to it with names such as event report, notification, command, or response. When specific terminology is required or clear distinctions are necessary, such terms will be well-defined and explained.

Each service will have an indication about the layer: for example, A, which refers to an application layer; a verb such as ASSOCIATE; and a primitive such as request. An example of a service is thus A-ASSOCIATE. request. Each service has parameters which convey information, including data and controls.

OSI and ITU-T protocols use a *finite state machine* (FSM) to explain functional aspects of the protocols. FSM is a mathematical modeling concept used to describe properties and behaviors of a system. A *state* is a distinct stage in a set of possible circumstances. In an FSM, there is an initial or starting state. A system begins its operation from the initial state. Some examples of states are *active, busy,* and *idle.* Events occur because service primitives, such as A-ASSOCIATE. req, are received from a user. This event triggers an action or actions. An action causes a transition or change of state to happen.

FSMs are represented graphically by a *state transition diagram* and *state transition tables.* State transition tables use tabular structure, listing all the states in columns, and the events in rows. The intersections of rows and columns represent possible actions, which may also include transitions.

OSI management framework

In a systems management standardization effort, this document is a good starting point. It basically covers the following areas:

- Terms and general concepts
- Systems management model
- Informational model
- Systems management functional areas
- Systems management standardization framework

OSI management was motivated by the need to control, coordinate, and monitor the resources of open systems. Management information exchange using systems management communication protocols is done between sys*tems management application entities* (SMAEs). SMAEs are located in the application layer of our OSI seven-layer model.

A manager has the responsibilities for activities such as configuration management. To collect the data on configuration, a manager has to send commands or operations to collect it. In return, the manager receives replies to its commands. In between, if something goes wrong, the manager may get unsolicited information or notifications. As an example, if component X has gone down, the manager would need to update its configuration database. For this, component X, which is represented as a managed object, may send a notification to *an agent.* Component X may be in the same system as the agent or may be in another system. The agent, in turn, will send a notification to the manager with the information that component X has gone down. Accordingly, the manager may update its configuration database.

Hence, a manager collects and collates the information received from the agents. A manager's responsibilities also include system administration functions. A manager may control the operation of remote agents. It may send commands and actions on the basis of information received from agents.

An agent can be on a workstation and must be present wherever accessing of resources is required. The agent has its own important role. It performs the following functions:

- An agent must manage its own environment, in which it must interact with managed objects. A workstation may have many objects defined, such as a printer, modem, mouse, and so on. The agent interacts with managed objects representing these resources and controls their operations. However, this interface is not standardized by the OSI.
- When an agent gets commands from a manager, it acts upon these commands and accordingly manages the managed objects. A manager may send a command to an agent to set the font in an object such as a printer. Here, *font* may be an attribute of the managed object *printer*.
- An agent may get some notifications from the managed objects. It forwards them to the manager. As an example, a printer attached to a workstation may be defined as a managed object. In turn, this managed object may send a notification or a message, which says that it has run out of paper. This must be forwarded by the agent to the manager.

However, in OSI standards, the roles of a manager or the boundaries between manager and agent roles are not strict. A SMAE that is a manager in one interaction may take up the role of an agent in another interaction. Similarly, a SMAE that was an agent may take up the role of a manager. OSI standards do not cover how an agent deals with a managed object. OSI standards also do not state how an agent handles the managed objects that are outside the managed system boundary. As an example, an agent may ask for details on objects from another agent. In this case, the other agent forwards its data to the agent that asked for details. This is also not within the purview of standards.

For a manager and agents to communicate, each must know about the other; thus, the *application context* (AC) must be known. AC refers to the application service elements used between a manager and agents and the protocols used. Also there is a need to know which functions and functional units are supported by a manager and agents. Then, a knowledge of the managed object classes supported by agents and the relationships between functions and managed objects should be known. This is known as *shared management knowledge* between a manager and an agent.

This shared management knowledge is made known before an association is started and is stored in some file and restored every time an association is made between a manager and agent, or during the association establishment phase. While establishing an association, it must be possible to change the shared management knowledge.

There are different terms associated with the starting of a manager and agent communication. Before system management operations, the manager and agents should know what to expect and how each one behaves. Each one will have to know the parameters, such as security features, that will be used. This is done differently in different protocols, and we will examine each one of them in respective chapters. The terms associated with the initial phase of manager and agent communication are:

- *Association:* Associated with CMIP
- *Affiliation:* Used in CMIP over LLC
- *Community:* Popular term for association in SNMP

Systems management model

OSI management comprises systems management, (N)-layer management, and (N)-layer operation. This threefold division should account for all possible situations that could arise in management, as we will see later. Systems management covers managed objects in all seven OSI layers, including the application layer. It assumes reliable connection-oriented end-to-end transfer of management information. There is a caveat here: The OSI management framework does not preclude the use of connectionless services.

In layer management, the management of managed objects is limited to those in a particular layer. The management protocols make use of the communication protocols of lower layers. (N)-layer management is useful when it is not possible to go for all seven OSI layers. In such a case, we can use the layer management protocol, because this is strictly applicable to a particular layer. Layer management should not duplicate the systems management. An example of layer management is LAN/MAN management protocols which are limited to layers 1 and 2. Finally, (N)-layer operation is limited to monitoring and controlling a single instance of communication of management information within a layer. Layer operation is sometimes required, because some layer protocols may contain management information. An example of management information is the parameters that are exchanged in protocol data units while establishing connections. The standards within (N)-layer management and (N)-layer operation are beyond the scope of OSI systems management standards. However, the OSI management information model can be used by layer management.

The basic systems management model assumes management operations and notifications between peer systems, This model facilitates the distributed aspect of systems management. Sometimes, these peer systems are designated as managing systems and managed systems. For systems management purposes, the roles of peer open systems are defined. One peer open system is assumed to take the role of a manager and the other peer open system is assumed to take the role of an agent for a given interaction. An agent may be distributed throughout the OSI environment.

Management information model

A managed object is an OSI way of viewing resources for management purposes. A resource can be described as a managed object. A managed object is an instance of a *managed object class*. A managed object class is a collection of packages, which can be mandatory or conditional. In packages, similar characteristics are grouped together. If we define *printer* as a managed object class, a Lexmark Laser Jet printer is an object instance; an HP Deskjet 560C would be another object instance.

For controlling the activities of resources, the manager and agents need to be aware of the details of the resources. The details of these managed objects, which are required for management purposes, are stored in a conceptual repOSItory known as the *management information base* (MIB). The MIB is a conceptual model and it has no relation to how the data is physically or logically formatted and stored. Standards do not cover the storage aspect. Nevertheless, the syntax and semantics of how the information is exchanged are governed by the OSI protocols. However, these managed objects must be properly formatted for management purposes. The retrieval of data from the managed objects may involve the use of communication services provided by the layers below.

For OSI management, we have to take into consideration all the resources in the computer systems, including those related to data processing, data storage, and data communication. As an example, in fault management, we should consider the utilization of processors, bard disks, or CD-ROMs.

Managed object

The definition of a managed object must include properties. These properties with specific values that can be exchanged are known as *attributes*. The type of printer—e.g., dot matrix, laser jet, or laser printer—can be one of the properties. A managed object class definition must also include *operations* that can be performed on a managed object. Modifying or querying attribute values are examples of operations.

Managed objects can send *notifications* if a certain event occurs. A notification is an unsolicited message, which contains details of the message, including why a notification has occurred, where it occurred, and for whom the notification is intended. When the characteristics of a managed object, such as attributes, operations, and notifications, are defined, there must be a way to express their semantics and how they are related. This is done by *behavior*. These characteristics must be capable of manipulation by management operations.

There are two types of managed objects. One type of object, known as an *(N)-layer managed object is* relevant to one OSI layer. The other type of object is known as a systems *managed object*. Here, the systems managed object is used for systems management purposes and covers more than one layer.

For definition of managed objects, we perceive conceptually the managed objects as having a boundary. The characteristics of managed objects used for systems management are visible at and beyond the boundary. These characteristics include attributes, operations, notifications, and behavior. Hence, what is of interest are the properties at or beyond the conceptual boundaries. What is inside the managed object boundary is not needed for systems management purposes.

The process of creating a managed object as per rues is known as *instantiation*. For example, when a Create on a managed object class, tokenRing, is done, then a managed object created with, say, tokenRingID = 1594 is known as an *instance* of a managed object class tokenRing.

Management knowledge management function

The management knowledge management function can be used by an application process for systems management purposes. ISO 10164-16.2 primarily provides the model for the management knowledge objects, defines the management knowledge manage[object classes required, and maps management knowledge management function services to CMIS services. ISO 10164-16.2 ties up many loose ends and basically provides information on how a manager and agents can know about each other and how a manager can extract information on the managed objects managed by agents.

Management knowledge refers to the management information required by an open system to associate and perform management operations on another peer open system. There are three types of management knowledge:

- *Repertoire knowledge:* This relates to the capabilities of a managed system, which pertain to the classes supported, the systems management functions supported, and the name bindings. Repertoire knowledge assists a manager in identifying the capabilities of managed systems without accessing them.
- *Definition knowledge:* This refers to the formal specifications of managed object classes, name bindings, test categories, relationship classes, and the management information definitions understood by a managed system.
- *Instance knowledge:* This provides the information on the managed objects in a managed system.

Management knowledge has further subdivisions for repertoire knowledge and instance knowledge. Repertoire knowledge subdivisions are:

- *Managed object class knowledge:* This provides details on the managed object classes supported by a managed system, such as initial values of the instances of objects, the packages supported, the allomorphs supported by each managed object class, and the constraints on each of the managed object classes.

- *Naming schema knowledge:* This relates to the naming relationship between the managed objects made available by a managed system.
- *Relationship knowledge:* This refers to the relationship between managed object classes supported by a managed system and also the relationship of role bindings between managed object classes.
- *MIS-user knowledge:* This provides the titles, presentation address, application contexts, the functional units supported, and the management profiles of the SMAEs supported.

Relationship knowledge and MIS-user knowledge have instance knowledge. Instance knowledge relates to the object instances associated with relationship managed object classes and instances of agents. Instance knowledge has the following subdivision:

- *Managed object instance knowledge:* This provides details on the instances of managed objects which are made visible by a managed system.

For realizing the management knowledge manage-ment function, ISO 10164-16.2 defines 15 managed object classes under *top* and two repertoire directory managed object classes. Basically, the groups of managed object classes are:

- *Repertoire managed objects:* This refers to the information on the capabilities of a managed system, such as the managed objects supported and their name bindings.
- *Definition managed objects:* This provides details on management information supported by managed objects. These definition managed objects are useful while forming associations. Three types of definition managed objects are document objects, template objects, and ASN. 1 module objects.
- *Discovery managed objects:* This group has details on the managed objects made visible by a managed system.
- *Management knowledge directory objects:* These provide information on the capabilities and definition knowledge of the management systems. There are basically repertoire directory objects and definition directory objects under this category.

OSI systems management functional areas (SMFAs)

For the convenience of standardizing management, systems management activities are subdivided into different functional areas. Each functional area has specific responsibilities. The systems management functional areas are:

- Configuration management

- Fault management
- Performance management
- Accounting management
- Security management

Configuration management

Computer networks are expanding and becoming more complex. These networks need to be managed. The different components of networks cannot be managed without knowing where the various components are. Configuration management is used to locate the resources, including the failed ones, and also to keep track of the types of resources and their details. One of the key objectives of systems management is to maintain continuous operation of a network. We have already seen that components of a network are modeled as managed objects. These managed objects will have addresses and names to distinguish them. These can be stored in directories, and these directories can be built using OSI directory services.

The data on managed objects, such as their state and how they are related to one another, is collected on a regular basis and, where there are changes, they can be collected in a manager, using unsolicited messages such as event reports. These changes must be reflected in the database on topology and status. These services may be used by other systems management functions such as fault management.

In addition, we may activate and deactivate managed objects. Sometimes, these may have to be done in a controlled manner. Also, we may want to change the configuration of the network. For example, a workstation may no longer be attached to network A; instead, it is now attached to network B. This change has to be known and accordingly reflected in the configuration. In addition, we may wish to change the parameters of systems. Most of these activities have been standardized by the configuration management functional area of systems management. We also need to manage day-to-day operations of the systems and resources. The configuration management function provides the support services to keep the systems and resources operational.

Software management. This function is within the configuration management functional area of OSI systems management. With the widespread use of computers, this is becoming an important function. When new computers are set up, software needs to be installed. It is not possible to hand-carry the diskettes for installing software; there should be a way to distribute the new software for installing new systems.

Once we have systems installed, they need to have the latest versions of software. In some cases, we need to apply fixes to software problems that have cropped up. The distribution of software fixes is a part of this function. Fixes usually should not be applied when a system is busy; this should be done at a particular time and requires a scheduling operation. We also need to keep track of the software installed, as well as fixes and versions. Sometimes this is referred to as *license management*, which is also a part of *change management*. Basically, change management involves all the activities that are required to keep track of changes in computer networks and the resources associated with them.

Fault management

Though some of the goals of fault management appear to be part of other areas of systems management, each area must perform its part of the function, and sometimes cooperative functioning and management are required. For example, after we analyze system performance, we need to identify problem areas and take corrective actions to overcome them. We may use log services or a cache to store the data.

We may also need the help of configuration management to identify precisely where a problem has occurred. Some form of automation routines may be required to apply fixes. For example, a token-ring lobe becomes nonfunctional. We may use automation to bypass the problem lobe and take some other corrective action to prevent a station from being disabled permanently.

Fault management is broadly concerned with the detection, isolation using analysis, and correction of unusual operational behaviours of systems in the OSI environment. These unusual operational behaviors include conditions such as deterioration of service and error situations. Effective fault management may require that errors be logged in a database.

This error log may be in an agent or manager, depending on the situation. In some cases, an agent may not have much memory. In such a case, the error log may be off-loaded to a manager. In some other cases, error logs may be in agents and a summary is maintained in the manager. Where to locate the error log depends on requirements and implementation decisions.

For detecting and isolating complex faults, it may be necessary to examine error logs and run diagnostic tests. Sometimes traces may be helpful. After the problems are isolated, they are corrected. One of the trends in systems management is to automate as much as possible fault management functions. By automation, we mean a set of procedures which are triggered to correct impending and actual problems without human intervention. This set of procedures may be accomplished by hardware, microcode, software, or a combination of them.

Performance management

When computers are working, we need to know how they are operating—for example, is the system getting overloaded? Is there enough workload? How is the performance during peak hours? How is the LAN behaving? Are there too many collisions while transmitting data? The answers to these questions fall within the realm of performance management.

To undertake capacity planning, we need to collect performance-related data. What are our response time targets? Are we achieving them? Can we improve the performance with better load balancing? Is any system becoming a bottleneck? How can we improve the performance by removing the bottleneck? Some of these questions require historic data to be answered. The historic data has to be stored in databases so that it can be analyzed, and correct answers can be arrived at. Performance management is also concerned with the behavior and evaluation of the effectiveness of resources. For this, we may need to gather statistical data on the behavior of resources and store the data in databases. We can use the data to evaluate the performance of systems and networks and fine-tune them to maximize overall performance.

Accounting management

Here we must consider how much of the resources are being used and how much must be charged for using these resources. The accounting information can be from individual, department, section, and company levels, depending on the rate structure. Accounting management includes informing relevant users and authorities about the usage of resources and the costs associated with their usage. In some cases, it may be enough to send monthly reports about computer facilities usage to managers instead of to individual users. In order cases, these reports may have to be sent to individual users and managers in the administrative chain. All these are included in accounting management. In some cases, especially where computing resources may be necessary to set limits on the usage of resources. This is common practice in universities, where authorities do not want students to overload the centralized computing facilities. There are also cases where computing resources are out-sourced from some vendors and tight control on the usage of resources is desirable.

Furthermore, costs on resource usage may sometimes need to be combined and consolidated. As an example, some people work from home using modems. It may be necessary to consolidate the cost of telephone tariffs for this kind of work with other costs.

Security management

Security management must be very carefully and patiently implemented. It has become an important issue, especially in distributed computing environments with thousands of workstations. There are different levels of security to correspond to different levels of computing environments. There are threats of viruses creeping into networks. Without adequate precautions, important company information may be lost, or proprietary work that is being done may be stolen. Security management is a very important function for dealing with these threats. Though systems management security is closely related to network security and computer system security, we will focus on security issues related to systems management functions, such as those dealing with accounting management and managed objects.

Some security management functions are:

- Reporting any security violations, using event reports to the manager, and maintaining logs. Unusual security violations must be brought to the attention of the network manager for prompt action.
- Creating, deleting, and maintaining security-related services like encryption, key management, and access control.
- Distributing passwords and secret keys as necessary when bringing up systems and at regular intervals afterwards.

Business management

The business management function is a collection of aspects from the configuration management, accounting management, and security management functional areas of the OSI systems management function. Business management is an important function with much potential, and it needs to be included in OSI systems management. First, all the hardware, software, and computing resources used are registered. Then, whenever there is a new user, this user is registered along with the details of the resources being used.

After collecting the details of all the computing resources, we use them to manage the cost. This is where financial administration enters the picture. The total cost of using the resources and how much is used by each individual user, department, or division needs to be computed. Business management involves more long-range and strategic planning than does accounting management. A workload may increase or decrease, depending on the business climate. In such cases, short-term as well as long-term planning of data processing needs are appropriate. Once such plans are in place, they must be continuously monitored and updated.

Facilities planning is also a part of business management. How Much of the resources will be located in a particular place? flow best to place the resources? These concerns are very important where working space is at a premium. Some functions of business management will be discussed in this book as they are applicable to other functions.

OSI systems management standards overview

Systems management standards are pertinent to the application layer of the OSI. These standards can be broadly grouped into different areas. This classification indicates how these standards can be grouped to arrive at different systems management functional areas. Basic and general systems management services relate to the general explanation of systems management functions. The documents under this category furnish general guidelines on systems management standards. Many OSI standards, such as OSI layer standards, systems management standards, and standards or domains, fall under this classification. The next category relates to the management information model. Standards under this classification provide definitions of managed object classes and generic managed object classes that can be used for systems management. They all have a starting number of 10165 and are grouped under the *structure of management information* (SMI).

Another group of standards relates to the specific systems management functions and includes object definitions required for them. They all start with 10164. Providing a systems management function such as performance management may require the help of more than one standard in the 10164 grouping. As an example, performance management may require 10164-11, which is the workload monitoring function, and 10164-13, which is the summarization function.

Other standards are needed to implement interoperable systems management functions, including standards for association and for the syntax of data being transferred, and the protocols used for communication between manager and agent. ACSE, ROSE, CMISE, and CMIP are categorized under additional service functions. Security is a major consideration, especially when distributed computing receives wider acceptance. All of these issues are included under additional service functions.

These classifications are combined to make up the *systems management functional areas.* These SMFAs must be modular so that additional functionalities can be added more easily. For example, in the first release, all the bells and whistles required for security management may not be in place. These may be added in the second release or as the standards firm up. In some cases, depending on the needs and additional requirements, committees are set up to examine and formulate standards. This takes time, and must be considered when providing the systems management functions. Once all the functions are provided, it is essential to ensure that for operations under different conditions and multivendor environ-ments, they conform to the provided standards.

In India there are more than 43,000 computers linked to the internet, This includes dial-up and leased connection. This access is expected to increase considerably in the next two years. Besides there is no doubt that with the announcement of ISP policy and improvements in India's telecom connectivity through implementation of NII and the high speed telecom backbone is bound to bring a multi-fold increase in internet users in India. At present there are three types of internet accounts for which the price varies from Rs 15,000 to 550 for 500 hours. Now that the license fee for the entry of the ISPs has been waived for a period of five years instead of two years a lot of hope of hope has been raised. But the Internet Service Providers have to give a bank guarantee which is equivalent to one year's license fee. According to speculations the VSNL is going to lower the internet connection to Rs 10,000. Internationally people pay only 1520 dollars a month which is indeed very cheap. A regular internet user says, "Already companies like UPS, the largest courier service providers are linked to the internet. So a customer only has to log into the internet and find out the status of his parcel." Many Indian software companies have taken the lead for creating products on internet and selling products through internet. Also many of them have shown the desire to become service providers for internet together with the VSNL, the nodal agency of the government. In the software industry, promotional efforts constitute as much as 70 per cent of the total product cost. But with the low cost of internet based marketing and high visibility of Indian software companies, internet gives a distinct edge to companies to market and distribute products in a cost-efficient manner and thus reduce the costs to as low as 30 per cent of the total cost.

Most of the computer hardware manufacturers are modifying their computer configurations to make them more Internet friendly. In 1996 alone, the market was flooded with many Web Servers. Before the launch of internet services in India by VSNL in 1995, there were only under 10,000 users in India. The current number of subscribers base in India boasts of around 43,000.

Some of the most popular uses of internet in India are Web browsing, E-mail and FTP. "Currently the immediate fall out of the private ISPs will bc that the browsing will increase more. Secondly there will increase more. Secondly there will be more quality sites coming up in India. With more Indian sites there will be more Indian sites there will be more Indian content of international standard. Also the large ISPs are going to provide virtual private network to corporate clients. This will increase the company's intra net. Also there will be extra nets to service their distributors, customers and partners therefore," True, the fallout will be the use of internet for more resource intensive tasks. Internet will be deployed for commercial purposes which would include Home Banking, Tele-shopping, Electronic Commerce, Internet, Netvertising Internet Telephone/Video Conferencing, Collaborative Efforts, Real time Event relay. Web Varsities etc. This is important for a country where there is a great deal of cultural and economic disparity. According to current estimates, about 125 establishments in India have either set up or are in the process of setting up intranets. These are expected to increase to at least 12,000 by the turn of the century. The reason being that with PC penetration exploding in India, 'networked organisations and electronic commerce are becoming a way of life, increased focus on computeri-sation by the government departments and the corporate houses, intranet is seen as a viable and cost effective tool to exploit such strengths. Also the acceptability of internet and its popular constituent, WWW, has been beneficial for the Indian industry to market its products and services. It has already helped Indian companies to create brand awareness, invite potential partners, etc.

Internet will provide new opportunities to the telecom service providers and the value added service providers because they will have additional source of revenue. Internet being on the international superhigh-way has really increased by leaps and bounds all over the world which means additional revenue to all the telecom service 'providers. But the private operators have to pay attention to the quality to keep up to the international standards so that the people can use it for longer duration of time, with clarity of transmission and at a high speed.

President of Combit Advertising Network Limited says, "The government has yet to lay down the terms and conditions clearly although it has come out with outline, it has left a lot of grey areas. Liberalisation is the catalyst to the process where a wide array of society can get involved. If private operators come in then there will be more users which will help enlarge the market. in fact, it is only then that the real activity on the internet will come forth. Besides the techno-literate can provide decisive product and services."

With the liberalization of the economy and emerging business and economic opportunities, the government has been considering the creation of a National Information Backbone (National communication carrying capacity). This backbone would be used for national information infrastructure and promotion of Internet Services.

The tele commission chairman, Mr. G.V. Gokak called for a comprehensive approach to integrate cyber-technology to lead proliferation of Internet users in the country. Commenting on throwing the sector open to private participation. Mr. Gokak said that it ' was the best possible way to ensure proliferation of Internet users in the country.

Further elaborating the government' stand Vital says, "All this while the government has been playing on the security aspect as being the reason for not opening the sector. But in an era of no secrecy this excuse is very lame. There is no policing of software export elsewhere so why should we do it in India."

Dewang Mehta the Executive Director of NASSCOM remarked. Today in the world it is impossible to survive in the computer business without having the internet connection. The same applies for the business side. In the west all visiting cards have an internet number! "So in this era of globalisation India has to quickly get out of the agriculture age to enter the information age we have to concentrate on not only on the quantity of internet connection but also the quality."

Predicts Nahata, "Growth of internet is going to be phenomenal and the usage is going to increase terrifically because new services are available on the internet including possibility of the voice communication. But this will most probably not be allowed as the it will come in direct conflict with the direct service operators. DoT and VSNL. However, even without that there are a lot of services available at a very cheap rate which will ensure the phenomenal growth beyond what we can contemplate today. A is going to explode. Also success would depend on the good quality of the service available.

"Today there is lack of a good transmission network. The way I foresee the demand of internet. DoT will also have to increase their capacity in intra-state transmission network. Of course. Private operators are then going to provide good network."

But laments Dewang Mehta, "Somehow in this country. It is not that the demand is less. A survey done in the four metros show that the immediate demand for interest is 500,000. So it is not the demand ' that is bottleneck rather it is the supply which is the bottleneck and when that happens then we ought to go far privatisation as government agencies do not have the infrastructure or the resources nor the willpower to take up this task."

Defending the role of VSNL Director (Development). R. K. Gupta opined. "The VSNL is unnecessarily being blamed and the criticisms are totally unfounded. In many countries the internet connections are owned by the government. So why not in India. We are providing competitive rates, quality."

On the increasing use of internet services Vittal says. "Internet is no doubt becoming a competitor to voice telephoning. In India do we want to create an assumed monopoly of DoT. On one hand we have an aspiration that India should have the internet but will not allow them to grow by putting limitations. Because of the US, Germany, Europe and Japan are changing so we too need a wider vision if we want to link ourselves to internet."

Internet connection in India is only about 45 thousand in a country 1 billion when compared to the world. We are a great power in software, intellectually very sound, we have the second largest English speaking manpower in the world yet the percentage of the users are very low." Today in the World there are 40 million internet connections, which means 40m computers are connected to internet.

Mehta comments, "Private sectors should be allowed to do the pricing themselves and let the market forces decide. The market equilibrium should not be interfered with the government. Unfortunately DoT is old fashioned and is not used to privatisation. They do not want to loose power." True if DoT does not hasten up technology will overtake them so much that they would loose power anyway.

Index